Introduction to Personality and Intelligence

SAGE Foundations of Psychology Series

Series Editors: Craig McGarty, Murdoch University, S. Alexander Haslam, University of Exeter

SAGE Foundations of Psychology is a major new series intended to provide introductory textbooks in all the main areas of psychology. Books in the series are scholarly, written in a lively and readable style, assuming little or no background knowledge. They are suitable for all university students beginning psychology courses, for those studying psychology as a supplement to other courses, and for readers who require a general and up-to-date overview of the major concerns and issues in contemporary psychology.

Already published:

Statistics with Confidence: An Introduction for Psychologists
Michael J. Smithson (Australian National University)

An Introduction to Child Development
Thomas Keenan (Niagara College, Canada)

Research Methods and Statistics in Psychology
S. Alexander Haslam & Craig McGarty (University of Exeter, UK & Murdoch University, Australia)

Forthcoming:

An Introduction to Child Development 2nd Edition
Thomas Keenan (Niagara College, Canada)

An Introduction to Social Psychology
John Turner (Australian National University)

An Introduction to Biological Psychology
Lisa Wise (University of Melbourne, Australia)

Understanding Cognitive Neuropsychology: Studying Damaged Brains
Ashok Jansari (University of East London)

Introduction to Personality and Intelligence

Nick Haslam

Los Angeles | London | New Delhi
Singapore | Washington DC

First published 2007
Reprinted 2008, 2009, 2010, 2011

SAGE Publications Ltd
1 Oliver's Yard
55 City Road
London EC1Y 1SP

SAGE Publications Inc.
2455 Teller Road
Thousand Oaks, California 91320

SAGE Publications India Pvt Ltd
B 1/I 1 Mohan Cooperative Industrial Area
Mathura Road, New Delhi 110 044
India

SAGE Publications Asia-Pacific Pte Ltd
33 Pekin Street #02-01
Far East Square
Singapore 048763

British Library Cataloguing in Publication data

A catalogue record for this book is available from the British Library

ISBN 978-0-7619-6057-7
ISBN 978-0-7619-6058-4 (pbk)

Library of Congress Control Number: 2006930600

Typeset by C&M Digitals (P) Ltd, Chennai, India
Printed in Great Britain by Ashford Colour Press Ltd.

Contents

Acknowledgements

Many people deserve hearty thanks for helping me to imagine, plan, and finish this book. Craig McGarty and Alex Haslam convinced me that I was up to the task, and showed superhuman patience and faith when all the evidence seemed to suggest otherwise. Michael Carmichael, Claire Reeve, and Natalie Aguilera at SAGE gave good-natured encouragement and steered me towards completion. Bill Gottdiener, Bill Hirst, Nick Humphrey, and Louis Rothschild read chapters and corrected some of my errors. Timothy Bates strengthened the book by stepping in to write an excellent chapter on intelligence and cognitive abilities. The spirit of Charles Langley, who got me started in the field, sat like an amused parrot on my shoulder while I wrote. Vikki sustained me throughout the writing period, which included two intercontinental moves, two children, two academic positions, two muggings, and one terrorist incident. Max and Alastair made concentration difficult, laughter easy, and life interesting for the duration. This one is for them: fascinating little personalities both.

A Word on Statistics by Wisława Szymborska

Out of every hundred people
those who always know better:
fifty-two.

Unsure of every step:
almost all the rest.

Ready to help,
if it doesn't take too long:
forty-nine.

Always good,
because they cannot be otherwise:
four – well, maybe five.

Able to admire without envy:
eighteen.

Led to error
by youth (which passes):
sixty, plus or minus.

Those not to be messed with:
four-and-forty.

Living in constant fear
of someone or something:
seventy-seven.

Capable of happiness:
twenty-some-odd at most.

Harmless alone,
turning savage in crowds:
more than half, for sure.

Cruel
when forced by circumstances:
it's better not to know,
not even approximately.

Wise in hindsight:
not many more
than wise in foresight.

Getting nothing out of life except
things:
thirty
(though I would like to be wrong).

Balled up in pain
and without a flashlight in the dark:
eighty-three, sooner or later.

Those who are just:
quite a few, thirty-five.

But if it takes effort to understand:
three.

Worthy of empathy:
ninety-nine.

Mortal:
one hundred out of one hundred –
a figure that has never varied yet.

Guided Tour

1

What is Personality?

Learning Objectives

- To develop an understanding of how the concept of 'personality' has developed over the course of history.
- To understand how personality is conceptualized within psychology, and how personality differs from other forms of psychological variation.
- To distinguish between personality and related concepts, such as character and temperament.
- To recognize how personality fits within psychology as a whole, and how it differs from related subdisciplines.
- To develop an overview of the book's organization.

This chapter introduces and clarifies the concept of 'personality', which defines the subject matter of personality psychology. The historical background and alternative meanings of the concept are discussed, followed by an analysis of how personality relates to and is distinct from other kinds of differences between people, such as those that are physical rather than psychological, or transient rather than lasting. Personality is distinguished from the related concepts of character and temperament, and the place that the study of personality occupies in psychology as a whole is examined. Personality psychology is

Chapter introductions:
Chapter introductions concisely summarize the material covered in the chapter, in order of presentation.

2

Trait Psychology

Learning Objectives

- To develop a working understanding of the concept of 'personality trait' and the hierarchical structure of traits.
- To understand how psychologists have developed models of the dimensional structure of personality traits, including the statistical methods employed.
- To comprehend the 'Big Five' personality dimensions and their differences from existing three-factor models.
- To recognize the importance of trait taxonomies for advancing psychological understanding and prediction.
- To have a working knowledge of specific traits in additional to the broad personality dimensions.

This chapter turns to the fundamental question of how individual differences in personality should be described. The concept of personality 'trait' - the primary unit of personality description - is introduced and defined, and the hierarchical nature of traits is explained. The long-standing efforts to uncover the structure or organization of personality traits, by reducing the bewildering variety of possible traits into a few basic personality dimensions, are then explored. Along the way, the statistical methods used to conduct this

Bulleted learning objectives:
Bullet points at the beginning of each chapter outline its main topic areas and lay out the learning goals that it aims to achieve.

coefficients for all pairs of variables in a set. One half of the matrix is empty because the correlation between B and C, for example, is the same as the correlation between C and B so there is no need to present both. Correlations falling on the diagonal are all +1 because a variable always correlates perfectly with itself.

Looking at Table 2.2 what you probably see is a big mess. Some variables correlate quite strongly, some not much at all, some negatively and some positively. This is where factor analysis enters the scene. What it attempts to do is find patterns of correlations within the matrix that may not be readily obvious to the observer (i.e., what psychologists sometimes facetiously call 'eyeball analysis'). The technical and computational details of factor analysis need not concern us here, but in this particular correlation matrix the procedure would find clear evidence of two distinct groups of variables. Variables A, C and F form one group, and variables B, D and E the other. Table 2.3 simply rearranges Table 2.2 to demonstrate the patterns that factor analysis would uncover.

Illustrative Study: Personality traits and emotion regulation across cultures

'Emotion regulation' is the ability to manage emotional reactions in order to achieve one's goals. People are often faced with situations when it is desirable to modify or suppress the expression of an emotion: failing to do so may lead us to give up on an important task, say something offensive, escalate an argument or do something socially inappropriate. Emotion regulation is also something on which cultures may differ. It has been argued, for example, that some cultures discourage emotional expression more than others, or require that individual emotion be subordinated to collective demands.

The American cross-cultural psychologist David Matsumoto (2006) examined differences in emotion regulation between Americans and Japanese. Previous research had suggested that Japanese participants score lower on emotion regulation than Americans, and Matsumoto aimed to explain why this might be. There is reliable evidence of differences in the mean level of Five Factor Model (FFM) dimensions between cultures, and Americans have been found to score higher on average than Japanese on Extraversion and Conscientiousness, and lower on Neuroticism. Given the role of Extraversion and Neuroticism in emotionality, these cultural differences in mean levels of personality traits might account for cultural differences in emotion regulation.

One boxed description of an illustrative study per chapter:

In each chapter, a recent cutting-edge study is presented in a boxed section, which describes the study's methods, findings, and further implications.

---

intellectual (i.e., involving cognitive abilities) and those that are not, with a grey area of ambiguous characteristics in the middle. Some personality differences can be considered aspects of character or temperament. Enduring psychological differences are, in addition, related to more transient and specific behaviours, cognitions and emotions.

Chapter Summary

- 'Personality' is a complicated concept that has had several distinct meanings over the course of history. Within psychology, however, it refers to individual differences in psychological dispositions: that is, enduring ways in which people differ from one another in their typical ways of behaving, thinking and feeling. These differences often reflect core features of who we are as persons, and are central to our self-concepts.
- This understanding of personality often excludes individual differences in intelligence and cognitive ability, although these are also of interest to many personality psychologists.
- In addition, personality psychologists are interested not only in individual differences, but also in the underlying causes or dynamics that explain these differences between people.
- Personality can be loosely distinguished from character (morally-relevant dispositions having to do with self-control, will and integrity) and temperament (biologically-based dispositions that often involve emotional expression and are present early in life).
- Within psychology, the study of personality is distinctive for its focus on human individuality and its concern for the person as a functioning whole. It differs from social psychology, a neighbouring subdiscipline, by emphasizing the contribution that the person's internal dispositions make to behaviour, rather than the contribution of the person's external situation or context.

Bulleted chapter summaries:

Bullet points at the end of each chapter distil the main issues raised and set out the chapter's primary claims and conclusions.

FURTHER READING

Major reference works

For students wishing to obtain a more thorough and advanced review of personality psychology, the following major handbooks may be of interest:

- R. Hogan, J. Johnson & S. Briggs (Eds.) (1999). *Handbook of personality psychology*. New York: Academic Press.
- Pervin, L. A. (Ed.) (1999). *Handbook of personality: Theory and research* (2nd ed.). New York: Guilford.

Journals

To get a sense of current research in personality psychology, and the sorts of research methods that it uses, you should take a look at recent issues of prominent scientific journals such as the following:

- *European Journal of Personality*
- *Journal of Personality*
- *Journal of Personality and Social Psychology*
- *Journal of Research in Personality*
- *Personality and Individual Differences*
- *Personality and Social Psychology Bulletin*
- *Personality and Social Psychology Review*

Annotated further readings:

At the end of each chapter a short list of recommended readings is provided, with a brief summary of each one's perspective and its main implications.

Glossary

Affect: A general term to refer to emotions and moods.

Agreeableness: One of the Big Five personality factors, involving dispositions to be cooperative, interpersonally warm, and empathic.

Anal stage: The second stage of psychosexual development in psychoanalytic theory's genetic model, in which the focus of interest is the anus and the primary developmental issue is control.

Attachment style: The tendency to approach close or romantic relationships in a particular way, as indicated by trust, dependence, and desired closeness to relationship partners. Three styles are generally recognized: secure, avoidant and anxious-ambivalent.

Attributional style: The tendency to explain events using particular combinations of causal dimensions, the standard dimensions being internal vs. external, stable vs. unstable, and global vs. specific. A pessimistic attributional style is one in which negative events are habitually explained in terms of internal, stable and global causes. This concept is sometimes also referred to as 'explanatory style'.

Authoritarianism: A personality trait involving rigidity, punitiveness, conventionality, distrust of introspection, and submission to authority.

Behavioural approach system (BAS):   In Gray's theory, a neuropsychological system that underpins impulsivity, is sensitive to the possibility of rewards, and motivates people to seek them.

Behavioural inhibition system (BIS):   For Gray the neuropsychological system that is the basis for anxiety, is sensitive to the possibility of punishment, and motivates people to avoid it.

Behaviourism: A school of theory and research that addressed the relationships between environmental stimuli and observable behaviour, and held that mental states were not appropriate subjects of psychological investigation.

A Glossary of key concepts:

Major concepts discussed in the book are defined in a Glossary at the end of the book.

Introductory Remarks

Why begin a book about the psychology of personality and individual differences with a poem? Isn't that just a little bit old-fashioned, or pretentious, or pretty? Haven't you been solemnly told that psychology is a hard science, not a soft humanity?

Maybe these criticisms have some merit. However, *this* poem, by the Nobel Prize-winning Polish poet Wisława Szymborska, goes straight to the heart of the book you hold in your hands. Although the title suggests that it is about statistics, the poem beautifully captures the basic themes of personality psychology. First, it focuses on how people differ in their ways of behaving, thinking, and feeling. Second, it presents these differences as things that can be measured and subjected to systematic scientific study. (You can probably also detect in the poem a quietly sceptical attitude to the idea that personalities can be quantified precisely, a doubt that is shared by some psychologists.) Third, the poem reveals a set of basic assumptions about human nature, assumptions about what people are really like, what essential characteristics we all share. Szymborska's view of humankind is rather tragic and a little cynical; we are a cruel, selfish, anguished, lazy, unprincipled, and herd-like species, made equal by the inevitability of death. Few personality psychologists hold this bleak view of human nature, but all go beyond the scientific study of human differences to take positions, explicit or implicit, on what members of our species have in common. These three elements – the focus on differences between people, the somewhat ambivalent reliance on scientific methods of inquiry, and the alternative visions of human nature – define the basic themes of personality psychology and of this book.

Leaving aside the poem's relevance to this book, we can also step back for a minute and contemplate whether the literary concerns of the poet and the scientific preoccupations of the personality psychologist are really so different. After all, poets and other writers of fiction strive to make sense of experience, action, and the forces that shape mind and character, just as personality psychologists do. Most psychologists would probably agree that many of the great insights about human personality, behaviour, and mental life have come from the pens of novelists, and that works of fiction often contain penetrating and wonderfully rendered portraits of imagined individuals. The main difference between the fiction-writer and the personality psychologist may simply be one of method rather than focus. Fiction writers generally want to paint vivid verbal portraits of individual persons, based on informal scrutiny of others, introspection, and creative imagination. Personality psychologists, in contrast, typically want to develop scientifically sound generalizations about people, based on systematic observation, controlled measurement, and careful reasoning. The products of these two enterprises – works of fiction on the one hand, scientific studies and theories on the other – differ substantially, but the drive to understand human individuality powers them both.

On a more abstract level, '*poem*' derives from the ancient Greek '*poiema*', from '*poiesis*' meaning 'to make'. A poem is something made, constructed, put together, given form. So, according to the psychology of personality, is a person. Personality psychologists study how people are put together, what forms they take, how these forms are shaped by the forces of biology, culture, and experience, how each individual is the unique product of an enormously complicated process of person-making. Perhaps poems and personalities do belong in the same book.

In the pages that follow I want to introduce you to the fundamental issues, concepts, and theories of personality psychology, and to present research findings that illuminate them. The book doesn't aim to cover the field exhaustively, hoping instead to give you a first taste of the psychology of personality and individual differences that will stimulate your appetite and make you want to come back for more. I will be more than satisfied if this book makes you a little more inquisitive, more introspective, more reflective, or more critical in your everyday thinking about people.

I will even be happy if you emerge at the other end of the book more confused about the psychology of persons than when you started. After all, confusion is a sign of a mind in ferment, actively thinking through ambiguities and puzzles in search of some sort of truth or clarity. Out of confusion often comes curiosity, insight, and the will to learn, things that every teacher prizes. But it is also true that confusion sometimes breeds frustration and a disappointed turning of one's back on whatever it is that produced the confusion. I will be sorry if that is how you feel at the end of this book. Either I will have failed in my goals, or perhaps the psychology of personality is just not for you.

The book is organized into four sections. The first section has to do with the basic questions of how personalities should be described. For example, what do we mean by 'personality'? How should we characterize people's individuality? Is there a universal vocabulary or framework for capturing differences between them? All of these questions are fundamental. However, working out how to describe something is only a first step towards really understanding it. To do that, we need explanations and theories that account for *why* things are as they are. So the second section of the book focuses on theoretical approaches to the study of personality, approaches that tell quite different stories about the roots, causes, and underpinnings of individual differences in personality.

Personality psychology is not simply an abstract, academic enterprise of describing and explaining differences between people, however. It is intimately connected to a variety of practical activities in contemporary society, such as the treatment of mental disorders, the selection of job candidates, and the making sense of lives in biographical writing. These applied and practical aspects of personality psychology are discussed in the book's third section. The book's fourth and final section shifts focus from personality to intelligence and cognitive ability. Many of the issues that arise in the psychology of personality also appear in the study of intelligence, and many psychologists are intensely interested in both topics, placing them both under the broader umbrella of 'individual differences'. This section of the book therefore examines many of the same topics discussed in the three preceding sections, but in relation to intelligence: how differences in cognitive ability should be described, how they should be explained, and how they should be assessed in practice.

Each chapter contains several features that can help you direct and consolidate your learning and exploration. Each one starts with a set of learning objectives to guide your reading, and a brief chapter summary that captures the main topics to be covered. Every chapter ends with a summary of the main points, and an annotated list of suggested further readings, most of which are very recent works accessible to the beginning student of personality. Each chapter (except Chapter 1) also presents a recent piece of research that illustrates the chapter's themes, using studies conducted in many diverse countries. Key concepts are defined and explicated in a Glossary at the end of the book.

So without further ado, let's begin our journey by trying to understand what personality is.

SECTION 1
DESCRIBING PERSONALITY

1

What is Personality?

Learning objectives

- To develop an understanding of how the concept of 'personality' has developed over the course of history.
- To understand how personality is conceptualized within psychology, and how personality differs from other forms of psychological variation.
- To distinguish between personality and related concepts, such as character and temperament.
- To recognize how personality fits within psychology as a whole, and how it differs from related subdisciplines.
- To develop an overview of the book's organization.

This chapter introduces and clarifies the concept of 'personality', which defines the subject matter of personality psychology. The historical background and alternative meanings of the concept are discussed, followed by an analysis of how personality relates to and is distinct from other kinds of differences between people, such as those that are physical rather than psychological, or transient rather than lasting. Personality is distinguished from the related concepts of character and temperament, and the place that the study of personality occupies in psychology as a whole is examined. Personality psychology is argued to be distinguished by its emphasis on individual differences, and by its focus on whole persons as behaving, thinking, and feeling beings. Finally, an overview of the book's organization is presented.

A friend of mine once told me a sad story about a boy he knew as a child. Apparently, this boy's mother took him aside at an early age, looked him in the eye, and addressed to him the following words: 'Son, you're not very good-looking, you're not very smart, you have no personality, and you'll probably never have many friends, and I thought I should tell you this while you are young so you don't develop any unrealistic hopes for the future'.

This rather harsh assessment immediately raises a few questions. What kind of harm did the boy suffer from this statement? Did he grow up to be an alcoholic, an axe murderer, a dentist? What kind of mother would say this to her child? Is this story made up? However, one question that may not have struck you is this: What would it mean to have no personality? Or, turning the question around, what does it mean to have a personality?

THE CONCEPT OF PERSONALITY

To answer this question we have to explore the meanings of the word 'personality', because it turns out that there are several. One particularly instructive way to sort out these meanings and to think through their implications is to examine the word's history. Once upon a time, personality was something everyone had. When the word first appeared in English in the 14th century, it meant the quality of being a person, as distinct from an inanimate thing. 'Personality' referred to the capacities – such as consciousness and rational thought – that were believed to give humans a special place in creation (Williams, 1976). In this theological sense, then, personality refers to our shared humanity.

In time, however, this sense of personality as personhood gave way to one that has a more modern feel to it. Over a period of centuries, personality came to refer less to the human capacities that we share and that distinguish us from animals, and more to the characteristics that give each one of us our individuality. In this sense, personality implies a focus on the individual human being: the 'person'. Interestingly, however, the word 'person' did not originally refer to the individual in the way we tend to use it today. Instead, 'person' came, via French, from the Latin word *'persona'*, which referred to the mask worn by an actor to portray a particular character. In this theatrical sense, personality has to do with the role or character that the person plays in life's drama. The person's individuality, in this sense, is a matter of the roles or characters that he or she assumes.

While 'personality' gradually acquired the sense of individuality, it sometimes took on a more specific connotation. Rather than referring equally to all kinds of individuality, it increasingly referred to vivacity or charisma. As a popular song of the 1960s by Lloyd Price put it: 'I'll be a fool for you, 'Cause you've got – [ecstatic chorus] Personality! – Walk – Personality! – Talk – Personality! – Smile – Personality! – Charm – Personality!', and so on. People who had these qualities in abundance were said to have more personality, and self-improvement books gave directions for acquiring this precious quantity. Presumably it is in this sense that our unfortunate boy was said to have 'no personality', and why celebrities are commonly referred to as 'personalities'.

Clearly 'personality' has had several distinct meanings: personhood, individuality, and personal charm. These are all meanings that laypeople understand and use in their everyday speech. But what does personality mean in the specialized language of psychology, the science that should, presumably, have something to say about human individuality and what it is to be a person? What is it, precisely, that personality psychologists study?

'PERSONALITY' IN PSYCHOLOGY

If you ask an ornithologist or an architect what their fields are basically all about they will probably give you a simple, unhesitating answer: birds and buildings. Ask a personality psychologist and you are likely to hear a pause, an embarrassed clearing of the throat, and then a rather lengthy and abstract formulation. Ask ten personality psychologists, and you may well hear ten different formulations. Personality is a slippery concept, which is difficult to capture within a simple definition. In spite of this, a common thread runs through all psychologists' definitions. Psychologists agree that personality is fundamentally a matter of human individuality, or 'individual differences', to use the phrase that most prefer.

However, this definition of personality as human individuality immediately runs into problems unless we flesh it out a little. For a start, it is obvious that not all differences between people are differences of personality. We differ in our physical attributes, our ages, our nationalities, and our genders, and none of these differences really seem to be about personality. Of course, it is possible that these differences are in some way *related* to personality, but they are not themselves differences of personality. We are sometimes told that men are from Mars and women from Venus – the former aggressive and dominating, the latter loving and nurturing – but even if these crude stereotypes were true, biological sex would not be a personality characteristic. So we must immediately qualify our definition so that personality refers only to *psychological* differences between people, differences having to do with thought, emotion, motivation, and behaviour.

Even here our definition is not quite sufficient as far as most psychologists are concerned. Traditionally, psychologists have considered certain psychological differences between people to be outside of the realm of personality, specifically those involving *intelligence* and *cognitive abilities*. For many years psychological researchers and theorists have tried to understand and measure people's intellectual capabilities, individual differences that predict successful performance on a variety of tasks, and particularly those that involve formal schooling. Individual differences of this sort will be examined in a later section of this book (Chapter 11), and are certainly of interest to many personality psychologists, but they are generally treated separately from individual differences in personality. Excluding these ability-related differences, then, we are left with a definition of personality as non-intellectual psychological differences between people.

If this distinction between intellectual and non-intellectual differences makes you uneasy, you are not alone. Many psychologists consider it to be somewhat arbitrary. Which side of the conceptual divide does creativity fall on, for example? It seems to be partly a matter of mental abilities, and partly a matter of non-intellectual qualities such as openness to new experiences, mental flexibility, and drive. In addition, some psychologists argue that certain personality differences – differences that do not involve competencies in particular cognitive tasks – can be fruitfully understood as abilities or intelligences. For instance, some psychologists have recently proposed interpersonal and emotional intelligences. Nevertheless, although the boundary between the intellectual and non-intellectual domains is a vague and permeable one, it is a boundary that most psychologists continue to take seriously.

Have we finished our conceptual labour now that we have a working definition of personality as non-intellectual psychological differences between people? Sadly, not quite. Consider the case of emotions and moods. Emotions and moods are non-intellectual states of mind, and at any particular time individuals differ on them (you may be angry, another person anxious, yet another person content). Shouldn't emotions and moods therefore be aspects of personality? Psychologists argue that they are not, precisely because they refer to fleeting *states* rather than to enduring characteristics of the person. Only characteristics that have some degree of stability and consistency – characteristics that can be thought of as lasting *dispositions* of the person – are considered to be aspects of personality. Once again, people's emotional states may *reflect* enduring emotional dispositions (e.g., you might be an anger-prone person) or they may be *related* to their personalities in a specific way (e.g., you might be angry now because you are the sort of person who is quick to take offence). However, emotional states are too short-lived to be considered as aspects of personality themselves.

A related issue arises with psychological characteristics such as attitudes (e.g., being for or against immigration restrictions), beliefs (e.g., whether or not

God exists), tastes (e.g., preferring the Beastie Boys or Beethoven), and habits (e.g., going to bed early or late). All of these characteristics, unlike emotions and moods, are at least somewhat stable over time, and they clearly reflect non-intellectual differences between people. However, psychologists still do not usually consider them true components of personality. The reason this time is that attitudes, beliefs, tastes, and habits are normally quite narrow and restricted in their psychological relevance. Attitudes and beliefs concern specific propositions, tastes concern specific experiences, and habits concern specific actions. Personality characteristics, in contrast, have relatively broad relevance; they refer to *generalized patterns* of psychological functioning. For instance, people might be said to have 'authoritarian' personalities if, in addition to their specifically anti-immigration sentiments, they hold a variety of prejudiced, repressive, and highly conventional attitudes. Similarly, people who go to bed late might be said to be ambitious if this habit is part of a larger pattern of hard work and competitive striving, or extraverted and sensation-seeking if it is part of a pattern of relentless partying.

As you can see, the understanding of personality that psychologists employ is quite complex. The appealing simplicity that 'individual differences' implies is a little deceptive. From the perspective of personality psychology, that is, personality refers to those individual differences that (1) are psychological in nature, (2) fall outside the intellectual domain, (3) are enduring dispositions rather than transient states, and (4) form relatively broad or generalized patterns. This set of distinctions is presented schematically in Figure 1.1.

Does this complex set of distinctions add up to a satisfactory definition of personality? It certainly comes close. However, we need to make one more important addition to it. Some psychologists argue that the definition of personality should not only refer to individual differences in dispositions, but should also refer to the underlying psychological mechanisms and processes that give rise to them. That is, someone's personality is not simply a set of *characteristics* that they possess, but also a set of *dynamics* that account for these characteristics. If we allow for this sensible addition, then it is hard to do much better than Funder (1997), who defines personality as 'an individual's characteristic pattern of thought, emotion, and behavior, together with the psychological mechanisms – hidden or not – behind those patterns' (pp. 1–2).

After reading all of the conceptual distinctions we have made so far while defining personality, the definition that we have come up with may seem to narrow personality down to a small and insignificant subset of the differences between people. However, if you think about it for a minute, you might change your mind. In fact, those aspects of your psychological individuality that are enduring, broad, and non-intellectual are particularly important ones. If you were asked to describe yourself, you would probably mention many attributes that are not aspects of your personality – such as groups you belong to (e.g.,

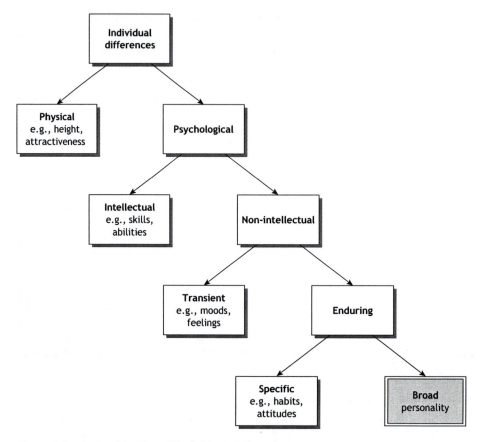

Figure 1.1   A classification of individual differences

national, ethnic, gender, age) and physical descriptions – but you would almost certainly mention quite a few personality characteristics. It is unlikely, on the other hand, that you would mention many of the psychological characteristics that we excluded from our definition of personality, such as current mood states, specific attitudes, or particular habits. Imagine how you would feel if someone responded to a request to describe who she is by stating that she feels worried, thinks that Britney Spears is a fine singer, and brushes her teeth five times a day. You would probably think that this person wasn't really answering the question appropriately: she isn't really giving you a good sense of who she is as a person and seems to be referring to incidental details of her life.

This is an important point. The reason why personality characteristics as we have defined them are particularly significant is that they seem to be central to who we are as persons, rather than merely being minor or incidental details. Why this is so is no great mystery. Characteristics that are not enduring dispositions are, almost by definition, not very informative about who we are as persons who endure through time: our transient psychological states may well not reflect how we normally are. Characteristics that are highly specific are usually not central to our sense of ourselves because they also tend to reflect isolated features of our make-up rather than ways in which our behaviour and our identity are coherent. Even if we did think of ourselves in terms of a list of specific attitudes, tastes, beliefs, and the like, it would be such a long and formless list that it would not amount to any good sense of who we are as individuals. This is why we tend to define ourselves in terms of broader patterns of thinking, feeling, and behaving: in short, personality characteristics. Even the distinction between intellectual and non-intellectual differences is relevant to our sense of self. People tend to define themselves much more in terms of a vast range of (non-intellectual) personality characteristics than the relatively narrow domain of cognitive abilities (although almost all of us, of course, think of ourselves as 'intelligent').

To summarize, personality is a particularly important domain of individual differences, even if on the surface it seems to be rather narrow according to our definition. It is important because it encompasses the sorts of psychological characteristics that are most informative about who we are as individuals, individuals whose behaviour is coherent, patterned, and governed by a stable sense of self or personal identity.

RELATED CONCEPTS

Having closed in on a sense of what personality is, it may be helpful to compare the concept to others with related meanings. Two concepts that quickly come to mind are '**temperament**' and '**character**'. In everyday language these terms are sometimes used more or less interchangeably with 'personality', and historically they have often been used in contexts where, in more recent times, 'personality' would be employed. Within psychology, however, they have somewhat distinct meanings. Temperament usually refers to those aspects of psychological individuality that are present at birth or at least early in child development, are related to emotional expression, and are presumed to have a biological basis. In short, temperamental characteristics are thought to be grounded in bodily processes.

Character, on the other hand, usually refers to those personal attributes that are relevant to moral conduct, self-mastery, will-power, and integrity. Someone of 'poor character', that is, might be deceitful, impulsive, and shiftless. Whereas temperamental characteristics are commonly assumed to have a biological basis, character is often assumed to be the result of socialization experiences, aspects of the person's psychological make-up that depend on learning socially appropriate forms of self-control and 'prosocial' conduct. Both assumptions are only partially true.

How do temperament and character relate to personality as we have defined it, and as it is understood by psychologists? Although the two concepts have rather distinct connotations, psychologists now tend to think of them as referring to different sorts of personality characteristics. In short, psychology's concept of personality contains temperament and character within it, and recognizes that personality characteristics can spring from biological and social influences, from genes and experiences, and, most often, both. We will have a lot more to say about this in later chapters.

PUTTING IT TOGETHER

Figure 1.2 tries to lay out the basics of our emerging sense of personality, as it is understood by personality psychologists. To the left is a set of psychological mechanisms and processes that produce enduring psychological differences between people. These differences can be roughly divided into those that are intellectual (i.e., involving cognitive abilities) and those that are not, with a grey area of ambiguous characteristics in the middle. Some personality differences can be considered aspects of character or temperament. Enduring psychological differences are, in addition, related to more transient and specific behaviours, cognitions, and emotions.

PERSONALITY PSYCHOLOGY'S PLACE IN PSYCHOLOGY

The definition of personality that we have been mulling over is psychology's. It may not correspond exactly to yours or anyone else's. However, it does define the subject matter of one of psychology's basic subdisciplines or areas of study, alongside cognitive, developmental, social, and physiological psychology, among others. So how is the psychology of personality, defined in this way, distinct from these other subdisciplines? Three distinctions are most important.

First, personality psychology is all about differences between people, as we have seen, whereas the other subdisciplines generally are not. Most psychological areas of study investigate what people have in common; the mechanisms, processes, and structures that we all share by virtue of being human. Cognitive psychologists may study how we perceive objects, social psychologists how we

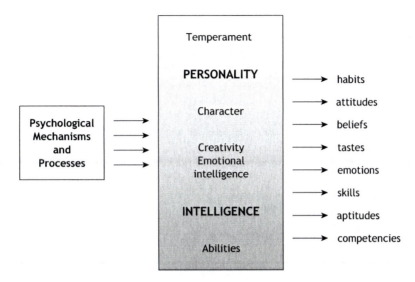

Figure 1.2   Psychology's model of individual differences

form stereotypes, and physiological psychologists how our brain chemicals are associated with our moods, where 'we' and 'our' are understood to refer to people in general. The focus of the studies that these psychologists conduct is usually on the average pattern of response that a group of study participants manifests. Variations among participants around that average are usually ignored and treated as a nuisance ('random error'). To personality psychologists, in contrast, such variations between people are precisely what is most interesting. Of course, understanding how we are all the same is at least as important as understanding how we differ, but personality psychology is virtually alone within psychology in focusing on questions of the second kind.

A second distinctive feature of personality psychology is that its focus is on the whole person as an integrated individual. This probably sounds rather vague and fluffy, but it is in clear contrast to some other areas of study in psychology. Most subdisciplines address a specific psychological function or domain, one piece of what makes up the functioning individual. These functions and domains include perception, thinking, emotion, and language. These are all important aspects of human psychology, of course, but they are also in some sense 'sub-personal', referring to components that are integrated into a coherent system that we call a person. Personality psychology, which takes individuals rather than their components as its subject matter, aspires to be broader and more encompassing. Arguably social and developmental psychology, by studying people in their social interactions and contexts and on their changes over time, share this focus on the whole person, although they do not usually emphasize individual differences. This is one reason why personality, social, and developmental psychology are all sometimes disparaged as 'soft' psychology, their methods seen as less rigorous and their findings less objective and reliable than those of the 'harder' subdisciplines. Because personality psychology and its allied subdisciplines deal with people in all their complexity – as creatures with social, cultural, and biological dimensions – they face greater scientific challenges than those subdisciplines that can isolate and study one part of the psyche.

A third distinctive feature of personality psychology contrasts it with social psychology. Personality and social psychology are close neighbours in some ways: many psychologists identify themselves with both, many professional journals are devoted to both, and both tend to share a focus on the whole person. However, as we have seen, personality psychology focuses on enduring characteristics of the person that are consistent across different situations. In contrast, social psychology tends to pay attention to those aspects of the person's thinking, feeling, and behaving that change over time and under different circumstances. Social psychologists are interested in how our mind and behaviour are shaped by the social contexts in which we are embedded and the social interactions in which we participate. Consequently, social psychologists emphasize the extent to which our attitudes, beliefs, emotions, and behaviours are malleable products of our social environment, and personality psychologists emphasize the extent to which they are stable attributes of the person. One way to think about this is that personality psychologists have a tendency or bias to see psychological phenomena as being due to *internal* factors – influences intrinsic to the person – whereas social psychologists have a corresponding tendency to see them as due to *external* factors located in the social environment.

In summary, then, the psychology of personality is an important and distinctive area of study within the broader field of psychology. It is distinctive in its focus on psychological variation, on the whole person or individual as the unit of analysis, and on the determinants of thinking, feeling, and behaving that are intrinsic to the person.

OVERVIEW OF THE BOOK

In the remaining chapters of the book we will explore the psychology of personality, keeping in mind the issues that have arisen in this introduction. In the remainder of this first section of the book ('Describing personality'), we discuss the efforts that psychologists have made to *describe* personality, that is, to define what it is and determine how its variations should be mapped out. Once we have decided that personality is essentially about certain kinds of differences between people – human individuality – we have to decide how these differences are most usefully characterized and classified. What units should we use to describe personalities, and can they be organized into an encompassing framework of personality description? Chapter 2 presents the tradition of psychological research that has attempted to characterize personality in terms of units called 'traits'. Psychologists who work in this tradition argue that traits provide the best language for describing personality variations, and that a few fundamental traits underlie these superficially limitless variations.

Chapter 3 reviews the psychology of traits and presents some of the criticisms that have been levelled against it. Is it true, for instance, that people's behaviour really is as patterned – consistent across different situations and stable over time – as trait psychology imagines? Are there alternative ways to describe personality that trait psychology leaves out? Are the supposedly fundamental traits that Western researchers have discovered truly universal, or are different traits needed to capture personality variations in non-Western cultures? These and several other challenges to the psychology of traits will be discussed.

Having reviewed attempts to *describe* personality, we turn in the book's second section to attempts to *explain* it. It is one thing to establish *how* something should be characterized, quite another thing to account for *why* it is as it is. For instance, to describe a landscape we might draw a map of its physical features (e.g., peaks, valleys, rivers, lakes), its vegetation (e.g., forests, woods, grasslands), and the incursions that people have made on it (e.g., settlements, roads, power-lines, district boundaries). However, to explain why the landscape is as it is, we need to go beyond and beneath its visible topography. Our explanation might refer to any number of influences, such as the geological forces that buckled and carved the surface of the land, the climate that surrounds it, and the historical, economic, and political realities that affected how humans modified it. In short, there may be many ways to account for why a phenomenon – a landscape or a personality – is the way it is.

The second section of the book ('Explaining personality') therefore reviews a variety of personality theories, which offer quite different answers to this 'why' question. Chapter 4 presents biological theories of personality, which maintain that personality variation is underpinned by individual differences in brain chemistry and functioning, and genetic inheritance. We review evidence regarding the degree to which personality characteristics are inherited, and what 'behavioural genetics' can tell us about the sources of personality. We also consider the degree to which fundamental traits have a neurochemical basis.

Chapter 5 discusses psychoanalytic theories, which account for personality in terms of child development, unconscious motives, and psychological defences and conflicts. Although linked in the popular mind with one man, Sigmund Freud, we discuss the many ways psychoanalytic theory has developed since he originated it and the many ways in which it accounts for personality processes and characteristics.

Chapter 6 introduces cognitive theories of personality, which explain personality variation as the result of differing patterns of thinking, perceiving, and believing. These patterns range from beliefs that guide our individual ways of understanding the world, to the social and emotional skills we bring to our interpersonal relationships, to the strategies we employ in trying to accomplish our goals and plans. They extend into our self-images and identities, and the stories that we construct to make autobiographical sense of our lives, past, present, and future.

The first two sections of the book focus on the fundamental concepts, theories, and findings of personality psychology. However, personality psychology is not simply an abstract science of how and why people differ psychologically. It also has important practical applications, which we will discuss in the book's third section ('Personality in practice'). The book's first two sections therefore provide a conceptual foundation for exploring these applications. Chapter 7 discusses the ways in which personality psychology can illuminate psychological development, and help us to understand personality stability and change. Does personality change in adulthood, or is it set in plaster during childhood? Can you predict adult personality from child temperament? What stages do people go through in personality development, and what are the characteristic themes and preoccupations of each stage?

Chapter 8 reviews the ways in which personality can be measured, and the contexts in which personality assessment has a very real impact on people's lives. Increasingly, personality tests are finding their ways into the selection of employees, as a supplement to interviews and other criteria. Personality testing is also commonly performed by clinical psychologists who need to evaluate the progress of clients in therapy, to diagnose their problems, or to assess their suitability for treatment. Many different forms of personality assessment have been developed, and their strengths, weaknesses, and goals are discussed at length in the chapter.

Chapter 9 discusses the various roles that personality plays in mental disorders, the destructive ways in which personality disturbances can manifest themselves, and the ways in which personality contributes to physical ill-health.

Chapter 10 critically reviews attempts to apply personality theory to the study of individual lives, a controversial practice known as 'psychobiography'. In discussing the difficulties, risks, and limitations of psychobiography – how hard it is to 'put it all together' and formulate persons in their entirety – we will come to an appreciation of the complexity of human lives and personalities. It is this complexity that makes the psychology of personality so daunting but also, I hope you will agree by the end of this book, so fascinating and challenging.

The book's fourth and final section contains a single chapter on the psychology of intelligence and cognitive abilities. Chapter 11 discusses several of the topics that were discussed earlier in the book in relation to personality. It reviews evidence on how individual differences in abilities should be described (i.e., the structure of ability), how they should be explained (i.e., the role of environmental and genetic factors), and the practical issues surrounding the study of abilities (i.e., intelligence testing).

Chapter summary

- 'Personality' is a complicated concept that has had several distinct meanings over the course of history. Within psychology, however, it refers to individual differences in psychological dispositions: that is, enduring ways in which people differ from one another in their typical ways of behaving, thinking, and feeling. These differences often reflect core features of who we are as persons, and are central to our self-concepts.
- This understanding of personality often excludes individual differences in intelligence and cognitive ability, although these are also of interest to many personality psychologists.
- In addition, personality psychologists are interested not only in individual differences, but also in the underlying causes or dynamics that explain these differences between people.
- Personality can be loosely distinguished from character (morally-relevant dispositions having to do with self-control, will, and integrity) and temperament (biologically-based dispositions that often involve emotional expression and are present early in life).
- Within psychology, the study of personality is distinctive for its focus on human individuality and its concern for the person as a functioning whole. It differs from social psychology, a neighbouring subdiscipline, by emphasizing the contribution that the person's internal dispositions make to behaviour, rather than the contribution of the person's external situation or context.

Further Reading

Major reference works

For students wishing to obtain a more thorough and advanced review of personality psychology, the following major handbooks may be of interest:

- Hogan, R., Johnson, J., & Briggs, S. (Eds.) (1999). *Handbook of personality psychology*. New York: Academic Press.
- Pervin, L.A. (Ed.) (1999). *Handbook of personality: Theory and research* (2nd ed.). New York: Guilford.

Journals

To get a sense of current research in personality psychology, and the sorts of research methods that it uses, you should take a look at recent issues of prominent scientific journals such as the following:

- *European Journal of Personality*
- *Journal of Personality*
- *Journal of Personality and Social Psychology*
- *Journal of Research in Personality*
- *Personality and Individual Differences*
- *Personality and Social Psychology Bulletin*
- *Personality and Social Psychology Review*

Websites

There are a couple of reasonably comprehensive websites that present personality-related material. The fourth and fifth sites can be searched for pages of individual personality psychologists:

- The personality project (www.personality-project.org)
- Great ideas in personality (www.personalityresearch.org)
- International Society for the Study of Individual Differences (issid. org/issid.html)
- Association for Research in Personality (www.personality-arp.org)
- Social Psychology Network (www.socialpsychology.org) and see especially www.socialpsychology.org/person.htm

2

Trait Psychology

Learning objectives

- To develop a working understanding of the concept of 'personality trait' and the hierarchical structure of traits.
- To understand how psychologists have developed models of the dimensional structure of personality traits, including the statistical methods employed.
- To comprehend the 'Big Five' personality dimensions and their differences from existing three-factor models.
- To recognize the importance of trait taxonomies for advancing psychological understanding and prediction.
- To have a working knowledge of specific traits in addition to the broad personality dimensions.

This chapter turns to the fundamental question of how individual differences in personality should be described. The concept of personality 'trait' — the primary unit of personality description — is introduced and defined, and the hierarchical nature of traits is explained. The long-standing efforts to uncover the structure or organization of personality traits, by reducing the bewildering variety of possible traits into a few basic personality dimensions, are then explored. Along the way, the statistical methods used to conduct this reduction are presented. One prominent outcome of this work, the five-factor model of personality, is presented, and contrasted with a rival model that proposes three rather than five basic dimensions along which people vary. We discuss the value of dimensional systems such as these, and demonstrate the many phenomena that one illustrative dimension helps to illuminate. Finally, we see that, in addition to such broad personality dimensions, a variety of more specific traits also offer valuable ways of capturing meaningful differences between people.

The previous chapter left us with an abstract understanding of what personality psychologists study. Our rather unwieldy definition tells us what personality is, according to the psychologists who study it. However, it does not even begin to tell us how to characterize a personality. How are we to describe the individual differences that make up people's personalities?

Description is a fundamental problem for any science, and personality psychology aspires to be scientific. Chemistry has its periodic table of elements, zoology its taxonomy of biological species, physics its classification of elementary particles. These systems of description systematically lay out the sorts of things that scientists encounter and work with when explaining phenomena. They describe the *structure* or *organization* of the world from the perspective of the respective sciences, and provide the units of analysis for theoretical and empirical work. So how are we to describe the structure of personality, and what are the proper units of description?

WHAT IS A TRAIT?

Many psychologists think that the best unit for describing personalities is the trait, and that the structure of personality is the organization of traits. At one level, the concept of trait is a simple one: a trait is a characteristic form of behaving, thinking, or feeling, such as 'friendliness', 'rigidity', or 'anxiousness'. At another level the situation is more complicated, and several important aspects of the concept need to be spelled out. Some of these should remind you of our discussion of the concept of personality in Chapter 1:

- A trait must be a relatively enduring characteristic of the person, as distinct from a transient state. Although vague, the 'relatively' is an important qualification here. Traits may change over time, but they shouldn't change rapidly or chaotically; they should tend to be stable attributes of the person.
- A trait represents a pattern of behaviour, thinking, or feeling that is relatively consistent over a variety of different situations. If a person behaves in a very different

manner when in similar situations – being very outgoing in some and very reserved and shy in others, for example – we should not attribute a trait to him or her. Once again, the 'relatively' is important because traits do not entail total situational consistency in a person's behavior. People need not be shy in *all* social situations for it to be appropriate to call them shy.

- A trait is a way in which people differ from one another – it is, as scientists would say, a 'variable' – so that different individuals will manifest different levels of the trait. To simplify communication, we may say that someone either has or doesn't have a particular trait, but psychologists typically assume that people differ by degrees on traits. People may have greater or lesser degrees of shyness, and in principle these degrees can be quantified.

- Traits are dispositions. That is, a trait is best thought of as a probabilistic *tendency* that a person has to act in a certain way when placed in a certain kind of situation. Cats, for instance, have dispositions to hiss and scratch, but will only express these dispositions in particular circumstances, and even in these circumstances they may not always do so. Consequently, a trait may remain unexpressed and unobserved if a person encounters few situations in which it might be expressed.

- Traits vary in their generality. Some traits only bear on narrow domains of life, and others are relevant to a very large proportion of the person's everyday activities. We can talk about a hierarchy of traits, with relatively specific traits that relate to a small number of behaviours falling under broader traits. For instance, shame-proneness could be considered one component of a more general trait of 'negative emotionality', the disposition to experience unpleasant emotional states. Such a hierarchy could have several levels, with particular behaviours or habits representing the bottom level: placing a raunchy personals advertisement is a behaviour that may reflect a narrow trait of sexual sensation-seeking, which is one component of a medium-level trait of sensation-seeking, which is itself a component of a high-level trait of extraversion. This hierarchical arrangement is illustrated in Figure 2.1.

DEFINING THE TRAIT UNIVERSE: PART 1

Our discussion so far should make it clearer how personality psychologists conceptualize traits. Defining what a trait is and choosing the trait as the unit of personality description is only the beginning, of course. To go further towards a system of personality description, we need a way to map the trait universe. In other words, we need to find a way to characterize the range of personality variation that traits cover. Does this universe of traits have any fundamental dimensions, groupings, coordinates, or axes, and what might they be?

A first step towards answering this question by English-speaking psychologists was taken by Allport and Odbert in 1936, who followed research in German by Baumgarten. Allport and Odbert sought to define the boundaries of the trait universe by collecting an exhaustive list of personality descriptors (see

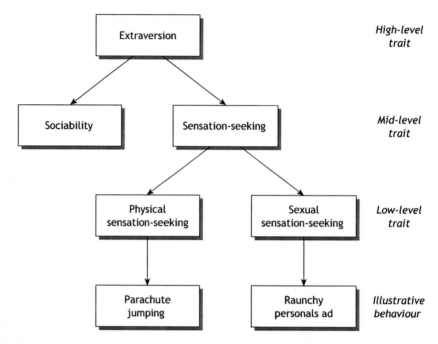

Figure 2.1   The hierarchical structure of traits

John, 1990, for more details). They did this by patiently combing through a large dictionary, containing about 550,000 entries, for terms that referred to ways in which one person's behaviour could be distinguished from another's. By this means they obtained almost 18,000 terms, an astonishing number if you think of it. As you might imagine, after reading Chapter 1, not all of these terms were personality characteristics. In fact, about three-quarters of them were not, according to the authors' understanding of personality. Some referred to physical characteristics, cognitive abilities or talents, transient states such as moods, specific behaviours, social roles, or highly evaluative terms used to describe people's effects on others rather than consistencies in their own behaviour (e.g., 'irritating'). Nevertheless, after all of these non-personality terms were removed from the list, roughly 4,500 trait terms remained.

Allport and Odbert's work creates a dilemma. If there really are 4,500 different trait terms circulating in English, and similar numbers in other languages, does this mean personality psychologists have to pay attention to all of them? That would seem to be a daunting task, and any descriptive system that needs

4,500 different terms would seem to fail an important scientific criterion: to be an economical and practical way to describe the phenomena of interest, in this case human personalities. Surely, also, many trait terms are redundant with others and refer to the same sorts of people. It is possible to draw subtle conceptual distinctions between 'hostile', 'aggressive', 'fierce', and 'belligerent', for example, but their meanings clearly overlap and it would be more than a little odd to hear someone described as 'hostile and aggressive but not at all fierce or belligerent'. If this is the case, it makes sense to imagine that hidden within the vast expanse of the trait term universe there might be a smaller number of fundamental personality characteristics, like constellations in the night sky. But how many such basic traits are there, what might they be, and how on earth might we be able to discover them?

A STATISTICAL DIGRESSION

Before we answer the first two of these questions we need to address the third, the 'methodological' question of how basic traits are to be determined. And to answer this question, we need to embark on a short digression into statistics. If the mere sight of this word makes your stomach turn, be reassured that this little excursion will not be technical. However, like all sciences, personality psychology has a significant quantitative component, and psychologists interested in determining the fundamental traits of personality have relied very heavily on two statistical procedures in particular. Statistical methods are indispensable to personality psychology as it has developed, as it is impossible to grasp efforts to examine personality structure without them.

The first procedure is called the *correlation coefficient* or **correlation** for short. A correlation represents the degree of association between two variables (i.e., things that vary) and is measured on a scale from −1 to +1. 'Association' refers to the degree to which one variable is *related to* or *predictable on the basis of* another. If I know that you are of above average height, for example, I can predict that you will be of above average weight too, because height and weight are associated in this sense. My predictions may be wrong in particular cases – there are plenty of heavy shorter people and skinny tall ones – but on average they should be better than chance (i.e., predicting randomly). This association of height and weight is a positive one, because the higher the quantity of one variable, the higher the quantity of the other is likely to be. A negative association – such as between a place's latitude and its average temperature – means that the higher the quantity of one variable, the lower the quantity of the other tends to be. When there is no association between two variables – such as shoe size and intelligence – they have a correlation of 0 and do not enable any

Table 2.1 *Hypothetical data sets illustrating correlations of different sizes*

Data set 1: small correlation (.1)

		Variable B Above average	Variable B Below average	Total
Variable A	Above average	55	45	100
	Below average	45	55	100
	Total	100	100	200

Data set 2: moderate correlation (.3)

		Variable B Above average	Variable B Below average	Total
Variable A	Above average	65	35	100
	Below average	35	65	100
	Total	100	100	200

Data set 3: large correlation (.5)

		Variable B Above average	Variable B Below average	Total
Variable A	Above average	75	25	100
	Below average	25	75	100
	Total	100	100	200

prediction of one another at all. A very large proportion of research in personality psychology involves looking for associations among variables, using the humble correlation coefficient.

The magnitude of a correlation coefficient matters a great deal. A positive association may exist between two variables, so the correlation is somewhere between 0 and +1, but the implications of it being .1 or .9 are very different. If it is .9, then each variable allows confident prediction of the other: the correlation is almost perfect. If it is .1, on the other hand, the two variables will yield prediction of one another that is barely above chance. By convention in psychology, correlations of .1, .3, and .5 are considered small, moderate, and large, respectively (Cohen, 1992). Correlations much higher than about .6 are quite rare, except between alternative measures of the same variable (e.g., two tests of depression). Because the size of correlations will be referred to on a few occasions throughout this book, it is worth getting some sense of what these values mean. Consider the three hypothetical situations presented in

Table 2.1 opposite, each of which represents 200 people measured on two variables, A and B. Each person's level on each variable is represented as being either 'above average' or 'below average', in the sense of falling in the top or bottom half of the 200 people. (Strictly speaking, this average is called the 'median'.) Note that this is a simplification: usually measures of personality variables take a continuous range of numerical values rather than crudely dichotomizing people.

Table 2.1 illustrates small, medium, and large correlations. Look at data set 1 first, which represents a small correlation of .1. If I know that someone is above average on Variable A, I can predict that he or she will also be above average on Variable B, because this is somewhat more likely (55%) than the reverse. However, this prediction is obviously not one that I can be very confident about, as it will be wrong 45% of the time. Still, it is better than nothing, because if I predicted at random I would be wrong 50% of the time.

Data set 2, which illustrates a .3 correlation, is quite a bit better than nothing. Knowing that someone is above average on A allows us to predict that he or she will be above average on B with more assurance. We will be correct 65% of the time, almost twice as often as we are incorrect (i.e., 65 ÷ 35 = 1.86). Data set 3, showing a strong .5 correlation, allows us to be correct 75% of the time: the odds of our prediction being correct are now 3:1. As you can see, the magnitude of a correlation has clear implications.

The little tables we've used to illustrate the meaning of correlation are called binomial effect size displays (BESDs; Rosenthal & Rubin, 1982). If you want to get a sense of what a correlation means in practical terms, a simple calculation lets you convert it into this way of thinking. All you need to do is divide the correlation by two and then add 0.5. This number estimates the proportion of cases who are above average on one variable who will be above average on the other; for example:

Correlation	Divide by 2	Add .5
.4	→ .2	→ .7
−.2	→ −.1	→ .4
.7	→ .35	→ .85
0	→ 0	→ .5

In these four examples, then, about 70%, 40%, 85%, and 50% of people, respectively, who score above the average on one variable will be above average on the other.

So much for the correlation coefficient, a simple measure of association that is the first statistical procedure that we need to review before returning to our

Table 2.2 *Hypothetical correlation matrix for variables A to F*

	A	B	C	D	E	F
A	1.0					
B	.1	1.0				
C	.5	−.2	1.0			
D	.2	.5	.1	1.0		
E	−.1	.4	−.1	.6	1.0	
F	.4	.1	.6	.2	−.2	1.0

exploration of personality structure. The second procedure that has been central to the study of personality structure is called factor analysis. In essence, factor analysis is a method for finding patterns within a group of correlations. It is perhaps best illustrated by a hypothetical example, illustrated above. Table 2.2 presents what is called a 'correlation matrix', which lays out correlation coefficients for all pairs of variables in a set. One half of the matrix is empty because the correlation between B and C, for example, is the same as the correlation between C and B, so there is no need to present both. Correlations falling on the diagonal are all +1 because a variable always correlates perfectly with itself.

Looking at Table 2.2 what you probably see is a big mess. Some variables correlate quite strongly, some not much at all, some negatively, and some positively. This is where factor analysis enters the scene. What it attempts to do is find patterns of correlations within the matrix that may not be readily obvious to the observer (i.e., what psychologists sometimes facetiously call 'eyeball analysis'). The technical and computational details of factor analysis need not concern us here, but in this particular correlation matrix the procedure would find clear evidence of two distinct groups of variables. Variables A, C, and F form one group, and variables B, D and E the other. Table 2.3 simply rearranges Table 2.2 to demonstrate the patterns that factor analysis would uncover.

As you can see, all of the correlations among variables A, C, and F are relatively strong and positive, averaging .5, as are the correlations among variables B, D, and E. However, the correlations of variables from one group with variables from the other, shown in the square at the lower left of the table, are all relatively weak, some positive and some negative, and they average close to 0. This indicates that there is no systematic pattern of association between the two variable groups: they are distinct and unrelated. In the language of factor analysis, these groups define separate factors.

Factor analysis searches through correlation matrices in an effort to locate variable groupings such as these. When it does so, it allows us to make certain inferences. First, we can guess that concealed within – or perhaps 'beneath' – the large set of variables, there is a smaller set of more basic 'latent' variables. Second, we can guess what these latent variables might be by paying attention

Table 2.3 *Rearranged correlation matrix*

	A	C	F	B	D	E
A	1.0					
C	.5	1.0				
F	.4	.6	1.0			
B	.1	−.2	.1	1.0		
D	.2	.1	.2	.5	1.0	
E	−.1	−.1	−.2	.4	.6	1.0

to what the variables within each group seem to have in common. If variables X, Y, and Z belong to one factor, that factor's identity or meaning can be guessed at by thinking about how the three variables are conceptually similar or about what they might jointly reflect.

As you may have guessed by now, factor analysis seems like a perfect way to begin the task, interrupted by this statistical digression, of uncovering and characterizing the fundamental traits that may underlie the wild profusion of trait terms.

DEFINING THE TRAIT UNIVERSE: PART 2

Sure enough, the first attempts to simplify the trait universe and discover the latent structure of personality relied heavily on factor analysis, and thus on correlation coefficients. The trail-blazer in this effort was Raymond Cattell, who tried to distil a smaller number of basic personality factors from Allport and Odbert's lengthy list of trait terms. Such a reduction could not easily be done by statistical means alone, so Cattell (1943) began by sorting the terms into semantically similar clusters of synonyms or near-synonyms, according to his personal judgment. He then sorted these clusters into pairs that appeared to be semantic opposites, or antonyms. In this fashion he derived 160 clusters, to which he added a few more from the psychological literature, and selected a representative term from each cluster.

At this point, the trait list drastically reduced from 4,500 to 171, statistical methods played their first, minor role. Cattell had 100 people rate one or two people they knew on the 171 trait terms, and then examined the correlations among the terms to identify a smaller set of 60 clusters. These were further reduced to 35 according to Cattell's judgment of which clusters were supported by the psychological literature. Only now did he employ factor analysis, again using a group of people's ratings of others' personalities. Through a complicated procedure, Cattell derived 12 factors from this analysis, to which he later added four more factors based on additional studies. At the end of this long and complicated process, then, we are left with 16 personality factors on which Cattell built a theory of personality.

Cattell's efforts to uncover the fundamental dimensions were Herculean, especially given the computational limitations of his time. Contemporary researchers can perform large factor analyses with a few pecks of a keyboard or clicks of a mouse, but in the mid-20th century analyses of moderately large data sets might take weeks of pencil-and-paper calculation. Cattell's work lives on in the tradition of factor-analytic research he pioneered, and in a still-popular personality test, the 16PF. Nevertheless, it has been eclipsed in recent personality psychology for three main reasons. First, many researchers have found Cattell's procedure for distilling his 16 factors to be somewhat arbitrary, relying on several steps that seem to involve too much subjective judgment. They have also had trouble replicating his factors in their own studies. Second, although 16 factors allow a much more economical description of personality than 4,500 trait terms, that number still seems too large for most theorists to juggle. It is certainly hard to keep so many dimensions in mind at once, leading many theorists to hope that a simpler system of description might emerge. Finally, many of Cattell's factors seemed to correlate, just as the trait terms within each factor correlate with one another. This fact raises the possibility that even more basic dimensions, or 'superfactors', might underpin Cattell's 16 factors. Ideally, perhaps, trait terms could be boiled down to truly independent, uncorrelated factors that are irreducible to any others.

The search for this bedrock of fundamental trait dimensions began with Fiske (1949) and was continued by many psychologists in the ensuing decades. Over time, researchers began to notice that factor analyses of personality ratings frequently converged on just five broad factors. Recognizing this regularity took some time, in part because different investigators chose different labels for their factors. Although factor analysis can tell researchers how many factors seem to be present in a correlation matrix, it is sadly incapable of telling precisely what they mean. Researchers must bestow a name, which they do based on some mixture of intelligent guesswork and theoretical predilections. Nevertheless, the recurrence of similar factors in many studies, using different methodologies and large and diverse samples of personality raters, eventually led some psychologists to dub them the '**Big Five**'. These five factors, it is claimed, represent the five fundamental ways along which people's personalities vary: the core of your personality can be represented by your position on these five dimensions. The primary label for each factor, alternative factor labels, and some trait terms that illustrate each factor, are presented in Table 2.4. Terms in italics represent the opposing pole of each factor.

Extraversion is a term that originated in the personality theory of Carl Jung, who meant by it an orientation to the outside world rather than to private

Table 2.4 *Summary of the Big Five personality factors (after John, 1990)*

Standard name	Alternative names	Illustrative trait terms
I. Extraversion	Surgency	sociable, assertive, enthusiastic, energetic, forceful, talkative *quiet, reserved, shy, retiring*
II. Agreeableness	Social adaptability	warm, modest, kind, appreciative, trusting, affectionate, helpful *cold, quarrelsome, unfriendly*
III. Conscientiousness	Dependability, Prudence, Will to Achieve	efficient, organized, thorough, planful, reliable *careless, irresponsible, frivolous*
IV. Neuroticism	Emotional instability	tense, irritable, shy, moody, nervous, high-strung *stable, calm, contented, unemotional*
V. Openness to Experience	Culture, Intellect	imaginative, intelligent, original, insightful, curious, sophisticated *narrow interests, simple, shallow*

experience, which he dubbed introversion. In the Big Five its connotations are somewhat different. As the table indicates, Extraversion is best exemplified by traits involving sociability, in particular a preference for large groups. However, it is much broader in scope than sociability, encompassing traits that involve energy and activity levels (hence the alternative title 'surgency'), sensation-seeking, interpersonal dominance, and a tendency to experience positive emotional states. Introverts tend to have low levels of these same traits.

Agreeableness, like Extraversion, primarily has to do with interpersonal qualities. Unlike Extraversion, it involves cooperativeness, altruism, and a generally warm, compliant, and trusting stance towards others. Disagreeable individuals are characterized as cold, callous, selfish, calculating, hostile, and competitive in their motivations.

Conscientiousness is a factor whose name has been the focus of some disagreement. However, there is little disagreement about the traits that characterize it, which generally reflect self-control, planfulness, and being organized, efficient, and deliberate in one's approach to tasks. Unconscientious people tend to be impulsive, disorganized, oriented to the present rather than the future, and careless towards their responsibilities. Conscientiousness is therefore a matter of caring about one's long-term goals and interests, resisting impulses that threaten to sabotage them, and harnessing one's efforts to accomplish these goals and interests competently. Different names for the factor draw attention to one or other of these aspects: 'dependability' emphasizes self-control and predictability, 'prudence' emphasizes planning and foresight, 'will to achieve' emphasizes the driven pursuit of goals.

Neuroticism has to do with people's emotional instability. Although 'neurosis' is an almost obsolete psychiatric term referring to pathological manifestations of anxiety, Neuroticism refers to a considerably wider range of negative emotions, including anger, sadness, shame, and embarrassment. It also does not imply the presence of any mental disorder. In this expanded sense, neurotic people are more prone to experience negative emotions, to be psychologically maladjusted and vulnerable, and to have low self-esteem. In contrast, people who are low in Neuroticism are emotionally stable, calm, and able to cope well with stress.

Openness to experience is a somewhat vague term for a factor that has proven to be controversial and difficult to name. Metaphorically, 'openness' implies a willingness to adopt novel and unconventional ways of thinking and behaving, manifest in such traits as creativity, imaginativeness, curiosity, and aesthetic appreciation. Open people are heavily invested in cultivating new experiences, and have a mild tendency to score relatively high on measures of intelligence. People who fall at the other end of this factor are conventional and narrow in their interests, and conservative and sometimes rigid in their approach to life's challenges and opportunities.

This set of 'Big Five' personality factors, which is sometimes referred to as the **'five-factor model'**, is probably the dominant model of personality structure in contemporary personality psychology. It is pleasingly economical, but also seems to leave few regions of the trait universe uncovered. Most of the trait terms we use in everyday speech can be related to the high or low end of these five factors, and most of the personality scales or tests that psychologists have developed seem to be measuring one or more of them to varying degrees. Research indicates that the factors can be derived from trait terms from several languages besides English, that they emerge reliably in studies of self-ratings as well as ratings of other people, that they are stable over time, and that they can predict many forms of behaviour. A questionnaire measure of the factors, the NEO PI-R (Costa & McCrae, 1992), is one of the most widely used personality scales. All told, the discovery of the five factors has been hailed as a major integrating achievement of personality psychology, a structure as objectively real as the seven continents.

ALTERNATIVES TO THE BIG FIVE

Although it has been widely adopted as a descriptive framework, the Big Five is not universally celebrated by psychologists working in the trait psychology tradition. Several alternative models have been propounded, the most well-supported of which propose that there are only three fundamental dimensions of personality. However, before we get to the details of these alternatives, we need to turn a critical eye on the origins of the Big Five. You will recall that the five factors emerged from statistical reductions of Allport and Odbert's list of trait terms. At the time you may not have questioned the merits of this list as a starting point for the exploration of personality structure. However, the idea that a language's repertoire of trait terms is the best place to search for basic personality dimensions can be challenged.

This idea is a key assumption of what has been called the *lexical* approach to personality description, from the Latin for 'word'. The lexical approach assumes that personality can be adequately encompassed by single words in natural language, and that languages encode in trait terms the personality distinctions that matter for their speakers. Every important personality characteristic should therefore be represented in the trait vocabulary, or 'lexicalized'. Is this so obvious? Might it not be the case that some important personality characteristics have evolved no corresponding term? Perhaps some characteristics, or traits, are not recognized or talked about by members of a language community, or maybe some are communicated about only by phrases or sentences. If this were true, and the trait term repertoire does not comprehensively reflect the trait universe, then factor analyses of trait terms might fail to capture some basic domains of personality, or might misrepresent others.

If the lexical approach is potentially flawed in this way, how else might the basic dimensions of personality be discovered? One approach is to examine people's responses to personality questionnaires rather than to trait lists. For at least a century psychologists have been developing scales or 'tests' to assess personality characteristics, which commonly contain a number of questionnaire items. These items usually take the form of statements to which people respond by endorsing one of a set of alternatives (e.g., yes/no, true/false, 1 = *strongly disagree* to 5 = *strongly agree*). Items might refer to a person's behaviours, feelings, attitudes, or beliefs. People's ratings of themselves or others on such items, or on the scales that are composed by combining multiple items, can be factor analysed, just like trait terms.

Advocates of this questionnaire approach to the study of personality structure argue that questionnaire items have one main advantage over trait terms. Simply put, they propose that items should be able to assess a greater range of personality characteristics. The greater semantic complexity of whole sentences should allow items to assess characteristics that have no corresponding single trait term, if such characteristics exist. This complexity also allows items to assess traits in particular contexts, whereas trait terms are context-free. Compare the task of rating how 'sociable' you are, which requires you to make a judgment that is abstracted from particular circumstances, with responding to 'I like to meet new people when I know I probably won't see them again'. Arguably statements such as these come closer to our ways of thinking about ourselves and others than lists of traits. It is therefore possible that people might respond in importantly different ways to questionnaire items and trait terms, and that using items might uncover traits to which the lexical approach is blind.

The most famous proponent of this questionnaire-based approach to personality description is Hans Eysenck. Eysenck, who died recently, was a colourful and very influential German-born English psychologist noted for his prolific, wide-ranging, and often controversial writings on such topics as the genetics of intelligence, psychoanalysis, crime, psychotherapy, and astrology. He is best known among psychologists for developing a two-factor model of personality. These factors, Extraversion–Introversion and Neuroticism, are now familiar to you, but they were first recognized and rigorously investigated by Eysenck (1947). On the strength of extensive factor-analytic research, he proposed that Cattell's 16 trait dimensions, many of which were moderately correlated, could be reduced to these two uncorrelated factors. In addition, he theorized that these factors were rooted in variations in the functioning of the nervous system, as we shall see in Chapter 4.

In subsequent work, Eysenck found a need for a third factor, which he labelled '**Psychoticism**'. By his account, the traits that composed this factor included aggressiveness, coldness, egocentricity, antisocial tendencies, creativity, lack of empathy, and tough-mindedness. These traits, according to Eysenck, reflect an underlying dimension stretching from psychological normality to psychotic disorders such as schizophrenia, which are marked by disabling symptoms such as hallucinations and bizarre delusions. Other theorists have disputed this understanding of the factor, proposing that it is more closely linked to 'psychopathic' tendencies – such as callousness, violence, and ruthlessness towards others – than to psychosis. Although some evidence supports Eysenck's proposed link between Psychoticism and schizophrenia, the factor's nature remains rather obscure. Its status is made more controversial by the factor's somewhat unreliable emergence in factor-analytic studies.

Despite the questions that surround Psychoticism, other psychologists have developed three-factor models of personality that closely resemble Eysenck's triad. Tellegen (1985), for example, found evidence for factors that he dubbed Positive Emotionality, Negative Emotionality, and Constraint. The first two are closely associated with Extraversion and Neuroticism, respectively, and emphasize the emotional susceptibilities associated with each. Constraint has a strong negative association with Psychoticism, representing a tendency to inhibit and control the expression of impulses and antisocial behaviour. Traits that illustrate Constraint include carefulness, cautiousness, reflectiveness, and lack of spontaneity. Watson and Clark (1993) developed a very similar model – cheekily dubbed the 'Big Three' – labelling their three factors Positive Temperament, Negative Temperament, and Disinhibition. Disinhibition's opposing pole, in this model, is Constraint. Although this profusion of factor names may seem confusing at first, they clearly converge on three distinct conceptual domains, and questionnaire measures of the corresponding factors all correlate strongly.

THREE FACTORS OR FIVE?

There is considerable empirical support for three-factor as well as five-factor models of personality, and proponents of each often find themselves in opposition. You might well ask, though, whether the differences between these models are really so deep. After all, three-factor and five-factor models both recognize that Extraversion and Neuroticism are fundamental dimensions of personality. Their real disagreement is therefore confined to a choice between a single Psychoticism, Disinhibition, or Constraint factor on the one hand, and distinct Agreeableness, Conscientiousness, and Openness to Experience factors, on the other. It turns out that Constraint or Psychoticism, from the three-factor models, seem to correspond to a combination of the five-factor model's Agreeableness and Conscientiousness factors. People who score high on Constraint, for example, are typically agreeable and conscientious, and those who score high on Psychoticism are disagreeable and unconscientious. In short, Constraint or Psychoticism can be seen as a broad trait dimension that encompasses two five-factor model factors. Indeed, measures of Agreeableness and Conscientiousness tend to correlate positively with one another (e.g., about .3; see John & Srivastava, 1999). This suggests that the two five-factor dimensions have the sort of affinity that makes it not entirely unreasonable to combine them into a superordinate dimension, although it is also true that they usually emerge as distinct factors in factor-analytic research.

The three-factor and five-factor models of personality are therefore not as different as they might first appear. They share two factors, and the three-factor model's third factor can be interpreted as a combination of two five-factor model factors. (Alternatively, these two factors can be seen as aspects, facets or components of this third factor.) Three-factor model advocates prefer the combined factor, which yields a more economical system of personality description and reduces the correlations among the system's factors. Five-factor model advocates, in contrast, prefer to keep Agreeableness and Conscientiousness conceptually distinct, even if they are empirically related. This distinction between 'lumpers' and 'splitters' – theorists who prefer fewer or more categories, respectively, when making classifications – appears frequently in personality and abnormal psychology. Here, as elsewhere, neither lumpers nor splitters have a monopoly on the truth, and judging who is right cannot be based exclusively on timeless 'facts'.

Only Openness to Experience is left out of the integration that we have laid out. It has no obvious home in the three-factor model, although its creativity component falls within Eysenck's understanding of Psychoticism. If you consider Openness to be an indispensable component of any system for describing personality you will tend to favour the five-factor model. If, on the other hand, you find it to be of relatively minor importance to personality description, you will consider its exclusion from three-factor models to be a reasonable omission. Whichever stance you take, however, what is not in doubt is that Openness to Experience is a meaningful broad personality factor. Only its importance is in question.

At this point you might be tempted to think that all of this quibbling about how many personality dimensions there are and how they should be characterized demonstrates either the irresolvable nature of the problem or the arbitrariness of psychologists' answers. Before you give in to this temptation, consider a couple of things. First, the five- or three-factor solutions have been obtained again and again by many independent researchers, with many different research populations, and using diverse sets of trait adjectives and questionnaires. Researchers don't tend to find two, four or six dimensions, and when they find three or five their composition almost always resembles those presented in this chapter. This is an impressive record of replication, a vital component of good science and a sign – although not a perfect one – that the solutions that have been reached are not arbitrary.

Further evidence against arbitrariness comes from studies that show quite consistently that factors akin to most of the Big Five can be detected in a variety of non-human animals (Gosling & John, 1999). These studies, which attempt to describe individual differences evident in ratings of animals' behaviour, find that factors closely resembling Extraversion, Neuroticism, and Agreeableness are detectable in most of the species studied. For example, Agreeableness-related factors have been obtained in chimpanzees, hyenas, dogs, pigs, rats, and five other species, but not in guppies and octopuses. Openness-related factors have emerged in seven of the 12 species studied, but Conscientiousness has only appeared in chimpanzees, our closest evolutionary relatives. Might these findings be due to the 'anthropomorphic' projection of human traits onto other animals? This possibility seems remote because studies have employed careful and objective ratings of specific behaviours – such as frequency of vocalization and number of nose contacts as indicators of piglets' 'extraversion' – rather than loose, subjective impressions. On balance, these findings provide remarkable support for the cross-species generality, and hence non-arbitrariness in humans, of most five-factor trait dimensions.

Whether there are three or five fundamental dimensions of personality, or some other number, is not a trivial issue, and it is possible that it will be conclusively resolved in the years to come. Hopefully you will now recognize that some of the differences between the rival models of personality structure are not so unbridgeable as they might seem, and that they are differences of theoretical predilection as much as fact. This should only increase our appreciation of just how far trait psychologists have moved towards their goal of understanding personality organization.

HOW DO MODELS OF BASIC TRAITS ADVANCE THE FIELD?

As we have seen, there is as yet no consensus among psychologists about the fundamental structure of personality, but there is substantial agreement and most of the disagreements that remain are not radical. At this point we need to ask what is gained by determining the structure of the trait universe. Is a model of personality structure just a descriptive classification – a factual statement about personality, equivalent to saying that there are two broad types of dinosaur or 130 chemical elements – or does it also promote our understanding of personality in other ways?

Before we explore this question we should remember that an empirically sound model of personality structure is a substantial intellectual achievement, and would remain substantial even if it did little more than enumerate and describe the fundamental ways in which personalities differ. Descriptive models and classifications are indispensable for science, and are interesting in and of themselves. Nevertheless, models of the basic trait dimensions go beyond simple classification in a number of valuable ways.

The first way in which models of personality structure advance the study of personality is by providing a conceptual net for capturing specific personality characteristics. If this sounds loose and metaphorical, imagine that you are beginning a study of a little-researched trait such as cynicism or envy-proneness. If you want to understand how your trait relates to other better-known traits, you would be well advised to find out whether a measure of it correlates with fundamental personality dimensions. Because these dimensions are broad and cover the personality domain comprehensively, they provide a framework for locating your trait. Perhaps it correlates with only one factor, as cynicism might correlate negatively with Agreeableness, for instance. In this case you could infer that your trait is similar to others that are associated with that factor, and that theory and research that apply to the factor – for example, ideas about its causes and correlates – may also apply to your trait. Or perhaps your trait correlates with two or more factors, suggesting that it represents a mixture of distinct characteristics. Shyness, for example, correlates negatively with Extraversion and positively with Neuroticism. This suggests that shyness represents a blend of lack of social interest (Introversion) and social anxiety (Neuroticism). Alternatively, shy people may come in two varieties: those who prefer being alone but tend not to be uncomfortable when in company, and those who are the reverse. Either way, locating the shyness trait's relationship to basic personality dimensions helps to clarify it. In principle then, models of personality structure can provide coordinates for any particular personality characteristic on a multidimensional map, and these coordinates can enlighten us about the nature of that characteristic.

A second way in which models of personality structure promote psychological understanding is closely related to the first. Just as the five-factor model or Eysenck's three factors provide frameworks for locating specific personality traits, they can help to understand psychological phenomena other than traits. Let's say there is a phenomenon that we want to be able to understand better, such as illegal drug use, or psychological well-being, or proneness to depression. The number of personality characteristics that might predict (i.e., correlate with) these phenomena is vast and unwieldy, but the basic personality dimensions offer an economical way to cover the personality domain. A researcher can therefore investigate whether any of these dimensions correlate with the phenomenon of interest, and possibly draw some helpful inferences about it.

Imagine, for example, that we want to understand vulnerability to depression. We could assess a group of people on a measure of the Big Five and on their history of depressive episodes. Let's say we find that people with more depression in their histories have relatively high levels of Neuroticism, and low levels of Extraversion and Openness. These findings would not allow us to say that these broad trait dimensions cause people to become depressed: maybe they are just associated with vulnerability. Nor could we confidently claim that these dimensions are the best way to conceptualize vulnerability: depression-proneness might be better understood in terms of more specific personality characteristics rather than broad factors. However, the findings would strongly suggest that personality characteristics linked to neuroticism, introversion, and lack of openness are associated with depression-proneness, and support more focused investigations of these characteristics. The findings would also count against any theory proposing that depression-proneness is a matter of having poor self-control or being overly competitive, because the factors associated with these characteristics (i.e., low Conscientiousness and Agreeableness) are not correlated with it. The broad trait dimensions can therefore help to clarify phenomena that could not be so easily clarified without them.

A third benefit that models of personality structure bring is that they point to the underlying *causes* of personality variation. If differences in people's observable behaviour reliably reveal a set of basic dimensions, it is reasonable to infer that there are distinct underlying processes or structures that give rise to these dimensions. The basic personality dimensions are clearly not arbitrary – they must have some objective basis – and just like any other psychological phenomenon it should be possible to locate their underpinnings. Models of personality structure therefore guide the search for explanations of personality. If there is a trait dimension of Extraversion, for example, there ought to be some psychological or biological structures and processes whose variations underlie variations in extraversion-related behaviour. Conversely, a satisfactory explanation of Extraversion must be capable of accounting for all of the forms of psychological variation that it encompasses (e.g., sociability, interpersonal dominance, high activity levels, sensation-seeking, positive emotionality, etc.). In short, models of personality description advance our knowledge of personality explanation.

AN ILLUSTRATIVE BROAD TRAIT: CONSCIENTIOUSNESS

To illustrate the use of basic trait dimensions as variables for predicting important forms of behaviour, let us consider Conscientiousness, one of the Big Five personality factors. Researchers who have employed measures of the factor in their studies have demonstrated its associations with a wide range of outcomes. Some of the strongest correlates of Conscientiousness are found in the workplace. Barrick and Mount (1991) showed that it was more reliably associated with work performance than other personality factors across different occupations, different occupational levels, and multiple performance criteria (e.g., productivity, success in training, time employed, and salary). In the educational domain, finally, personality research indicates that more Conscientious students tend to show greater educational attainment (e.g., Digman, 1989).

The correlates of Conscientiousness extend well beyond the office and the classroom, however. In the domain of mental health, John, Caspi, Robins, Moffitt, and Stouthamer-Loeber (1994) found that more Conscientious adolescent boys tended to have lower levels of 'internalizing' (e.g., depression and anxiety) and 'externalizing' (e.g., delinquency, illegal drug use) pathology. In the domain of physical health, Friedman, Tucker, Tomlinson-Keasey, Schwartz, Wingard, and Criqui (1993) found that Conscientiousness measured in middle childhood was associated with longer life, because more Conscientious people took more health precautions, avoided more health-risk behaviours, coped better with stress, and had lower rates of cardiovascular disease, cancer, and violent injury. In addition to its link to the avoidance of health risks, Marshall, Wortman, Vickers, Kusulas, and Hervig (1994) found that Conscientiousness was associated with traits such as optimism and low anger expression that are linked to physical well-being. More Conscientious people also tend to be more physically fit (Hogan, 1989). In the domain of general psychological well-being, Little, Lecci, and Watkinson (1991) found that more Conscientious undergraduates had personal goals that were more in keeping with their sense of self, more organized, and more viable.

(Continued)

The American cross-cultural psychologist David Matsumoto (2006) examined differences in emotion regulation between Americans and Japanese. Previous research had suggested that Japanese participants score lower on emotion regulation than Americans, and Matsumoto aimed to explain why this might be. There is reliable evidence of differences in the mean level of five-factor model (FFM) dimensions between cultures, and Americans have been found to score higher on average than Japanese on Extraversion and Conscientiousness, and lower on Neuroticism. Given the role of Extraversion and Neuroticism in emotionality, these cultural differences in mean levels of personality traits might account for cultural differences in emotion regulation.

Matsumoto assessed large samples of Japanese (6,409) and American (1,013) adults on a questionnaire measure of the FFM and two questionnaires measuring emotion regulation. As in previous research, he found that Americans scored higher on emotion regulation — although the Japanese scored higher on a scale assessing emotion suppression — and he replicated the cross-cultural differences on the three personality factors. Statistical analysis showed that the cross-cultural difference in emotion regulation was indeed accounted for by the cross-cultural differences in personality traits.

One interesting implication of Matsumoto's study is that some psychological differences between cultures may not be due to national differences in personality, nor culture *per se*. Rather than explaining differences in emotion regulation between Japan and the USA in terms of culture — shared beliefs, values, and social norms — perhaps we should refer to different average levels of traits. At some levels, such trait differences might themselves be grounded in culture: for example, in cultural differences in child-rearing beliefs and practices. Even so, this study shows how personality trait dimensions may illuminate cross-cultural research.

SPECIFIC TRAITS

From reading this chapter so far you may think that trait psychology consists entirely of efforts to determine the broad fundamental dimensions of personality structure. This has indeed been a major focus for researchers and theorists, but a great deal of trait psychology focuses on more specific traits. Many psychologists working within the tradition of trait psychology aim to clarify, explain, and determine the correlates of personality characteristics that refer to more delimited patterns of behaviour, feeling, and thinking. All it takes to work within this tradition is a belief that traits are useful units of personality description and a commitment to assess and study them, whether or not one clings to a particular model of basic personality dimensions.

There are two main reasons why psychologists are often inclined to focus on specific traits rather than broad personality factors. The first has to do with the *descriptive inadequacy* of broad factors, and the second with their *predictive inadequacy*. You have probably already had some doubts about the descriptive adequacy of models such as the Big Five. Are five dimensions really enough to characterize a personality in all its richness? The answer is obviously a resounding 'No'. As Allport and Odbert showed, human languages often supply vast numbers of trait terms to capture the subtle shades of meaning that people have found helpful in capturing one another's individuality. To believe that the Big Five is sufficient to describe individual personalities is to imagine falsely that the 4,500 trait terms are essentially synonyms of ten basic personality characteristics (i.e., high and low on each factor). We usually aren't satisfied to know that a person is relatively high in Neuroticism, but want to know in what forms and under what circumstances this emotionality is expressed (e.g., is the person typically shy, angry, jumpy, moody, sad, tense, guilty, high-strung, under-confident …?).

The predictive adequacy of broad personality factors may not have struck you as being as questionable as their descriptive adequacy. However, it is often true that broad personality factors correlate less strongly with psychological phenomena than the more specific traits that define them. For example, Paunonen and Ashton (2001) found that Conscientiousness and Openness to Experience predicted performance in an undergraduate psychology course modestly or not at all (correlations were .21 and −.04, respectively). However, narrower traits that were related to these factors – 'achievement' and 'need for understanding' – correlated somewhat more strongly (.26 and .23). Similarly, DeNeve and Cooper (1998) investigated personality predictors of subjective well-being, and found that Neuroticism and Extraversion correlated −.27 and .20, respectively. However, several specific traits demonstrated stronger correlations, including desire for control, hardiness, trust, repressive-defensiveness, and a tendency to think that events are primarily due to chance (the last two traits correlated negatively with well-being). In short, broad personality factors are often outperformed as predictors by the traits that are supposedly less basic.

These descriptive and predictive limitations of broad models of personality are unquestionably real. However, they are not really failures of the models, although personality psychologists who are opposed to them sometimes make this claim. The five-factor model and others make no claims to provide a sufficient set of dimensions for characterizing individuals or predicting particular psychological phenomena. They are organizing frameworks only, ways of classifying personality characteristics in an economical and encompassing fashion that aspires to reveal some deeper truth about the underlying structure (and maybe also the causes) of individual differences. Advocates of broad factors are not claiming that specific traits are *nothing but* the factors that they are associated with, just as no one claims that parrots and penguins are nothing but birds. Instead, they argue that each specific trait has its own specific content as well as some degree of overlap with broad factors, and that these factors reflect ways in which specific traits tend to go together. By analogy, parrots and penguins each have their own distinctive features, but they also share certain underlying similarities which make them both examples of the broad grouping of birds.

Similarly, advocates of broad personality factors make no claims about the predictive superiority of these factors. In fact, it would be surprising if more specific traits were *not* frequently better predictors of behaviour than broad factors. First, such factors comprise many specific traits, and unless every trait is equally predictive of the behaviour in question, some traits must be more predictive than the factor of which they are a part. Second, specific traits refer to narrower patterns of behaviour than traits, so they should be able to predict relatively narrow or context-specific kinds of behaviour in a more focused and hence stronger manner. Consider the case of sensation-seeking, presented in Figure 2.1 near the beginning of this chapter. If the behaviour to be predicted were taking out a raunchy personals ad in a magazine, then the specific trait that is narrowly focused on the sexual domain (i.e., sexual sensation-seeking) should predict better than the broader, less domain-focused trait (i.e., sensation-seeking). By incorporating non-sexual domains of sensation-seeking, whose relevance to sexuality is weaker than sexual sensation-seeking, the broader trait's capacity to predict sexual behaviour will be diluted. Extraversion, whose coverage of behavioural domains and contexts is even broader than sensation-seeking, should have an even more diluted capacity to predict sexual adventurism. By this reasoning, broader traits tend to predict specific behaviours more weakly than certain narrow traits. But by the same reasoning, as you may have noticed, broader traits will tend to predict a greater range of behaviour: more behaviours fall within their field of relevance. Thus, although broad personality factors often predict behaviour less strongly than specific traits, this is neither an embarrassment to proponents of these factors nor a sign of their overall predictive inferiority.

In any event, given that broad personality factors like the Big Five have some limitations, both in allowing fine-grained personality description and in predicting specific behaviours, psychologists have energetically pursued the study of specific traits. Often they have done so in the hope of illuminating a particular set of psychological phenomena. The number of traits that have been investigated is huge, but a small selection of some of the most interesting examples offers a flavour of the enterprise.

Authoritarianism

Authoritarianism is a specific trait that has been investigated by psychologists who want to understand the roots of prejudice. This programme of work was begun by Adorno Frenkel-Brunswik, Levinson, and Sanford (1950), who sought to explain the extreme and genocidal hatred of the Nazi regime towards Jews, Gypsies, homosexuals, and others. By their working understanding, embodied in a popular questionnaire (the California F-scale), the trait had several distinct components. These include an uncritical and submissive acceptance of societal authorities, deeply conventional values, thinking that is based on superstition and rigid categories, a tendency to project one's own impulses onto others and be punitive towards them, cynicism and misanthropy, and a reluctance to introspect. Although this formulation and the F-scale are controversial, recent work has shown authoritarianism to be a strong and reliable predictor of individual differences in prejudiced attitudes (Whitley, 1999). In Big Five terms, authoritarianism appears to be characterized primarily by low Openness and high Conscientiousness (Heaven & Bucci, 2001).

Self-monitoring

Self-monitoring is a trait that is most pertinent to the presentation of self in public behaviour. According to its originator (Snyder, 1974), the concept refers to the degree of consistency people display both between their inner selves and their public personas, and in their public behaviour across different situations. 'High self-monitors' show relatively little consistency, flexibly shaping their public presentation to fit the demands of the situation and their audience. 'Low self-monitors', in contrast, tend to display the same personal attitudes, beliefs, and dispositions regardless of the situation and audience, demonstrating what can be understood either as an admirable fidelity to their true selves or as a stubborn lack of social sensitivity. High self-monitoring predicts a variety of social psychological phenomena, such as being willing to use deception to get a date (Rowatt, Cunningham, & Druen, 1998) and being responsive to persuasive messages that emphasize enhancing one's personal image rather than expressing personal values (Lavine & Snyder, 1996).

Attachment styles

Attachment style refers to a set of personality characteristics that are particularly relevant to close relationships. Inspired by developmental psychology research on the different ways in which infants and toddlers react to separation from their caregivers, studies of attachment styles in adults present them as basic orientations to intimate relationships. Three styles are often recognized, each marked by distinctive approaches to forming and conducting emotional bonds, and responding to challenges to them (Hazan & Shaver, 1987). People with a 'secure' attachment style are comfortable with closeness and mutual dependency and are not preoccupied with the possibility of abandonment. The 'avoidant' style is associated with a lack of trust in others, and a reluctance to become close to or dependent on another. 'Anxious/ambivalent' people, finally, tend to desire more intimacy than their partner and want it more quickly, and are concerned about being abandoned or not loved enough.

These three traits are associated with a host of intriguing differences in psychological phenomena within close relationships. Not surprisingly, secure individuals experience the most trust, satisfaction, and commitment in their romantic relationships. Anxious/ambivalent people have the lowest self-esteem and satisfaction with their romantic relationships, are most prone to jealousy, obsessive preoccupation with and sexual attraction to others, and belief in love at first sight, and report having had fathers who were unfair. Avoidant people have the strongest fear of closeness, fail to seek support from a partner when under stress, and report having cold and rejecting mothers. When brought into a lab to discuss a relationship problem with their romantic partners (Simpson, Rholes, & Phillips, 1996), they show little negative emotion, remain distant and unsupportive (especially men), and report no change in feelings of love and commitment after the discussion. Anxious/ambivalent people, in contrast, show anger and upset during the discussion and reduced love and commitment after it, and securely attached people showed little distress and then more positive evaluations of the relationship.

In one fascinating study, Fraley and Shaver (1998) examined a setting where romantic couples frequently separate, and where attachment behaviour might therefore be particularly notable. They had a research assistant approach couples at an airport and ask them to complete a short questionnaire, which included a measure of attachment styles. Unknown to the couples, another research assistant then observed them until one or both of them departed, coding specific kinds of attachment-related behaviour. Fraley and Shaver found a number of correlations between participants' attachment styles and these behaviours for separating couples. More avoidantly attached women, for example, engaged in less 'contact seeking' behaviour (e.g., kissing, embracing, turning back after leaving), less 'caregiving' (e.g., stroking, whispering 'I love you'), and more 'avoidance' behaviours (e.g., looking away from the partner, breaking off contact, hurrying the separation). In short, attachment styles reveal themselves in naturalistic settings, and are clearly important specific traits for making sense of close relationships.

Type A

Type A personality is a characteristic that has been most intensively studied by psychologists interested in predicting risk for coronary heart disease, a major cause of death in most industrialized societies. Cardiologists had long suspected that people who suffered from heart disease tended to have a distinctive personality style, and Type A was an attempt to capture it (Friedman & Rosenman, 1974). Type A personalities are described as competitive, given to excessive achievement striving, vigorous in their activity and speech patterns, hostile, and impatient and pressured in their attitude towards time. Research has repeatedly linked Type A to a moderately increased risk for the development of heart disease, and suggests that hostility is the most toxic of its components, the one most strongly associated with coronary risk. This association may be partly due to an increased engagement in health-damaging behaviours and partly due to more direct physiological effects of chronic hostility on the body.

The specific traits sketched here illustrate a tiny fraction of the personality characteristics that have been studied by trait psychologists. Note how they illuminate psychological phenomena in specific domains – attitudes towards outgroups, self-presentation, close relationships, physical health – by focusing on specific kinds of thinking, feeling, and behaving. Note also how none of these specific traits corresponds precisely to any trait term in English. Instead, they are theoretical entities or 'constructs' that have been proposed, assessed, and studied by researchers. Specific traits need not be drawn from the everyday lexicon, which clearly does not exhaust the trait universe.

CONCLUSION

The psychology of traits starts from some intuitively sensible premises. It assumes that personality characteristics encoded in ordinary language are useful units of personality description, and that their structure can be determined by studying empirical consistencies in thinking, feeling, and behaving. On these pillars – the trait lexicon and the humble correlation coefficient (and its factor-analytic descendant) – elaborate and robust accounts of personality structure have been built. In addition, a great assortment of specific traits has been investigated. The language of personality description that has emerged from this enterprise seems to be both systematic and comprehensive. Its practical utility is shown by an enormous research literature that demonstrates the capacity of traits to predict a wide range of psychological phenomena. Trait psychology would appear to give us a very solid foundation for personality description.

Chapter summary

- A major task of personality psychology is to develop systematic ways of describing and classifying individual differences, or determining the 'structure' of personality.
- A major unit for the description of personality is the 'personality trait', an enduring disposition (or tendency) to think, feel, or behave in a particular, patterned way.
- Traits are hierarchically organized. They vary in how broad or general they are, some relating to very specific or narrow types of behaviour and others to wide ranges of behaviour, and broader traits may incorporate many more specific traits.
- Personality psychologists have made efforts to classify the structure of traits for more than 70 years, starting from the thousands of trait words available in everyday language and distilling these into a smaller number of broad trait dimensions.
- This process of distillation has involved the analysis of correlations (i.e., associations) among different traits. These correlations are examined using 'factor analysis', a statistical procedure that finds groupings of correlated traits and infers the presence of broad dimensions that underlie them.
- Factor-analytic research first distilled traits into 16 factors or dimensions, and then further reduced them to five. The five factors have increasingly come to represent the scientific consensus on personality structure, and are referred to as the 'Big Five' or the 'five-factor model'.
- The five factors are Extraversion, Agreeableness, Conscientiousness, Neuroticism, and Openness to Experience. They serve as a useful framework for personality description and explanation, and they are associated with a wide variety of psychological phenomena.
- Alternative models of personality structure based on only three factors have also been proposed.
- Although broad factors play an important role in personality description, many more specific traits have also been the focus of personality research and theory. These specific traits may be more effective in predicting behaviour than broader traits.

Further Reading

- Eysenck, H.J. (1990). Biological dimensions of personality. In L.A. Pervin (Ed.), *Handbook of personality: Theory and research* (pp. 244–76). New York: Guilford.

This long chapter reviews evidence supporting the validity and utility of Eysenck's three-factor model of personality trait dimensions, including discussions of their proposed biological bases.

- John, O.P., & Srivastava, S. (1999). The Big Five trait taxonomy: History, measurement, and theoretical perspectives. In L.A. Pervin (Ed.), *Handbook of personality: Theory and research* (2nd ed.) (pp. 102–38). New York: Guilford.

This chapter lays out the historical development of the five-factor model of personality, and reviews relevant research and theory on the nature of the factors and their optimal measurement.

- Matthews, G., Deary, I.J., & Whiteman, M.C. (2003). *Personality traits* (2nd ed.). New York: Cambridge University Press.

This is a thorough, up-to-date and readable presentation of contemporary personality psychology from the trait perspective.

- McCrae, R.R., & Costa, P.T. (2002). *Personality in adulthood: A five-factor theory* (2nd ed.). New York: Guilford.

For those who want a more comprehensive discussion of the five-factor model of personality, this book offers an up-to-date review of an enormous body of research.

3

Challenges and Alternatives to Trait Psychology

Learning objectives
• To develop a balanced understanding of the merits and limitations of personality traits as units of personality description.
• To understand how the concept of personality traits is called into question by the situationist critique of personality, and how that critique was over-stated.
• To recognize some of the controversies and criticisms surrounding personality traits and trait models of personality.
• To understand the extent to which these criticisms present serious challenges to the trait psychology perspective.
• To understand alternative units of personality description (e.g., values) and how these complement description in terms of traits.

This chapter outlines and examines several of the challenges that the trait psychology approach presented in Chapter 2 has faced. First, we discuss the criticism that behaviour is not very consistent across situations and over time, and that it is determined more by the situations or context in which people behave rather than by their traits. We then examine whether individual differences in personality are always a matter of degree, people being located along continuous trait dimensions, or whether some distinct personal 'types' or categories might also exist. Third, we examine whether trait dimensions are universal, or whether the structure of personality traits varies across cultures. Finally, we investigate whether traits are capable of explaining behaviour, as distinct from merely describing it. After discussing these challenges, we then examine several ways of describing personality that represent alternatives to traits. In particular, we discuss values, character strengths and virtues, interests, motives, and goals. These concepts capture important aspects of personality, and complement traits as units for individual differences.

As we saw in the last chapter, trait psychologists have made great progress in developing ways of describing human personality. Over the past few decades, psychologists have put forward a variety of systems for characterizing the basic dimensions of personality, which they have supported with extensive bodies of research. Although these systems differ in the number of dimensions that they propose, and in the labels that they attach to them, there is now considerable agreement among psychologists that personalities differ in a few fundamental ways that are increasingly well-understood.

To have reached such a level of agreement about the fundamental dimensions of personality is no small accomplishment. Every field of study needs to develop ways of describing and classifying the phenomena of interest to it. Some of the most important achievements of the sciences have been systematic ways of describing nature: the periodic table of elements in chemistry, the enumeration of elementary particles in physics, and the classification of species in biology. Just as these systematic descriptions provide foundations for their sciences, trait psychology aspires to be a foundation for the study of personality. However, the strength of this foundation has not gone unchallenged. Indeed, psychologists have raised many serious criticisms of trait psychology, and questioned whether it offers a firm ground on which to build a science of personality.

In this chapter we will review some of the challenges that have been mounted against the psychology of traits. These challenges range from the radical – for instance, the claim that traits are not intrinsic to persons but exist only in the eyes of those who judge them – to the relatively mild, pointing out minor limitations of the trait concept. Let us examine these challenges one by one.

DO TRAITS EXIST, AND DO THEY MATTER?

It seems intuitively obvious that people differ from one another in their typical ways of behaving, and that these differences matter. Most of us are implicit trait psychologists, thinking about one another in terms of general dispositions and using trait terms extensively in our daily lives. However, the most fundamental challenge to trait psychology argued that we are all quite mistaken: traits are much less solid and powerful than we, and academic trait psychologists, imagine.

This challenge, which came to be known as '**situationism**', was launched by Walter Mischel in a controversial book published in 1968. In his book, Mischel reviewed a large number of studies of behavioural consistency, the extent to which a person's behaviour is consistent in different situations or according to different measures. Although trait psychology assumes a high level of consistency, Mischel repeatedly found that behaviours expressing a single trait in different settings often correlated quite weakly (i.e., rarely more than .30). Another way of saying this is that there is a great deal of 'within-person variability' of behaviour across different situations. For instance, a well-known study of children's moral behaviour found that their likelihoods of cheating, lying, and stealing were only marginally correlated when assessed in diverse classroom, home, and social settings. Different children behaved immorally in different situations, and most individual children were not consistently moral or immoral. Similarly, Mischel found that alternative measures of particular traits rarely reached high levels of consistency, and usually correlated quite modestly. He concluded that behaviour is influenced only weakly by traits, and that situational determinants are usually more powerful. Behaviour is, in short, highly specific to situations, rather than springing from general dispositions as people tend to imagine. Consequently, even if such dispositions exist – a claim he never denied – they are of little practical value in predicting behaviour.

Needless to say, Mischel's conclusions were met with a chorus of disagreement from personality psychologists. (In contrast, social psychologists, who focus on situational determinants of behaviour, tended to applaud.) Mischel had, after all, cast doubt on the large and apparently successful research enterprise of trait psychology, as well as on the livelihood of psychologists who practised personality assessment in clinical, educational, and industrial settings. As a result, his findings were subjected to numerous criticisms over many years. Some psychologists argued that his review of the literature was selective, others that it focused too much on studies performed in artificial laboratory situations which might not generalize to everyday life. However, two criticisms are particularly telling.

First, is it true, as Mischel maintained, that the levels of behavioural consistency revealed in his review are too low to be practically useful? Some psychologists have argued that .30 correlations of the sort he dismissed may actually have considerable practical value. Remember that such a correlation allows a 30% reduction in prediction errors, and raises the odds of correct prediction from 1:1 to almost 2:1. In many practical settings these figures are very respectable. An extreme example comes from the study that first showed the role of aspirin in preventing heart attacks. In this case, a correlation of .034 between aspirin consumption and heart attack was enough to lead researchers to call off the study and announce their findings to the world (Rosenthal, 1990). Modest correlations can clearly be of great importance.

Second, it may well be that Mischel significantly under-estimated the degree to which behaviour can be predicted by traits. The studies that he reviewed correlated specific behaviours measured on a single occasion with one another, or with psychological tests. However, psychologists are often interested not in predicting single instances of particular behaviours, but in predicting *tendencies* to behave in a certain general manner over a period of time (i.e., 'aggregated' behaviour). A personnel psychologist assessing the conscientiousness of potential employees is usually not aiming to predict a specific occasion of dishonesty, for instance, but hopes instead to predict *patterns* of unconscientious behaviour (e.g., lying, lateness, absenteeism, theft, drinking). Now, aggregated behaviour is more predictable than specific instances, because the many unpredictable factors that influence each instance tend to even out in the long run. Think about how much less accurately you would probably predict the maximum temperature on this day next year than the average maximum temperature for this month next year. For this reason, aggregated behaviour is more consistent, and more strongly correlated with trait measures, than Mischel claimed.

It is now generally accepted that traits survived the 'person–situation debate' with few lasting injuries. Evidence for the consistency of behaviour has accumulated, and growing evidence for the stability of personality traits over time has strengthened the position that traits are influential and predictively valuable sources of behaviour. At the same time, trait psychologists have developed a healthy recognition of the level of inconsistency or within-person variability (Fleeson, 2001) in behaviour and the vital importance of the context in which behaviour occurs. Some have acknowledged the role of the situation and reconciled it with the trait approach in a variety of ways. For instance, some note that traits will tend to predict behaviour best in situations that are not governed by constraining rules and expectations. Others propose what has been called **'interactionism'**, according to which people's traits express themselves in ways that are situation-specific, so that behavioural consistency is to be found in particular *combinations* of traits and situations. For instance, some people are consistently anxious in social settings, others in settings involving physical danger. All in all, then, trait psychologists have learned from the situationist critique, and its challenge has been successfully rebutted.

ARE TRAIT DIMENSIONS CULTURALLY UNIVERSAL?

Trait psychology aspires to give us a universal language for describing differences between people. Trait theories such as the five-factor model aim to provide a map of *human* personality, rather than one that is only appropriate to members of a particular cultural, national, or linguistic group. Some psychologists have challenged this claim of universality, arguing either that Western trait dimensions are not appropriate to particular non-Western cultures, or, more radically, that the trait concept itself is not applicable in these cultures. Such challenges – which represent what can be called the *relativist critique* – are important ones. If they are valid they imply that trait theories apply only within rather narrow cultural and geographical boundaries, and have more to do with culturally-specific beliefs and ways of life than with the fundamentals of human nature.

There are certainly reasons to suspect that there might be significant cultural variations in the ways in which personality is conceptualized. Anthropologists and cultural psychologists have pointed out many differences between Western and non-Western people's typical ways of understanding themselves, their minds, and their behaviour, ways that may collectively be called their 'folk psychologies'. Compared to Westerners, non-Western people tend (1) to explain their behaviour in terms of 'external' factors such as the situation it occurred in, and the social constraints and relationships that influenced it; (2) to talk about concrete behaviour without referring to underlying psychological causes such as intentions, desires, and traits; and (3) to possess relatively restricted trait vocabularies (see Lillard, 1998, and Fiske, Kitayama, Markus, & Nisbett, 1998, for reviews). In contrast, Westerners tend to interpret behaviour in terms of an elaborate folk psychology of dispositions and mental processes. That is, they tend to see people as autonomous agents whose actions spring from abstract internal attributes that distinguish them from one another. On the surface, then, trait psychology would seem to be less appropriate to non-Western cultures, with their preference for contextual and situational explanations and their less individualistic values.

All of this evidence suggests that Western trait psychologies could in some respects be specific to their cultural origins. But is it true, for instance, that trait theories such as the five-factor model only hold up in Western contexts? This turns out to be quite a difficult question to answer. On the one hand, when standard personality tests are translated into non-Western languages, they usually yield more or less identical underlying factors, suggesting that Western trait dimensions are indeed universal and can be exported with few reservations. For example, questionnaire measures of the 'Big Five' have yielded factors closely resembling these dimensions when translated from English into

Chinese, Croatian, Dutch, Filipino, French, German, Hebrew, Japanese, Korean, and Spanish. Translated versions of Eysenck's measure of Extraversion, Neuroticism, and Psychoticism have yielded quite consistent factors in an even wider variety of languages. Although this evidence for universal factors is generally strong, however, it is also worth noting that it is somewhat less strong for non-European samples. For instance, there is some indication that the Big Five Extraversion and Agreeableness factors do not appear in Filipino, Japanese, and Korean samples, but seem to be replaced by factors that might be better labelled Love (a blend of Extraversion and high Agreeableness) and Dominance (a blend of Extraversion and low Agreeableness).

Translated versions of Western personality measures provide evidence that trait dimensions proposed by Western psychologists are reasonably general, and also reveal some subtle cultural variations. However, it can be argued that such translations are not the best places to look for cultural differences in personality structure. After all, these measures contain items that have been selected by Western psychologists to reflect the characteristics that they consider to be most relevant for describing individual differences within their own cultures. For this reason, some psychologists have claimed that translations of Western measures essentially impose a restricted and potentially quite alien set of descriptions on the non-Western people who respond to them. Consequently, these psychologists argue, translation of imported Western measures may exaggerate the consistency of personality structure across cultures. More importantly, it may fail to detect trait dimensions that are specific to a culture because items relevant to these dimensions are not included in the original Western measure. In response to these problems, some cross-cultural psychologists have proposed investigating personality from an *indigenous* perspective, studying personality characteristics and trait terms that are recognized *within* the culture of interest.

Studies of indigenous personality characteristics typically begin with the collection of trait terms that occur naturally in the language of interest, often following a detailed 'ethnographic' analysis of the characteristics that are most culturally salient. Participants then rate themselves or others on the resulting terms, and correlations among these are examined for evidence of broader dimensions, whose resemblance to those obtained in other cultures can be assessed. Several such 'lexical' studies have now been performed, and the findings are very interesting. On the one hand, they show a fairly high level of consistency with the Big Five dimensions in many cases, especially in European languages. On the other hand, they are often inconsistent, failing to yield equivalents of specific Big Five dimensions or yielding indigenous dimensions that resemble Big Five dimensions in some respects but differ in others. For instance, the Big Five dimension of Openness to Experience is not consistently represented in an assortment of European languages, and a study of Chinese trait terms yielded dimensions such as 'optimism' and 'self-control' that clearly overlap with the Big Five but do not obviously correspond to them in a one-to-one fashion. Most strikingly, some indigenous research has yielded entirely unique dimensions, such as a dimension of 'Chinese Tradition' (incorporating 'harmony', 'relationship orientation', and 'thrift') among Chinese people, and a dimension of 'Filipino Cultural Norms' (incorporating 'respectfulness', 'restraint', 'perseverance', 'responsibility', and 'humility') among Filipinos. Studies of indigenous personality dimensions therefore pose a challenge to the universality of Western trait theories. Although the dimensions that they produce are often similar to those developed by Western psychologists in broad outline, they differ significantly in the finer detail.

At this point it is worth pausing to consider what all of this research indicates. On balance, does it support or refute the generality of trait psychology's dimensions? Sadly the research gives no conclusive answer either way, offering evidence to confirm the pre-existing beliefs of both universalists and relativists. Before coming to your own judgment, however, consider two more complexities.

First, note that there is no culturally universal concept of 'personality', so the terms that a researcher uses in a study of one culture's indigenous trait lexicon may not be considered legitimate aspects of personality in a different culture. For example, perhaps one reason why 'Chinese Tradition' appears to be a unique indigenous dimension is that Westerners consider it to contain aspects of values, shared beliefs, or ideologies rather than personality traits. As a result, cultures may seem to differ in their indigenous dimensions simply because of differences in what they understand personality to be, thereby magnifying apparent differences between them. Perhaps there would be more cross-cultural consistency in the structure of personality if all cultures agreed on what characteristics are relevant to personality.

Second, note that while we have been discussing the generality of personality structure across cultures we have focused exclusively on broad personality dimensions such as the Big Five. Although there is evidence for significant generality of most of these dimensions, there is unlikely to be the same level of generality for the narrower traits or 'facets' that make up these dimensions. Remember that the broader dimensions are essentially scientific discoveries for which, in most cases, new labels were coined, whereas the narrower traits usually correspond to terms used in everyday language. For instance, 'neuroticism' was coined by Eysenck to label a dimension that emerged in his factor-analytic research, whereas the trait facets that compose it in the five-factor model – anxiety, angry hostility, depression, self-consciousness, impulsiveness, and vulnerability – are commonplace English trait terms expressed in noun form. Everyday terms such as these are unlikely to be readily translated into other languages without losing at least some of their meaning and cultural resonance. Indeed, the more different two language communities are, the less likely it is that their trait lexicons will align with one another in any mutually translatable way.

For instance, cultures differ markedly in how they classify emotions, so emotional traits, such as those that make up neuroticism, may in one culture be divided up in ways that have no clear equivalents in another culture. English concepts such as depression, self-consciousness, and vulnerability may have no corresponding concepts in another language, in which case these traits will have little cross-cultural generality. Some anthropologists have gone so far as to argue that such obstacles to the translation of trait language show that each culture's personality system must be understood only within its own indigenous framework. Because cultures are not commensurable, they maintain, it is inappropriate to try to compare them within a common framework, such as the five-factor model. This highly relativist conclusion seems extreme, especially given how much evidence of generality is found when such comparisons are made. However, it makes the important point that at some level of analysis traits are clearly not universal. By focusing on broad psychometric dimensions rather than the narrower traits that make up each culture's repertoire of everyday personality description, the research that we reviewed earlier probably over-states the cross-cultural generality of traits.

In sum, all cultures use trait terms to describe differences between people, and do so in ways that reveal a moderate to strong level of consistency. This consistency indicates an encouraging but by no means overwhelming cross-cultural generality for the broad trait dimensions advocated by Western trait psychologists. However, the inconsistencies that remain are significant, especially when traits are investigated from an indigenous perspective, and they show that trait psychology can not at this stage claim to have conclusively demonstrated universal personality dimensions. This conclusion neither invalidates trait theories such as the five-factor model nor does it imply that measures of these traits should only be used in Western cultures. It simply represents a real limitation of trait psychology.

TRAITS OR TYPES?

In essence, traits are ways in which people differ from one another. When psychologists talk about a trait, they are thinking of a dimension on which people differ: some people are very high on the dimension, some are very low, and most vary by degrees in the intermediate range. A trait is therefore understood to be a continuum, so that scores on a personality test correspond to approximate positions on the underlying trait that it measures. In short, traits are differences that are *differences of degree*, differences that can be thought of as *continuous* or *quantitative*, like the weight of an object, the brightness of a light, or the volume of a noise.

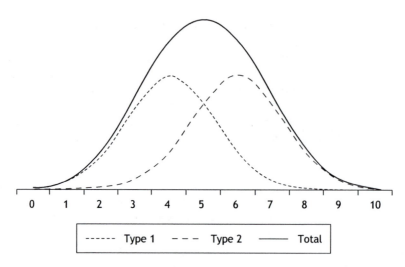

Figure 3.1 Illustration of psychological types

Although this view of traits often goes unchallenged, some psychologists have pointed out that not all differences between people are differences of degree. Some differences – like biological sex and blood type – are not continuous variations on a dimension, but involve a small number of discrete alternatives (e.g., male and female sex; blood types A, B, AB, and O). In differences of this sort, people either belong to one kind or to another. Differences such as these are therefore called *differences of kind*, and may also be described as *discontinuous, typological,* or *qualitative* (Meehl, 1992).

Figure 3.1 illustrates this sense of personality **types**. Imagine that some personality characteristic is assessed on a scale from 0 to 10, and we plot the distribution of people who receive each score. This 'observed distribution' is represented by the solid line, marked 'Total' in the figure legend, and it conforms to the bell shape that many individual differences display: most people fall in the middle of the distribution and relatively few score very high or very low. However, hidden beneath this observed distribution are two 'latent distributions' that correspond to distinct types of people. Members of Type 1 have an average score of 4, whereas members of Type 2 have an average score of 6. When the two latent distributions are added together, they yield the observed distribution. This is similar to what happens when the height of a sample of adults is examined: the observed distribution is roughly bell-shaped, but it is composed of two categorically distinct subgroups that differ in average height: men and women. As you can see from the figure, the two latent distributions overlap. Many members of the low-scoring type obtain higher scores on the scale than many members of the high-scoring type, just as many women are taller than many men. The important thing to note, however, is that whenever we observe a distribution of scores on a personality scale and see that it is smooth and bell-shaped, we cannot be sure whether people differ on the scale only by degree, or whether two different kinds of people are hidden within that distribution.

Given that there are two distinct sorts of differences, and that traits are usually understood to represent difference of degree only, perhaps the trait concept does not adequately characterize some personality differences. Perhaps some differences between people are better understood as differences of kind, grouping people into discrete personality types rather than dispersing them on a dimension. This possibility has been explored in some recent research, which has statistically investigated whether particular personality characteristics are better understood in terms of traits or types (Haslam & Kim, 2002). This research has found strong support for the existence of several typological differences between people, such as:

- *inhibited temperament*, a pattern of reserved, shy, and novelty-averse behaviour that is observable even in young children;
- *Type A personality*, a characteristic that combines impatience, hostility, and competitive drive;
- *self-monitoring*, the tendency to closely monitor social situations for signs of how to behave appropriately and to adapt one's behaviour to the context, rather than behaving consistently across situations; and
- *schizotypy*, a complex characteristic combining peculiar thinking patterns with social awkwardness and anxiety.

It seems fair to say that trait psychology's assumption that personality characteristics are best understood as differences of degree is sometimes mistaken. Some personality characteristics appear to reflect differences of kind. The existence of these differences indicates that efforts to describe personality must incorporate traits *and* types, and not automatically favour one sort of difference over another, as trait psychology has tended to do.

Do personality types present a serious challenge to trait psychology? The answer is surely mixed. On the one hand, they do point to a basic limitation of the trait concept as it has usually been employed. On the other hand, we should remember that personality types resemble personality traits in most respects. Both traits and types represent enduring, cross-situational dispositions, so the distinction between them is relatively subtle. In addition, it is worth noting that psychologists have not always blindly assumed that personality differences are differences of degree. For instance, psychologists have typically assumed that male sexual orientation – men's tendency to be erotically attracted to men or women – is a matter of kind, sorting men into homosexual and heterosexual categories, when research suggests that it is better understood as a matter of degree (Haslam, 1997).

In sum, the existence of personality types does not pose a radical challenge to trait psychology. However, it does point out a limitation with significant implications for how personality should be described. As a result, we need to think critically about personality differences and question our assumptions about them in the light of research evidence.

DO TRAITS EXPLAIN BEHAVIOUR?

Some trait psychologists take it as a given that traits explain behaviour. After all, psychological tests that measure traits generally predict behaviour to some extent, and you might think being able to predict something implies being able to explain it. In addition, traits are conceptualized as general dispositions that underlie specific behaviours, and it seems reasonable to explain the specific events, such as behaviours, by the more general tendencies. Gravity, for example, involves a general disposition for things to move towards the ground: knowing about gravity allows us to predict with high confidence that a spilled drink will fall to the floor rather than float around the room or splash upon the ceiling, and allows us to explain why. Is the explanation of behaviour by traits any different?

Some psychologists have argued that it is quite different, in several respects. First, trait explanation can often seem rather circular. Does it really explain a person's agreeable behaviour to say that he or she has a high level of trait agreeableness? This sounds a little bit like the medieval thinkers who argued that fire heated things up because it had 'calorific power', where this power was defined as the tendency to heat things up. Similarly, agreeableness just *is* the tendency to act agreeably; it is not a cause or explanation of the agreeable behaviour. In short, to refer to the trait may not really offer an explanation of the agreeable behaviour, but be just an observation that the behaviour is consistent with a pattern that the person has displayed in the past.

A second objection to the explanatory power of traits involves a fundamental question about what a trait is. Two main alternative views can be distinguished (Wiggins, 1997). On one view, traits are hypothetical 'latent variables': we cannot observe them but on the basis of regularities in someone's observable behaviour we hypothesize that they exist as explanatory entities within the person. To attribute a trait to someone involves inferring something that underlies and accounts for their behaviour. This is somewhat like how we explain the dropped drink: we infer the existence of an unobserved force (gravity) that causes the drink to fall. On the other view (Hampshire, 1953), however, traits are not inferred hypothetical entities. They do not cause behaviour, but simply provide a summary description of it. To attribute agreeableness to a person is not to infer something unobservable that resides within them, but just to state that in the past the person has tended to behave in an agreeable manner. Such a summary of past behaviour cannot explain present or future behaviour, but only point to its consistency or inconsistency with that behaviour.

A third criticism of the capacity for traits to explain behaviour argues that traits are static (i.e., fixed) attributes or entities that tell us very little about the *processes* that underlie behaviour. Even if we accept that traits are underlying variables and not mere behavioural summaries, there is often still something unsatisfying about explanations of behaviour that refer to traits: they don't tell us about the multiple steps and mechanisms that gave rise to that behaviour. You could explain why a car moves fast by referring to its horsepower or number of cylinders – both fixed attributes – but this explanation does not help to understand the many processes and mechanisms that combine to enable the car to move quickly. Similarly, if a researcher found that people high in neuroticism were less likely to get tested for a disease than those lower in neuroticism, this would not enlighten us about the processes that might underpin that difference in behaviour. Perhaps more neurotic people worry more about receiving an undesirable test result and therefore avoid testing, or perhaps they estimate defensively that they have a lower risk of having the disease (i.e., denial) and so don't bother getting tested, or perhaps they lack close friends who could encourage them to get tested. As a static attribute of the person, neuroticism is certainly relevant to the explanation of this behaviour, but a fuller explanation requires some added detail about psychological processes.

All of these criticisms of the explanatory power of traits have some merit, but it is important to put them in perspective. Trait explanations are certainly not always circular, for example. If we refer to a trait to explain a behaviour that is not merely an example of that trait – using Conscientiousness to explain longer life, for instance – then there is no circularity. Living longer is not an example of Conscientious behaviour, it appears to be an outcome or consequence of it. Similarly, most personality psychologists would argue that traits are not just summaries of past behaviour, that they allow the prediction of future behaviour, and that there is nothing unusual about inferring unobservable entities and giving them explanatory power, as we do with gravity. Finally, most psychologists would accept that traits can play an important role in the explanation of behaviour, even if it is only a partial explanation that needs to be supplemented by other psychological processes.

These issues surrounding the adequacy of trait psychology are also relevant to all of us in our daily lives. There is plenty of evidence from social psychology that laypeople – particularly in Western countries – make sense of one another's behaviour in much the same way as trait psychology, and with some of the same limitations and biases. We often under-estimate the extent to which

other people's behaviour is due to situational factors, over-estimate the extent to which it is due to their traits, and act as if describing people in terms of their traits is a sufficient explanation for their behaviour. When a shop assistant responds to a question with an unhelpful comment or an annoyed expression, we are often quick to explain that behaviour in trait terms – they acted in this way *because* they are 'arrogant' or 'stuck-up' – without considering that they might be tired, caffeine-deprived, or responding to our own unpleasant tone of voice. This tendency has been referred to as 'lay dispositionism': people tend to see behaviour (especially other people's behaviour) as caused by static, unchanging dispositions that lie deep within the person, as if people's traits are fixed essences (Haslam, Bastian, & Bissett, 2004). Stereotypes are largely made up of just these sorts of essences: particular groups are seen as lazy, devious, effeminate, impulsive, stupid, stingy, over-emotional, and so on, although often these trait-based stereotypes are inaccurate (Terracciano et al., 2005). One aspect of prejudice is the tendency to automatically attribute the behaviour of group members to these stereotypic traits (Leyens, Yzerbyt, & Schadron, 1994). Just as it is important for us to recognize the limitations of the trait approach to personality – to remember that situational factors are important, that people's behaviour is quite variable, that traits cannot always explain behaviour satisfactorily – it is important to be wary of our own tendencies to jump to conclusions about other people's traits.

ARE TRAITS SUFFICIENT FOR DESCRIBING PERSONALITY?

Up to this point we have discussed several criticisms of trait psychology and the concept of traits. We have seen that behaviour is somewhat consistent across situations and that traits are predictive of behaviour more than Mischel's critique might suggest, but that the levels of consistency and prediction are often quite modest. We have seen that although trait dimensions do not vary greatly across cultures, there is evidence for meaningful cultural differences in how traits are structured. We discussed how some enduring differences between people are not captured well by trait dimensions, but that in some respects people fall into discrete personality types. Finally, we noted that it is questionable whether traits explain behaviour, as distinct from describing or summarizing behaviour patterns. All of these issues relate to the adequacy of trait psychology as an account of individual differences in personality.

It is also possible to pose a different question about trait psychology. Even if traits were adequate in all of these senses, are they *sufficient* for describing human personality? When we describe a personality, do we need to refer to characteristics beyond traits, or is trait description enough? Although few psychologists deny that trait psychology offers an important and perhaps necessary vocabulary for describing individual differences, many have denied that traits encompass all that we need to consider when we attempt to describe human individuality. Traits may be indispensable, but they may not be the whole story when it comes to personality description. To supplement trait descriptions, theorists have proposed a wide variety of alternative descriptive units, concepts, and structures. Some of these alternatives will be discussed in greater detail in later chapters, but it is worth introducing a few of them here to give you a flavour of how they extend and complement trait psychology.

ALTERNATIVES TO TRAITS

Values

Values are units of personality description that are importantly different from traits. A value is an abstract goal that applies across a variety of situations, and that motivates people who hold it to behave in a way that pursues or expresses it. If you value freedom, for example, you believe that people should generally be at liberty to do what they want, and you will be inclined to pursue activities that allow you to express yourself freely.

Conceptually, values differ from traits in five main ways. First, they are not behavioural dispositions, but cognitions. Whereas traits are simply tendencies to behave in particular ways, values are beliefs about what is desirable that are represented in people's minds. Second, values are intimately connected to people's motives and needs, reflecting the goals that they strive towards. Traits may *express* motives – extraversion may reflect a drive for social power, for example – but they are not themselves motivating. Third, as a related matter, values are intrinsically desirable, at least to the people who hold them, whereas many traits are negative or undesirable. Fourth, values are things that people tend to be able to verbalize: they are often embedded in political or social beliefs and ideologies, and are the focus of public debate and discussion. Traits, in contrast, are often difficult to verbalize and they are rarely held up for public argument. Finally, values are often conceptualized as more changeable than traits. Whereas traits are often seen as deeply rooted in the person, and at least partly genetic in origin, values tend to be seen as learned and relatively malleable. Because they are cognitions, changing one's values should be more like changing one's mind than changing one's fundamental behavioural tendencies. Indeed, the university years are often considered a time when students undergo rapid value change in response to new experiences and new knowledge.

The most popular psychological model of values was developed by Schwartz and colleagues (e.g., Schwartz, 1992, 1994). Based on a comprehensive study of

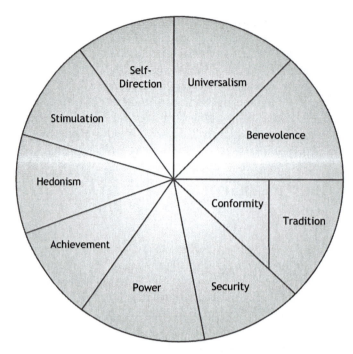

Figure 3.2   Schwartz's value circumplex

values in a wide variety of countries, Schwartz found evidence of a cross-culturally universal structure of values. Values seem to differ from one another on two dimensions, and can be placed in ten distinct segments around the perimeter of a circle defined on these dimensions. This 'circumplex' structure is illustrated in Figure 3.2, and the values that compose each segment are summarized in Table 3.1. Values in neighbouring segments of the circumplex – such as Stimulation and Hedonism values – are similar, and values in segments that are opposite on the circle – such as Stimulation and Tradition values – tend to conflict. Values in the lower left of the circumplex (Hedonism, Achievement, & Power) are sometimes described as 'self-enhancing' because they involve seeking personal goals, whereas those in the upper right (Universalism & Benevolence) are 'self-transcending' because they involve striving for the welfare of others. Values in the upper left (Stimulation & Self-Direction) and lower right (Security, Conformity, & Tradition) differ on a dimension of 'openness to change' versus 'conservation'. People with the former values seek novelty whereas those with the latter seek to preserve existing arrangements.

Values provide a vantage point on personality that differs in useful ways from the trait psychology perspective. Values are important ways in which

Table 3.1   *Summary of Schwartz's value classification*

Value segment	Core themes	Illustrative values
Power	Social status, control, dominance	Social Power, Authority, Wealth
Achievement	Personal success through competence	Successful, Capable, Ambitious
Hedonism	Pleasure, sensuous gratification	Pleasure, Enjoying Life
Stimulation	Excitement, novelty, challenge	Daring, a Varied Life, an Exciting Life
Self-Direction	Independence, choice, exploring	Creativity, Freedom, Independent, Curious
Universalism	Understanding, tolerance	Equality, Peace, Wisdom, Social Justice
Benevolence	Welfare of close others	Helpful, Honest, Forgiving, Loyal
Tradition	Acceptance of traditional customs and culture	Humble, Devout, Respect for Tradition
Conformity	Restraint, not violating social norms	Obedient, Politeness, Self-Discipline
Security	Safety, harmony, stability	Family and National Security, Social Order

cultures differ – for example, 'individualist' Western cultures tend to emphasize self-enhancing values more than relatively 'collectivist' cultures, such as those in East Asia – so they allow personality psychologists to examine the cultural dimension of their work. In addition, values are significant ways in which people differ from one another. Individual differences in values are associated with traits – for example, Openness is modestly correlated with Self-Direction values, Agreeableness with Benevolence values, and Conscientiousness with Achievement values – but these associations are generally quite weak. Values and traits may also allow us to predict different sorts of phenomena, as the Illustrative Study shows. The important message here is that values are components of personality that tell us something important about people beyond what standard personality traits can tell.

Illustrative study: how do values and traits differ in the prediction of behaviour?

Sonia Roccas and colleagues in Israel (Roccas, Sagiv, Schwartz, & Knafo, 2002) sought to clarify the relationships between personality traits and human values, and to examine whether they complement one another

(Continued)

(Continued)

in predicting behaviour. Values are conceptually different from traits — reflecting broad goals that people hold (how they desire to be) rather than dispositions to behave in a particular way (how they are) — but they might be expected to be empirically associated with one another. In addition, they might be expected to help us predict different sorts of behaviour. Roccas et al. predicted that values should be relatively useful for predicting goal-directed behaviour that is chosen or under the person's control, whereas traits should be relatively useful for predicting spontaneous and emotionally driven behaviours. They argue that religiosity (degree of religious belief, observance, and identity) is a good example of the former, and positive affect (the tendency to experience positive emotional states) is a good example of the latter.

Roccas et al. had a sample of 246 university students complete questionnaire measures of Schwartz's values and of the five-factor model. Participants also completed short measures of religiosity and positive affect. Correlations among the value and trait measures revealed a modest degree of overlap: traits and values were associated sparingly but in intelligible ways. For example, extraverts tend to value stimulation, agreeable people tend to hold benevolence values, and open people tend to value self-direction. Moreover, consistent with their prediction, Roccas et al. found that the values predicted religiosity much better than the five-factor traits, and the traits predicted positive affect better than the values. This study therefore makes a powerful argument that traits and values are distinct and important units for describing personality, and complement one another in making sense of human behaviour.

Character strengths

In Chapter 1 we saw how scientific psychologists distinguished 'personality' from 'character', which was a more evaluative concept involving desirable or morally relevant attributes. Most trait psychologists have taken pains to maintain this distinction, and have argued that social or moral value has no place in the scientific study of personality. As Allport (1931: 371) wrote:

> a trait of personality, psychologically considered, is not the same as a moral quality … Where possible it would be well for us to find our trait first, and then seek devaluated terms with which to characterize our discoveries.

Table 3.2   *The Values in Action classification of virtues and character strengths*

Virtue class	Core themes	Exemplary character strengths
Wisdom	Strengths that entail the acquisition and use of knowledge	Creativity, curiosity, judgment, social intelligence, perspective
Courage	Strengths that involve exercise of will in the face of opposition	Integrity, vitality, industry, valour
Humanity	Strengths that are interpersonal in nature	Kindness, love
Justice	Strengths that are civic in nature	Fairness, leadership, teamwork
Temperance	Strengths that protect from excesses	Modesty, prudence, self-regulation
Transcendence	Strengths that connect us to the larger universe	Forgiveness, appreciation of beauty, hope, gratitude, spirituality, playfulness

Increasingly, some psychologists, and especially those in the new 'positive psychology' movement, have been arguing that this divorce of personality and evaluation is illegitimate. Many personality characteristics, they propose, are socially desirable or 'normative' and should be actively nurtured. Peterson and Seligman (2002) have recently developed a classification of virtues and character strengths, which can be thought of as lying somewhere between personality traits and values: like traits, they are dispositions rather than beliefs or goals, but they are intimately bound up with values. This 'Values in Action' (VIA) classification is intended as a positive counterpart of psychiatric classifications, which focus exclusively on the forms of misery and human weakness. Peterson and Seligman propose that for a disposition to qualify as a character strength it must contribute to fulfilment in one's life, be valued in its own right rather than merely as a means to some other end, and not diminish anyone else in society when it is exercised. They argue that character strengths are environmentally shaped, can be cultivated (i.e., developed in a positive direction by self-improvement and social institutions), and fall into six distinct categories, which they refer to as virtues. Their classification is presented in Table 3.2.

The study of character strengths and virtues is in its infancy, but as was the case with values, there is reason to believe that they add something to our understanding of the person to what standard trait psychology offers. Character strengths overlap with personality traits and values (Haslam, Bain, & Neal, 2004), but also appear to be somewhat distinct, and they may therefore be useful ways in which personality can be described.

Highly evaluative personality characteristics

Values, virtues, and character strengths are all more saturated with evaluation than standard traits. As we have seen, personality psychologists are increasingly arguing that we need to recognize that personality characteristics are often evaluative, and that it is inappropriate to think about personality removed from evaluation. However, although values, virtues, and strengths are all positive, personality evaluation is often negative, as anyone who has been gossiped about knows only too well.

Recently, Benet-Martínez and Waller (2002) have proposed that highly evaluative personality descriptors, both positive and negative, need to be considered if we are to have a complete vocabulary for describing personalities. Doing this is necessary for two reasons. First, everyday description of and communication about personality, as in gossip, is intensely evaluative, involving the sizing up of people's reputations and the exchange of information that is often heavy with emotion. Ordinary people's understanding and use of personality impressions is fundamentally evaluative – about *judging* people, not just describing them dispassionately – and psychology should acknowledge this fact. Second, the lists of trait terms from which classifications such as the Big Five were later developed (Allport & Odbert, 1936), explicitly removed all terms that were judged to be highly evaluative, as you will remember from Chapter 2. In short, highly evaluative personality terms have been omitted from most efforts to chart personality structure.

To remedy this omission Benet-Martínez and Waller (2002) examined people's ratings of large samples of descriptors that had been excluded from standard trait lists for being too evaluative. They found that these descriptors varied along five dimensions which appeared to be distinct from the five factors that are obtained when less evaluative terms are factor-analysed. These dimensions, and illustrative descriptors, are presented in Table 3.3. Each dimension had a primary evaluative direction, with four dimensions containing descriptors that were predominantly negative and one containing positively evaluated descriptors. (This imbalance between negative and positive terms is also found when psychologists examine emotion terms, and may reflect a general tendency to give greater weight to negative phenomena; Rozin & Royzman, 2001.) Personality evaluation clearly is not simply positive or negative, but has a complex structure, based on distinct domains of power (distinction and worthlessness), intelligence (stupidity), morality (depravity), and normalcy (unconventionality).

Benet-Martínez and Waller (2002) argue that their dimensions may have important applications in professional psychology, where personality evaluations of job candidates or patients must be made, and in the study of everyday personality judgment. Once again, as with values and character strengths, the evaluative dimensions provide ways of describing personality that go beyond those that standard trait psychology offers.

Table 3.3 *Dimensions of highly evaluative personality descriptors*

Dimension	Evaluation	Core themes	Illustrative terms
Distinction	+	Social recognition	Remarkable, stellar, first-rate, magnificent
Stupidity	−	Lack of intelligence	Half-witted, blockheaded, moronic, brainless
Worthlessness	−	Tarnished reputation	Lacklustre, subnormal, pointless, meaningless
Unconventionality	−	Peculiarity, abnormality	Odd, bizarre, peculiar, cracked, off
Depravity	−	Moral taint	Rat, scoundrel, pukish, beastly, disgraceful

Interests

Up until now, the additional non-trait units of personality description have all involved evaluation in one way or another. However, there are other ways of describing aspects of personality that also complement the psychology of traits. One such aspect is people's **interests**. Interests represent the preferences people have for particular kinds of activity. They are therefore less abstract than values, and more to do with what engages people and attracts their attention rather than what they find desirable or good. Interests involving occupational or vocational preferences are particularly significant, because they often play a large role in determining what careers people pursue, and whether or not they are satisfied with the work that they do. Understanding and assessing people's vocational interests is therefore an important task for psychologists who study individual differences.

One popular model of vocational interests was developed by Holland (1997), who proposed that there are six main interest types. Holland described the structure of these 'vocational personalities' as a hexagon, and presents them as they are shown in Figure 3.3, but they can be understood just as well as a circumplex, as in Schwartz's model of values. The typical characteristics and most suitable occupations are laid out in Table 3.4. Thus, people with artistic interests, for example, are most similar to those with investigative and social interests, and most dissimilar to those with conventional interests. Holland's model underlies a popular assessment tool for career counsellors to assess people's profiles of interests – people rarely have interests that are specific to one interest type – and can help to illuminate the reasons why people may fail to adjust successfully to their work environments. If their interests are a poor fit to their work role or environment – for instance, someone with

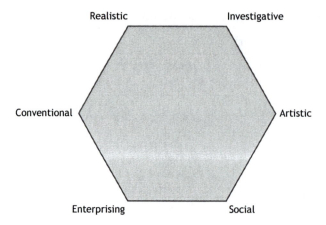

Figure 3.3   Holland's model of vocational interests

Table 3.4   *Summary of Holland's model of vocational interests*

Interest type	Typical attributes	Occupations
Realistic	Hard-headed, conforming, practical, materialistic; prefers work with physical objects	Mechanic, electrician, farmer
Investigative	Analytical, rational, curious, cautious, critical; prefers work involving systematic observation and problem-solving that is not too social or repetitive	Scientist, lab assistant, anthropologist
Artistic	Intuitive, independent, open, imaginative, idealistic, sensitive, impractical; prefers work that is creative and unsystematic	Artist, musician, writer
Social	Friendly, kind, empathic, responsible; prefers work that involves helping or teaching others	Teacher, clinical psychologist, nurse
Enterprising	Extraverted, energetic, optimistic, ambitious, confident; prefers work involving leadership, manipulation of others, and seeking power	Executive, manager, salesperson
Conventional	Orderly, efficient, pragmatic, careful; prefers work that is systematic and unambiguous	Financial analyst, book-keeper, accountant

artistic interests working in a position more suited to someone with conventional interests, or in an organization that adopts an inflexibly conventional workplace culture – then they are likely to be dissatisfied and to work poorly. The study of interest patterns is therefore a practically valuable adjunct to the standard psychology of traits.

Motives and goals

Personality traits reflect behavioural consistencies from which dispositions are inferred. They therefore describe *how* people behave rather than *why* they do so. You will remember that some critics of trait psychology have questioned whether traits explain behaviour, and the fact that they do not directly answer such questions partly underlies their criticisms. Some personality psychologists have therefore argued that we must pay attention to **motives**, the sources of behaviour. By their account, trait psychology overlooks this vital component of human individuality.

Motivational concepts have been brought into the study of personality in two main forms. Some psychologists propose motivations of a kind that people may not be aware of, but that underlie and propel their behaviour. These sorts of motives are commonly referred to as *instincts*, *needs*, or *drives*. Murray (1938), for example, proposed that people have as many as 20 basic needs, such as the need for autonomy (to be free of constraint and to be independent), the need for order (to have things well organized, neat, and precise), and the need for abasement (to submit passively to external forces). These needs will vary in strength for each person, giving the individual a unique profile of needs. In a similar spirit, McClelland (1985) developed an influential analysis of three fundamental needs: for achievement (a drive for efficient accomplishment and mastery), for affiliation (a drive for warm, interpersonal relationships), and for power (a drive for control and dominance). McClelland and his colleagues researched individual differences in these motives not by asking people about the strength of their needs – after all, people might not be aware of this – but by developing subtle ways of inferring need strength from the stories they told about ambiguous pictures (see Chapter 8 for a discussion of such 'projective' tests).

Other personality psychologists have discussed motivations in terms of *goals* and *strivings* rather than needs and drives. Whereas needs metaphorically 'push' people to behave in particular ways, acting on them in ways that may be outside of their conscious awareness, goals and strivings 'pull' people from the future: the person has a conscious awareness of a future state that they desire, and are motivated to achieve. For example, Markus and Nurius (1986) propose that people hold mental representations of their 'possible selves', the people they would like to be (or dread becoming) sometime in the future. These selves are often concrete images of what the person might become and they provide incentives that motivate the person to take the necessary steps to realize or preclude them. Conceptually, possible selves are sharply different from traits: they are ideas rather than dispositions, they refer to the future rather than describing the person's present dispositions, and they are highly specific to each person, rather than measured on a standard set of dimensions.

Another form of goal-related motivational concept is the 'personal project' (Little, 1989). Personal projects are extended series of goal-directed actions that people see themselves as working towards. Rather than just being images of a desired end-state, like possible selves, personal projects also include the intermediate steps that need to be taken to achieve this goal. Projects vary in their duration ('finish this essay' vs. 'finish this degree'), in their generality ('finish this essay' vs. 'become wise'), in their degree of personal importance, and in the extent to which the person sees progress in accomplishing them. The state of a person's projects seems to have serious implications for their well-being, as people who do not see such progress, whose projects are mostly of long-term duration, and whose projects are incompatible with one another tend to be less satisfied with life (Palys & Little, 1983).

The concepts of needs, possible selves, and personal projects merely scratch the surface of the motivational concepts that have been employed by personality psychologists (Emmons, 1999). The important point to recognize is simply that these motivational concepts provide information about personality that is not captured by personality traits, namely the forces and goals that drive behaviour. Such needs and goals are not entirely unrelated to personality traits – personal projects do correlate with Big Five trait dimensions, for example (Little et al., 1991) – but they need not be closely linked. Although having a certain strong need may drive the person to behave in a way that is consistent with that need, the person's typical behaviour (i.e., their traits) may not match it. For example, someone who has a strong power motive will be driven to exert control over others, but may be timid and inhibited and therefore unable to express this motive successfully. It is not difficult to understand how such a mismatch or conflict between motives and traits could be problematic and distressing for people. Indeed, this combination of inhibited power motivation has been shown to predict high blood pressure and ill health (Jemmott, 1987). In sum, people's motives are psychologically distinct from their traits, and they tell us something basic about human individuality that complements what we learn from trait psychology.

In this section we have reviewed an assortment of ways of describing personality besides traits. The aim of this exercise was to show that there are many other interesting descriptive units for making sense of the person's individuality. In an important paper, McAdams (1995) argued that in fact traits represent just one level of personality description, and that personality psychologists should also pay heed to other levels. At Level I, dispositional traits represent broad, cross-situationally consistent attributes that are useful for getting a first impression of someone. Research shows that we can perceive other people's personality traits when we only observe them for a few moments, or even when we do not directly observe them at all, but only see the environments that they make for themselves. For example, people can form accurate impressions of others from their personal websites (Vazire & Gosling, 2004) and from the state of their offices and bedrooms (e.g., organized and uncluttered = high Conscientiousness; distinctive and with lots of books = high Openness; Gosling, Ko, Mannarelli, & Morris, 2002). However, if we are to understand someone in greater detail and depth, McAdams suggests, it is necessary to move to Level II, which he refers to as the level of 'personal concerns'. Personal concerns differ from traits in being more specific to particular contexts (e.g., particular social roles, situations, life domains, life stages, or temporal contexts [such as the future]) and in relating to the dynamics of personality: the factors that account for *why* people act in certain ways, not just *what* they do. McAdams mentions motives, values, and personal projects as prime examples of personal concerns, and interests could be added to that list, given their specific relation to the context of work. In short, the concepts reviewed in this chapter offer a different kind of description of personality that is distinct from the trait level, and complements it.

CONCLUSIONS

In this chapter we have reviewed several challenges to the trait psychology approach to the study of personality. Has trait psychology succumbed to the sheer number and variety of these challenges? The simple answer is 'No': the trait approach has had a remarkable resurgence in the past decade, and is being pursued with renewed confidence. Does this mean that the challenges were all ultimately weak or mistaken? No again. Many challenges have been successfully addressed, but others must be taken seriously. In particular, it is important to recognize that behaviour has a great deal of within-person and cross-situational variability, and that traits have limitations as explanations of behaviour. In addition, it is important to recognize that there is more to personality than traits. People's personalities can also be described in terms of their values, their character strengths (and weaknesses) and other highly evaluative terms, their interests, their goals, and their motives. This is just a subset of the different facets of personality that theorists and researchers have proposed: later chapters will introduce you to others (i.e., unconscious processes such as defence mechanisms in Chapter 5, cognitive processes in Chapter 6, life narratives in Chapter 10). It should be clear by now that although trait psychologists sometimes write as if traits are all there is to personality – or that personality *is* traits – traits alone cannot encapsulate a person's individuality. This is not a deep criticism of trait psychology, just an acknowledgement that it has a somewhat limited scope. Trait psychology offers an unquestionably important perspective for describing and understanding personality, but there are others.

Chapter summary

- Although the psychology of traits has made major contributions to the study of personality, it has also come under criticism on a variety of fronts.
- Some psychologists have argued that behaviour is not very consistent across different contexts, and that it is therefore determined primarily by the situation in which it occurs rather than by enduring traits of the behaving person. According to this 'situationist' critique, behaviour is not very 'traited' and traits are only weak predictors of behaviour.
- Rebuttals of the situationist critique argue that it under-estimates the consistency of behaviour as well as the predictive power of traits. Traits can, in fact, predict behaviour well when the behaviour is assessed as aggregate patterns rather than single actions.
- Other psychologists have argued that trait dimensions are not culturally universal, and that explaining behaviour with reference to personality is characteristically Western. At least at the level of broad trait factors, however, cross-cultural research tends to support the view that these factors are reasonably universal, with a few subtle exceptions. However, there are likely to be more substantial differences between cultures in the traits that are indigenously recognized.
- Trait psychologists usually assume that individual differences in personality fall along continuous dimensions: they are matters of degree, like height. However, some research supports the existence of several distinct personality 'types': categories that people either do or do not belong to.
- It has sometimes been argued that traits merely describe or summarize behaviour rather than explaining it: explaining someone's tendency to behave in an agreeable manner because they have high levels of agreeableness seems circular. However, personality traits can be understood as 'latent' variables that are inferred to underlie behaviour and explain behaviour in the same, non-circular way that other inferred variables do.
- Traits are not the only descriptive units that can be used to capture aspects of people's personalities, and psychologists have developed useful models of several alternative units. These include values, character strengths and virtues, interests, motives, and goals. These concepts offer ways of describing personality that complement the psychology of traits.

Further Reading

- Church, A.T., & Lonner, W.J. (1998). Personality and its measurement in cross-cultural perspective. Special issue of the *Journal of Cross-Cultural Psychology, 29.*

This journal issue presents a fascinating variety of articles on the cross-cultural variability (or consistency) of personality structure.

- Meehl, P.E. (1992). Factors and taxa, traits and types, differences of degree and differences in kind. *Journal of Personality, 60*, 117–74.

This is a conceptually difficult but nevertheless valuable discussion of the distinction between dimensional and categorical views of personality, and of why that distinction matters. For a related review of research on the possible existence of personality types, see Haslam, N., & Williams, B. (2006). Taxometrics. In S.N. Strack (Ed.), Differentiating normal and abnormal personality. New York: Springer.

- Mischel, W. (1968). *Personality and assessment.* New York: Wiley.

This monograph is mainly of historical value now, but is worth a look to see what seemed at the time to be a crushing blow to the concept of personality (and traits in particular) when it first appeared.

- Peterson, C., & Seligman, M.E.P. (2002). *Character strengths and virtues: A handbook and classification.* New York: Oxford University Press & American Psychological Association.

This book lays out a classification of strengths and virtues from the standpoint of the new 'positive psychology'. In addition to presenting reviews of individual strengths, the book contains illuminating reviews of accounts of strengths and virtues from psychology, philosophy, and religious traditions.

- Schwartz, S.H. (1992). Universals in the content and structure of values: Theoretical advances and empirical tests in 20 countries. In M. Zanna (Ed.) *Advances in experimental social psychology, Vol. 25* (pp. 1–65). New York: Academic Press.

Schwartz reviews the large body of work on his influential model of human values, which represent an important unit of personality description beyond traits.

(Continued)

(Continued)

- Wiggins, J.S. (1997). In defence of traits. In R. Hogan, J. Johnson, & S. Briggs (Eds.), *Handbook of personality psychology* (pp. 95–115). New York: Academic Press.

Wiggins vigorously defends the concept of personality traits against some of the criticisms discussed early in the present chapter, arguing that most of these criticisms are weaker than some had supposed.

SECTION 2
EXPLAINING PERSONALITY

4

Biological Approaches to Personality

Learning objectives

- To understand the behavioural genetic approach to the study of personality, and the research methods it employs to determine the heritability of traits.
- To recognize the nature and limitations of genetic influences on personality, and the ways in which behavioural genetics clarifies the role of environmental factors in personality.
- To understand major theories of how patterns of brain functioning are associated with individual differences in personality.
- To clarify how personality variations can be understood in terms of evolutionary adaptations.

This chapter is the first of three that examine alternative ways of explaining personality, and focuses on biological processes and mechanisms. We first review evidence for genetic contributions to personality, examining their magnitude (i.e., the 'heritability' of personality traits) and the research methods employed to assess them. Evidence on the nature of environmental contributions has also emerged from this research, and it is examined along with recent research on the role of specific genes in personality. We then turn to the role of brain functioning in personality, reviewing three theories of the biological (i.e., physiological and neurochemical) underpinnings of major personality traits. Finally, we investigate how evolutionary theory – the theory of how organisms evolve and how their adaptations emerge and function – can help to make sense of individual differences.

In the first section of this book we discussed how individual differences in personality should be described and represented. Now we move on to consider the ways in which these differences can be explained. To explain a phenomenon is to give an account of how and why it arises. However, explanation is not a simple concept, and explanations may take a variety of forms. To explain phenomena such as flight in birds and mechanical alarm clocks, for instance, it may be appropriate to refer to *structures* (e.g., feathers, hollow bones, and wing muscles; cogs, wind-up motors, and clock-hands), underlying *processes* or *mechanisms* (e.g., coordinated patterns of muscle contraction and relaxation; the interconnections of the rotating components), and *functions* (e.g., to allow swift escape from predators and access to distant or inaccessible food; to tell time and wake people up). All of these elements of explanations – structures, processes, and functions – contribute to a full account of why a phenomenon is as it is, and how it is produced. To explain personality differences, then, we must account for the structures, processes and functions that underlie them. We will explore a wide variety of explanatory approaches in the next three chapters.

One way to explain personality variation is to look for its biological basis. All behaviour is produced by living, embodied organisms – the objects of biological investigation – so it would be surprising if behavioural variation were not in some way underpinned by biological differences. Nevertheless, this claim has been controversial, and many psychologists have objected strongly to the implication that cultural and social influences on behaviour ('nurture') are overshadowed by biological influences ('nature'). The nature–nurture debate is a complicated and heated one, and to keep a balanced view we should keep a few thoughts in mind. First, to say that biological differences underlie personality is not to imply that social and cultural influences on personality are unimportant. Second, it is possible to investigate the biological bases of personality without claiming that they directly *determine* personality variation ('determinism'), or that personality can be *reduced* to them ('reductionism'). Third, the division between biological and sociocultural influences and explanations is to some extent a false one. Humans are innately and intrinsically social, our capacity for culture as much a part of our biological fabric as our capacity for breathing. Social influences affect our biology, just as biological influences affect our social behaviour. Biological accounts of personality simply represent one among several legitimate ways of understanding the sources of human variation.

Biology provides three main vantage points for investigating the underpinnings of personality. We can ask whether personality traits are subject to *genetic influences*, and therefore partially inherited. We can also ask whether personality characteristics are reflected in distinct patterns of *brain activity*, such as differences in the functioning and chemical composition of the brain's circuitry. In addition, we can ask how individual differences in personality might make sense in the light of *evolution*. These three perspectives correspond to the three types of explanation mentioned earlier: genes represent the structures that underlie personality differences, patterns of brain activity represent the underlying processes and mechanisms, and evolution offers an explanation of what functions personality variation might serve. We will examine each of these biological approaches to the explanation of personality in the pages to come.

THE GENETICS OF PERSONALITY

It is well known that many differences between people are inherited. Characteristics such as biological sex, height, eye colour, and susceptibility to a variety of diseases are clearly under the control of biological structures that are passed on to us by our parents. These structures are known as genes, which are segments of a long two-stranded molecule known as DNA. The strands of the DNA molecule are held apart by pairs of four simpler molecules known as bases. The sequence of these base pairs contains information in a code that our cells 'read' to synthesize the proteins that build, maintain, and regulate our bodies. Human DNA contains about 30,000 genes composed of a total of about 3 billion base pairs. Roughly 99.9% of these base pairs are identical for all people, and therefore cannot be the source of individual differences in personality or any other characteristics. The remaining 3 million or so base pairs take two or more alternative forms as a result of genetic mutations, and are therefore known as 'polymorphisms'. Genetically-based differences between people are based on the modifications in gene functioning that result from these polymorphisms.

Behavioural genetics is the field that attempts to understand the influence that these inherited genetic differences have on psychological characteristics such as cognitive abilities, mental disorders, and personality traits. Although researchers have not, until recently, attempted to identify specific polymorphisms and determine the effects that they have on gene functioning, they have taken great steps towards illuminating how genetic differences, as a set, contribute to individual differences in behaviour. Behavioural geneticists have three main methods for studying these contributions: family studies, twin studies, and adoption studies. The three kinds of studies represent alternative ways of estimating the extent of genetic and environmental influences on the characteristic of interest.

Behavioural genetic research methods

Family studies assess the resemblance of family members on the characteristic of interest – for example, correlations between them on a personality questionnaire – as a function of their degree of genetic relatedness. The 'first-degree' relatives of a particular family member – the person's brothers and sisters, parents, and children – are 50% genetically similar. 'Second-degree' relatives – grandparents, uncles and aunts, nephews and nieces, and grandchildren – are 25% similar, and more distant relatives have correspondingly weaker genetic similarity. If genes contribute to the characteristic of interest, then closer relatives should more closely resemble one another on it, with unrelated people having no systematic resemblance at all. Although family studies can begin to establish genetic influence on a characteristic in this way, they have a significant deficiency in that they fail to disentangle genetic from environmental influences. Closer relatives – such as brothers, or parents and children – resemble one another more closely than distant relatives in their genes, but also in their family environment, social class, and life experiences. Consequently, it is risky to infer that their greater resemblance on the characteristic of interest is due to shared genes, because it might partly or wholly be due to shared environmental influences.

Twin studies offer an alternative means of testing and estimating genetic contributions to a characteristic. They capitalize on the well-known distinction between two kinds of twins: identical (or monozygotic; MZ) and fraternal (dizygotic; DZ) twins. Because MZ twins are genetically identical – derived from a single fertilized egg – whereas DZ twins, derived from two separately fertilized eggs, are no more genetically similar than non-twin brothers and sisters (50%), genetic influence can be shown if the former resemble one another more than the latter. Unlike family studies, twin studies take steps to rule out environmental influences on the characteristic of interest, because both MZ and DZ twins do not typically differ significantly in the environmental influences that impinge on them (i.e., the 'equal environments assumption'). Therefore, geneticists can be confident that differences in the resemblance of MZ and DZ twins are primarily genetic in origin.

A third form of behavioural genetic investigation is the *adoption study*, in which the resemblance of adopted children to their biological and adoptive parents is examined and compared. The extent to which children resemble the biological parents who gave them up at birth reveals the extent of genetic influence, because there should be little systematic environmental resemblance between them. Similarly, children's resemblance to their adoptive parents, with whom they have no systematic genetic similarity, reveals the extent of environmental influence. Therefore, if children resemble their biological parents more than their adoptive parents then we have grounds for concluding that genes outweigh environmental factors in their influence on the characteristic of interest. Studies are sometimes performed with separately adopted twins to yield especially interesting evidence about genetic and environmental effects.

These three kinds of behavioural genetic study all have potential limitations. As noted earlier, family studies fail to disentangle genetic and environmental influences because closer relatives are more similar both genetically and environmentally. Twin studies are vulnerable to violations of the equal environments assumption and to the criticism that twins are unrepresentative of the general population. Perhaps identical twins are treated more similarly by their parents than fraternal twins, which would exaggerate the difference in their degree of resemblance, and perhaps twins are so unlike other children that it is unwise to generalize from them. Research tends to discount both of these possibilities, finding, for example, that MZ twins misclassified by their parents as fraternal are just as similar as correctly classified MZ twins, and that twins do not differ significantly from non-twins in personality. Nevertheless, twin studies must guard themselves against these limitations. Adoption studies, in turn, are vulnerable to the same representativeness problems as twin studies, and to the possibility that adoptive and biological parents might systematically resemble one another, the problem of 'selective placement'. If in some way adoptive and biological families are matched on such criteria as social class, education, or intelligence, we can no longer have confidence that the resemblance of children to their biological parents is purely genetic or that their resemblance to their adoptive parents is purely environmental. In addition, it should be noted that biological parents not only contribute their genes to their adopted-away children, but also contribute the prenatal environment in which these children spend nine important months. Consequently, the supposedly 'genetic' resemblance of biological parents to their adopted-away children may in fact be partially environmental.

Genetic influences and heritability

Clearly behavioural genetic studies face some very real methodological complications. Nevertheless, behavioural geneticists are able to perform highly sophisticated statistical analyses that take many of these complications into account when estimating the relative contribution of genetic and environmental influences. These contributions are usually quantified as the proportion of observed variation in the characteristic of interest that can be accounted for by variation in the two kinds of influences. For genetic influences, this proportion is known as the characteristic's **heritability**. If genetic differences between people do not account for differences in their standing on the characteristic – for example, if adopted children do not resemble their biological parents or if MZ twins resemble one another no more than DZ twins – then heritability is .0.

If genetic differences underlie all variation in the characteristic then the heritability is 1.0. As a guide, the heritabilities of height, weight, and performance in secondary school mathematics are about .9, .7, and .4, respectively.

When behavioural geneticists have studied the inheritance of personality characteristics they have obtained a quite consistent and, to many people, surprising body of findings. Most importantly, they have consistently found that virtually every personality trait studied has a substantial heritability, generally in the range of .3 to .5 (Plomin, DeFries, McClearn, & Rutter, 1997). That is, between about one-third and one-half of personality variation is due to genetic influences. This holds true not only for the Big Five personality traits, but also for more specific characteristics that might intuitively seem completely unrelated to genetic influence, such as religiosity, vocational interests, and attitudes towards the death penalty. This does not mean that there are genes for faith, librarianship, and execution. It does mean that a large proportion of the differences between people on personality-related characteristics such as these is due to many polymorphic genes that influence brain processes in as-yet unknown ways.

Often when people hear about the substantial heritability of personality traits they disagree and point out how different they are from their family members. However, high heritabilities do not entail high correlations among close relatives. Extraversion, for instance, has a heritability of about .5, but the correlation of biological parents with their children is only .16, and the correlation between their biological children is only .20 (Loehlin, 1992). These correlations indicate that if you are an extrovert (i.e., above the population mean on extraversion), the probability that any particular sibling or parent of yours is also an extrovert is roughly 58-60%, not much better than chance. This number is so low because environmental influences are also strong and because your genetic similarity to these first-degree relatives is only 50% (the chance of your identical twin being extraverted rises to 76%). In short, family resemblances need not be strong for genetic influences to be considerable.

Heritability is a valuable concept for representing the relative contribution of genetic influences to variation within a population. However, it is easily misunderstood and abused. Heritability does not imply anything about the extent of genetic contribution to any *individual's* personality, but only to variability *between* individuals. Both genes and environments are indispensable to the creation of individual personalities (and lives): neither can be expressed without the other. Heritability also says nothing about how changeable a characteristic is. Highly heritable characteristics may be readily modified, both at the individual level and the collective level. For example, there are very effective treatments for many highly heritable disorders, both mental and physical, and average height has increased dramatically over the past century as a result of improved nutrition. That is, heritability only implies a statistical propensity to have a certain characteristic, not an inescapable necessity. Finally, heritability is particular to the time and place in which it is estimated. It represents the proportion of variation in a characteristic that *happens to be* due to genetic influences in a particular sample of people, not what the proportion *could be if* the sample's environmental conditions were different or *would be* in a different sample. For instance, in places where the range of environmental influences that people are subject to is very broad, the proportion of genetic influence on variation in a characteristic will correspondingly shrink and heritabilities will be relatively low. Heritability estimates will therefore be relatively high in places where environmental conditions are more homogeneous and socially equitable. In sum, heritability is an important index of genetic influence, but its meaning is quite specific and limited.

The role of the environment

Behavioural genetic research on personality not only illuminates the heritable influences on personality, but has also generated some intriguing findings about the nature of the relevant environmental influences. Two findings are particularly important. First, the environmental factors that are most influential for personality are not those that people within a family have in common but those that are distinctive to individual family members and make them different from one another. Second, many apparently 'environmental' influences are, in fact, genetically influenced.

The first finding – that **'shared environment'** contributes very little to personality variation relative to 'non-shared environment' – is surprising because many psychologists have assumed that personality is primarily influenced by such factors as child-rearing practices, parental beliefs and values, social status, and shared experiences such as economic deprivation and divorce. If factors such as these were important determinants of personality we would expect adoptive parents to closely resemble their children, and we would expect these biologically unrelated children to closely resemble one another. However, studies consistently show virtually no such resemblance, indicating that the shared environment of the adoptive family has very little influence on personality. The same conclusion emerges from studies of non-adoptive families.

Evidence for the importance of non-shared environmental influences, on the other hand, is very strong. For instance, MZ twins reared together are often far from identical in personality, typically correlating only about .45 (Plomin et al., 1997), despite having identical genes and essentially identical shared environments. Given that the heritability of a typical personality trait is .4 and the contribution of shared environment to personality variation is close to zero, the proportional contribution of non-shared environment to personality variation – i.e., the remainder – must approach .6. That is, perhaps a little more than half of the variation in personality is due to environmental influences that are not shared within a family, such as personal accidents, illnesses, distinctive school experiences and peer groups, and differential treatment of children by their parents (e.g., favouritism). In short, life circumstances and experiences strongly influence our personalities, but in ways that make us different from, not similar to, other members of our families.

The second major finding of behavioural genetics is that some environmental influences are themselves subject to genetic effects. For one thing, the negative life events that befall and shape us are partially heritable. For example, susceptibility to accidents and divorce are partly heritable, probably because they are associated with heritable personality traits. Similarly, we actively expose ourselves to environments that match or fit our genetic dispositions. For example, extraverts gravitate towards more excitement- and people-filled work and social environments than introverts. Genetic dispositions also influence the responses that we evoke from the environment. For example, children with difficult temperaments tend to engage in risky and antisocial activities and to join delinquent peer groups, and thereby evoke more punitive and critical responses from their parents and teachers. In addition to influencing the environments that we passively endure, actively seek and evoke from others, genes influence how we *experience* life events, so that people with different genetic dispositions may respond very differently to the same events. The picture that emerges from this research is that people's genetic dispositions, revealed in their personalities, can profoundly affect the environments that they inhabit. Genetic and environmental influences are entangled and often difficult to separate.

Specific personality-related genes

The research that we have reviewed shows that genetic differences between people are a major source of personality variation. Twin and adoption studies demonstrate that genetic resemblance strongly influences resemblance in personality. Although this evidence is compelling, it is also incomplete. After all, it indicates that *some* genes influence personality, but not which ones or how they work. The next step in behavioural genetic research on personality is therefore to locate specific genes that contribute to personality variation. Recently, this step has been taken by several pioneering genetic researchers (Hamer, 1997). These researchers have located specific genes that are associated with individual differences in novelty-seeking – a trait that involves an interest in new experiences and risk-taking – and in anxiety-related traits such as neuroticism. Both genes are linked to differences in the transmission of chemical messages within the brain by chemicals known as **'neurotransmitters'**. In the case of novelty-seeking, the variants of the gene produce molecules that make the brain sensitive to the presence of dopamine, a neurotransmitter involved in reward and subjective pleasure. One variant produces a long version of the molecule that is more sensitive to dopamine than the short version produced by the gene's other variant. People with the long version score higher on measures of novelty-seeking, presumably because they are more alert and sensitive to the rewarding, pleasurable possibilities of behaviour. In the case of anxiety-related traits, the gene is involved in the production of a protein that influences the functioning of serotonin, another neurotransmitter. One variant of the gene, linked to higher levels of neuroticism and childhood shyness (Lesch et al., 1996; Arbelle, Benjamin, Crolin, Kremev, Belmaker, & Ebstein, 2003), results in increased serotonin levels. Each of these genes is responsible for only a small fraction of the genetic influence on the respective traits, but their discoveries represent landmarks in the biological explanation of personality.

The nature of genetic influence

The accumulation of evidence for genetic influence on personality has not been greeted with universal joy by psychologists or by the general population. The discovery of specific personality-related genes in particular opens up nightmare scenarios of parents aborting foetuses whose genes place them at 'risk' of having undesirable personality characteristics. The discovery of a gene linked to the complex personality disposition of sexual orientation (i.e., heterosexuality/homosexuality) makes this fear especially real to many people. Although societies will have to respond to the ethical threats of this accelerating body of research with vigilance, it is equally important that individuals put the role of genetic influences on personality in clear-headed perspective. Several popular misconceptions must be dispelled. The following points are worth remembering.

First, genetic influences on personality are not overwhelming: usually more than half of the variation in personality characteristics is non-genetic. Second, genes do not 'determine' personality in the sense of fixing it within narrow limits before birth. They simply exert influences that push and pull personality development and brain functioning in particular directions, influences that for each individual gene are typically small. Third, and as a consequence of the second point, 'genetic' does not mean immutable. Genetic influences, being non-determining and accompanied or mediated by environmental influences, can be modified and compensated for by a variety of environmental interventions. The mistaken popular view that genes are powerful and immutable determinants of personality stems in part from the much-used metaphor of the genetic 'blueprint' (Rose, 1998). This metaphor implies that genes carry a full set of instructions for building the finished human being, who is present in miniature at the fateful moment of conception. The construction of a personality, although it is undeniably influenced by genes, is a much more flexible and multi-determined process that the blueprint metaphor implies, and more guided by personal choices, the social environment, and blind luck.

Illustrative study: The interaction of personality genes and life stress in depression

Avshalom Caspi and colleagues based in England and New Zealand have conducted important longitudinal research on the development of personality and mental disorders in a representative sample of New Zealand young people, who have been followed from age 3 to age 26. In one article (Caspi et al., 2003), they investigated how people with different versions of a gene (5-HTT) known to be associated with neuroticism respond differently to life stress. People (and monkeys) with a short allele ('s') version of the gene show reduced serotonergic function and greater response to stress than those with a long allele ('l'). Caspi et al. divided their sample of 847 26-year-old participants into three groups based on which pair of alleles they had (ss, sl, or ll), measured the number of stressful life experiences they had faced in the previous five years, and used a diagnostic interview to assess whether they had suffered from depression in the previous year.

Caspi et al. found that the more stressful life events participants faced, the more depressed they were likely to be. However, this association was stronger among people with the short allele, especially among those with two copies of it (i.e., ss). By implication, this version of the gene makes people respond more negatively to stressful experiences. Gene version was not consistently associated with higher levels of depression, but only among people who had experienced high levels of adversity. The same pattern of findings was obtained when Caspi and colleagues examined their participants' history of being maltreated as children (age 3 to 11) rather than their recent life stress: maltreated children only experienced more depression as adults if they had a short allele version of 5-HTT. This study is therefore a striking example of the complex interplay of genes and environment.

PERSONALITY AND BRAIN FUNCTIONING

As the previous section demonstrated, genetic influence on personality is now well-established. However, although their influence is substantial, genes offer incomplete explanations of personality differences. The fact that personality is heritable shows that information coded in people's genes partially accounts for their personality characteristics. However, the mere existence of genetic influences does not illuminate the biological *processes* that underlie personality variation. Genes do not directly affect behavioural dispositions; they only do so indirectly by influencing brain development, brain structure, and brain chemistry. The recent findings of genes associated with novelty-seeking and neuroticism bear out this point: the genes are not *for* the two traits, they are for the production of particular molecules that influence brain processes. Genes code for the production of proteins that regulate brain functioning – indeed, about one-third of all our genes are expressed only in the brain – and if we want to account for the biological processes that underpin personality it is at brain functioning that we should look. After explaining personality in terms of genetic *structures*, that is, let us now examine brain *processes*.

Most attempts to find the roots of personality in brain processes have focused on the major personality dimensions identified by trait psychologists. Because these dimensions reflect pervasive behavioural tendencies that are empirically well-established and valid across a variety of diverse cultures, they are prime candidates for biological explanation. As a result, most explanations of the biological bases of personality have addressed extraversion, neuroticism, and constraint, or variants of these three dimensions.

Eysenck's theory

One of the first and most influential theories of the brain processes underlying personality was proposed by Hans Eysenck (1967). Eysenck argued that his dimensions of extraversion and neuroticism correspond to two distinct aspects of brain functioning. According to his theory, our standing on the dimension of extraversion–introversion is a behavioural expression of our brain's chronic level of physiological arousal or excitation. This arousal level is regulated by a brain structure known as the 'reticular activating system', which acts like a volume control on the level of diffuse electrical activity in the brain's cortex. Extraverts, contrary to what one might expect, are hypothesized to have relatively low levels of brain arousal, so that they are drawn to situations and activities that are exciting, novel, and stimulating, and that therefore raise their arousal. Introverts, in contrast, have relatively high chronic levels of arousal, and are therefore more inclined towards familiar and solitary activities. On account of their differences in arousal, extraverts will be more prone to boredom and introverts more prone to find novel activities unpleasantly over-stimulating. In short, the traits that make up extraversion – such as sociability, liveliness, activity, and sensation-seeking – represent people's compensatory responses to having an under-stimulated or 'stimulus hungry' brain.

Eysenck's account of neuroticism refers to a distinct set of brain structures which he dubs the 'visceral brain'. Roughly corresponding to parts of the limbic system, a primitive region of the brain intimately involved in emotional and motivational processes, the visceral brain controls the body's autonomic activation, which is reflected in anxiety and other negative emotional states. Eysenck proposed that neuroticism is underpinned by variation in the reactivity of the visceral brain. If the visceral brain is highly reactive, it will tend to activate the autonomic nervous system strongly and in response to relatively mild stresses. As a result, the person will be prone to emotional instability.

Eysenck's theory has generated a large volume of research on the physiological correlates of personality traits, which shows moderate support for some of his claims. Evidence is strongest for his account of extraversion. For instance, studies tend to show higher resting levels of brain arousal and stronger physiological responses to unpredicted stimulation among introverts (Eysenck, 1990). Also consistent with Eysenck's theory, drugs which stimulate or depress brain arousal (e.g., caffeine vs. alcohol) tend to induce more introverted and extraverted behaviour, respectively. In addition, a wide variety of intriguing findings is predictable from the theory, such as extraverts having greater pain tolerance, being easier to sedate, having less dilated pupils, and being at greater risk of tooth decay due to lower saliva production! Research evidence linking measures of neuroticism to autonomic activation and reactivity is more scarce and inconclusive than the research on extraversion, and the theoretical basis for the association is less well-articulated. Nevertheless, Eysenck's account of the biological mechanisms underlying of extraversion and neuroticism has been very fruitful and served as a springboard for theoretical developments.

Gray's theory

One such development was proposed by Jeffrey Gray (1981). Gray based his theory on Eysenck's personality dimensions, but conceptualized them in somewhat different terms and gave his versions of them different biological explanations. Although he acknowledged that extraversion and neuroticism are fundamental dimensions for *describing* human personality, he argued that the dimensions appropriate for *explaining* personality in terms of underlying brain systems are blends of these dimensions. In place of extraversion and neuroticism he proposed dimensions of 'impulsivity' and 'anxiety'. Impulsivity corresponds to the combination of neuroticism and extraversion, so that stable introverts are particularly unimpulsive. A person's position on this dimension reflects the strength of a set of brain mechanisms that Gray called the **'behavioural approach system' (BAS)**. Anxiety corresponds to the combination of neuroticism and introversion, and reflects what Gray termed the **'behavioural**

inhibition system' (BIS). Gray has conducted a great deal of research, much of it on non-human animals, to characterize the neuropsychology of these two systems.

In Gray's theory, the two behavioural systems are common to all mammals, and involve sensitivities to different kinds of environmental conditions and patterns of response to them. The BAS involves sensitivity to signals of reward: the positive, desirable, or pleasurable consequences that can be achieved by behaviour. When rewarding possibilities for behaviour are detected, the BAS endows them with motivational force and facilitates the actions that can obtain them. Therefore, the BAS's function is to seek out and obtain beneficial opportunities for behaviour. In contrast, the BIS involves sensitivity to signals of punishment and novelty – the negative, aversive, or unpredictable consequences of behaviour – and inhibits tendencies to respond. The function of the BIS is to prepare the organism to respond to threatening and stressful events and to interrupt its ongoing behaviour while it pays close attention to them.

Individual differences in the strength of these two behavioural systems underlie differences in impulsivity and anxiety, according to Gray. People who have a relatively strong BAS tend to be more sensitive to signals of reward than to signals of punishment. Because they tend to pursue pleasurable goals without being restrained by consideration of their costs, their behaviour is often impulsive and risky. People whose BIS is relatively strong, on the other hand, live in a motivational landscape where the costs of behaviour loom larger than the benefits. They tend to have anxious and inhibited personalities because the possibility of suffering, loss, and unpleasant surprises is more salient to them than the possibility of pleasure and gain. In contrast to Eysenck's theory, then, Gray's emphasizes the organism's sensitivity to the motivationally-relevant aspects of the environment rather than its internal states of arousal and autonomic activation.

Gray's theory has motivated a lot of research on the neuropsychology of personality and of a variety of mental disorders, and has been praised for its innovativeness and sophistication. It has also been somewhat controversial. Theorists such as Eysenck have asked why, if impulsivity and anxiety are fundamental personality dimensions, extraversion and neuroticism emerge far more often in analyses of personality structure. Eysenck has also noted that Gray's two dimensions do not represent equal blends of neuroticism and extraversion. Anxiety is much more strongly associated with neuroticism than with introversion, and impulsivity is more associated with extraversion and Eysenck's third dimension of psychoticism than with neuroticism. Nevertheless, Gray's work has significantly advanced our understanding of the neuropsychological systems that underlie behavioural variation in humans and other animals.

Depue's theory

The biological theories of Eysenck and Gray emphasize the neuroanatomical structures and pathways that underlie individual differences in personality. Some recent research has focused more attention on the neurochemical aspects of brain functioning. Neurobiological systems are not just brain structures and the neural pathways that connect them. They are also networks through which information is transmitted by neurotransmitters, the chemicals introduced briefly in our discussion of specific personality-related genes. Neurotransmitters are often specific to particular brain systems and pathways, and distinctive patterns of behaviour occur when their functioning is altered by recreational drugs or psychiatric medications. Many neurotransmitters are found in a broad range of species, and research on animals has generated a great deal of information about their role in the regulation of behaviour.

Richard Depue (e.g., Depue & Collins, 1999) has argued that three main neurotransmitters are each implicated in a basic 'neurobehavioural system', and that individual differences in these systems are associated with the three superfactors of personality: extraversion, neuroticism, and constraint. The three brain chemicals are *dopamine, norepinephrine,* and *serotonin.* Dopamine (DA) is fundamental to what Depue refers to as the 'behavioural facilitation system', a system that is closely akin to Gray's BAS. Like the BAS, this system is concerned with positive or 'incentive' motivation and is expressed in behaviours that direct the organism towards rewarding goals, such as exploration, forward motion, social activity, and flexible problem-solving. In contrast to Gray's presentation of the BAS, Depue emphasizes that activation of the behavioural facilitation system is associated with positive emotional experiences and pleasure, and links the system to extraversion rather than impulsivity. Individual differences in the strength of this system are therefore expressed as differences in extraversion-related traits such as positive emotionality, liveliness, drive, achievement motivation, optimism, and novelty-seeking. The brain pathways that make up the system primarily use DA for neurotransmission, and research indicates that DA functioning is greater in more extraverted people and in animals that show stronger tendencies to explore and approach rewarding stimuli.

Norepinephrine (NE) is a second neurotransmitter that appears to be linked in a rather specific way to broad personality characteristics, in this case to neuroticism or 'negative emotionality'. Depue conceptualizes NE as the neurochemical component of a neurobehavioural warning or alarm system. This system motivates the organism to direct attention towards potential threat in the environment when environmental conditions are changing or uncertain. The system is therefore expressed in vigilant and cautious behaviour, and in negative emotional states such as fear and anger. Once again, this system bears a strong resemblance to Gray's BIS, but with greater emphasis on the link with negative emotional states and with the dimension of neuroticism, rather than with Gray's anxiety dimension.

The third neurotransmitter that Depue discusses is serotonin (5-HT). Whereas DA and NE appear to be involved in brain systems that underlie emotionality, Depue argues that 5-HT is associated with a non-emotional system that modulates the flow of information in the brain. 5-HT appears to play a central role in inhibiting the brain's reactions to stimulation and to emotional arousal. Reduced 5-HT functioning in animals is associated with over-sensitivity to stimulation and exaggerated emotional expression. On the strength of a large body of human and animal research findings, Depue proposes that 5-HT functioning in humans is associated with personality differences in Tellegen's constraint dimension. High levels of 5-HT functioning are reflected in restricted emotional expression and rigidity, whereas low levels are manifested in impulsivity, aggressiveness, irritability, and emotional instability, phenomena that are attributed to 'disinhibition'. One way to understand the role of 5-HT is to see it as setting a threshold for facilitating emotional responses, both positive and negative. When 5-HT levels are low the threshold is also low, so that the brain systems involved in positive and negative emotionality are easily and strongly activated, resulting in impulsive reward-seeking and unstable emotional states. With higher 5-HT levels the threshold is higher, so that the brain activation in these systems is damped down and impulsivity and emotional expression are restrained. In short, 5-HT, like DA and NE, appears to play a significant part in the neurobiological processes that underlie the major sources of personality trait variation.

The neurobiological theories that we have briefly reviewed have made great strides towards explaining the brain mechanisms and processes that underlie personality. However, it is important to recognize that they are all simplifications of the enormously complicated workings of the human brain. As Zuckerman (1991) has noted, we should not imagine that there are any straightforward correspondences between particular personality traits and specific brain structures, systems, or chemicals. All brain activity represents the organized interaction of many densely interconnected pathways and mechanisms, and when we isolate one pathway or mechanism from its broader functional context we risk misunderstanding it. Current theories are probably guilty of over-simplification to some extent, but they offer helpful large-scale maps of a territory that future research will eventually describe in finer detail.

PERSONALITY AND EVOLUTION

Neurobiology and behavioural genetics offer two important explanatory perspectives on personality. Neurobiology tells us about the brain processes that give rise to behaviour and its variations, and behavioural genetics tells us about the inherited structures that give rise to these brain processes. That is, genes influence personality by influencing the brain processes that underlie it. We can even go one explanatory step further and ask what gives rise to genetic influences on personality. To do this – to ask why there is inherited personality variation – we have to consider evolution.

Evolution by natural selection is a process that operates on the genetic variation (i.e., polymorphisms) that occurs within a species. Over a multitude of generations, genes that promote the survival and reproduction of organisms and their relatives – genes that contribute to 'adaptive fitness'– are gradually selected as part of the species' genetic constitution, and genes that have harmful or merely less adaptive effects are eliminated. Genes that enhance adaptive fitness ensure their continuation into future generations because organisms that have them are more reproductively successful than organisms that do not. In short, evolution works in a slow, blind, and trial-and-error manner to improve the 'design' of a biological species, ensuring that its genes underpin an array of functional adaptations.

Given that evolution tends to yield adaptations grounded in genes, and that personality clearly has a genetic component, we can ask whether personality is adaptive and, if so, what adaptive functions it serves. This question is a difficult one to answer. Notice that it is not the same as asking whether the behavioural systems on which personality differences are based are adaptive. If our brains did not have systems that motivate us to actively seek and pursue rewarding activities and to be alert for and avoid threats, our behaviour would be very maladaptive indeed. The question, instead, is whether individual *differences* in personality are adaptive. Are some personality traits more fitness-promoting than others?

On the surface, we might give a cautious 'yes' to this question. It is certainly conceivable that variation in some normal personality traits is associated with greater reproductive success – perhaps extraverts are better at attracting mates than introverts, for instance – and it is highly likely that some pathological personality characteristics (see Chapter 9) are decidedly maladaptive. However, hard evidence is very scarce on this question, and there are some theoretical reasons to argue that normal personality variation is unlikely to be adaptive. That is, evolution tends to yield a single best form of any one gene, gradually eliminating less fitness-promoting alternatives. Remember that humans are identical on 99.9% of their DNA base pairs. Consequently, genetic differences that remain between people, such as those associated with personality differences, are probably 'adaptively neutral', unrelated to adaptive fitness.

This position has been put forward strongly by evolutionary psychologists Tooby and Cosmides (1990), who argue that evolution has produced an innate 'human nature' that we all share. Just as all people – with a few pathological exceptions – are born with an identical configuration of bodily organs, our shared genetic constitution also endows us with an identical set of psychological mechanisms and capacities, or 'mental organs'. Because our genes were selected to bestow on us a universal human design, most genetic differences between us are not adaptive, but simply represent random mutations or by-products of evolution. Tooby and Cosmides therefore contend that genetically-based personality traits are probably rather trivial differences of degree in the operation of universal psychological capacities. For instance, certain adaptively neutral mutations might influence the tuning or threshold of a particular brain system, subtly influencing its sensitivity to certain stimuli or its typical level of activation.

Tooby and Cosmides also point out that personality variation might be partly grounded in our genes without being heritable. That is, shared genes need not produce the same behavioural effects in different people. One apparent truth about the human genetic endowment is that it has a high level of what is known as 'phenotypic plasticity': genes (the 'genotype') can yield quite different observed expressions ('phenotypes') depending on the environment in which the organism develops. That is, our genes make us sensitive and responsive to our environmental conditions rather than dictating inflexible, fixed forms of behaviour. Striking examples of this kind of plasticity can be seen in other organisms, in which a single genetic constitution can yield drastically different physical and behavioural forms depending on some kind of environmental 'switch'. For example, whether a given female ant becomes a worker or a queen depends on its diet, and whether an alligator embryo becomes male or female depends on the temperature at which its egg is incubated. By this account, environmental influences play a large role in human personality because of our shared genetic constitution, which 'instructs' it to take distinctly different forms according to its early experiences. In short, some personality variations may be adaptive, rooted in inherited characteristics, but not based on genetic differences between people.

Although Tooby and Cosmides are generally sceptical about the adaptiveness of genetically-based personality variation, other writers are more open to the possibility. Wilson (1994) argues that some heritable personality characteristics are indeed adaptive, but not in the sense that one form of a personality-related gene will in any simple way be more adaptive than another. Instead, he contends that genetically-based behavioural variations may reflect different adaptive strategies that are specialized for different environmental niches. Alternate forms of a gene may therefore produce equally adaptive phenotypes.

As an example, Wilson discusses the garter snake, whose markings range from a long stripe on the back to a mottled pattern of blotches. The striped form tends to escape predators by slithering in a straight line, making it difficult to locate its exact position, whereas the mottled form exploits its camouflage by remaining motionless. Both genetically-based marking variants are adaptive because they successfully occupy somewhat distinct ecological roles. By this account, human personality differences may represent adaptive ways of specializing for different roles and activities within the social world. Wilson suggests that more inhibited or introverted people may be specialized for acting in more structured, risk-free settings, whereas bolder, more extraverted people may be adapted to social positions in which greater initiative and tolerance of risk and novelty are involved. It is certainly plausible that people with differing personalities are best suited to different social roles, and given the enormous complexity of human social life there are likely to be many such social niches in which different personality variants might thrive.

In addition to heritable personality differences being adaptive in different specialized social roles or positions, it is also conceivable that some personality characteristic might be adaptive simply because it is rare. This possibility corresponds to an evolutionary phenomenon known as 'frequency dependent selection'. To illustrate, consider a moth that comes in two differently coloured forms (Tooby & Cosmides, 1990). If its predators tend to search for the more common colour, the rarer colour will be more adaptive because it is less often detected. However, in time the originally rarer colour will come to predominate and the predators will search for it. Consequently, the two forms of the moth will come to co-exist in a stable equilibrium in which both are equally adaptive.

A similar explanation has been given for the apparently maladaptive personality characteristic of psychopathy or antisocial personality disorder (see Chapter 9). Psychopaths are interpersonally callous, exploitative, remorseless, and deceitful; hardly traits that foster social approval. However, this form of behaviour might serve as an effective adaptive strategy – especially, perhaps, as a way for men to acquire unearned resources and reproduce without commitment – *if not too many people follow it* (Mealey, 1995). Although psychopathy might be a profitable strategy when it is uncommon and most people are trusting and gullible, if it became common there would be fewer mugs left to cheat and deceive, and they would be more vigilant for the possibility of being duped. As a result, the frequency of psychopathy should reach an equilibrium point at which the behavioural strategy that it represents is as adaptive as the alternative.

This account of psychopathy is highly speculative, and the adaptiveness of heritable personality differences is still very much an open question. However, the evolutionary approach to personality is an intriguing and increasingly popular one, which has wide-ranging implications for the study of behavioural variation.

CONCLUSIONS

The biological bases of personality can be considered from three complementary angles: the genetic structures that predispose people to develop particular personality variations, the neurobiological processes and mechanisms that directly underlie such variations, and the evolved adaptive functions that these variations might serve. Of the three perspectives, the behavioural genetic and the neurobiological are by far the most fully developed. Behavioural genetic researchers have established that personality differences are subject to considerable genetic influence and identified specific personality-related genes and their mode of action. Neurobiological researchers, in turn, have closed in on a variety of brain pathways and neurotransmitters, understood as integrated neurobehavioural systems that underpin major personality dimensions. Variation along these dimensions is linked to differences in the functioning of these systems that are being mapped in increasingly fine detail. Evolutionary approaches to personality are mostly at the conceptual stage, but pose intriguing questions about why personality variation exists. Evolutionary considerations force us to think seriously about the fundamental nature of human behavioural differences, and to remember that, despite the stubborn reality of individual differences, all humans are deeply the same.

One of the most interesting aspects of biological research on personality is, paradoxically, how it illuminates the importance of environmental factors. As we saw earlier, behavioural genetic research is responsible for the finding that most of the non-genetic contributions to personality are due to non-shared components of the environment (i.e., factors that are not shared within families). This kind of research has also helped to pin down the precise environmental factors responsible for personality variation. A study by Caspi, Taylor, Moffitt, and Plomin (2000), for example, showed that living in a socio-economically deprived neighbourhood contributes to children's behaviour problems over and above the contribution of genetic factors. Other research shows the closeness and complexity of the interrelationships of biological and environmental factors. As we saw earlier, Caspi et al. (2003) showed how genes may alter people's susceptibility to environmental events: being maltreated as a child was only associated with depression among adults who had a particular form of the gene. Finally, there is some evidence (Driessen et al., 2000) that certain brain structures are reduced in size among people with a particular form of abnormal personality (borderline personality disorder: see Chapter 9). Interestingly, this reduction is probably due to these people having been exposed to traumatic experiences as children: brain anatomy responds to environmental events. What these studies show is that biological and environmental determinants of personality – nature and nurture – are intimately entangled.

Chapter summary

- One important set of explanations for individual differences in personality refers to its biological basis. This basis can be examined from the perspectives of genetics, brain functioning, and evolution.
- Behavioural genetic research uses a variety of methods to study the contribution of genetic variation to personality. Family studies examine the extent to which people of different levels of genetic relatedness within families resemble one another, twin studies compare the resemblance of identical and fraternal twins, and adoption studies investigate the extent to which adopted children resemble their biological and adoptive parents.
- This research consistently finds that the heritability of personality characteristics (i.e., the proportion of their variation that is explained by genes) is between .3 and .5. It also demonstrates that most of the non-genetic contributions to personality are due to 'non-shared environment': influences that are distinctive to individuals rather than shared within families.
- A number of specific genes have now been located that exert influences on personality. However, the nature of genetic influence on personality is complicated, and environmental and genetic factors interact in intricate ways.
- Several theories linking major personality dimensions to patterns of brain functioning (i.e., physiology and neurochemistry) have been developed. Eysenck and Gray linked trait dimensions to distinct patterns or systems of brain arousal and activation. Others have linked personality dimensions to levels of neurotransmitters in the brain.
- From the standpoint of evolutionary psychology, we all share a genetically encoded 'human nature', composed of psychological adaptations. Genetic variations such as those related to personality will not tend to be adaptively relevant. However, some evolutionary psychologists have developed novel theories to account for individual differences in personality. For example, some traits may represent 'adaptive strategies' that fit people to particular environments.

Further Reading

- Hamer, D. (1997). The search for personality genes: Adventures of a molecular biologist. *Current Directions in Psychological Science, 6,* 111–14.

(Continued)

(Continued)

Although it is somewhat out of date in a rapidly moving field, this short and accessible article conveys some of the excitement of contemporary behavioural genetics, which is moving beyond simply demonstrating the genetic contribution to personality and is starting to locate specific genes.

- Kaufman, J., Yang, B.Z., Douglas-Palumberi, H., Houshyar, S., Lipschitz, D., Krystal, J.H., & Gelernter, J. (2004). Social supports and serotonin transporter gene moderate depression in maltreated children. *Proceedings of the National Academy of Sciences, 101*(49), 17316–21.

This article shows how the search for specific genes may hold interesting surprises: here, an environmental variable (maltreatment) is shown to have different effects on children depending on which version of a gene they carry (i.e., a gene–environment interaction).

- Plomin, R., DeFries, J.C., McClearn, G.E., & Rutter, M. (1997). *Behavioral genetics* (3rd ed.). New York: W.H. Freeman.

Plomin and colleagues present a masterful review of the literature on behavioural genetics, with significant coverage of personality.

- Zuckerman, M. (2005). *Psychobiology of personality* (2nd ed.). New York: Cambridge University Press.

This book presents a comprehensive review of psychobiological research and theory on personality traits, written by one of its most prominent contributors.

5

Psychoanalytic Approaches to Personality

Learning objectives

- To understand the historical development of psychoanalytic theory.
- To understand the multiple 'models' that make up the psychoanalytic account of the mind, and the Freudian account of personality development.
- To develop a basic understanding of the directions that psychoanalytic theory has taken in different schools of post-Freudian psychoanalysis.
- To recognize the theoretical limitations of psychoanalytic theory, and the problematic nature of its evidence base from the point of view of scientific method.
- To come to a balanced understanding of the weaknesses of psychoanalytic theory as well as its unique vantage point on human personality.

This chapter presents psychoanalytic theory, an influential but controversial account of the structure, functioning, and development of personality. After describing the origins of psychoanalysis in Sigmund Freud's clinical work with hysterics, we review three distinct 'models' of the mind that he developed:

the topographic model, which presents the different levels of mental life; the structural model, which proposes three different and often conflicting mental agencies; and the genetic model, which lays out the stages of childhood development that form the adult personality. Along the way, the nature of psychological conflict and the ways in which people protect themselves against undesirable thoughts and desires ('defence mechanisms') are explained. Psychoanalysis does not end with Freud, however, so several post-Freudian schools are presented. We then turn to criticisms of psychoanalytic theory, focusing on its account of motivation, on the problematic nature of the evidence on which the theory is based, and the deficiencies of the theory from a scientific viewpoint (e.g., whether it can be tested or falsified).

In 1896, Sigmund Freud was a Viennese neurologist specializing in the treatment of hysteria. The cause of this condition, which was most often diagnosed in women, was something of a mystery. The ancient Greeks believed it to result from the uterus becoming dislodged and roaming malevolently through the body, and the doctors of Freud's day debated several alternative theories. The manifestations of the condition were also puzzling and often bizarre. Freud wrote about one patient, Anna O., whose symptoms included loss of feeling in her limbs; inability to drink water; medically unexplained pains, paralyses, and muscular twitches; hallucinations of slithering black snakes; failure to see or hear nearby things; loss of the capacity to speak her native German while retaining facility with English; and 'absences' in which she lapsed into a trance-like state.

Freud treated his hysterics using hypnosis, and noticed that in the hypnotic state many patients recalled childhood memories of a sexual nature. He found that when his patients were led to recount these memories, a flood of emotion was often released, and their hysterical symptoms often vanished. Intrigued about what these apparent therapeutic successes might imply about the nature and origins of hysteria, Freud set about developing a theory of the condition. His first attempt, usually referred to euphemistically as the 'seduction' theory, proposed that hysterics suffered from traumatic memories of childhood sexual abuse, typically perpetrated by fathers. Soon after, however, Freud abandoned this theory for a number of reasons, including his doubts that childhood 'seductions' could be as common as the theory implied. Instead, he argued that the origins of hysteria were to be found not in memories of actual events but in childhood fantasies. These fantasies, in turn, expressed and satisfied the child's perverse sexual wishes and impulses. Hysterics suffered not from memories, as Freud had first thought, but from the disowned products of their childhood desires.

This episode, which took place when Freud was just embarking on the work that would make him a household name, captures in a nutshell many of the distinctive properties of the psychoanalytic theory of personality. First, both of Freud's accounts of the origins of hysteria propose that the sources of the condition are to be found in phenomena that are outside the person's consciousness. The hysteric is a mystery to herself, her disturbed experience and behaviour produced by causes of which she is unaware, and which are accessible only by special procedures such as hypnosis. Second, these underlying causes are proposed to be meaningful psychological phenomena – memories or fantasies – rather than the sorts of biological causes that we discussed in the previous chapter. Rather than being explained by neurochemistry – or a wandering uterus – Freud argued that the source of hysteria could be traced back, often circuitously, to interpretable experiences, whether real or imagined. Third, Freud's second theory of hysteria implies that the mind is a place of conflict: the hysteric has wishes that are forbidden and perverse, and that she cannot consciously acknowledge. The price of this conflict between the wish and the social prohibition that forbids it is suffering and symptoms. Fourth, childhood experience is given a privileged place in the explanation of adult behaviour. Fifth, the sexual dimensions of experience are also given a large role in psychoanalytic explanation, with Freud maintaining that children are not innocent of sexual desires and experiences. These basic elements of psychoanalytic theory – the unconscious, the meaningfulness of behaviour, and the importance of psychological conflict, childhood experience, and sexuality – give it its distinctive flavour. A sixth property of psychoanalytic theory that the seduction theory episode demonstrates might also be mentioned at this point: it is unfailingly controversial.

BIOGRAPHICAL DETAILS

Psychoanalysis was, from the beginning, the brainchild of Sigmund Freud. Freud was born to a middle-class Jewish family in Freiburg, Moravia (then Austria-Hungary), in 1856, moving in early childhood to Vienna, where he lived for most of his life. A good and intensely curious student, he entered university for medical training and soon became fascinated with biological research. His first research was on the sexual organs of the eel, but he subsequently became interested in the nervous system and spent several years doing laboratory science on its anatomy. Following graduation Freud did several years of clinical work with patients suffering from neurological disorders and continued to conduct research on questions including the possible medical uses of cocaine. After a period of study with the famous neurologist Jean-Martin Charcot in Paris, he commenced a private practice in which he primarily treated hysteria and other neuroses, using hypnotic methods that were controversial at the time.

Following the abandonment of the seduction theory of hysteria, Freud began to develop psychoanalytic ideas in numerous books and papers. After publishing an early volume on hysteria, his next three books, the first to be truly psychoanalytic, were on topics that appeared to be incidental to personality and mental disorder. Nevertheless, these studies of dream interpretation, slips of the tongue and related errors, and jokes, laid out a systematic psychology and showed how even apparently trivial phenomena such as these seemed at the time could be richly revealing about mental life. His later writings continued to develop and popularize his ideas, including his clinical writings on the psychoanalytic treatment of mental disorders. Meanwhile, Freud cultivated a group of thinkers and clinicians interested in his work and aggressively strove to develop a world wide psychoanalytic movement with their help. Although some of his early supporters, most famously Carl Jung and Alfred Adler, had bitter breaks with this movement, within a couple of decades institutes for the training of Freudian psychoanalysts were widespread in Europe and the USA. When the Nazis invaded Austria in 1938 Freud escaped to London, where his daughter Anna went on to a distinguished career in the psychoanalysis of children. In 1939 he died of throat cancer, probably due to smoking the cigars about which, in reference to his theories of symbolism, he famously said, 'Sometimes a cigar is just a cigar'.

ELEMENTS OF PSYCHOANALYTIC THEORY

Before we begin our examination of psychoanalytic theory, it is important to recognize that the theory has an unusually broad focus. Psychoanalysis certainly contains a theory of personality, but it also offers theoretical tools for understanding culture, society, art, and literature. It is also a clinical theory that aspires to explain the nature and origins of mental disorders, and that is associated with an approach to their treatment. To give a sense of Freud's breadth, consider that he wrote extensively on topics as diverse as the meaning of dreams and jokes, the origins of religion, Shakespeare's plays, the psychology of groups, homosexuality, the causes of phobias and obsessions, and much more besides. Even as a theory of personality, psychoanalysis is primarily an account of the processes and mechanisms of the mind, rather than an account of individual differences.

In addition to its breadth of focus, Freud's psychoanalytic theory has many distinct components, making it difficult to integrate into a unitary model of the mind. Although they are all interconnected in complex ways, these theoretical components – often referred to as 'models' – are best introduced individually. To do justice to the richness and complexity of psychoanalytic theory, we will discuss three of these models.

The topographic model

The first model of the mind that we will consider is called the 'topographic' model because it refers to levels or layers of mental life. Freud proposed that mental content – ideas, wishes, emotions, impulses, memories, and so on – can be located at one of three levels: Conscious, Preconscious, and Unconscious. Before we examine each of these levels, it is important to understand that Freud used these terms to describe degrees of awareness or unawareness, but also to refer to distinct mental systems with their own distinct laws of operation. Unconscious cognition is categorically different from Conscious cognition, in addition to operating on mental content that exists beneath awareness. To convey this point, Freud often referred to the three levels of his topographic model as the 'systems' Cs., Pcs., and Ucs.

The Conscious

According to Freud, consciousness was merely the proverbial 'tip of the iceberg' of mental activity. The contents of the Conscious are simply the small fraction of things that the person is currently paying attention to: objects perceived, events recalled, the stream of thought that we engage in as a running commentary on everyday life.

The Preconscious

Not all of our mental life occurs under the spotlight of attention and awareness, of course. There are many things to which we could readily pay attention but do not, such as ideas or plans we have set aside or memories of what we were doing yesterday. Without any great effort these things, which in the present are out of consciousness, can be made conscious. They form the domain of the **Preconscious**.

The boundary between the Conscious and the Preconscious is a permeable one. Thoughts, memories, and perceptions can cross it without great difficulty, according to the momentary needs and intentions of the individual. They also share a common mode of cognition, which Freud called the 'secondary process'. Secondary process cognition is the sort of everyday, more-or-less rational thinking that generally obeys the laws of logic.

The Unconscious

The **Unconscious** is perhaps Freud's most celebrated theoretical concept. He did not invent or 'discover' the unconscious as is sometimes claimed – versions of the concept had been floating around intellectual circles for some time – but he gave it a much deeper theoretical analysis than anyone before him. Freud distinguished between mental contents and processes that are *descriptively* unconscious and those that are *dynamically* unconscious. The former simply exist outside of consciousness as a matter of fact, and therefore include Preconscious material that can become conscious if it is attended to. Freud's crucial contribution was to argue that some thoughts, memories, wishes, and mental processes are not only descriptively unconscious, but also *cannot* be made conscious because a countervailing force keeps them out of awareness. In short, mental life that is dynamically unconscious is a subset of what is descriptively unconscious, one whose entry to consciousness is actively thwarted. The Freudian Unconscious corresponds to the dynamic unconscious in this sense.

Freud held that the Unconscious contains a large but unacknowledged proportion of mental life that operates according to its own psychological laws. The barrier between it and the Preconscious is much more fortified and difficult to penetrate than the border between the Preconscious and Conscious. In addition, it is policed by a mental function that Freud likened to a 'censor'. The censor's role is to determine whether contents of the Unconscious would be threatening or objectionable to the person if they became conscious. If the censor judges them to be dangerous in this way, the person will experience anxiety without knowing what caused it. In this case, these thoughts, wishes, and so on, will normally be repelled back into the Unconscious, a process referred to as 'repression'. Unconscious material, by Freud's account, has an intrinsic force propelling it to become conscious. Consequently, repression required an active opposing force to resist it, just as effort is required to prevent a hollow ball from rising to the surface when it is submerged in water.

Under the unremitting pressure of Unconscious material bubbling up towards the Preconscious, the censor cannot simply bar entry to everything. Instead, it allows some Unconscious material to cross the barrier after it has been transformed or disguised in some way so as to be less objectionable. This crossing might take the form of a relatively harmless impulsive behaviour, or in the form of private fantasy, the telling of a joke, or in a slip of the tongue, where the person says something 'unintentionally' that reveals to the trained eye their repressed concerns and wishes. Psychoanalytic training teaches how phenomena such as these can be interpreted, a process that involves uncovering the unconscious material that is concealed within their disguises.

To Freud, dreams represent a particularly good example of the disguised expression of Unconscious wishes. They offered, he wrote, 'a royal road to the Unconscious'. One reason for this is that during sleep the censor relaxes and allows more repressed Unconscious material to cross the barrier. This material, given a less threatening form by a process referred to as the 'dream-work', then appears as a train of images in the peculiar form of consciousness that we call dreaming. By Freud's account, each dream has a 'latent content' of Unconscious wishes that is transformed into the 'manifest content' of the experienced dream. This transformation must allow the Unconscious wishes to be fulfilled while concealing their threateningness. If it fails to conceal the latent content sufficiently, the sleeper will register the threat and be awoken. To avoid this, the dream-work may change the identities of the people represented in a wish. For example, if a person has an Unconscious wish to harm a loved one, the dream-work might produce a dream in which the person harms someone else or in which the loved one is harmed by another person. Neutralized in this way, the Unconscious wish finds conscious expression.

Dreams also showcase the distinct form of thinking that operates in the Unconscious. 'Primary process' thinking, unlike the secondary process that governs the Conscious and Preconscious, shows no respect for the laws of logic and rationality. In primary process thinking, something can stand for something else, including its opposite, and can even represent two distinct things at once. Contradictory thoughts can co-exist, and there is no orderly sense of the passage of time or of causation. Described in this way, primary process thinking captures the magical, chaotic quality of many dreams, the mysterious images that seem somehow significant, the fractured story lines, the impossible and disconnected events. To Freud, dreams are not simply night-time curiosities, but reveal how the greater part of our mental life proceeds beneath the shallows of consciousness.

The structural model

The topographic model of the mind was part of Freud's psychoanalytic theory almost from the beginning, the Unconscious being one of the fundamental concepts of the theory. Several decades later, in 1923, Freud proposed another three-way dissection of the mind, this time defined in terms of distinct mental functions instead of levels of awareness and their associated processes. In English, these three mental structures were translated as the Id, Ego, and Super-Ego, forbidding terms that encourage a mistaken view of the structures as mental organs or entities. In Freud's original German, the terms – das Es, Ich, and Über-Ich; literally the It, I, and Over-I – come across as less alien and thing-like. As we examine each of these structures, it is important to remember that they were not proposed as real underlying entities, but rather as a sort of conceptual shorthand for talking about different kinds of mental processes.

Although it is convenient to talk of the Ego, Id, or Super-Ego 'doing' such-and-such or being 'in charge of' so-and-so, remember that they were not intended to refer to distinct sub-personalities within the individual.

The Id

The **Id** represents the part of the personality that is closely linked to the instinctual drives that are the fundamental sources of motivation in Freudian theory. According to Freud, these drives were chiefly sexual and aggressive in nature. On the one hand, he proposed a set of 'life instincts' concerned with preserving life and with binding together new 'vital unities', the foremost expression of this concern being sexual union. Opposed to these life instincts are a set of 'death instincts', whose corresponding concern is with breaking down life and destroying connections, its goal a state of entropy or nirvana, the complete absence of tension. The clearest expression of these instincts were aggressiveness expressed inward towards the self or outward towards others. Freud proposed that the instinctual drives were powered by a reservoir of instinctual 'psychic energy' grounded in basic biological processes. The sexual form of this energy was referred to as the libido.

Although Freud proposed that the Id has a biological underpinning, its contents are psychological phenomena such as wishes, ideas, intentions, and impulses. These phenomena are therefore sometimes described as 'instinct-derivatives'. Some of these phenomena are innate, whereas others have been consigned to the Id by the process of repression. All of the Id's contents, however, are unconscious.

Freud proposed that the Id operated according to what he called the 'pleasure principle'. Simply stated, this principle states that the Id's urges strive to obtain pleasure and avoid 'unpleasure' without delay. Pleasure, in Freud's understanding, represented a discharge of instinctual energy which is accompanied by a release of tension. In short, the Id strives to satisfy its drives by enabling the immediate, pleasurable release of their instinctual energy. Its essence is nicely captured by a quote from a friend's charming young son: 'I want my ****ing sweets, and I want them now!'

The Ego

The **Ego** complicates this cheerful picture of immediate gratification. According to Freud, this 'psychic agency' arises over the course of development as the child learns that it is often necessary and desirable to delay gratifications. The bottle or breast does not always appear the instant that hunger is first experienced, and sometimes it is better to resist the urge to urinate at the bladder's

Table 5.1   *Selected Ego defence mechanisms*

Denial	Refusing to acknowledge that some unpleasant or threatening event has occurred; common in grief reactions.
Isolation of affect	Mentally severing an idea from its threatening emotional associations so that it can be held without experiencing its unpleasantness; common in obsessional people.
Projection	Disavowing one's impulses or thoughts and attributing them to another person; common in paranoia.
Reaction formation	Unconsciously developing wishes or thoughts that are opposite to those that one finds undesirable in oneself; common in people with rigid moral codes.
Repression	Repelling threatening thoughts from consciousness, motivated forgetting; common in post-traumatic reactions.
Sublimation	Unconsciously deflecting a sexual or aggressive impulses towards different, socially acceptable expressions; central to artistic creation and sports.

first bidding if one is to avoid the unpleasure of wet pants, embarrassment, and a parent's howls of dismay. The Ego crystallizes out of this emerging capacity for delay, and in time becomes a restraint on the Id's impatient striving for discharge. It cannot be an inflexible restraint, however. Its task is not to delay the fulfilment of wishes and impulses endlessly, but to determine when and how it would be most sensible or prudent to do so, given the demands of the external environment. It operates, that is, on the 'reality principle', which simply requires that the Ego regulate the person's behaviour in accordance with external conditions.

Freud emphasized that the Ego is not the dominant force in the personality, although he believed it should strive to be. (His famous statement of the goal of psychoanalytic treatment is 'Where Id was, there Ego shall be'.) By his account, the Ego not only emerges out of the Id – beforehand, the infant is pure Id – but it also derives all of its energy from the Id. Freud had a gift for metaphor, and he likened the Ego's relation to the Id as a rider's relation to a wilful horse. The horse supplies all of the pair's force, but the rider may be able to channel it in a particular direction.

Fortunately, this rider has a repertoire of skills at its disposal. Freud proposed that the Ego could employ a variety of **'defence mechanisms'** in the service of the reality principle. A few of these mechanisms are presented in Table 5.1. Despite their diversity, they all represent operations that the Ego performs to deal with threats to the rational expression of the person's desires, whether from the Id, the Ego, or the external environment. Although the table presents situations in which Freud believed the mechanisms to be especially prominent, he proposed that they were common processes in everyday mental life.

Illustrative study: defence mechanisms and social adjustment

American psychologists Marlene Sandstrom and Phebe Cramer (2003) sought to investigate the defence mechanisms people employ in response to experiences of rejection, and whether socially maladjusted people respond differently from others. Their chosen study sample contained 50 grade-four girls, who first completed a 'sociometric' interview in which they reported who among their classmates they liked or disliked. The data from this interview enabled the researchers to classify the girls according to their levels of popularity or social rejection. Each girl was then run through a procedure in which she was told that she would later have a chance to communicate over 'closed circuit TV' with another girl who was doing the study at the same time in another location. In fact this girl was a child actor who had been videotaped making a standard presentation. The actual participant was instructed to describe herself to this bogus participant over the TV, and then watched that participant 'respond' with her own, pre-recorded presentation. The actual participant was then instructed to ask the bogus one to join her for a play session, to which the bogus participant 'responded' as follows: 'No, I don't think so ... I don't want to play'.

Both prior to and following this harrowing rejection experience, the girls told stories about what was going on in a series of ambiguous images. (These images were chosen from the TAT, a well-known 'projective' personality test that aims to assess hidden psychological dynamics; see Chapter 8.) These stories were scored for the presence of two defence mechanisms using an established and validated coding manual. Denial was coded when, for instance, a story omitted major characters in the images or overly minimized negative aspects of the image, and projection was coded when, for instance, hostile feelings were attributed to characters in the image.

Sandstrom and Cramer's findings indicated that more socially maladjusted girls used more defences after the rejection experience than the more popular girls, but did not use more defences prior to that experience. By implication, the maladjusted girls were more disturbed by the rejection and therefore responded in a more defensive manner. Doing so might have negative implications, furthering these girls' rejection by their peers.

You will be relieved to hear that no little girls were harmed (at least in any lasting way) by this research. Before the study was over, each girl was told that the bogus participant actually thought she was 'a really neat kid', and wasn't able to play with her because she 'wasn't allowed to', not because she didn't want to.

The Super-Ego

As we have seen, the Ego's task is to regulate the expression of the Id's impulses in response to the demands and opportunities of the external environment. However, this task is complicated by the emergence of a third psychic agency during childhood. This agency, the **Super-Ego**, represents an early form of conscience, an internalized set of moral values, standards, and ideals. These moral precepts are not the sort of flexible, reasoned, and discussable rules of conduct that we tend to imagine when we think of adult morality, however. Internalized as they are in childhood – under developmental conditions that will become clearer when we discuss the next of Freud's models of the mind – they tend to be relatively harsh, absolute, and punishing; adult morality as refracted through the immature and fearful mind of a child. The Super-Ego therefore represents the shrill voice of societal rules and restrictions, a voice that condemns and forbids many of the sexual and destructive wishes, impulses, and thoughts that emerge from the Id.

The Ego now becomes the servant of three masters: the Id, the Super-Ego, and the external environment. It is not enough now to reconcile what is desired with what is possible under the circumstances. The Ego now also needs to take into consideration what is socially prohibited and impermissible. Instinctual drives must still be satisfied; that is a constant. However, the Ego now attempts to satisfy them in a manner that is flexibly 'realistic' – that is, in the person's best interests under existing conditions – but also socially permitted. These prohibitions are often quite unreasonable and inflexible, rejecting any expression of the drive with an unconditional 'No', either because the moral strictures of a culture are intrinsically rigid or because the child's internalization of these strictures is starkly black-and-white.

Given the multiple demands it faces, the Ego can either find a way to express the Id's desires successfully, or its attempts to arbitrate can fail. In this case, psychological trouble is likely to follow. If the Id wins the struggle, and the desire is expressed in a more-or-less unaltered form, the person may experience guilt, the Super-Ego's sign that it has been violated, and may also have to pay the price of a short-sighted, impulsive action. If the Super-Ego dominates, the person's conduct may become overly rigid, rule-bound, anxious, and joyless. The forbidden desires may well go 'underground' and manifest themselves in symptoms such as anxieties and compulsions, or in occasional 'out-of-character' impulsive behaviour or emotion.

Freud's account of the Id, Ego, and Super-Ego implies that conflict within the mind is inevitable, a view that has led some to describe his theoretical vision as 'tragic'. The demands of society – or 'civilization' as he preferred to say – are inevitably opposed to our natural drives. Indeed, intrapsychic conflict is one of the fundamental and defining concepts of psychoanalysis. For Freud, conflict is at the root of personality structure, mental disorder, and most psychological phenomena.

Before we proceed to the next model, the relationship between the first two should be clarified. Although the structural model is conceptually distinct from the topographic model, they do map onto one another to some degree. The content of the Id, of course, lies firmly within the Unconscious, forbidden entry to consciousness unless disguised in the form of dreams, slips of the tongue, symptoms, and so on. However, the Ego also has an Unconscious component, given that a great deal of psychological defence is conducted out of awareness and is inaccessible to introspection. The Super-Ego also has an Unconscious fraction, reflecting as it does an often 'primitive' and irrationally punishing morality at least as much as it reflects our reasoned beliefs and principles.

The genetic model

The third model that we will explore is usually called the 'genetic' model, a term that in this context means 'developmental' rather than having anything to do with genes. Freud proposed that the developing child proceeded through a series of distinct stages on its way to adulthood, each with its own themes and preoccupations. What is truly novel about Freud's stage theory is that the stages are understood to be organized around the child's emerging sexuality. As we have seen in our discussions of the structural model, 'sexuality' meant more than adult genital sexuality to Freud, referring broadly to pleasure in the body and to sensuality. He believed that adult sexuality merely represented the culmination of an orderly set of steps in which the child's 'psychosexual' focus shifted from one part of the body to another. These body parts or 'erotogenic zones' all have orifices lined with sensitive mucous membranes. (The nose alone lacks its own stage, although Freud did briefly speculate on nasal erotism.) Initially the infant's sensuality is centred on the mouth, followed by the anus and then the genitals in early childhood. After some interesting dramas at about age 5, the child's sexuality goes underground for a few years, reappearing with a vengeance when puberty hits. We will examine each stage in turn.

The oral stage

According to Freud, the infant's voracious sucking is not purely nutritional. Although the infant clearly has a basic need to feed, it also takes a pleasure in the act of feeding that Freud did not hesitate to call sexual. Babies appear to enjoy the stimulation of the lips and oral cavity, and will often happily engage in 'non-nutritive sucking' when they are no longer hungry and the milk supply is withdrawn. Beyond being an intense source of bodily pleasure – an expression of sexuality in Freud's enlarged sense – sucking also represents the infant's way of expressing love for and dependency on its feeder, normally its mother. It also signifies a general stance that the infant takes towards the world, one of 'incorporation' or the taking in of new experience.

In addition to this lovingly incorporative mode, the **oral stage** also has an aggressive component. This 'oral-sadistic' component involves the infant's pleasure in biting and devouring. Both of these themes – incorporation and sadism – are important elements of the oral stage.

The anal stage

With the **anal stage**, we move to the other end of the digestive tract. At around the age of 2, the child is developing an increasing degree of autonomous control over its muscles, including the sphincters that control excretion. After the incorporative passivity and dependency of the oral stage, the child begins to take a more active approach to life. According to Freud, these themes of activity, autonomy, and control play out most crucially around the anus. The child learns to control defecation, and finds that it can control its environment, in particular its parents, by expelling or withholding faeces. Moreover, it takes pleasure in this control, pleasure that Freud recognized as 'anal erotism'. An important conflict during this stage involves toilet-training, with struggles taking place over the parents' demand that the child control its defecation according to particular rules. However, the anal stage represents a set of themes, struggles, pleasures, and preoccupations that cannot be reduced in any simple way to toilet-training, as they sometimes are in caricatures of Freudian theory.

The phallic stage

Eventually, but still in the early childhood years, the primary location of sexual pleasure and interest shifts from the anus to the genitals. The little boy becomes fascinated with his penis and the little girl with her clitoris. However, Freud referred to this stage as 'phallic' rather than 'genital' because he maintained that both sexes were focused on the male organ; 'phallus' referring not to the actual anatomical penis but to its symbolic value. Briefly stated, the little boy has it but, knowing that girls lack it, believes he could possibly lose it. The little girl, in contrast, knows that she lacks it, and wishes she had it. This is the first time that the difference between the sexes, and the contrast between masculinity and femininity, really becomes an issue for the child. It is also the first stage at which Freud's psychosexual theory recognizes sexual differences, and marks the crucial point at which, according to the theory, children become gendered beings.

The little boy's and girl's differing relation to the phallus plays a vital role in an unfolding drama that takes place within the family during this stage, somewhere around the age of 3 to 5. It is dubbed the 'Oedipus complex', after the

Greek legend in which Oedipus unwittingly kills his father and marries his mother. The little boy is proposed to direct his phallic desires toward his mother, his original love-object after all, and is consequently jealous of his father, who seems to have his mother to himself. The boy's fearful recognition that he could lose his prized penis – 'castration anxiety' – becomes focused on the idea that his father could inflict this punishment if he recognizes the boy's desire for his mother. Faced with this fear, the boy renounces and represses this desire and instead identifies with his father, becoming his imitator rather than his rival. In this way the little boy learns masculinity and internalizes the societal rules and norms that the father represents (i.e., the Super-Ego).

The little girl's case is a little different. According to Freud, she feels her lack of a penis keenly ('penis envy') and blames her mother for leaving her so grievously unequipped. The father now becomes her primary love-object, and the mother her rival. A similar process to the little boy's now takes place, resulting in the repression of the little girl's love for her father and an identification with her mother and hence with femininity. However, given that the girl is under no castration threat, this process occurs under less emotional pressure. Consequently, Freud proposed that the Oedipus complex was resolved less conclusively and with less complete repression in girls than in boys, and that girls internalized a Super-Ego that was in some ways weaker or less punishing. Needless to say, this last claim was highly controversial, and is one reason why Freud's account of the Oedipal conflict in women has been the subject of much criticism and revision.

Latency

After the upheavals of the Oedipus complex, the sexual drives go into a prolonged semi-hibernation. During the pre-pubertal school years, children engage in less sexual activity and their relationships with others are also desexualized. Instead of desiring their parents, children now identify with them. This interruption of childhood sexuality is largely a result of the massive repression of sexual feelings that concluded the phallic stage. One consequence of this repression is that children come to forget about their earlier sexual feelings, a major source, Freud claimed, of our general amnesia for our early childhoods. Social arrangements such as formal schooling reinforce the repression of sexuality during **latency**, leading children to focus their energies on mastering culturally valued knowledge and skills. Freud observed that the desexualization of latency-age children was less complete among so-called 'primitive' peoples.

The genital stage

The latency period ends with the biologically-driven surge of sexual energy that accompanies puberty. This issues in the final stage of psychosexual development which, if all has gone well, leaves the person with a capacity for mature, sexual love. The focus of sexual pleasure is once more the genitals, as it was before latency, but now it is fused with a capacity for true affection for the object of desire. In addition, both sexes are now invested in their own genitals rather than sharing a focus on the penis, as occurred in the phallic stage. The genital stage therefore sees the end of the 'polymorphous perversity' of childhood sexuality. These earlier erotic elements are not abandoned entirely but are instead subordinated to genital sexuality, often finding expression, for example, in sexual foreplay.

According to the genetic model, people pass through each of the psychosexual stages on the way to maturity. However, we do not pass through them unscathed. There are many ways in which people have difficulties in particular stages, and when this occurs a 'fixation' develops. A fixation is simply an unresolved difficulty involving the characteristic issues of the stage, and represents a fault-line in the personality. If the person did not receive reliable nurturance and gratification during the oral stage – or alternatively if they were over-indulged – a fixation on that stage may develop. When a person is confronted with stresses, they may revert to the typical immature ways of dealing with the world of that period, a process that Freud referred to as 'regression'. In some cases, fixations might also lead to full-fledged mental disorders. Oral fixations are linked to depression and addictions, anal fixations to obsessive-compulsive disorder, and phallic fixations to hysteria.

Fixations do not only represent forms of behaviour and thinking that people regress to when faced with life's difficulties. The whole personality or 'character' – the term Freud preferred – may be organized around the themes of the stage at which people are most strongly fixated. As a result, Freud proposed a set of distinct stage-based character types. Oral characters tend to be marked by passivity and dependency, and liable to use relatively immature ego defences such as denial. Anal characters tend to be inflexible, stingy, obstinate and orderly, with a defensive style favouring isolation of affect and reaction formation. Phallic characters, finally, tend to be impulsive, vain and headstrong, with a preference for defence mechanisms such as repression. This three-part typology is the closest that the psychoanalytic theory of personality comes to being a psychology of individual differences.

POST-FREUDIAN DEVELOPMENTS

Up to this point we have treated psychoanalytic theory as if it were the product of one remarkable and solitary mind. Although it is true that psychoanalysis owes more to its founder than any other major theory of personality, it would be a mistake to imagine that psychoanalysis ends with Freud. Indeed, the psychoanalytic movement has been very active since Freud's death in 1939, and has spun off many new theoretical developments rather than standing still. Psychoanalytic theory has branched off in many directions, yielding a contemporary scene that is bewildering in its complexity and riven by sharp doctrinal differences. A complete review of these strands of thought is beyond the scope of this chapter, but brief reviews of some of the main historical trends and movements may give a sense of how varied Freud's legacy has been.

Neo-Freudian theories

First to be considered are a loose group of theorists, most of them European immigrants to the USA following World War II, who took psychoanalytic thought in more accessible and socially-engaged directions. Erich Fromm, for example, wedded Freudian thinking about the formation of character with sociological and political ideas about human freedom and the good society. In his work, he proposed that people's needs extend beyond the Freudian drives to include loving relatedness to others and a sense of identity. He further argued that many social and political arrangements distort or fail to satisfy our basic needs, and that people often go along with their own oppression out of a fear of freedom and the insecurity it brings.

Fromm wrote popular books extending psychoanalytic ideas into the study of society and harnessed them to the cause of progressive reform. In similar fashion, Karen Horney wrote a number of widely-read books – some of them verging on self-help manuals – that gave a larger role to social forces in mental life than Freud tended to allow. Both authors argued that social conflict – conflict between people or between people and their wider social environments – was as important for personality development and behaviour as the intrapsychic conflict that Freud emphasized. Many of Horney's most significant contributions involved challenges to Freud's questionable views on female sexuality and development, including forceful critiques of the concept of penis envy. Rather than envying and feeling inferior to men on anatomical grounds, she argued, many women suffer more from an over-emphasis on love and a general lack of confidence (Hall & Lindzey, 1978). Horney offered revisionist accounts of several other Freudian concepts, viewing needs for security and warmth as closer to the truth of human motivation than Freud's instinctual drives. Similarly, she attributed human misery to helplessness, isolation and neurotic needs for approval, achievement, and power rather than to compromises between wishes and super-ego prohibitions. Although she retained the core psychoanalytic commitment to the centrality of unconscious processes and conflict, it is clear that she and her fellow neo-Freudians have travelled a considerable theoretical distance from the master.

Ego psychology

Ego psychology was another primarily American development in psychoanalytic theory. Its main theoretical emphasis was on the functioning of the ego, a structure often described by Freud as at the mercy of the drives and responsible for the irrationality that repression and other defence mechanisms often generated. Ego psychologists such as Heinz Hartmann, Robert White, and George Klein gave a stronger role to the ego, presenting it as a source of psychological strength and potentially mature defence, and seeing in it a capacity to adapt to the demands of the outside world rather than merely resolving the mind's inner tensions. In addition to their emphasis on the adaptive capacities of the ego, these authors also argued that some of the ego's functions were relatively independent of psychic conflict, comprising the ego's 'conflict-free sphere'. The ego even had its own intrinsic drive towards competent mastery of tasks, rather than simply finding ways to channel sexual and aggressive impulses in socially acceptable and prudent ways, as Freud has proposed.

As their name suggests, many ego psychologists were, in fact, psychologists. This may not seem so surprising, but it has to be understood that at the time most psychoanalysts were medical doctors. This was especially the case in the USA, whose main psychoanalytic association uncharacteristically ignored Freud's advice that psychoanalysis should not be restricted to those with medical training. The presence of psychologists in their ranks led the ego psychologists to be more open to mainstream academic psychology than other schools of psychoanalysts. Consequently, ego psychologists made some of the first attempts to submit psychoanalytic hypotheses to systematic empirical tests. They also conducted psychological research in the trait psychology tradition by studying individual differences in 'cognitive style'. Klein, for example, proposed that how people typically perceive their environment was as important for understanding their behaviour as their drives, defences, and super-ego structures. He found that people differ systematically in their attentiveness to the detail of their environment, some seeing it in a relatively diffuse and impressionistic way and others focusing on the detail, sometimes at the expense of perceiving its broader context. The ego psychologists, in short, brought to psychoanalysis a greater appreciation of cognition, of adaptation to the environment, and of the need for empirical, psychological investigation.

Object relations theory

Ego psychology granted the ego a larger role in the theatre of mental life, but otherwise left much of classical Freudian psychoanalytic theory unchallenged. The theory of motivation, built on sexual and aggressive drives, largely remained intact, as did the view that the Oedipus complex was the crucial turning point for psychological development. The person was still understood as a more or less solitary individual beset by forbidden wishes and impulses, punitive super-ego prohibitions, and the demands of the outside world. Although they remained faithful to many basic psychoanalytic doctrines, theorists of the **object relations** school that began to emerge in Britain in the 1950s challenged these aspects of classical theory.

One way in which object relations theorists, such as Melanie Klein, Ronald Fairbairn, and Donald Winnicott, departed from classical psychoanalysis was by emphasizing pre-oedipal development. These theorists focused their attention on the first years of life in which, according to Freud, the child's life is wrapped up in an exclusive 'dyadic' relationship with a mothering figure, prior to entering the more complex domain of 'triadic' Oedipal relationships (i.e., the child–mother–father triangle). During this time, the child is developing a sense of itself as a distinct individual as well as learning how to relate to another person, getting its first taste of the conflict between independence and interdependence. According to object relations theorists, the infant initially experiences itself as merged with and indistinct from the mothering figure, and has to pass through a number of often painful stages as it 'hatches' into a stable sense of being separate and autonomous. Object relations theorists dissect the ways in which people mentally represent other people during these different stages and as adults, and how these 'object representations' govern the ways in which we relate to others. Because issues of autonomy and connectedness are so crucial to adult relationships, the object relations approach to psychoanalysis emphasizes interpersonal relationships much more than classical Freudian psychoanalysis.

This emphasis on relationships also colours the object relations theorists' views of motivation. Instead of recognizing sexuality and aggression as the sole or even primary drives, some object relations theorists propose a basic drive for relatedness. People desire interpersonal connections for their own sake, not simply as opportunities for the pleasurable discharge of instinctual tensions. This idea makes perfect evolutionary sense for the infant, given its profound helplessness and dependency on adult care, and provided a springboard for theorists such as John Bowlby (1969), who investigated the formation of attachments in children and non-human young. This work on children's attachments, in turn, led to the work on adult attachment styles that we discussed in Chapter 2.

Lacanian psychoanalysis

Another current of psychoanalytic thought that has been popular in recent decades, especially in Europe and South America, was initiated by the colourful French psychoanalyst Jacques Lacan. Lacan developed psychoanalytic theory in radically new directions, so radical in fact that many psychoanalysts working in different traditions dismiss it as hopelessly obscure and misconceived. Lacan forcefully challenged many of the established beliefs and practices of mainstream psychoanalysis, and in particular those associated with American ego psychology. He argued that by allowing for a conflict-free region of the ego and by understanding mental health in terms of the strong ego's capacity to master the demands of life, the ego psychologists turned psychoanalysis into a shallow psychology of self-improvement and adaptation to the social environment. To Lacan, these trends not only reflected a characteristically 'American' approach to life that he deplored – 'getting on and getting along' – but they also removed what was most threatening from Freud's theory. Lacan proposed a 'return to Freud' in response.

Lacan's version of Freud relied heavily on linguistic theory and on other intellectual trends in late 20th-century France, such as the structuralist movement. He proposed that the Unconscious is structured like a language, so that its operations can be likened to linguistic phenomena (for example, he likened repression to metaphor). One consequence of this view is that to uncover unconscious material the psychoanalyst must decipher a chain of clues with a great deal of verbal cleverness. Half-flippantly, he once suggested that analysts could prepare for their profession by doing crossword puzzles. Lacan also held that the ego is not so much an organ of self-control and adaptation, as the ego psychologists maintained, but an unstable and ultimately illusory sense of personal unity. Our sense of self is, to Lacan, a tissue of identifications with people we have known, and the only wholeness we imagine ourselves to have is a fiction, a comforting and self-deceiving way of narrating our personal story. Our selves are profoundly 'de-centred'.

Ideas such as these are quite unsettling. Are we really entrapped in webs of symbols and signs, lacking a stable centre of self and identity, at the mercy of powerful unconscious desires that are almost impossible to comprehend? By making these claims in a stark and uncompromising fashion, Lacan aimed to recapture some of the radicalism that Freud served up to his first readers. Lacanian theory remains radical within the psychoanalytic community. It has been widely employed by literary and cultural scholars, typically keeps its distance from academic psychology – the feeling is generally mutual – and is associated with an approach to psychoanalytic understanding that is unusually abstract and intellectual.

The four broad branches of psychoanalytic theory discussed here are only a sampling of the schools of thought that have emerged since Freud. However, they should make it clear to you that there is a diversity of belief within psychoanalysis, and that contemporary psychoanalysis cannot be reduced to the worshipful preservation of Freud's legacy. Indeed, since Freud's death over half a century ago, psychoanalysis has not only diverged along several different lines, but has also shown a few broad trends. Generally speaking, contemporary psychoanalytic theory pays more attention to interpersonal relationships, gives less credence to Freud's account of drives, dispenses with outdated concepts such as psychic energy and instinct, and has made efforts to reconcile with empirical psychology.

CRITIQUES OF PSYCHOANALYSIS

Psychoanalysis has been, without any doubt, the most criticized theory of personality, and perhaps the most criticized theory in psychology as a whole. The reasons for this are quite clear. Psychoanalysis has been around for a long time by the standards of most psychological theories, it makes many bold and challenging claims, and it was for a long time a dominant force in the study of personality and mental disorder. In short, it has been a large and juicy target. As a result, the list of critiques of psychoanalysis is a very long one, and impossible to review in a short space.

Thankfully, however, many of these criticisms are irrelevant for the purposes of evaluating the psychoanalytic theory of personality. For instance, criticisms of Freud as a person – for example, his shabby conduct towards some patients and stubborn and perhaps deceptive unwillingness to modify theories in light of new evidence – are not directly relevant to the adequacy of his theories, let alone those of other psychoanalysts. Similarly, criticisms of his clinical theory and practice – such as his dubious accounts of particular disorders and the scant evidence for the efficacy of psychoanalytic therapy – also have little bearing on the psychoanalytic theory of mental life as a whole. We shall focus instead on just a few major criticisms that have a more direct relevance to the psychoanalytic theory of personality. These include critiques of Freud's motivational theory, of psychoanalytic inference, and of the questionable scientific credentials of psychoanalytic theory.

The psychoanalytic account of motivation

Freud's account of human motivation, resting on his account of sexual and death instincts, has been a flashpoint for critics of psychoanalysis from the very beginning. Two of the earliest departures from the psychoanalytic movement were largely caused by disagreements over motivational concepts. Jung questioned the centrality of sexuality and argued the importance of spiritual drives, and Adler proposed a basic desire for social superiority and a 'will to power'. Later writers within the psychoanalytic tradition also sought to expand the theory of motivation to include drives for mastery and competence (i.e., ego psychologists) and for interpersonal relatedness (i.e., object relations theorists). Writers outside the psychoanalytic movement typically challenge the importance Freud ascribed to sexuality and the very existence of a death instinct.

These disputes can perhaps be broken down into two main issues. The first is whether the sexual and death instincts are plausible sources of human motivation. Second, we can ask whether they are sufficient explanations of motivation, or whether additional motives that are not reducible to these drives are needed.

With respect to the first issue, it is difficult to deny that sexual wishes and drives are powerful sources of motivation, especially if, following Freud, we include as 'sexual' desires for loving relationships and for bodily pleasure. From a biological or evolutionary standpoint, it could not be otherwise, as reproductive success is the basic currency of individual genetic fitness, not to mention species survival. From this perspective, the psychoanalytic emphasis on sexual drives, an emphasis shared by no other personality theory, is a strong point of the theory, even if we disagree about some of Freud's particular claims about sexual development or the antiquated idea of sexual 'energy'. From the same evolutionary standpoint, however, a death instinct makes no sense at all. It is entirely implausible that a creature would have a fundamental drive for its own destruction and decay. Note that this negative judgment on the death instinct, which is shared by many contemporary psychoanalysts, does not mean that we need to dispense with the idea of aggressive drives. Aggressiveness could be theorized not as a form of self-destructiveness, but as a way to strive for social dominance, to fend off attackers or intruders on one's territory, or to assert one's personal interests.

Our second issue is whether sexual and perhaps aggressive drives are broad enough to capture the full range of human motivations. At one level, the answer is clearly not. What about drives for achievement, social approval, nonsexual relatedness, creativity, self-esteem, and so on? More basically, are biologically-based motives that 'push' us towards certain kinds of behaviour sufficient? Do we not also need to include future-oriented motivational concepts, like goals and personal ideals, that 'pull' us towards desirable endpoints? When it is stated in this way, it becomes obvious that the Freudian account of human motivation is too limited in its scope, leaving out a range of motives that are socially shaped or personally determined, rather than being grounded in basic biological processes.

However, the issue is not quite so easy to resolve. Psychoanalysts might agree that motivations beyond the instinctual drives are needed to describe how our behaviour is guided, but argue that these motivations ultimately derive from the drives. For example, achievement striving could be understood psychoanalytically as a socially shaped motive that is underpinned and powered by aggressive urges. Similarly, creativity might be understood as a sublimated expression of the sexual drive, based on the sort of desire for unifying and making connections that Freud saw as the hallmark of the life instincts.

This issue is therefore complex. Most psychologists, and even many psychoanalysts, will tend to find any claim that human motivation is ultimately based on a few instinctual drives to be overly reductive. Even if this claim were true, it would probably still be more enlightening and accurate to describe a person's motivation in a more complex way. And the real problem is that there is really no way to establish that this claim *is*, in fact, true or false. The only reason to believe that motivations such as achievement striving or creativity are based on aggressive or sexual drives is a pre-existing commitment to psychoanalytic theory. Most psychologists therefore remain unconvinced that the Freudian account of motivation is adequate.

Psychoanalytic inference

Another focus of criticism of psychoanalysis reflects not so much the basic propositions of the theory, such as its claims about human motivation, but the way in which the theory is used to account for psychological phenomena. Critics often argue that inferences drawn from psychoanalytic theory – interpretations of dreams, symptoms, character traits, psychological test results, and other phenomena – are often not adequately supported by the available evidence. When psychoanalysts make judgments about what a phenomenon means, they argue, these judgments are not sufficiently constrained. Consequently, judgments will often be wild, arbitrary, and over-confident, and different analysts will reach entirely different interpretations of the same phenomenon. Critics argue that if psychoanalytic inference is unreliable in this way, then there is little reason to place confidence in *any* psychoanalytic interpretation.

This criticism clearly has some merit. Psychoanalysts from different schools of thought often offer radically different interpretations of the same phenomena, and psychoanalytic clinicians frequently disagree strikingly about how to make sense of a patient's presenting difficulties. Similarly, examples of silly psychoanalytic inferences are not hard to find. For example, one of Freud's colleagues proposed that a patient developed a swelling on his knee to symbolize the swollen head of his father, who had died in a fall from a ladder. Other analysts developed a theory of the psychodynamic origins of Down's syndrome shortly before it was determined to be due to a chromosomal abnormality. A psychoanalytic study of low productivity in the British coal-mining industry suggested that this was due to miners being hampered in their work by unconscious fantasies that they were tearing at their mothers' internal organs. If psychoanalytic inference can give rise to such flagrant absurdities, how can we have faith in others that seem superficially less ridiculous?

This critique of psychoanalytic inference is a serious one. Part of the reason for its problems is that psychoanalysis attempts to make sense of things that are intrinsically difficult to interpret. If the phenomena to be explained are in their very nature slippery – recollections of remote childhood events, dreams, baffling symptoms – attempts to grasp them will often lead to mistakes. However, the critique cannot be entirely brushed off by the intrinsic difficulty of psychoanalytic inference. The nature of psychoanalytic theory also makes wild and arbitrary inferences more likely. For a start, the concept of the Unconscious allows any phenomenon to be explained with reference to a cause that not only cannot be observed, but also cannot be verified in an independent, objective manner by someone other than the explainer. Explaining something in terms of unconscious processes therefore allows the explainer to make inferences that are not restrained by conventional standards of evidence. The concepts of primary process and of defence mechanisms also allow for a great deal of looseness in psychoanalytic inference in a similar fashion. If a phenomenon can mean something different from or even opposite to what it appears to mean, and if an idea or impulse can be distorted in myriad ways by reaction formation, projection, sublimation, and the like, it is inevitable that different interpreters will often come to different interpretations.

All of this places psychoanalysis in a dilemma. Some of its fundamental concepts, the ones that suggest that human psychology is more complex and mysterious than common sense would have it, are the very concepts that make inferences about human psychology unreliable and problematic. Psychoanalytic theory proposes that the Unconscious, defence mechanisms, and the like, are indispensable concepts for making sense of psychological phenomena, but as soon as we use them we seem to be vulnerable to real concerns about the adequacy of these explanations.

The scientific status of psychoanalysis

A final, and particularly crucial, set of criticisms of psychoanalytic theory concern its scientific status. These criticisms can be divided into two subsets. First, critics have questioned whether the kinds of evidence on which psychoanalytic theory was developed are sufficiently reliable to yield valid conclusions.

Second, critics have argued that psychoanalytic claims either have not stood up well to scientific investigation or that they are not scientifically testable in the first place.

Psychoanalytic evidence

Freud ardently believed that psychoanalysis was a science, and was an accomplished biological scientist before he developed his psychoanalytic theories. Biological ideas are woven throughout his work, as in his concepts of drive, instinct, and psychic energy. Nevertheless, the methods which he used to obtain evidence for his psychoanalytic proposals were very different from those he used as a laboratory scientist. As an anatomist and physiologist, he made systematic observations of living and dead organisms, and conducted controlled experiments. As a psychoanalyst, in contrast, he introspected and speculated about his own mental life, and listened closely to what his patients told him during sessions of psychoanalytic therapy. It goes without saying that dissecting an eel is importantly different from dissecting a personality, and that observing the stream of one's consciousness or another's speech is different from conducting a controlled experiment. Psychoanalytic evidence is clearly unlike the evidence on which most 'hard science' is based.

Many critics of psychoanalysis have pointed out the limitations of psychoanalytic evidence, and argued that much of it is too flimsy to serve as a foundation for developing or testing a scientifically adequate theory of personality. These limitations are several. First, whereas scientific evidence ought to be publicly available for checking by independent observers, most psychoanalytic sessions are intensely private and go unrecorded. Any reports on what happened in these sessions therefore cannot be independently re-examined and verified by people who might want to challenge how the analyst interpreted it. Second, scientific evidence ought to be objectively recorded, free from the possibility of distortion by the observer. Clearly this is not the case in the psychoanalytic session, where the analyst cannot help but interpret what is spoken according to subjective biases. Analysts, like everyone else, are prone to attend to and recall information selectively, to take heed of information that confirms their theoretical preconceptions, and to discount information that does not. Consequently, analysts' claims that their clinical experience repeatedly confirms a particular psychoanalytic hypothesis are scientifically tainted.

A third limitation of psychoanalytic evidence is more complicated. Even if the evidence of millions of psychoanalytic sessions were publicly accessible and objectively recorded, it would still be compromised by the nature of the psychoanalytic relationship between analyst and patient. What patients say in psychoanalytic sessions is influenced in often subtle ways by how the analyst responds to them and by their expectations for psychoanalytic treatment. This influence has been called 'suggestion', referring to the ways in which ideas can be insinuated into the mind. Suggestion can take a variety of forms. Most crudely, analysts might directly suggest to patients that they have a certain kind of wish, feeling, or recollection, and patients might oblige by reporting these things, perhaps even coming to believe in their reality. Less directly, the patient might infer from the thrust of the analyst's comments the sort of thing they ought to be saying, or learn to focus, even without being aware of it, on the sort of topic in which the analyst seems to take particular interest. In addition, it is a rare patient who comes to psychoanalytic therapy without being at least somewhat knowledgeable about psychoanalytic theory, and a large fraction of patients nowadays are training to be analysts. As a result, most patients enter psychoanalytic treatment with at least an implicit understanding of what is expected of them, with some familiarity with psychoanalytic ideas, and with a positive disposition towards psychoanalytic theory.

None of this implies that patients deliberately tailor their behaviour in psychoanalytic sessions to be consistent with psychoanalytic theory. However, under these circumstances it is clear that patients' reports of their experience in psychoanalytic sessions might conform to psychoanalytic hypotheses for reasons other than the truth of those hypotheses. It is no surprise, perhaps, that patients of Freudian analysts report Oedipal dreams, those of Jungian analysts report mythological and spiritual dreams, and those of Adlerian analysts report dreams about struggles for superiority.

Psychoanalysts are well aware of the problem of suggestion, and strive to assume a stance of 'neutrality' towards the patient, trying not to introduce any particular social demands or personal elements into the therapeutic relationship. Nevertheless, influential critics such as Adolf Grünbaum (1984) and Malcolm Macmillan (1997) have argued that analysts seriously under-estimate the problem. In their view, psychoanalytic evidence is deeply contaminated from a scientific standpoint, and claims by Freud and his followers that psychoanalytic hypotheses are confirmed by clinical experience are rather weak.

As we have seen, psychoanalytic evidence is problematic, and does not offer a very solid foundation on which to construct or test psychoanalytic theories. These criticisms aside, it is important to recognize that there is also something quite special about psychoanalytic evidence, for all its flaws. A completed psychoanalytic treatment may occupy four or five sessions each week over a period of several years, amounting to perhaps 1,000 hours in which the analyst listens closely to the patient's innermost thoughts. These thoughts, often too intimate and raw to be shared even with loved ones, range widely over the patient's personal history and lived experience. They are recounted in a wide variety of mood-states and frames of mind. These millions of spoken words and feelings may not represent the kind of systematically and objectively collected data on which a scientific theory of personality can easily be built. However, it is difficult to accept that the analyst does not understand the patient's personality better than someone who might interpret the patient's responses, dashed off in a few minutes, to a trait questionnaire. There *is* something valuable about psychoanalytic evidence, but it is devilishly difficult to build reliable theory out of it.

Scientific support and testability

The clinical evidence on which many psychoanalytic theories were developed is clearly problematic from the perspective of empirical science. Critics of psychoanalysis have also claimed that the theories themselves are often not scientifically testable. The influential philosopher Karl Popper argued that for a theory to be scientific, its propositions had to be falsifiable – that is, capable of being refuted by evidence – and by this criterion, critics argued, psychoanalysis is not a science. We mentioned some of the reasons for this claim in the preceding section on psychoanalytic inference. The Unconscious and concepts such as defence mechanisms make it very difficult, if not impossible, to falsify any psychoanalytic claim, because the analyst can always explain away evidence that contradicts the theory. For instance, if a certain mental disorder is proposed to be caused by a certain kind of wish or childhood event and a patient with the disorder shows no evidence of the wish or event, it can always be claimed that these supposed causes have been repressed or disguised in some way.

Often accompanying this philosophical criticism regarding scientific testability is a factual criticism that psychoanalysts have seldom tried to test their theories scientifically. This criticism has some truth to it. Many psychoanalysts have responded to the call for more scientific research by asserting that it is unnecessary and that clinical evidence is quite sufficient. Other analysts have argued that scientific support for their theories is irrelevant. Psychoanalysis, they suggest, is not a science, so it is inappropriate to judge it by scientific standards. Some see psychoanalysis as a 'hermeneutic' discipline, an approach to interpretation rather like a school of literary criticism or biblical scholarship. To them, psychoanalytic theory is a way to decipher mental life, an interpretive technique for uncovering meaning. Its goal, they say, is to understand psychological phenomena in terms of their underlying reasons rather than explaining them scientifically in terms of causes. Some have gone so far as to suggest that the goal of psychoanalytic understanding is not to ascertain literal or scientific truth – for example, what 'really happened' in a person's past to make them the way they are today – but instead to formulate 'narrative truth', a story that gives coherent meaning to the person's experience (Spence, 1980).

Increasingly, however, some psychoanalytic thinkers and sympathizers are beginning to find ways to test psychoanalytic hypotheses in rigorously scientific ways, despite all the difficulties that this involves. This research is now very extensive, and is therefore difficult to summarize. However, two very broad conclusions can be drawn from it. First, specific Freudian claims typically fail to receive experimental support. For example, repression, castration anxiety, and penis envy cannot be experimentally demonstrated, dreaming does not seem to preserve sleep by disguising latent wishes, and there is very little evidence to back up the theory of psychosexual stages. However, more general Freudian concepts often receive a good deal of support. There is plentiful evidence for the existence of unconscious mental processes, for the existence of conflict between these processes and conscious cognition, and for existence of processes resembling some of the defence mechanisms.

Three studies can give a flavour of this work. First, Fazio, Jackson, Dunton, and Williams (1995) found that people who sincerely profess to having no racial prejudice can be shown to associate negative attributes with Black faces more than White faces in a laboratory task. This well-replicated finding shows that people's conscious attitudes may conflict with their 'implicit' attitudes. A second illustration comes from the work of Silverman and his colleagues (e.g., Silverman & Weinberger, 1985), who attempt to activate unconscious material subliminally. They do this by presenting their experimental subjects stimuli having to do with sex, aggression, and feelings towards parents for durations that are too short to be consciously perceived. They find that subjects exposed to these stimuli behave in a variety of predictably different ways from subjects exposed to comparable stimuli that are not psychoanalytically meaningful. These differences generally do not occur when stimuli are presented for long enough to be consciously recognized. In a third study, Adams, Wright, and Lohr (1996) hooked male subjects up to a daunting instrument called a penis plethysmograph, which measures sexual arousal by gauging penile circumference. They found that men who reported strong anti-gay ('homophobic') attitudes demonstrated increased arousal when shown videos of homosexual acts, whereas non-homophobic men did not. This finding seems to reveal the defensive operations consistent with the psychoanalytic view that homophobia is a reaction formation against homoerotic desires.

None of these illustrative studies are conclusive, and all have been controversial and subject to different interpretations. For example, perhaps the increased penile blood flow of Adams et al.'s homophobic subjects was due to anxiety, shock, or anger rather than sexual arousal pure and simple. Nevertheless, they show that with enough ingenuity at least some psychoanalytic propositions can be scientifically tested. Doing so should contribute to the important task of sifting what is worth retaining in the psychoanalytic theory of personality from what isn't.

CONCLUSIONS

The psychoanalytic theory of personality is an enormously complicated and ambitious one. It aims to make sense of a much broader array of psychological and social phenomena than other theories, and does so with a large collection of explanatory concepts. If nothing else, the sheer scope of psychoanalytic theory – its aspiration to be a total account of mental life – needs to be recognized and applauded. By comparison, most other approaches to the study of personality look decidedly timid and limited in focus. Although other approaches generally have better scientific credentials, they tend to leave out much that we might want to include in a comprehensive theory of human behaviour. To many people, any account of personality that fails to acknowledge that we are something like how psychoanalytic theory sees us – driven by deeply rooted motives, inhabiting bodies that bring us pleasure and shame, shaped by our early development, troubled by personal conflicts, and often a mystery to ourselves – is fundamentally limited.

The price of all this depth and scope in psychoanalytic theory, of course, is some quite serious theoretical and empirical weaknesses, reviewed towards the end of this chapter. Many psychoanalytic claims are questionable, psychoanalytic evidence is often too contaminated to support the theories that have been developed from them, and these theories often permit the drawing of inferences that are unconstrained. Some of these problems are due in part to the intrinsic difficulty of what psychoanalytic theory tries to explain. Others could be at least partly overcome if researchers made a more concerted effort to determine which psychoanalytic ideas stand up to closer, scientific scrutiny. If we are to evaluate psychoanalytic theory only on the basis of its current scientific standing, most of it will be found wanting. However, it would be a mistake to abandon it impatiently, given how much a suitably revised and empirically updated theory of psychodynamics might deepen the future scientific study of personality.

The last word goes to the psychodynamic psychologist Drew Westen (1998: 362):

> Grand theorists like Freud ... are ... the grandest purveyors of falsehood in the business. This reflects simple mathematics: The more propositions one advances (and the bolder these hypotheses are), the higher the probability that several will be wrong. But on some of the central postulates of psychodynamic theory, such as the view that much of mental life is unconscious, Freud has left an important ... mark on human self-understanding. As psychology moves into its second century, we would do well to attend to and integrate some of these disavowed psychodynamic ideas.

Chapter summary

- Psychoanalysis is a theory of the underlying dynamics of personality that was originally developed by Sigmund Freud, whose theory consists of several distinct models of the mind and its functioning.
- The topographic model divides the mind's contents into levels of awareness, from conscious, potentially conscious ('preconscious') to unconscious. Unconscious content is not just out of awareness, but actively prevented from reaching awareness except in disguised form, as in dreams, jokes, slips of the tongue, and neurotic symptoms.
- The structural model describes three interacting mental 'agencies'. The Id is the repository of desires, wishes, and impulses that are connected with sexual and aggressive instinctual drives, and seeks expression of these desires and so on. The Super-Ego is a harsh and primitive form of conscience that opposes the expression of desire. The Ego mediates between Id, Super-Ego, and the constraints of reality.
- Among the Ego's tools for dealing with the conflicting demands of desire and prohibition is a repertoire of defence mechanisms.
- According to Freud's genetic model children progress through a series of psychosexual stages that are referenced to different body parts: oral, anal, and phallic. Each stage has its distinctive themes, and failure to successfully negotiate each stage is associated with distinctive forms of disturbed personality.
- Psychoanalysis is often identified with Freud, but it has undergone numerous developments since his death, and is composed of several distinct theoretical schools.
- Psychoanalytic theory has drawn many criticisms. The sexual instinct-based account of motivation has been very controversial, and the reliability of psychoanalytic inference – the ability of interpretations to yield dependable knowledge about the mind – has been seriously challenged.
- Psychoanalytic theory is often difficult to test scientifically or to falsify, and much of its evidence base is problematic. Nevertheless, it is an ambitious theory that attempts to capture aspects of human motivation and cognition that have often been ignored by other theories.

Further Reading

- Freud, S. Just about anything.

Freud's work is more often criticized or adulated than read. It is an instructive exercise to read some of his work to get a flavour of the psychoanalytic approach, and an appreciation of his stylistic brilliance (he won a Nobel Prize for Literature). A good place to start is the 'Introductory lectures'.

- Luborsky, L., & Barrett, M. (2006). The history and empirical status of key psychoanalytic concepts. *Annual Review of Clinical Psychology, 2,* 1–19.

Luborsky and Barrett defend the accessibility of some psychoanalytic concepts to scientific investigation, and review a (rather modest) body of evidence related to them. In general, they find a reasonable degree of support for at least some psychoanalytic propositions.

- Macmillan, M. (1997). *Freud evaluated: The completed arc.* Cambridge, MA: MIT Press.

This book is a pitched at a fairly advanced level, but presents a concerted critique of psychoanalytic theory and evidence that cannot be ignored.

- Westen, D. (1998). The scientific legacy of Sigmund Freud: Toward a psychodynamically informed psychological science. *Psychological Bulletin, 124,* 333–71.

Westen is a clinical psychologist and personality theorist who is adamant that there is something worthwhile to be salvaged from psychoanalytic theory, despite is flaws and limitations. This article forcefully defends the possibility of a scientifically defensible form of 'psychodynamics'.

6

Cognitive Approaches to Personality

Learning objectives

- To understand how the cognitive approaches to personality differ from trait and other approaches.
- To develop a working understanding of the basic concepts of personal construct theory.
- To understand the concept of 'attribution' and the dimensions of attributional style.
- To understand the concept of 'coping' and the main forms of coping strategy.
- To understand the concept of 'self' and personality variables involving the evaluation and structure of the self (i.e., self-esteem and self-complexity).
- To understand the concept of 'emotional intelligence'.

This final chapter in the 'Explaining personality' section presents several ways of accounting for individual differences that share an emphasis on cognition. They all focus on the ways in which people actively make sense of their world; interpreting it, explaining events, coping with adversities, representing information about themselves, and perceiving and reasoning about emotions. We first discuss the theoretical perspectives that provide the historical context from which the cognitive approach emerged, namely behaviourist, humanistic, and social learning theories. We then turn to the work of a cognitive pioneer, George Kelly, and his psychology of 'personal constructs': ways of making sense of people and events by perceiving their similarities and differences. Following this, we investigate 'attributional style', a concept that refers to individual differences in ways of explaining the causes of events: whether something is due to factors internal to the person or to their external environment, to causes that are temporary or enduring, and so on. The implications of different styles for physical and mental well-being are discussed. We outline the varied strategies people use to deal with stress in a section on coping, and the mixed implications of viewing oneself in a positive or multifaceted fashion ('self-esteem' and 'self-complexity'). Finally, we examine the concept of 'emotional intelligence', a set of skills in perceiving and thinking about emotions that appears to be associated with a range of desirable life outcomes.

In a classic paper published in 1990, the American psychologist Nancy Cantor drew an important distinction between two ways of studying personality. One way, she wrote, is to study things that people 'have', another is to study things that they 'do'. A psychology of 'having' investigates the attributes that people possess – the characteristics that compose them and distinguish them from others. You will recognize this from Chapter 2 as trait psychology, a vigorous and successful tradition of personality research and theory that has yielded vital insights into the structure of individual differences.

You will also recall from Chapter 3 that trait psychology is not without its critics. Some criticisms have to do with the supposed abstractness and lack of explanatory power of traits. Critics contend that trait psychology represents people as collections of static properties, and fails to capture the processes that give rise to how we think, feel, and act. In a sense, traits describe the 'what' rather than the 'how' of personality. This is where Cantor's psychology of 'doing' comes to the rescue. She argues that personality psychology needs an approach that complements trait psychology by revealing the mental processes that account for how we do things. This approach, she proposes, is a cognitive one.

By 'cognition' psychologists mean mental activities such as thinking, believing, judging, interpreting, remembering, planning, and the like. A distinctly cognitive approach to psychology arose in the 1950s and 1960s, fuelled by the growing recognition that cognitive processes are indispensable for explaining behaviour. It had become clear from analyses of the nature of language and language learning that human activity is highly creative, flexible, and complex, and requires a very complex information processing system to underlie it. A basic tenet of cognitive psychology is that learning and memory are active processes. People do not relate to their environments in a passive manner, merely registering what happens to them, but meet it head on, determined to make meaning out of it. We actively filter and pay attention to incoming information according to our current concerns, actively impose patterns and meanings on it on the basis of our knowledge and expectations, and actively search our memories in order to do so. Cognitive psychologists developed many new research methods that allowed these mental processes to be studied in an impeccably controlled and scientific fashion.

Cognitive approaches to personality similarly emphasize the active, meaning-making processes that people employ in their daily lives. Proponents of these approaches study the processes people employ in interpreting their environments, explaining events, coping with life's challenges, imagining and planning for their futures, and using strategies to accomplish their goals. These emphases on cognitive process and active meaning-making distinguish cognitive approaches to personality from the biological and psychoanalytic approaches that we discussed in the previous chapters.

Unlike the biological approach, the cognitive approach refers to phenomena that are close to subjective experience. Biological theorists and researchers address the underpinnings of personality dispositions, and make no attempt to study how behaviour, thought, and emotion are expressed and lived. Biological approaches also have much more to say about structures and traits ('having') than processes, focusing as they currently do on enduring genes and physiological patterns. Psychoanalytic approaches certainly make a great deal of reference to cognitive processes – the defence mechanisms, primary and secondary process thinking, and so on – but not in a systematic fashion. Instead, psychoanalytic theorists emphasize the role of emotion and drives in the personality. Cognition in psychoanalytic theory is generally viewed as being at the mercy of desires and urges, reactive rather than pro-active, and is understood to be primarily unconscious. This view of cognition contrasts sharply with cognitive psychology's emphasis on its active, goal-pursuing, and (often) subjectively accessible nature.

To understand the cognitive approach to the study of personality, it is necessary to take a brief detour through some of the theoretical approaches to personality that led up to its development. These approaches are no longer prominent, but they provide a historical context in which the distinctness of the cognitive perspective can be appreciated.

BEHAVIOURISM

Cognitive psychology began in part as a rebellion against the previously dominant 'behaviourist' school of psychology. **Behaviourism** itself began as an attempt to develop a more rigorous, experimental approach to psychology than the approaches that preceded it. In their quest for rigour, behaviourists – most famously the American psychologist B.F. Skinner (1904–90) – argued that psychology should be the science of behaviour, rather than mind. Indeed, mental processes are so irredeemably subjective, unobservable, and difficult to pin down, they maintained, that they were not appropriate phenomena for scientific study or psychological theorizing. Psychological science should, instead, focus on what we can observe and control, specifically manifest behaviour and its relationship to observable events in the environment. Whatever happened within the organism, between the perception of an event and the 'emitting' of a behavioural response to it, was scientifically out of bounds.

Behaviourism was primarily an empirical analysis to how organisms respond to their environment, and in particular how these behavioural responses change with changes in the environment. In short, it was a psychology of learning. Behaviourists exhaustively studied how creatures modify their behaviour in response to different patterns of reward and punishment. Its understanding of learning was passive and deterministic: patterns of reward and punishment directly influence our behaviour, and our behaviour is merely a function of the rewards and punishments that we have experienced in our lifetime. The organism is not an active participant in learning, and the theory leaves no room for it to have purposes or the freedom to act as it chooses.

Behaviourism had rather serious limitations as a psychology of personality, quite apart from its portrayal of the organism as passive and determined. First, it had very little to do with what is distinctively human, and was an approach to the study of learning processes across many organisms more than a theory of human individuality. Much of its evidence base was derived from studies of rats and pigeons, and it tended to fail miserably in accounting for phenomena that are unique to our species. It is no accident that a decisive blow for cognitive psychology was struck by Noam Chomsky when he demonstrated the inability of behaviourism to make sense of human language. Second, behaviourism had no account of personality structure: the person is a collection of specific behavioural tendencies rather than having broad dimensions (as in trait psychology) or underlying components (as in psychoanalysis). Third, the behaviourist view of motivation is implausibly simple. People merely seek reward and avoid punishment, and there is no room for more elaborate needs, goals, and desires. Finally, the behaviourism approach seems to minimize the contribution of the person to behaviour. Our behaviour simply reflects our learning history, so we are essentially mere products of our environment. Individuality does not reside within the person so much as in that person's history of encounters with the external world.

It should by now be clear how cognitive psychology, and the cognitive approach to the study of personality, departed from behaviourism. Cognitivists declared mental processes to be legitimate topics for study, emphasized the active and (relatively) free nature of the person and encouraged a focus on uniquely human attributes and capacities. Despite all of its limitations, however, behaviourism did leave two important legacies to the cognitive approach to personality. First, proponents of cognitive approaches to personality retain a commitment to the scientific method as a means of studying people. Second, they retain the behaviourist belief that learning is a fundamentally important process. More than many other theories of personality, cognitive theories propose that people do not have fixed attributes but are malleable. Changing someone's personality is as easy (or as difficult) as changing their mind (i.e., their cognitions). We return to this issue of personality change in Chapter 7.

HUMANISTIC THEORIES

As we have seen, the cognitive approach to personality differs sharply from behaviourism in some respects but also has some affinities with it. Another approach to the psychology of personality that has some important similarities and differences with the cognitive approach is often called the 'humanistic' approach. Like behaviourism, **humanistic psychology** is no longer prominent with the field of personality psychology, but it again offers historical context for the emergence of the cognitive approach.

Two key figures in the humanistic approach to personality were Abraham Maslow (1908–70) and Carl Rogers (1902–87). Both theorists reacted against behaviourism by emphasizing the active, free, and creative aspects of human nature, by taking rationality and consciousness to be central processes in human behaviour, and by rejecting coercive attempts to control people by reward and punishment. Both theorists view people as intrinsically motivated to grow and develop in positive ways, and saw the environment not so much as a determining force in shaping people, but as a context that can enable growth and self-realization. In addition, both theorists made use of cognitive concepts.

According to Maslow's (1962) psychology, people have an internal drive to realize their potential ('self-actualization'), and will naturally tend to do this unless their social environment constrains their opportunities and choices. Providing that our basic needs for bodily sustenance, safety and security, and closeness to and esteem from others are met, we will strive for personal growth in this fashion. Social arrangements that fail to meet these needs cause neurotic suffering. As people come closer to self-actualizing, they adopt different ways of thinking, becoming less judgmental and critical.

Rogers' approach to the psychology of personality (Rogers, 1961) is similar in its optimism and belief in an intrinsic tendency to self-actualize. His personality theory unapologetically emphasized the role of subjective experience over the external environment, arguing that it is how situations and events are perceived and interpreted that determines the person's behaviour, not these external facts in themselves. The self plays a particularly central role in Rogers' psychology. It is the focus of one of our strongest needs – the need for 'positive regard' – and well-being follows when others esteem us unconditionally, enabling us to act in accordance with our 'true self'.

The humanistic approach to personality shares with the cognitive approach a rejection of the behaviourists' passive and deterministic view of people, and they also have in common the position that mental processes and subjective experience are vitally important phenomena to study. Its theorists give a central role to cognitive concepts such as self, creativity, choice, judgment, and goals. Some personality theorists who take a cognitive approach share at least part of the optimistic growth orientation of the humanistic psychologists, who in some ways can be considered precursors of that approach. The main difference between the approaches is in their relationship to the scientific method. Whereas the humanistic psychologists tended to have an ambivalent or negative relationship to scientific investigation, cognitive psychologists have tended to embrace it. In this respect, the humanistic approach to the study of personality departs further from behaviourism than the cognitive approach, although in a somewhat similar direction.

SOCIAL LEARNING THEORIES

Both behaviourism and humanistic psychology are precursors of the cognitive approach to the study of personality, but both are importantly different as we have seen. More direct forerunners of the cognitive approach are the so-called **'social learning theory'** and 'social-cognitive theory'. Both of these theoretical approaches are rigorously scientific, like behaviourism, but they adopt cognitive concepts in ways that bridge behaviourist and cognitive psychology.

The main proponent of social learning theory was Julian Rotter (1916–). In some respects Rotter's views were clearly behaviourist: he saw behaviour as being motivated by rewards and punishments. However, he introduced an important added complexity to this simple view. Behaviour is not governed by these rewarding or punishing consequences directly, but by our 'expectancy' that our behaviour will bring them about. Expectancy is a cognitive concept: it refers to a subjective judgment about the probability of a future event. When people decide whether or not to do something, that is, they form an expectation of whether that behaviour is likely to yield a desirable outcome (e.g., 'will the movie be any good?'). The likelihood that someone will act in a particular way in a particular situation – the act's 'behavioural potential', in Rotter's terms – therefore depends both on the desirability of the behaviour's possible outcome and on how probable this outcome is judged to be.

Rotter argued that expectancies exist not only for particular behaviours, but also for behaviour in general (Rotter, 1966). One such 'generalized expectancy' is '**locus of control**', the person's beliefs about whether the outcomes of behaviour are typically under their control ('internal') or under the control of the environment ('external'). People with an internal locus believe that they are primarily responsible for what they get in life, whereas those with an external locus believe that their life outcomes are determined by other people, fate, luck, or some other factor that they cannot control. You will notice, again, that locus of control is essentially a cognitive concept, a belief about the self and the world that may not directly reflect any objective state of affairs.

The social-cognitive theory of Albert Bandura (1925–) moves us even further in a cognitive direction. More than Rotter, Bandura (1986) emphasizes the importance of the self as an active agent and as a focus of people's beliefs and expectations. Against the behaviourist view that behaviour is determined by reward and punishment, he argues that it is primarily 'self-regulated': the person, not the environment, is its primary determinant. Bandura paid special attention to beliefs about the self's capacity to bring about particular outcomes. People who are high in '**self-efficacy**' strongly believe that they are capable of behaving effectively, for instance succeeding at a demanding work task. People who are low in self-efficacy, in contrast, have low expectations that they can produce the desired behaviour, and consequently they are likely not to attempt it. Efficacy expectations such as these need not correspond closely to people's actual capabilities, so that many people may be plagued by self-doubt and fail to realize their capabilities. Bandura and colleagues have repeatedly shown that self-efficacy predicts positive outcomes in a wide variety of domains – health, job performance, academic achievement – and that by enhancing people's self-efficacy it is possible to improve their chances of benefiting from psychological treatment. Like social learning theory, then, Bandura's theory places cognitions centre stage in the study of human behaviour.

We have seen how behaviourist, humanistic, social learning, and social-cognitive theories provide a backdrop for the emergence of a distinctively cognitive approach to the study of personality. There is no single cognitive theory of personality, however. Rather, there are several distinct lines of cognitive inquiry, each focusing attention and research on specific cognitive personality characteristics. In the remainder of this chapter we will examine several ways in which the cognitive approach has contributed to and enriched the psychology of personality. These illustrative lines of theory and research will be discussed under headings that refer to a particular kind of cognitive activity.

CONSTRUING: PERSONAL CONSTRUCTS

The first systematic cognitive theory of personality was developed by George Kelly (1955). Kelly's theory rests on a supremely cognitive metaphor for human nature. Biological theorists of personality represent the person as an organism and psychoanalysts as a battlefield, but Kelly saw people as scientists. Although most of us lack white coats and PhDs, we are all engaged in developing and testing theories about the world, trying to produce the best understanding of our environments and ourselves. The best personal theories are like the best scientific ones, too: they are those that are most accurate and that allow us to predict and control our environments best. As personal scientists, that is, our goal is to anticipate the future so we can best deal with it. Theories that fail to meet this goal are revised in the face of the evidence, and are ceaselessly put to the test of daily life.

The basic unit in Kelly's psychology of personality is the 'personal construct', Kelly's preferred term for the theories that everyday people develop. He once defined a construct as a way that two things are alike and different from a third thing. This may not strike you as a very enlightening definition, but it goes to the heart of Kelly's psychology. Human cognition, he argued, searches for similarities and differences, or contrasts. It is bipolar and categorical, meaning that we think and represent the world in terms of opposed categories and tend to perceive objects, events, and people as belonging to one or the other rather than falling on a continuum between them. The distinct contrasts through which we see the world are our personal construct systems.

The term 'construct' is a good one because it captures two important aspects of Kelly's theory. First, a construct is something with which – or through which – we *construe* our world; that is, how we interpret or make sense of it. By implication, personality is how we subjectively interpret the world. Second, constructs *construct* the world for us, in the sense that by interpreting our world we are actively and creatively building a coherent picture of what it is like. To a large extent, this subjective world is the one we inhabit, and our reactions to objective events and circumstances only make sense in terms of this personally constructed world. Different people may inhabit very differently constructed worlds.

Kelly laid out his theory of personal constructs as a 'fundamental postulate' and a series of 'corollaries'. The fundamental postulate expresses the basic cognitive claim that people's processes are 'channelized' – that is, formed into consistent patterns – by the way they anticipate events (i.e., their constructs). Some of the more important corollaries are easily laid out, and give a sense of Kelly's approach. First, anticipation of the future is based on construal of the past: our constructs are active and changing interpretations of evidence, and we try to improve these interpretations over time. Second, these constructs are organized in hierarchies: some are broader and basic (good vs. bad) and others more refined and specific (well-dressed vs. scruffy). Third, we tend to favour one pole of every construct: constructs are evaluative. Fourth, people construe events in different ways, and the more their construct systems diverge the more psychologically different they are. Fifth, understanding another person requires us to understand how that person construes the world, but not necessarily to share their constructs. Sixth, a person's constructs may vary in their openness to revision (i.e., their rigidity), and may conflict with one another.

All of this is fairly abstract and perhaps not very thrilling until you consider what it *doesn't* mention. There are no drives, goals, or motives of any sort, unless you count the desire to anticipate events better and grasp the world more accurately. There is no unconscious, no defence mechanisms, no emotion, no biology. All the theory refers to is our subjective ways of representing and interpreting the world. And of course that encompasses a great deal of what makes us who we are as individuals, in spite of all the theoretical concepts it leaves out. Kelly's system carves out a domain of subjectivity – our internal mental worlds – that is relatively neglected by most other theories of personality, and it does so because it is a cognitive theory.

It is worth stepping back for a moment here and thinking through how personal constructs differ from traits as units of personality. Traits are objective ways of behaving, whereas constructs are subjective ways of seeing. Traits are ways in which individuals differ along continuous dimensions, whereas constructs are ways in which each individual fits experiences into discrete categories. Traits are sources of stability and consistency that tend to change at a glacial pace, whereas constructs can in principle change as rapidly as a theory can be abandoned. Traits and personal constructs, in short, are very different theoretical concepts.

Kelly developed his theory not just to be a conceptual radical, however. His main goal was to understand individual clients in clinical settings. He recommended that therapists and counsellors assess clients' construct systems so as to understand them better, and launched a highly original method for doing so (see Chapter 8). The end result of such an assessment offers a map of the client's distinctive ways of making sense of their environment, with a focus on the social environment, and of whom the client perceives to embody the poles of each construct. The role of the therapist or counsellor was to determine how this construct system was not functioning well. Someone might have a system that is too simple, with a few overly dominant constructs, and someone else might have one that is full of contradictions. A client might be inhibited or prejudiced because a construct is so rigid that it narrows their thinking and prevents their construct system from developing. Someone might be disabled by anxiety because events in their lives can't be grasped by their existing constructs. Another person might be riddled with guilt because they can no longer perceive themselves as occupying the favoured pole of one of their most basic constructs. Personality psychologists in the Kellyan tradition are masters at painting revealing psychological portraits of clients' inner subjective worlds and at formulating innovative construct-based theories of conditions as diverse as stuttering and suicide.

One of the most interesting features of Kelly's cognitive approach to personality that is connected to his clinical focus may have escaped your notice. From a trait psychology perspective, a personality is characterized by locating it on a set of dimensions such as the Big Five: very high on one, low on another, average on a third, and so on. These same dimensions provide a standard descriptive framework for everyone: in principle, everyone has a location within the five-dimensional space. For Kelly, however, each person has a set of constructs that is unique to him or her. Your construct system is in principle different from mine and everyone else's. It is your signature way of construing your personal world.

Some psychologists find this aspect of Kelly's theory enormously attractive and much less restrictive than the standardized formulation of personalities that trait psychology affords. Its main disadvantage is that it makes systematic personality research quite difficult. If each personality must be characterized in it own terms, it is hard to see how generalizations about the structure or correlates of personality can be made, or even how two personalities can be compared. Generalizations and comparisons can be drawn, but Kellyan theory makes it complicated. This conflict between an approach to personality that emphasizes the uniqueness of the individual and another that seeks generalized conclusions is a real one in the psychology of personality. There are even two forbidding terms – **'idiographic'** (literally 'own-writing') and **'nomothetic'** (literally 'law-making') – that refer to these alternatives. The nomothetic or generalizing approach is dominant in personality psychology, a field inhabited largely by quantitative researchers, but the idiothetic or individualizing approach that Kelly represents still has its champions. We will return to the challenges of understanding the uniqueness of the individual in Chapter 10.

Kelly's approach has relatively few adherents among contemporary personality psychologists. Nevertheless, he is far from being merely a historical curiosity. His personality theory made a deep impact on the field by opening up subjectivity – the person's distinct ways of making sense of the world – as an important and legitimate field of study for personality theorists and researchers. In doing so, he contributed to the viability and popularity of the cognitive approaches to personality that followed him. We will explore some of these in the next few pages.

EXPLAINING: ATTRIBUTIONAL STYLE

Kelly's psychology of personal constructs gives a broad account of how we make sense of our worlds. Constructs govern how we perceive others, ourselves, and our environments, and how we fit new experiences into established beliefs and ways of thinking. Other psychologists have focused attention on a narrower form of making sense of the world, namely how we explain events. Humans, they argue, are not content to merely observe what happens around them, the passive stance towards the world that cognitive psychology debunks. Instead, we are driven to understand the *causes* of events, to actively try to grasp why they happened when or how they did. There is a reason for this, of course. If we can grasp the causes of events we are in a good position to predict and control them. We will know when similar events are likely to happen again and what sorts of responses might prevent them if they are undesirable, enable them if they are desirable, and deal with their consequences in either case.

Explanations and the causes they propose vary in many respects, but psychologists (Abramson, Seligman, & Teasdale, 1978) have argued that three dimensions are especially important. Some explanations make reference to causes that are internal to the person, such as his or her beliefs, desires, intentions, traits, and physical attributes, and some to causes that are external. External causes include other people's psychological or physical attributes as well as life events, economic or social conditions, supernatural forces, luck, and so on. Some explanations refer to causes that are stable over time and difficult to change (e.g., intelligence, genes, capitalism), whereas others refer to causes that are short-lived or unstable (e.g., moods, the weather, ill-fortune). Finally, some explanations propose causes that are broad in their implications for the person, likely to have deep and wide-ranging effects on him or her (e.g., stupidity, fate, schizophrenia), whereas others propose causes with relatively limited or specific implications for the person (e.g., spelling problems, random errors, chicken phobia).

These three dimensions are usually presented as a series of oppositions: internal vs. external, stable vs. unstable, global vs. specific. Their importance in human cognition has been established by decades of research in social psychology, especially a branch of it called '**attribution theory**', which studies how people attribute meaning, causation, and responsibility to actions and events. Any particular explanation or cause can in principle be located on each of the three dimensions. Therefore, there should be eight distinct kinds of explanation, representing combinations of the three opposed pairs (e.g., external–unstable–specific).

Many events almost demand a particular kind of explanation. Almost everyone would agree that being struck by lightning is caused by random bad luck (i.e., external–unstable–specific). However, many events are causally ambiguous, and can be explained in multiple ways. For this reason, people often differ in how they account for events that they experience. Some of these differences are systematic: people may have a typical style of explaining events. Such 'explanatory styles' have been the focus of a great deal of research by cognitively-oriented personality psychologists.

Although any consistent way of explaining events could be considered to be an explanatory style, most psychologists have focused on a particular style that they refer to as 'pessimistic'. Pessimists tend to explain negative and positive events in quite distinctive ways. They tend to explain negative events – events that are undesirable from their perspective – in terms of causes that are internal, stable, and global. Such explanations see the negative event as caused by the self, likely to last, and likely to have widespread negative implications. In other words, pessimistic explanations lead people to blame themselves for their troubles, and to believe that these troubles are large (encouraging helplessness) and enduring (encouraging hopelessness). An example would be explaining a disappointing performance on an exam as being due to one's lack of intelligence. Pessimists tend to explain positive events very differently, with reference to external, unstable, and specific causes. Good things, that is, are seen as being out of the pessimist's control, fleeting, and having only limited implications for his or her well-being. Doing better than expected on an exam might be explained as due to a scoring error or to lucky guesses.

Optimists show the opposite pattern. Negative events are explained as externally caused, transient, and limited in their implications ('That stupid exam was unfair') and positive events as internal, stable, and global ('Because I am brilliant'). Notice that both of these patterns are equally unbalanced and both are likely to be inaccurate, biased, or irrational to some extent. The extreme pessimist irrationally discounts successes and catastrophizes and takes excessive responsibility for failures, whereas the extreme optimist is self-serving, taking excessive credit for successes and making excuses for failures.

Optimism in this sense is not just a dispositional term like a trait, involving relentless cheerfulness and hope. It is, instead, a specific way of explaining events, a set of carefully described cognitive *processes*. Note how optimistic explanation by this account – e.g., ascribing negative events to causes that are external, short-lived, and narrow in their implications – has nothing directly to do with positive mood or general expectations that things will get better. Optimism here is a way of making causal sense of events, a process that can be observed whenever explanation takes place, rather than just a static trait that describes a hopeful stance towards the future.

Researchers have demonstrated that explanatory style has many important implications. Pessimistic explanatory style is a vulnerability factor for depression (Metalsky, Halberstadt, & Abramson, 1987). Pessimism at age 25 predicts worse physical health at age 45 (Peterson, Seligman, & Vaillant, 1988). Among university students it is associated with worse health and more doctor visits, even among students who are matched for initial health. Among students it also predicts poorer academic performance, less specific academic goals, fewer contacts with academic advisers, and dropping out prematurely (Peterson & Barrett, 1987). More pessimistic life insurance salesmen sell less insurance (Seligman & Schulman, 1986), and pessimistic competitive swimmers are more likely to perform below expectation in races, especially after another disappointing race (Seligman, Nolen-Hoeksema, Thornton, & Thornton, 1990).

Researchers have also developed ways to measure the pessimism of people who are unlikely to complete explanatory-style questionnaires, including historical figures, by rating spontaneous explanations extracted from speeches, diaries, letters, interviews, and even song lyrics. By this means, it has been found that most successful American presidential candidates gave a more optimistic nomination speech at their political party's pre-election convention than their rival (Zullow & Seligman, 1990). Similarly, famous American baseball players who were rated as more optimistic from explanations they gave in newspaper interviews, tended to live longer than their more pessimistic but equally successful peers (see Reivich, 1995). This method also can assess the optimism of cultures and historical periods: when top-40 song lyrics contain relatively high levels of pessimistic explanation, economic growth and consumer confidence tend to fall in the years that follow (Zullow, 1990).

All of this glowing talk about the benefits of optimism makes some students grumpy. Surely, they ask, optimism isn't always the path to everlasting health, wealth, and happiness? Aren't realism or even pessimism sometimes better approaches to take towards life? One response to these questions is to reiterate the point that optimism is often irrational and biased, reflecting a tendency to explain negative and positive events in different, self-serving ways. If it is important to you to be objective and free of illusion then you will probably not have an unusually optimistic explanatory style. However, even if optimism may be *irrational* in the sense of being distorted or inaccurate, research suggests that it may be *rational* in the sense of serving our adaptive interests most effectively. Evidence has accumulated that 'positive illusions' such as unrealistic optimism are associated with better mental health (Taylor & Brown, 1988), and that it is mildly or moderately depressed people who have the most realistic assessment of themselves and their environments (Ackermann & DeRubeis, 1991). If you strive for accurate, truthful self-knowledge you may indeed find true happiness and well-being, but research suggests you will have to push against a kind of psychological gravity to do so.

On the other hand, theorists interested in cognitive strategies have determined one way in which pessimism might not be a disadvantage in life. Cognitive strategies are defined as ways in which people apply what they know about themselves to performing specific tasks in a way that satisfies their goals. A strategy is therefore a planful way of implementing cognitive processes in real-world situations. One intriguing strategy has been called 'defensive pessimism' (Norem & Cantor, 1986). Defensive pessimists perform well on a particular kind of task, but nevertheless hold unrealistically low expectations about how well they will do each time they face new challenges. They may consistently do well on written exams, but forecast that they will do badly whenever a new one approaches. Such people imagine the worst, feel intensely worried about it, but unlike other pessimists they do not tend to withdraw effort from it and make it a self-fulfilling prophecy. Indeed, they tend to perform as well as those who pursue an optimistic strategy.

It therefore appears that defensive pessimists approach the task of performing well with the implicit goal of minimizing the disappointment they would feel if they fell short of their hopes. In a sense, they pay for a reduction in possible disappointment in the future with an increase in actual misery in the present. Presumably, they employ this strategy because it makes the most sense to them given their anticipated emotional reactions. They suffer, but they do well. This may be the best reassurance that personality psychology can offer to the pessimistic reader.

COPING: COPING STRATEGIES

Construing and explaining are two sets of cognitive processes that are quite broad and general in their implications. Kelly's personal constructs influence how we make sense of more or less everything that we encounter in life, and other people in particular. Similarly, explanatory style is relevant to more or less every event that we observe: in theory at least, we are forever seeking the causes of what happens. The next set of cognitive personality phenomena that we discuss are more specific in their focus, referring to the ways we deal with the challenges and difficulties that life throws at us. **Coping** has been defined as 'the thoughts and behaviours used to manage the internal and external demands of situations that are appraised as stressful' (Folkman & Moskowitz, 2004, p. 745). In short, people engage in efforts to cope whenever they perceive a situation as taxing their capacity to deal with life problems, and these efforts may target the situations themselves or people's internal responses to them, such as emotional distress.

Reading this definition you might see parallels with the psychoanalytic concept of defence, which was discussed in Chapter 5. The concepts of coping and defence are indeed related, but there are some important differences that reflect the theoretical differences between cognitive and psychoanalytic approaches to personality. First, coping strategies primarily deal with external stresses that the person faces – challenging events and our responses to them – whereas defence mechanisms primarily deal with internal threats such as impulses and repugnant thoughts. Second, whereas most defence mechanisms are employed unconsciously, out of the person's awareness, coping strategies are generally employed consciously. Third, 'defence' implies a reactive, damage-controlling response, whereas 'coping' implies a response that is to some extent active and future-oriented. In short, the concept of coping reflects a more active, conscious, and externally-oriented set of processes than the concept of defence mechanisms.

Coping does not refer to a single phenomenon, but to any response that people make to stressful events. These responses, known usually as 'ways of coping' or 'coping strategies' are extraordinarily diverse. One recent review of the scientific literature found more than 400 distinct labels that have been used to describe ways of coping (Skinner, Edge, Altman, & Sherwood, 2003), and there have been numerous attempts to classify these into a more manageable set. The most widely used classification distinguishes between problem-focused and emotion-focused ways of coping (Folkman & Lazarus, 1980). Problem-focused forms of coping directly and actively address the problem that is causing the distress, and try to change it. Examples might include confronting someone about their unpleasant behaviour towards you, developing a plan of action, or actively trying to solve the problem. Emotion-focused coping, in contrast, attempts to modify the person's emotional response to the stressful situation, rather than the situation itself. For example, a person might engage in wishful thinking (i.e., imagine that an unpleasant situation would magically disappear), try to reduce their distress by drinking, distract themselves from stressful thoughts, try to relax, or try to reappraise the situation so that it doesn't seem so bad.

One reason why researchers have studied coping is to learn which ways of coping are most effective in dealing with stress. A huge volume of work has investigated the effectiveness of different ways of coping in relation to an enormous variety of stressful situations, including bereavement, cancer diagnosis, looking after an ill family member, motherhood, workplace problems, and everyday life hassles. Four main conclusions can be drawn from this work. First, most coping strategies are not intrinsically effective or ineffective, but vary according to the specific nature of the stressful situation. Particular strategies work best in particular contexts. Second, although the first point appears to be true, there is still a modest tendency for problem-focused ways of coping to be somewhat more effective than emotion-focused ways.

The third point helps to make sense of the first two. Whether a particular coping strategy is effective seems to depend on whether the person judges the stressful situation to be controllable or uncontrollable. When the situation is perceived to be potentially under the person's control (e.g., 'If I tell him off he'll stop bullying me'), then it makes sense to engage in active, problem-focused forms of coping. If, on the other hand, the person judges the situation to be unchangeable (e.g., 'Nothing I do can stop him bullying me'), these forms of coping are likely to be unproductive, and it is more appropriate for people to adapt themselves to the situation using emotion-focused strategies. Coping researchers talk about this issue in terms of the 'goodness of fit' between coping efforts and the situation: a close fit exists when people tend to engage in problem-focused coping for stressors they appraise as controllable and in emotion-focused coping for stressors they judge to be uncontrollable. Some research indicates that better fit is associated with better coping outcomes. In short, successful coping involves a capacity to engage in ways of coping that are tailored to the situation, rather than a tendency to employ a single kind of strategy in an inflexible manner.

Although the distinction between problem-focused and emotion-focused coping has been dominant in the literature, it may also be a little too coarse to encompass the diversity of coping efforts. Several additional types of coping strategies may also need to be considered, and we will briefly discuss three of them here. First, some writers have argued that although emotion-focused coping strategies often seem rather passive and inadequate, some are notably worse than others. It is possible to refer to 'avoidant' forms of coping that involve attempts to escape, either cognitively or behaviourally, from the stressful situation rather than facing it or adapting oneself to it. For example, wishful thinking, pretending the problem does not exist, avoiding people who remind you of a stressful situation, excessive sleeping, substance abuse, and simple denial, are all examples of avoidant coping. As you might expect, avoidant coping is almost always an ineffective strategy.

More effective may be a second additional kind of coping, namely the seeking of social support. Although the coping literature has tended to see coping as a relatively non-social process, in which individuals try to manage their lives single-handedly using an assortment of clever strategies, people are of course embedded in social relationships and networks. There is ample evidence that having close relationships and being a connected part of broader networks buffers people against stress and its consequences, and efforts to seek out other people appear to represent a distinct type of coping. Interestingly, support-seeking cuts across the distinction between problem- and emotion-focused coping. Other people could be sought to give active assistance in dealing with a problem we are facing, or they could be sought to console and comfort us, and to listen to our tales of woe, thereby helping us to manage our emotions.

A third, additional kind of coping involves finding meaning in adversity. Often people who are experiencing life stress, and especially stress that is lasting and severe, report that they have come to a new understanding of themselves or of life as a result of their experiences. A quote from a cancer patient, reported by Taylor (1983), is a good illustration:

You take a long look at your life and realize that many things that you thought were important before are totally insignificant. That's probably been the major change in my life. What you do is put things in perspective. You find out that things like relationships are the most important things you have. (p. 1163)

Such efforts to find meaning and to put life and self in a new perspective are not problem-focused ways of changing the situation itself, and neither are they ways of managing emotions. Instead, they represent ways for people to reappraise or accept their fate and to reinterpret the stressful event so as to make it personally significant. Although all of this may sound woolly and philosophical, the discovery of meaning in adversity appears to have important practical implications. In a study of HIV+ men whose partners had died of AIDS, Bower, Kemeny, Taylor, and Fahey (1998) found that those men who actively engaged in cognitive processing about the meaning of their loss were more likely to find meaning in it, as indicated by a significant shift in their values and life priorities (e.g., a greater appreciation of loved ones or enhanced spirituality). Moreover, those men who found meaning showed less rapid decline in immune functioning over the next three years, and were less likely to die of AIDS-related causes (i.e., 19% of the men who found meaning compared to 50% of those who did not). Finding meaning in adversity is clearly not just a matter of philosophical navel-gazing.

The psychology of coping is an exciting area of research with important applications in a variety of applied fields. One of the most attractive features of the coping concept, and of the cognitive approach to personality more broadly, is that coping strategies are skills or ways of thinking that should be teachable. Strategies that are found to be effective by researchers could become targets for interventions aimed at people who are experiencing particular kinds of stress, so that their coping can be enhanced. The psychology of coping is therefore a solid foundation for a very practical way of improving people's lives.

REPRESENTING THE SELF: SELF-ESTEEM AND SELF-COMPLEXITY

The three sets of concepts that we have discussed to this point in the chapter – personal constructs, explanations and attributions, and coping skills and styles – all reflect cognitive processes. All of them refer to ways in which people make active sense of their environment and respond to its challenges. However, processes are only one component of cognition, and we can also speak of cognitive products. In addition to cognitive processes, that is, people have organized knowledge of themselves and their world, and this knowledge reflects the ways in which they make sense of the world. Cognitive psychologists often refer to this structured knowledge in terms of 'representations'. People store representations of the world in their memory, and these representations, built up and modified throughout the course of our development, guide the way we process new information.

One of the most interesting and important knowledge structures or representations is the self. The self is a notoriously slippery phenomenon, and might seem to be very difficult to pin down, but when it is understood as a 'self-concept' – that is, as an organized body of knowledge about one's attributes – it becomes amenable to study by personality and social psychologists. At the most basic level, we can simply ask people to list the characteristics that they see as aspects of themselves (i.e., answers to the question 'I am _____'). Typically, people have no difficulty listing a large number of attributes. Some of these attributes refer to personal characteristics, both psychological and physical (e.g., traits, attitudes, abilities, height, hair colour), others refer to groups to which the person belongs (e.g., nationality, ethnicity, gender), and still others refer to the person's roles or relationships (e.g., father, employee, girlfriend). Sometimes these three components of the self are referred to as personal, collective, and relational selves, respectively.

Importantly, however, the self-concept is not merely a list of disconnected attributes or labels, but a structured set of beliefs. Certain attributes may be especially central to a person's self-concept but incidental to someone else's. A person's gender, or their physical appearance, or their toughness, or their ethnic group membership may be a core, defining property of their identity, for example, all other properties being secondary. In addition, the attributes within a person's self-concept are inter-connected to varying degrees, and in ways that may be highly distinctive for each person. In one woman's self-concept, for example, female gender may be prominently associated with traits of modesty and self-control, so that she feels most feminine when exercising self-restraint, whereas for another woman, for whom being female is an equally important aspect of self, femininity may be associated with spontaneity and seductiveness. In short, people can represent their self-knowledge in quite unique and personally revealing ways.

An enormous amount of research within personality psychology has gone into studying the self, and it is well beyond the scope of this introductory textbook to discuss most of it. However, two topics are perhaps particularly interesting and important. One refers to how we evaluate our self-concept (self-esteem), and the other to how complicated this concept is (self-complexity).

Self-esteem

Self-esteem is a concept that has successfully made the jump from the psychological literature into everyday speech, where it has thrived. People can often be heard to explain one another's behaviour in terms of the concept, and low self-esteem is commonly invoked as an explanation of everything from eating disorders to academic under-achievement. In essence, self-esteem refers to the person's overall or 'global' evaluation of their self-concept: whether they believe that their self, as they conceptualize it, is overall a good one or a not-so-good one. To have high self-esteem, then, implies that you are satisfied with and proud of the attributes that you believe yourself to possess.

When it is put this way it seems obvious that high self-esteem is a good thing. Thinking highly of oneself surely feels better than the opposite, and we would expect people who are confident in themselves to be more secure and interpersonally warm, and less prone to act in self-defeating or antisocial ways. Many people have taken the next step and argued that we should aim to promote and increase self-esteem. In the 1980s, in California, a state government task force was founded to raise self-esteem, in the hope that social pathologies as varied as teen pregnancy, crime, and poor school performance might be reduced as a result, and since then numerous organizations have advanced similar agendas. Over the past 30 years or so, for example, parents and teachers have increasingly been instructed to enhance children's self-esteem by frequent praise and by cushioning them from potentially hurtful feedback on their academic performance. Indeed, there is evidence that a cultural shift has taken place, at least in some parts of the Western world, and that self-esteem levels have been rising. Twenge and Campbell (2001) investigated the mean scores on popular self-esteem tests for American undergraduate students assessed between the 1960s and the 1990s, and found that these scores have been steadily rising. At least within this population, it would seem that the prayers of the self-esteem movement are being answered, and people are becoming more positive about themselves.

Recently, however, psychologists have begun to take a more critical view of self-esteem. First, they note that apparent rises in self-esteem over the past decades do not seem to have produced reductions in problem behaviours in which low self-esteem was implicated. Indeed, on many social indicators, the problems have become worse over this period. In the period covered by Twenge and Campbell's analysis, for example, rates of depression, anxiety, adolescent crime, and teen pregnancy rose, while scores on tests of educational attainment dropped. Second, evidence emerged that far from being a universal human motive, the desire for high self-esteem was difficult to establish in some cultures, such as Japan (e.g., Heine, Lehman, Markus, & Kitayama, 1999). Third, and most importantly, a body of personality and social psychology research began to challenge the causal role that self-esteem has often been assumed to play in positive behaviour. That is, self-esteem has often been understood as a psychological phenomenon that is responsible for desirable outcomes, and if it does not have such a causal role in bringing about positive outcomes then it makes little sense to raise it.

Research on this important question has recently been reviewed by Baumeister, Campbell, Krueger, and Vohs (2003). They concluded that although self-esteem has rather modest positive correlations with academic performance in school, there is little or no evidence that self-esteem is causally responsible for better performance and more evidence that it results from school performance. Efforts to raise self-esteem tend to produce no lasting improvement in performance. Similarly, there is little evidence that self-esteem boosts work performance. People with high self-esteem tend to see themselves as having high levels of interpersonal skill and popularity, but this view is not supported by other people's impressions of their social skills, and in some conditions, specifically when they are threatened with a loss of face, high self-esteem people are rated less likeable than low self-esteem people. There is some evidence that low self-esteem is weakly associated with delinquency, but high self-esteem people are no less likely to be aggressive than others and raising self-esteem does not lead to reductions in aggression for perpetrators of domestic violence. High self-esteem is not associated with a lower risk of alcohol and drug use, and may be linked to risky sexual behaviour. There is little evidence that it plays a significant causal role in physical health. The only desirable things that high self-esteem is clearly associated with, claim Baumeister et al., are positive mood and a tendency to speak up more assertively in groups. Self-esteem seems to be far from the cure of all social and personal ills that its advocates sometimes claim it to be: it appears to be more associated with feeling good than with behaving well, and to be more the result than the cause of the desirable properties with which it is associated.

What might account for the mixed implications of self-esteem? Several possibilities have been proposed. One possibility is that high self-esteem is beneficial when it is stable, but not when it is fragile. Kernis, Cornell, Sun, Berry, and Harlow (1993) have argued that some people with high self-esteem have a vulnerable sense of self-worth, which fluctuates in response to everyday hassles, problems, and self-doubts. For example, holding overall level of self-esteem constant, people with less stable self-esteem tend to report lower levels of well-being (Paradise & Kernis, 2002). Another explanation for the mixed implications of self-esteem is that some people who report high levels of self-esteem on questionnaires ('explicit' self-esteem) in fact have low levels of self-esteem at a less conscious or 'implicit' level. Implicit self-esteem can be assessed using an experimental procedure that examines how readily people associate themselves with desirable and undesirable stimuli (Greenwald & Farnham, 2000), and interestingly it does not correlate strongly with explicit self-esteem. People who have high explicit but low implicit self-esteem have been said to have 'defensive' self-esteem (Jordan, Spencer, Zanna, Hoshino-Browne, & Correll, 2003), because they are prone to respond more defensively than people with secure high self-esteem. Such people also appear to be high in 'narcissism', a complex trait involving arrogance, a sense of superiority and entitlement, and an exaggerated sensitivity to criticism. Narcissists tend to be particularly likely to react aggressively when their self-esteem is threatened by an insult (Bushman & Baumeister, 1998).

Self-esteem is obviously more complicated than it first appears. It does not seem to be an entirely desirable trait because it has two faces: one healthy and solid, the other unhealthily sensitive to perceived threats. It may be that high self-esteem *is* desirable, but only when it is also stable and held both explicitly and implicitly.

Self-complexity

Self-esteem refers to the person's overall *evaluation* of his or her self, but we can also ask about how, independent of its evaluation, the person's self-concept is organized or *structured*. Some personality psychologists have studied the implications of having a more or less complex self-concept. **Self-complexity** has been conceptualized and measured in several different ways, but one influential definition is 'having more self-aspects and maintaining greater distinction among self-aspects' (Linville, 1987, p. 664), where a self-aspect refers to a role or setting that defines the self (e.g., me-at-work, me-as-a-student, me-as-a-daughter). By this definition, people who report a greater number of self-aspects, and who describe these self-aspects in ways that do not overlap very much, have a more complex representation of self.

Linville, who first presented the concept, proposed that high self-complexity is beneficial because it should buffer the person against stressful events. When these events happen to someone with a complex self they may negatively affect one of the person's self-aspects, but the person has numerous other self-aspects and these should remain largely unaffected if they do not overlap. A person's self-as-student aspect may suffer in response to a bad mark on an exam, but if that person has numerous additional, unrelated self-aspects, any distress the person experiences will be confined to the one aspect. If the person's identity is almost completely wrapped up in being a student, on the other hand, and her few other self-aspects are closely related to this self-aspect (e.g., being 'smart' is an important trait for how she sees herself as a worker and family member), then the bad mark's effects should spill over to make the person generally miserable. In short, having a self that is low in complexity is like putting all one's (self-knowledge) eggs into one (cognitive) basket.

Linville's research (e.g., 1987) supported her argument that greater self-complexity buffers people against extreme emotional responses to stress, and some other studies have agreed. For example, Smith and Cohen (1993) found that people who mentally separated their romantic self-aspect from other self-aspects responded less negatively to relationship break-ups than those who did not. However, findings such as these have not been consistently obtained in other research (Rafaeli-Mor & Steinberg, 2002). Many studies have failed to find evidence that greater self-complexity reduces the negative impact of unpleasant events, and there is, instead, more evidence that it reduces the positive impact of pleasant events (i.e., the consequences of good news for one self-aspect do not spill over into self-aspects that are unrelated to it). This finding suggests that self-complexity may itself have complex and mixed implications.

This conclusion is also drawn by a number of researchers who argue that having a self composed of unrelated, non-overlapping aspects might not be a good thing. Rather than being complex, it might also be described as fragmented, disunited, conflicted, divided, confused, diffuse, or incoherent, characteristics that might seem pathological rather than healthy (Donaghue, Robins, Roberts, & John, 1993). For example, Campbell (1990) argued that it is healthy for people to have 'self-concept clarity', namely a self that the person can describe confidently and clearly and that is internally coherent, in the sense of not containing attributes that are contradictory. Clarity in this sense refers to an integrated rather than differentiated self, and there is some evidence that it is positively associated with psychological health and well-being. Some researchers have found that self-complexity is associated with higher levels of depression, consistent with this position (Woolfolk, Novalany, Gara, Allen, & Polino, 1995). The overall picture, then, is rather similar to the one that self-esteem presents. Having a more complex and differentiated self, like having a more positive self-evaluation, may not always be desirable, if this complexity involves a lack of integration or clarity in the self-concept.

THINKING ABOUT EMOTIONS: EMOTIONAL INTELLIGENCE

In Chapter 2, as we attempted to clarify the meaning of 'personality', we drew a basic distinction between two kinds of psychological differences between people: those that are intellectual and those that are non-intellectual. Intellectual characteristics include cognitive abilities and skills, particularly those that underlie competent performance in academic or school-related activities. Whereas non-intellectual characteristics, such as personality traits, involve dispositions to behave, think, and feel in particular ways, abilities involve capacities to find objectively correct solutions to problems, and to do so with ease and rapidity. Mathematical ability involves the capacity to process information about numbers and to solve mathematical problems, and verbal ability involves the capacity to process verbal information and to solve verbal problems. Both sorts of ability are cultivated by formal schooling.

In Chapter 2 we also discussed how the distinction between intellectual and non-intellectual characteristics is not always crisp. Some characteristics, such as creativity, have an obvious cognitive ability component, but they also seem to incorporate styles of thinking and feeling beyond narrow abilities (flexibility and openness, say, when it comes to creativity). Other writers have argued that personality includes abilities other than those that are specific to the academic or school-related context. Inspired in part by theorists who proposed the existence of multiple intelligences (Gardner, 1983), some writers have recently developed the concept of **'emotional intelligence'**, a set of abilities that involve the skilful processing of emotion-related information (Goleman, 1995).

Proponents of emotional intelligence argue that it meets the traditional criteria for considering something to qualify as an intelligence. They define it as 'an ability to recognize the meanings of emotion and their relationships, and to reason and problem-solve on the basis of them' (Mayer, Caruso, & Salovey, 1999). These theorists propose that emotional intelligence, or EI, has four fundamental components or 'branches'. The first branch, the ability to accurately perceive emotions, refers to the capacity to recognize the emotional states of others non-verbally, by observing the facial expressions, voice, and movements of others, and also to recognize one's own emotional states. The second branch, the use of emotions to facilitate one's thinking, refers to the ability to use information about one's emotional states to make plans of action and to direct our attention to relevant information. The third branch, understanding emotions, involves the ability to reason accurately about the meaning of people's emotional states, such as figuring out how someone is likely to feel when a certain event takes place and what the implications of that emotion are likely to be. The fourth branch, managing emotions, refers to the ability to regulate or control one's own and others' emotions so as to accomplish one's goals. People who are high in emotional intelligence, that is, accurately identify emotions, know how to use them to advantage, understand their personal and interpersonal implications, and are adept at regulating them.

The concept of emotional intelligence, and the development of measures which assess it as a set of abilities to figure out correct answers to emotion-related problems or tasks, has given rise to a rapidly growing body of research evidence, much of it encouraging (Mayer, Salovey, & Caruso, 2004). The component abilities (i.e., branches) appear to form a coherent set (i.e., a single factor in a factor analysis), are distinct from other intelligences (e.g., verbal ability or general IQ), and are largely independent of standard personality trait dimensions, such as the Big Five (EI is correlated with Openness and Agreeableness, for example, but quite weakly). There is some evidence that emotional intelligence is associated with better academic and job performance, and lower levels of antisocial behaviour. More emotionally intelligent people appear to have greater interpersonal sensitivity and they are rated as more socially desirable by others (Lopes, Salovey, Cote, & Beers, 2005).

Although this work suggests that emotion-related abilities may be valuable components of personality, the concept of emotional intelligence has also been quite controversial for several reasons. First, the concept has been widely popularized by writers who have made exaggerated claims for its importance, and who have arguably distorted its meaning. Some writers have claimed that EI is the most important factor in personal or job-related success, and have given it such an elastic definition that it includes just about every desirable characteristic you could imagine, apart from IQ. Second, some psychologists have approached EI not as a set of abilities that should be assessed by objective performance on emotion-processing tasks (e.g., accuracy in identifying emotions), but as a trait that can be assessed using self-report questionnaires. Such questionnaires assess *self-perceived* emotional intelligence, but they do not appear to assess *actual* EI abilities accurately. Questionnaire measures of EI therefore seem to overlap to a large extent with standard personality dimensions such as Agreeableness and (low) Neuroticism (De Raad, 2005). This overlap, and the discrepancies between different definitions and measures of emotional intelligence, has led critics to charge that EI is either incoherent or not meaningfully distinct from ordinary traits (Matthews, Roberts, & Zeidner, 2004).

At present the concept of emotional intelligence is in a state of flux. Many psychologists believe it to be an important set of abilities that add something to more familiar trait approaches to personality, and many consultants are eager to develop (and sell!) programmes for increasing the EI of workers and for teaching it in schools. Other psychologists are sceptical. Nevertheless, the idea that some aspects of personality might be understood as cognitive abilities dedicated to making sense of real-world emotional and interpersonal phenomena, strikes many people as intriguing and original.

Illustrative study: how does emotional intelligence relate to job performance?

Canadian organizational behaviour researchers Stéphane Côté and Christopher Miners (2006) examined whether, as has often been asserted, emotional intelligence is associated with superior job performance. Research evidence on this question has been rather mixed. In addition, Côté and Miners were interested in how emotional and cognitive

(Continued)

(Continued)

intelligence might interact in predicting job performance, asking whether, if someone is relatively low in one form, then the other form might compensate. If this were true, emotional intelligence might be more important for job performance among people with lower levels of cognitive intelligence.

Côté and Miners recruited 175 employees of a large university, who worked in managerial, administrative, or professional roles, and brought them into a laboratory to complete measures of the two forms of intelligence. They also obtained ratings of the employees' job performance and 'organizational citizenship' (i.e., contributing positively to the organization and its members) from their work supervisors.

Findings of the study indicated that both emotional and cognitive intelligence were positive correlated with the measures of job performance and organizational citizenship. Consistent with the researchers' predictions, they found evidence that emotional intelligence may compensate for lower levels of cognitive intelligence. Emotional intelligence was more strongly associated with job performance among people of lower cognitive intelligence. The importance of emotional intelligence for occupational success may therefore depend on workers' levels of cognitive intelligence.

CONCLUSIONS

In this chapter we have reviewed a variety of cognitive concepts that have been employed within personality psychology. All of them – personal constructs, explanatory styles, self-conceptions, coping strategies, and emotional intelligence – refer to distinctive kinds of mental process that are involved in making sense of our world and acting competently within it. These cognitive concepts are theoretically important in that although they provide ways to describe individual differences in personality, they also offer explanations of personality in terms of the mental processes or mechanisms that generate individual differences in emotion and behaviour. These explanations are notably different from those we reviewed Chapters 4 and 5. They explain individuals in psychological rather than biological terms, and in terms of generally conscious cognitive mechanisms rather than generally unconscious motivations. Emphasizing the cognitive underpinnings of personality like this is theoretically and practically important because it has clear implications for intervention. If someone is engaging in ineffective coping strategies, has inflexible personal constructs or poor skills in perceiving emotion, we can in principle improve their life by altering these cognitions. Altering cognitions is something that humans do rather well, and have a wide variety of methods at their disposal. Education is a prime example. In theory, it should be possible to adapt methods such as these to the correction of maladaptive ways of thinking. In short, the cognitive approach to personality implies an optimistic view of the possibility of changing people's personality, and treating their psychological disturbances.

Chapter summary

- The cognitive approach to personality differs from others in emphasizing the ways in which people actively make sense of themselves and their worlds. It explains individual differences in terms of cognitions such as beliefs, concepts, attitudes, explanations, and abilities.
- The cognitive approach arose in part out of a rebellion against the passive and deterministic view of human nature in behaviourist theory, and also resonates with some aspects of humanistic personality theories. Social learning and social-cognitive theories also introduced cognitive concepts into the study of personality.
- There is no single cognitive theory of personality, only a number of concepts that have inspired active programmes of research.
- 'Personal constructs' are cognitive structures that people use to interpret, perceive, or 'construe' the world. They are bipolar — composed of one attribute and a contrasting attribute (e.g., warm vs. cold) — and each individual has a unique, subjective repertoire of them. According to personal construct theory our main motivation is to grasp and anticipate events in the world accurately, like scientists.
- 'Attributions' are explanations that people give for events. An event may be attributed to causes that differ in several ways. How people habitually explain events is their 'attributional [or explanatory] style'. People who typically attribute negative events to causes that are internal to themselves, lasting and broad in their implications (i.e., pessimists) are vulnerable to a variety of negative outcomes.
- 'Coping strategies' are ways of dealing with adversity, implemented when events are judged to be stressful. Different strategies are associated with better and worse coping with particular kinds of stressors.

(Continued)

(Continued)

- The self is a cognition: a mental representation of what the person is like. Self-esteem and self-complexity are ways in which these representations differ between people: how positively the self is evaluated, and how many distinct aspects compose it. Both are associated with important life outcomes in interesting ways: self-esteem, for example, is not the recipe for unbridled happiness and success that it is sometimes claimed to be.
- 'Emotional intelligence' refers to the capacity to recognize and reason about emotions in oneself and in others. It is conceptualized as a cognitive ability, and has multiple components. These appear to be associated with interpersonal and work-related success.

Further reading

- Baumeister, R.F., Campbell, J.D., Krueger, J.I., & Vohs, K.D. (2003). Does high self-esteem cause better performance, interpersonal success, happiness, or healthier lifestyles? *Psychological Science in the Public Interest, 4,* 1–44.

Baumeister and colleagues challenge the widespread belief that self-esteem is an entirely desirable quality that social institutions should make sure to raise. They review evidence showing that self-esteem often does not contribute to positive outcomes, and that in some cases it is associated with negative ones.

- Buchanan, G.M., & Seligman, M.E.P. (Eds.) (1995). *Explanatory style.* Hillsdale, NJ: Erlbaum.

This edited collection shows the wide range of topics that explanatory style can illuminate, and reviews a substantial body of research on this cognitive approach to personality.

- Butt, T., & Burr, V. (2005). *An invitation to personal construct psychology* (2nd ed.). New York: Wiley.

This is an accessible introduction to Kelly's personal construct psychology, with plenty of illuminating examples of this distinctive approach.

(Continued)

(Continued)

- Folkman, S., & Moskowitz, J.T. (2004). Coping: Pitfalls and promise. *Annual Review of Psychology, 55,* 745–74.

Folkman and Moskowitz review research on coping processes and styles, including which coping strategies are most effective in particular conditions.

- Goleman, D. (1995). *Emotional intelligence.* New York: Bantam.

Although this is a popular work, rather than an academic tract, it is a very readable book that is largely responsible for starting the widespread interest in the concept of emotional intelligence.

- Mayer, J.D., Salovey, P., & Caruso, D.R. (2004). Emotional intelligence: Theory, findings, and implications. *Psychological Inquiry, 15,* 197–215.

Mayer and colleagues' article complements Goleman's book, laying out recent scientific work on emotional intelligence for an academic audience.

SECTION 3
PERSONALITY IN PRACTICE

7

Personality Change and Development

Learning objectives

- To comprehend the extent to which personality traits are stable over time, and the factors that contribute to this stability.
- To understand the extent of personality change, and the factors that contribute to it.
- To understand the different senses of stability and change: rank-order and mean-level.
- To understand how personality develops out of childhood temperament, and the stages that development follows.
- To recognize the broader implications of personality change and stability, and of our beliefs about them.

The first of four chapters on practical issues surrounding personality, this chapter investigates the important question of how stable (or changeable) personality is, and how it develops from childhood. Evidence for high levels of stability in adult personality is discussed along with some of the factors that contribute to it. Equally strong evidence that the average levels of personality traits change with age is then laid out. Possible causes of these changes are discussed, including those that involve broad changes in society and culture. The chapter next reviews the ways in which child temperament develops into adult personality, and one prominent theory of the stages through which personality development proceeds. We conclude with a discussion of why the issue of change versus stability matters, pondering on some of the possible costs of believing personality to be fixed.

You are 4 years old. Your bladder control is not yet perfect. You think dinosaurs and trains are the coolest things, or play with dolls whose waists are improbably thin. You have not discovered irony or sarcasm. Your repertoire of rude words is tiny, and focused on bottoms. When you stand straight up your eyes are at the level of your parents' hips.

A researcher comes to your preschool and leads you into a room that is furnished with a table, a chair, a small bell, and a mirror. She sits you down at the table and shows you first one marshmallow and then two. She asks you which of these alternatives you prefer. You are too young to think that this is a stupid question, and say you would prefer to have two. She then says to you that she has to leave the room, but if you wait until she comes back you can have the two marshmallows. If you don't want to wait, she says, you can ring the bell and bring her back any time you want to, but if you do you only get one marshmallow. She leaves the sugary alternatives in front of you on the table and exits the room. In an act of treachery that would shock your trusting and innocent little mind, she then retreats behind the one-way mirror and times how long you withstand this torture. If you have not broken your resolve in 20 minutes she returns to the room. The average child gives up and rings the bell after eight and a half long minutes.

This experiment was conducted by Shoda, Mischel, and Peake (1990), who did an innovative thing. Not content to simply observe how long or by what means children delayed gratification, they followed up their experimental participants 11 or 14 years later, assessing their personality and their academic aptitude. Length of delay at 4 years of age correlated with parental ratings of mid- to late-adolescents' planfulness, thinking ahead, using and responding to reason, tolerating stress, and being able to delay gratification. It was also correlated with standardized tests of verbal and quantitative reasoning that play a major role in college admissions in the USA, where the experiment was conducted. These correlations were substantial, averaging about .4: a child who delayed longer than average was more than twice as likely as one who didn't to be above average on these personality and academic strengths as an adolescent.

These results may surprise you, and they certainly surprised many psychologists. People often think of children as malleable creatures who undergo so many transformations over the course of development that little stability should be apparent across the 14-year gulf separating early childhood from late adolescence. Moreover, the observed correlations may *under-estimate* the real level of stability, given that the experiment represents a single observation of the children's delay tendencies. As we know from the great trait controversy (see Chapter 3), behavioural prediction improves when multiple observations, taken in different contexts and at different times, are aggregated together. Isn't it remarkable how much the adolescents' personality was foretold by one highly peculiar childhood experience?

Maybe not. Almost by definition personality is relatively stable and enduring, a source of personal continuity and predictability through time. However, this 'relatively' obscures a host of questions. Just *how* stable is personality? Is it less stable during some stages of life, such as childhood, than at others? Is there an age at which it is essentially fixed or 'set in plaster', a metaphor employed by the famous psychologist William James, who gave 30 as the answer? Even if personalities don't *tend* to change over time, does that mean that they *can't* change? To the extent that personality is stable, does this stability reflect a kind of constant momentum that traits have or a continuous process of stabilization by the person's social environment and life choices? To the extent that personality changes, what factors promote or trigger change? Does personality have the same structure in children and adults, or does the very nature of personality change? How does personality develop? This chapter will try to provide some answers to these important questions.

THE STABILITY OF PERSONALITY

To determine the stability of personality, researchers must conduct longitudinal studies like Shoda et al.'s (1990), in which the same people are tracked over significant periods of time. Needless to say these studies are costly and difficult to carry out, and they demand a great deal of delay of gratification on the part of researchers. University promotion committees are also generally unimpressed when scientists tell them that they expect to publish some fascinating and important findings in ten years, when the study is complete. Nevertheless, a number of longitudinal studies of personality have been conducted in recent years, often covering spans as long as 20 years. Typically they administer the same personality measure at the beginning and end of the time span and correlate participants' scores on the two occasions. These 'retest correlations' represent the degree to which participants retain the same position relative to the other participants on the trait in question. If all participants hold the identical rank-order from the beginning to the end of the study then the correlation is perfect.

Many longitudinal studies of adult personality have used the Big Five traits reviewed in Chapter 2. Their findings have been quite consistent. Over a period of almost 20 years, the five factors all show retest correlations of about .65 (Costa & McCrae, 1994a). If you score above average on a particular trait at 30, that is, you have roughly an 83% likelihood of being above average when you turn 50. This likelihood is almost five times as great as someone who at 30 scores below average. This is surely quite impressive evidence for the stability of personality, especially as the retest correlations are probably under-estimates once again. All personality measures are subject to measurement error – random influences such as variations in mood states and attentiveness that cause a person's scores to fluctuate even over short periods – and this error reduces or 'attenuates' their ability to correlate with other measures (or with themselves years later in longitudinal studies). When measurement error is statistically removed, the 'disattenuated' correlations (i.e., estimated correlations had the trait in question been measured perfectly) rise even higher. In short, adult personality appears to be remarkably stable.

Is personality equally stable prior to adulthood, however? The evidence suggests that it isn't. Studies that track high-school-age adolescents or young adults tend to report lower retest correlations than those that follow people beginning in middle age, even when the former studies have shorter durations. These studies seem to demonstrate somewhat less stability in the personalities of people in their teens and 20s than in those in middle and old age. Costa and McCrae (1994b) conclude that 'by age 30, personality is essentially fixed' (p. 146). Although there is nothing magical about this age – you won't turn into a pumpkin on your 30th birthday – it does seem to be true that personality traits are approaching their maximum level of stability during the early-to-mid-adult years (Roberts & DelVecchio, 2000).

SOURCES OF STABILITY

If personality is indeed more or less fixed by early-to-mid adulthood, why is this so? One possibility, based on William James' metaphor, is that personality 'sets like plaster' at a certain time of life, remaining constant thereafter. Or to use a different metaphor, personalities moving through time, like objects moving through space, have their own momentums, carried by a steady internal force in a constant direction. These metaphors imply that in adulthood personality is intrinsically stable.

Although this way of thinking about the continuity of adult personality is pleasantly straightforward, other possibilities exist, captured by quite different metaphors. Consider water moving along a channel or a ball rolling down a groove. In both of these images, something moves in a consistent and predictable direction. However, the water and the ball do this not because it is in their intrinsic natures to be consistent and predictable, but because some external forces constrain or direct them. The channel prevents the water from flowing in different directions, despite its intrinsic capacity to do so, and the physical forces that the groove imparts on the rolling ball compel it to continue following the groove. If someone dug another channel that branched off from the main one, the water might begin to flow down this new one instead, and if the groove became shallower the ball might roll over its edge to freedom. Is it possible that the stability of personality reflects some sort of channelling process?

Maybe so. After all, people tend to inhabit environments that are quite stable over time, living under the same or similar physical and economic conditions and interacting with the same or similar people. Continuities in their personalities might therefore simply reflect continuities in the environmental influences that bear on them. In an intriguing longitudinal study of married couples, for instance, Caspi and Herbener (1990) found that people who married more similar partners showed greater stability in their personalities over the ten-year period than people who married less similar partners. By this account, then, personality stability might be at least partially shaped by the environments – or channels – in which our behaviour is expressed. Interestingly, this might help to explain the apparent increase in the stability of personality over the course of adulthood. People tend to undergo more frequent major life events and transitions in youth and early adulthood than in later adulthood – entering the workforce and long-term relationships, becoming parents, moving house, and so on – so we might expect their personalities to be more stable later in life.

Although this environmental channelling account of personality stability has some plausibility, there has been little research to establish its validity and it faces a major conceptual problem. Environments and personalities may both tend to be stable during the adult years, but can we confidently infer that the stability of the former *causes* the stability of the latter? Isn't the opposite inference equally plausible? That is, one reason why environments tend to remain stable is that people select environmental niches that suit them and express their basic dispositions. Extraverts surround themselves with friends, people high in Conscientiousness gravitate to demanding work-roles. People also elicit reactions from the environment according to their dispositions: timid people tend to be dominated by others and socially dominant people have leadership positions thrust upon them. In short, it is very risky to suppose that environmental channelling is directly responsible for the stability of personality because to some degree people's dispositions determine which channels they enter.

If environmental channelling isn't an entirely convincing account of personality continuity – although it is surely part of the explanation – other kinds of explanation are needed. Besides the intrinsic 'set like plaster' account, which might reflect genetic and maturational influences, a couple of other proposals have been put forward. One is that over the course of life people's self-perceptions tend to become crystallized (Glenn, 1980). Several implications flow from this simple claim. First, older adults should tend to open themselves to fewer new experiences that might generate personality change, because of a fixed sense of how they are and how they should live. That is, a crystallized sense of self may make people more likely to remain in their channel, or to have a more restricted view of it. By doing so, they expose themselves to familiar experiences that further reinforce the stability of their dispositions. Second, older adults' more fixed sense of self may lead them to ignore evidence of personal change that challenges their self-perceptions. This discounting of self-discrepant information may even bias people's responses to self-report personality questionnaires to minimize actual change, so that the apparent stability of personality in longitudinal studies might be exaggerated.

This explanation of the stability of personality is an important one. It suggests that personality in adulthood might be relatively stable not simply because of environmental channelling or the intrinsic fixedness of personality, but because of the basic conservatism of our ways of thinking, especially about ourselves. Our sense of who we are and what we are like tends to stabilize with age, and constrains and stabilizes the expression of our dispositions to be consistent with it. By implication, personality itself may not be intrinsically or necessarily stable in adulthood, but tends to be consistent for reasons that *are* intrinsic to human psychology, namely the self-stabilizing processes of the self-concept. The factors contributing to the continuity of personality are evidently many and complicated.

PERSONALITY CHANGE

The research that we have reviewed to this point paints a picture of continuity of the personality, particularly in middle and later adulthood, and offers several explanations for this apparent stability. The evidence for stability seems quite overwhelming. However, 'stability' turns out to be a less straightforward concept than you might imagine, and it comes in different varieties. Retest correlations reflect what is called '**rank-order stability**': they are high to the extent that people tend to maintain the same rank over time, so that people who rank high at the beginning of a longitudinal study still rank high at the end. However, a ranking is a *relative* ordering, referring to how people place relative to others. It is possible that people's ranks on a personality trait might be stable from one time to another, but the group's *absolute* level on the trait might change. The same people might tend to be high and low relative to their peers, but their peers might tend to undergo a shift.

As it turns out, the same studies that have found substantial rank-order stability in adult personality have also obtained evidence of significant changes in the average levels of five-factor traits. Although these changes are not huge, they complicate the picture of apparent stability that retest correlations give us, and point to typical patterns of maturational change over the course of adulthood. A particularly important study of mean-level personality change was conducted by Srivastava, John, Gosling, and Potter (2003), whose results challenged not only the 'hard plaster' view of personality – in which it is fixed at 30 – but also the 'soft plaster' view that the pace of personality change invariably slows after 30. They found that Conscientiousness rose from age 21 to 30 and continued to rise at a slower rate thereafter, but Agreeableness actually rose faster after 30 than before. Similarly, Neuroticism declined at an even rate over the adult life course (only for women), Openness declined more steeply after 30 than before. One way to summarize these developmental trajectories is to say that people tend to become more self-controlled and prudent, more interpersonally warm, less emotionally volatile, and less open to new experiences and ways of thinking. Alternatively, and more economically, one could say that with increased age people tend to have a narrower emotional range – less positive *and* negative affect – and become more socialized. More economically still, but perhaps a little uncharitably, one could say people become duller. However we look at it, though, the clear message is that some personality change – however small and gradual it may be – is normal, even during adulthood.

In addition to this work on normal, absolute changes in personality over the life-course, research on the rank-order stability of personality also reveals evidence of change. Although this research demonstrates that in adulthood broad personality traits tend to be quite stable, even in the late adult years retest correlations do not approach perfection (i.e., 1.0). Even at this time of life, a small but significant fraction of people undergo some amount of personality change. If nothing else, this shows that personality change in adulthood is entirely possible, even if it is not large or common.

This conclusion is reinforced when we look at the rank-order stability of personality prior to adulthood. In a review of 152 longitudinal studies, Roberts and DelVecchio (2000) found that retest correlations for studies of adults aged between 30 and 73 averaged about .67. The average for young adults aged 18 to 29 was about .57, and the average for children and adolescents (aged 3 to 17) was about .45. Among infants and toddlers (aged 0 to 2) the average was only .31. (All of these correlations were adjusted to refer to a retest duration of about seven years.) As you can see, personality is less and less stable the closer we get to the beginning of life, to the point that traits measured in early childhood generally do not allow confident predictions about personality in middle childhood, let alone in adulthood. Personality traits assessed at age 2 should correlate about .31 with the same traits assessed at age 9, and *this* assessment should correlate about .45 with an assessment at age 16. The stability of traits over long periods will therefore be progressively diluted. Wordsworth wrote that 'the child is father of the man', implying that adults' dispositions can be extrapolated from their childhood tendencies, but the research evidence does not bear it out strongly. This should be a comfort to parents of bratty or difficult children, and challenge the complacency of parents of little angels. Perhaps it should also challenge our willingness to extrapolate backwards from how we or others are as adults to how we were, or 'must have been', as children. The scientific study of personality suggests that such continuities may often be exaggerated or imaginary.

Personality change, both absolute and relative to one's peers (i.e., rank-order instability), seems to be quite possible. If this is the case, what might account for it? One possible influence on personality change might be genes. Although genes are often thought of only as sources of stability, they could conceivably produce distinct patterns of personality change over time, just as they may partly control the timing of pubertal changes. However, research has found little evidence for genetic influences on personality change, suggesting that change must be either random or primarily driven by environmental influences.

Several kinds of environmental influence may be responsible for changes in personality. One kind that perhaps operates most in childhood involves other people's direct attempts to change the individual's personality characteristics. A great deal of socialization and parenting can be understood in these terms, and there is considerable evidence that childhood personality can be responsive to them. For example, Kagan (1994) found that toddlers with inhibited temperament who subsequently became less inhibited had parents who exposed them to novel situations rather than being overly protective. Children whose parents allowed them to avoid the novelty that distressed them tended to remain inhibited.

Another kind of environmental influence that can account for personality change is stressful life experience. Research suggests that life stress is associated with reduced stability of the personality, and that major life transitions and changes can produce lasting reductions in self-esteem (Harter, 1993) and increases in need for intimacy (Franz, 1994). Consistent with our metaphor of the environmental channelling of personality, disruptions in the environment can produce instability and personality change.

A third kind of environmental influence can be found in the changing social roles that people occupy over the course of life. The adjustments that people make to the demands and expectations of new social positions can yield lasting changes in traits, motives, and personal preoccupations. For example, Helson, Mitchell, and Moane (1984) tracked women from their university years through their late 20s and found that those who became mothers tended to show increases in responsibility, self-control, and femininity, and decreases in self-acceptance and sociability. Women who had not become mothers did not change in this manner, suggesting that the experience of motherhood was responsible for it. The same research group found that non-mothers tend to show greater increases in independence than mothers. In another longitudinal study of male managers (Howard & Bray, 1988), those who were more success-ful showed a reduction in nurturance from their 20s to their 40s, whereas less successful managers showed a small increase. These various changes can be rea-sonably interpreted as responses to changing life challenges and opportunities.

The idea that personality can change in response to changing social circum-stances is consistent with some fascinating recent work on changes in personal-ity over the course of recent history. Just as changing social roles can bring about personality change within an individual's life, changing societal or cultural con-ditions appear to bring about changes in the average personality of people who grow up in different generations (different 'birth cohorts' is the preferred term). Jean Twenge and her colleagues have carried out a series of studies – using a for-midable-sounding technique called 'cross-temporal meta-analysis' – that allows them to examine mean scores on personality tests for young people (usually American undergraduates) who completed these tests in many studies span-ning several decades. They find striking changes in mean levels of a variety of personality traits from the 1960s to today. For example, young people in recent years report considerably higher average levels of self-esteem and extraversion than they did 40 years ago (Twenge, 2001b; Twenge & Campbell, 2001). Young women became more assertive over this period (Twenge, 2001a), and showed steady increases in other stereotypically masculine traits so that gender differ-ences in personality tended to decrease (Twenge, 1997). Other changes were arguably less positive: samples of young people assessed in the early 1990s reported substantially higher levels of anxiety and neuroticism than those assessed 40 years previously (Twenge, 2000), and recent samples were more likely to report that their lives were controlled by outside forces rather than by internal factors such as their personal desires and abilities (Twenge, Zhang, & Im, 2004). All of these changes indicate that mean-level personality change occurs over historical time, presumably in ways that reflect social and cultural changes. In the last half century, that is, Western societies have tended to place increasing emphasis on individual self-assertion and the feminist movement has contributed to encouraging this, especially in women. At the same time, many people are feeling more alienated – less connected to one another, and more con-cerned that their destinies are not in their own hands. Social conditions have changed, and our personalities have changed with them.

These three forms of environmental influence laid out here – socialization, stressful life events, and changes in social roles or conditions – offer a way to think about and account for some of the rank-order instability and absolute changes in personality that we discussed earlier. It is also possible that some personality change is at least partially self-initiated rather than merely responding to environment influences. Many people report undergoing a relatively sudden change, akin to a conversion experience, in which they believed their personality to be transformed by a new insight or sense of meaning. Although these experiences often appear to be provoked by a particular event, and by a pre-existing state of emotional distress, it would be a mistake to see them merely as passive reactions to external conditions, or to doubt their validity too strenuously. They may indeed be perfectly real and lasting, however rare: psychotherapists certainly hope so! It is clearly possible for personalities to change, even in adulthood, and just as we now recognize the forces that hold them steady, we are also beginning to understand the sources of instability.

Illustrative study: how do personality traits change over time?

American psychologists Brent Roberts and colleagues (Roberts, Walton, & Viechtbauer, 2006) set out to describe patterns of **mean-level change** in major personality traits. They employed a statistical methodology known as 'meta-analysis', which allows researchers to combine the findings of existing studies in a rigorous, quantitative fashion. They thoroughly combed the literature for studies that reported mean-level change information, and managed to locate 92 of them. They then carefully read the studies to extract information about the extent of change observed in different age ranges for six personality traits (i.e., essentially the Big Five but with extraversion divided into 'social vitality' and 'social dominance' facets).

The findings of this meta-analysis revealed systematic patterns of change from adolescence to old age. Levels to conscientiousness, social dominance, and emotional stability tend to increase with age, although most strongly in young adulthood. Levels of agreeableness increase only in old age. Levels of openness to experience and social vitality tend to rise in adolescence, only to fall again in later life. These findings add to the growing evidence that personality traits are malleable and follow predictable trajectories over time. This evidence is especially noteworthy because – thanks to meta-analysis – it is based on a diverse assortment of studies with an enormous combined sample of 50,120 participants.

TEMPERAMENT AND PERSONALITY

At this point you should have an appreciation of the ways in which personality both changes over time and remains consistent, and of the factors that influence continuity and change. However, all of these ideas about the trajectory of personality through time assume that personality itself is essentially the same sort of thing throughout the life-span. To be able to say that the average level of Extraversion decreases over the course of adulthood, or that it shows moderate rank-order stability from the teens to the 30s, requires that Extraversion be a meaningful personality trait throughout this period. If this were not the case, comparisons of 'Extraversion' over time would be invalid in a very basic way. So is it true that personality structure – the basic organization of individual differences – is constant through the life-span?

Let's think more about Extraversion, and assume for the minute that it is a valid personality factor from adolescence to senescence. Would the kinds of behaviour that express or exemplify it be the same in a 15-year-old as in a 75-year-old? On the one hand, many behavioural characteristics might well be equally expressive of Extraversion at both ends of this age spectrum, perhaps including talkativeness, number of friends, activity level, and interpersonal dominance. Remember that this does not imply the same absolute levels of these characteristics in extraverted people of each age. On the other hand, there would surely also be age differences in the behavioural manifestations of Extraversion. Teenagers are unlikely to express gregariousness by attending bingo games, or older people to express high energy levels by participating in team sports.

These differences in the behaviours that express traits at different ages can make the task of longitudinal comparison somewhat tricky. However, they do not necessarily cast doubt on a trait's continued reality or its validity as a basis for comparison. For example, if factor analyses of age-relevant behaviours in samples of teenagers reveal a factor that closely resembles one obtained in similar studies of older adults, it would be difficult to deny that the factor corresponds to essentially the same trait at both ages. This would be true even if the specific behaviours that define the factors in the two age groups differ somewhat. What matters is simply that broadly equivalent forms of behaviour define the factors at both times (e.g., the factors both encompass gregariousness, expressed in characteristically adolescent or elderly ways).

The idea that the same dimensions capture variations in personality from adolescence to old age is probably not very controversial to you. But what if we move from adolescence back to infancy, and compare babies' personalities with adults'. Do babies even have 'personalities'? It is certainly hard to imagine that systems of personality description like the Big Five can make much sense of infant behaviour. Conscientiousness would not seem to be a promising way to describe differences among little savages who lack consciences, and the relevance of Openness to Experience to creatures whose lives revolve around sucking, sleeping, screaming, and excreting is questionable.

Nevertheless, as any parent will tell you, each infant comes into the world with its own distinctive behavioural style. Far from being, as the English philosopher John Locke imagined, a blank slate (*'tabula rasa'*), waiting for experience to inscribe a distinctive psychological signature on its emptiness, a baby has individuality from birth. Some rarely cry, sleep long and with regularity, and reward any face with a smile, while others fuss and scream constantly, sleep without consistency, and cry, turn purple, and grow little horns on their foreheads when they lay eyes on a friendly stranger.

Behavioural tendencies such as these – with the possible exception of horn-growth – are normally thought of as variations of temperament rather than personality. This distinction is usually based on an understanding that temperament is early-appearing, biologically grounded, and primarily related to emotional response. Our earlier question about the continuity of personality structure therefore becomes a matter of determining how temperament in infancy and early childhood is associated with adult personality. Despite appearances, the structure of temperament might map straightforwardly onto the structure of personality. Alternatively, the basic dimensions of temperament might show little correspondence with systems like the Big Five, just as the characteristics on which caterpillars differ are not the same as those that differentiate butterflies. (In a sense babies are, after all, human larvae.)

Numerous researchers have examined the structure of temperament in babies and young children. Their task is importantly different from that of the psychologists who pioneered the analysis of adult personality structure. Because infants and young children cannot rate one another's temperaments or complete self-report questionnaires, researchers must rely on ratings made by adults, usually parents or the researchers themselves. These methodological constraints present challenges, but a great deal of progress has been made in mapping temperament in spite of them. At first blush, some of these maps seem to bear little relationship to the broad adult personality factors that make up the Big Five or Big Three. Temperament researchers have identified dimensions such as distractibility, activity level, sensory sensitivity, attention span, and rhythmicity (i.e., the degree of regularity in the infant's sleeping, eating, and habits). None of these seem to have obvious parallels in adult trait dimensions.

The existence of apparently childhood-specific dimensions suggests that the structure of child temperament may differ substantially from the structure of adult personality. Research presents a more balanced picture. Martin, Wisenbaker, and Huttunen (1994) reviewed several factor-analytic studies of

Table 7.1 *Replicated child temperament factors, behaviours that illustrate them, and associated adult personality factors*

Temperament Factor	Illustrative Behaviour	Associated Personality Factor
Activity Level	shows vigorous motor activity	Extraversion
Negative Emotionality	reacts intensely to upsets	Neuroticism
Task Persistence	is attentive and endures frustration	Conscientiousness
Adaptability	adjusts quickly and easily to change	Agreeableness + low Neuroticism
Inhibition	avoids novel situations	low Extraversion + Neuroticism
Biological Rhythmicity	has regular sleeping habits	none
Biological Threshold	is highly sensitive to new foods	none

child temperament and found that seven dimensions emerged repeatedly. These, and the adult personality factors with which they appear to be associated, are presented in Table 7.1.

Table 7.1 indicates that, despite appearances, the structure of temperament in childhood may be not so very different from the structure of adult personality traits. Three replicated temperament factors are clearly related to a single factor of the Big Five, although you should note that Activity Level is only one component of adult Extraversion. Two more temperament factors seem to be related to combinations of Big Five factors. Openness is alone among the Big Five in having no associated temperament dimension. Only biological rhythmicity and threshold seem to have no clearly corresponding adult dimensions. This may be because the variations that they capture – how well established daily cycles are and how sensitive people are to sensory stimuli – are developmentally relevant only to infants. These temperament factors also may not have sufficiently extensive behavioural implications in adulthood to emerge as broad personality dimensions.

A reasonable conclusion to draw from research on the structure of temperament is that it does not differ radically from the structure of adult personality, as represented by broad trait factors. There are differences, to be sure, and the pathways that lead from childhood temperament dimensions to adult personality factors are indistinct at times. For example, we don't know how and when Openness emerges, or whether biological threshold vanishes as a meaningful dimension at some stage of development. However, the structure of individual differences seems to be more stable over the course of development than it is unstable. Generally speaking, similar dimensions endure throughout life, even if, as we saw earlier, they are exemplified by different behaviours at different ages and individuals do not always occupy enduring positions on them.

PERSONALITY DEVELOPMENT

So far in this chapter we have focused most of our attention on change and stability in traits, with an emphasis on the broad factors identified by trait psychologists. However, these broad traits might not tell the whole story about personality change, continuity, and development. If you cast your mind back to McAdams' (1995) critique of trait psychology, you will remember that he identified levels of personality description beyond traits. For instance, he identified a level of 'personal concerns', such as motives, values, strivings, developmental issues, and life tasks. Such concerns, he argued, are more tied than traits are to specific contexts, such as particular social roles or stages of life. Consequently, McAdams suggested, the trait level of description might be the level on which the stability of personality is the most evident. Perhaps, then, a fuller picture of personality change and development might come from examining personal concerns. That is, there might be ways of thinking about personality that permit subtle – or even not-so-subtle – changes to be observed even in the face of trait stability.

Relatively little research has been conducted on the stability or change of personal concerns. However, theorists have made a variety of proposals about how such concerns might tend to undergo distinct shifts over the course of the lifespan. The best-known of these theorists is Erik Erikson, who proposed that personality development consists of the person's navigation through eight distinct stages of life, each with its defining theme or issue. By this account, personality change is a basic fact of life and continues through the adult years rather than ceasing at age 30 as trait psychologists tend to maintain. Moreover, this change is not simply a gradual process of increase or decrease in certain characteristics, but reflects instead a series of qualitative transformations as the person moves from one stage to another. This is truly a different way of thinking about personality development and change.

Erikson is a romantic and charismatic figure in the history of personality psychology. Born in Germany to Danish parents, he travelled widely as a young man and subsequently moved to the USA, along the way adopting a surname that indicates his sense of self-creation (Erik son of Erik). His professional life was unusually broad, including teaching children, training as a psychoanalyst with Freud's daughter Anna in Vienna, conducting research on Native American children, and writing psychologically informed biographies of historical figures such as Mahatma Gandhi and Martin Luther. Although deeply influenced by psychoanalytic theory, he departed from it by focusing on the entirety of the life cycle and on the social and cultural aspects of psychological development rather than its sexual dimensions. Thus, his account of personality development proposes 'psychosocial' stages extending into old age rather than the Freudian stages of 'psychosexual' development that extend no further than childhood. Each of Erikson's stages deserves its own brief explanation.

Basic trust vs. basic mistrust

The first stage covers the period of infancy that corresponds to Freud's oral stage. Rather than focusing attention on the baby's sensuality, however, Erikson concerns himself with its sense of being consistently and sensitively cared for by parenting figures. Basic trust, trust that one's needs will be looked after and that the world itself is a beneficent place, arises when the infant comes to believe in the reliability and familiarity of these figures, in the continuity and stable routine that they bring to its life. By Erikson's account, successful resolution of this stage confers on the infant the beginnings of a sense of coherent selfhood and a capacity for hope. Difficulties in the stage, in contrast, leave the person vulnerable to serious mental disorders.

Autonomy vs. shame and doubt

Erikson's second stage again represents a re-framing of a Freudian stage, in this case the anal stage, which roughly corresponds to the toddler period. It is set in motion by the young child's maturing musculature, and the increased capacity for independent and freely chosen physical activity that it allows. The child strives to express its new capabilities, and does so with a will to master new actions. At the same time, it is being socialized by its parents and others, who communicate to it expectations that certain behaviours are forbidden and that self-restraint must be practised. If this socialization is carried out in a way that allows the child to exercise and take pride in its capacities and learn self-control, a sense of personal autonomy emerges. If, on the other hand, the child's behaviour and will are suppressed by overly harsh, constraining, or critical parenting, the child becomes vulnerable to feelings of shame, humiliation, and self-doubt. A 'precocious conscience' develops that takes a critical and belittling stance towards the child's behaviour, and may lead it to behave in an over-controlled way.

Initiative vs. guilt

In the third stage, the child ideally develops a capacity to pursue goals in a purposeful, future-oriented, and planful manner. Adding to its capacity for autonomous action, it sets tasks and goals, usually in the form of play activities, and strives to accomplish them. According to Erikson, however, children may have their capacities for initiative stifled by fears of punishment or by the guilt that they feel for pursuing their goals and tasks with too much aggression. Ideally, children emerge from this stage with a capacity for responsible striving that is regulated by social and moral obligations. Otherwise, children become inhibited, reluctant to engage in self-initiated activities for fear of breaking rules.

Industry vs. inferiority

Corresponding roughly to the school years, Erikson's fourth stage is a time when the child must learn to work in a determined and effective manner. During this stage the child's overarching task is to acquire specific socially-valued skills, many of which require prolonged effort and practice for mastery. Children who accomplish this task have developed a sense of industriousness, diligence, and, most of all, competence. Those who do not succeed at this task develop a sense of being incapable. This is not only a matter of lacking a sense of personal mastery, but also involves a comparison with others on a hierarchy of competence, so that people who feel incapable also feel socially inferior.

Identity vs. identity confusion

To many, Erikson is best known for his analysis of 'identity', by which he meant a sense of being a unique individual with a meaningful role to play in society and life. For Erikson, identity in this sense was not a given but a developmental achievement and milestone, which was the consuming task of his fifth stage. Located roughly during adolescence, the stage involves the gradual development of a coherent sense of personal goals, motives, interests, tastes, and social roles: in short, a worked-through sense of who one is as a distinctive, self-reflective, and future-oriented being. This identity often incorporates an image of the sort of work one will do as an adult. To Erikson, achieving identity was the primary struggle in the transition from childhood to adulthood, and laid the foundation for the adolescent's full participation in adult life. Adolescents who have difficulty with this struggle suffer 'identity confusion', a sense of emptiness, alienation, and being stuck due to having no clear and unifying picture of one's self and one's future. Others, Erikson argued, escape this state of confusion by prematurely opting for a relatively unexamined identity. These 'foreclosers' often organize their identities around a particular vocational goal, in which their identity is submerged. Erikson maintained that an exploratory period in which alternative roles, personal styles, and interests are 'tried on for size' is developmentally superior to foreclosure. He noted approvingly how the university years served for many as a 'moratorium' period, a postponement of normal adult life, in which such an exploration of possible identities could be pursued. How well this image matches the modern, vocationally-oriented university is perhaps debatable.

Intimacy vs. isolation

Ideally with a bedrock sense of identity established, the young adult moves into Erikson's sixth stage, in which the primary task is to form relationships that are loving, intimate, committed, and lasting. Such relationships provide a solid foundation for productive work and the rearing of children. Sexuality is a fundamental component of these relationships, but it is no longer based simply on pleasure and self-exploration, as in earlier stages. Instead, it is part of a deeper pattern of mutuality that amounts to full life-partnership and shared identity. Faced with this challenge, the person may withdraw into isolation and self-absorption out of a fear that being intimate and committed to another person entails a dangerous loss of personal identity. Needless to say, if the previous stage has not supplied the person with a solid sense of identity this vulnerability or 'ego loss' may be particularly intense and the avoidance of intimacy particularly desperate. Such a person may either directly avoid all close relationships, or may engage in them in shallow, self-centred, or self-sabotaging ways which ensure that no deep mutuality develops.

Generativity vs. stagnation

With the seventh stage we enter the mid-life years, whose prominent themes, according to Erikson, have to do with generating. This is not understood in the limited sense of production at work, but also includes the bringing into existence of children, ideas, artistic creations, and social arrangements. For Erikson, generativity did not consist of merely piling up accomplishments, driven by conventional success or self-aggrandizement, but of showing care to others by contributing to the continuance and advancement of one's society and culture. Generative people invest their energies, and the accumulated skill and wisdom that their life experience has given them, in making meaningful contributions to the wider world. People who lack a sense that they are making meaningful contributions, whether because their efforts to produce are directed only towards personal advancement or because their efforts to contribute are stifled, risk feeling that their life's work is meaningless drudgery. A pervasive sense of being 'stuck', stagnant, and unfulfilled results, even in people whose careers seem on the surface to be distinguished by great success.

Integrity vs. despair

The task of the final stage of development is to achieve a sense that one's life, now nearing its end, had a deeper order and meaning. To Erikson, this sense of coherence went well beyond a self-satisfied belief that one's life had gone well. Instead, it involved a deep acceptance of the entirety of this life, with all its pains, failures, and disappointments, and an understanding that it had meaning of a sort that transcends individual lives. People who achieve integrity have a detached and wise understanding of their place in a wider scheme of things, which might or might not be understood in spiritual terms, and a recognition that their life was part of the continuing story of human history. People who fail to reach this sort of integrity and understanding experience a sense of existential despair and emptiness. They believe that their life had no greater meaning outside of its specific details, and know that it is too late to go back and relive their lives differently. For them, death is feared or grimly surrendered to rather than accepted.

By Erikson's account, these 'eight ages of man' reflect a maturational blueprint or timetable, a series of stages through which people can be expected to progress as they grow older. However, successful resolution of each stage is far from certain. People negotiate each stage, and the developmental task it represents, with more or less favourable outcomes. Ideally, they lay down solid foundations of basic trust, autonomy, initiative, and so on. However, if people have difficulty navigating a stage's shoals, their personalities will be marked by the stage's characteristic weaknesses. Failure to achieve a sense of personal autonomy in early childhood creates a fault-line in the personality that might be cracked open under stress in later life, leaving the person prone to shame and intense self-doubt. Erikson did not insist that such weaknesses could not be overcome by corrective experiences in later stages, but he argued that failure to resolve one stage would be likely to endanger the resolution of later stages. Lacking a sense of personal autonomy, someone would be expected to have difficulty establishing a sense of industry, identity, and generativity, for instance. Thus, each successive stage builds on those that came before.

Why would someone have difficulty negotiating a stage? According to Erikson, successful and unsuccessful passage through a stage depends crucially on the quality of help that the person's environment – social, cultural, and physical – provides. The immediate environment of the family is especially important in the earlier stages. A sense of trust develops, he argued, primarily out of the infant's perception that its needs are reliably and sensitively nurtured by its caregivers. Conversely, inadequate, cold, chaotic, or overly rigid caregiving will leave a psychic scar of mistrust. The school environment will have a major role in determining a child's successful achievement of a sense of industry, for example. And the opportunities that the workplace environment affords may be particularly critical for establishing a sense of generativity.

However, Erikson's analysis of the factors that enable or impede personality development did not focus exclusively on people's immediate social surrounds. He also drew attention to the forces and trends of the culture at large. If a culture's standard child-rearing practices do not provide the sort of responsiveness that Erikson believed to be crucial to the infant's maturational needs, patterns of mistrustfulness might characterize personality formation in that culture. If a culture offers no space for its youth to explore alternative ways of being before submitting to the discipline of the workplace, then its adults could be expected to lack a deep sense of self-coherence. Similarly, if cultures fail to provide their adults with avenues for productive work and service to others, then a widespread sense of stagnation can be expected.

Note how this analysis can be extended to a comparison of historical periods *within* a culture. Erikson's account implies that personalities will tend to take predictably different forms as social and cultural transformations produce different environments for personality development. Increased access to higher education over the past century in many industrialized societies should have produced changes in their members' sense of self and identity over that time. (And perhaps the increasingly vocational, career-focused quality of much higher education is pushing the pendulum back again.) Great shifts over the same period in societal expectations about how parents should interact with young children should have produced additional changes. Decreased levels of authoritarian parenting should, by Erikson's account, have given children more beneficial opportunities to exercise and develop their personal autonomy, with potentially huge implications for the society that these children made as adults.

To many psychologists the openness of Erikson's understanding of personality development, the way it encompasses history, culture, society, and the lifespan, is very attractive. It is a rich and complex account, unlike the economical but static and reductive descriptive grids offered by trait psychology. However, richness and complexity have their price, and this includes the greater difficulty of pinning down and studying Eriksonian concepts. It is harder to rigorously assess people's developmentally-linked preoccupations – reflecting subtle life themes about which they may lack introspective awareness – than it is to assess standard traits with self-report questionnaires. Consequently, less research has been done on personality development from Erikson's perspective than on the stability of trait dimensions, and it has been less validated. Some supporting research has been conducted, however. For example, McAdams, de St. Aubin, and Logan (1993) found that generativity themes were more prominent in the personal strivings and autobiographical scripts of people in middle age than in those of younger and older adults. Other studies (e.g., Stewart, Franz, & Layton, 1988) have found evidence of increased intimacy and generativity concerns, and decreasing identity concerns, over the course of adulthood, again in general support of Erikson's approach. Nevertheless, this approach remains less a body of scientifically validated fact than a fruitful set of concepts for making sense of development and personality change.

How can we reconcile Erikson's portrayal of personality development as constant transformation with the trait psychology picture of considerable stability? The first thing to remember here is that there may not be much conflict to reconcile: the first five of Erikson's eight stages take place in the years over which longitudinal studies show only moderate trait stability. A second consideration is that Erikson's stage theory is more relevant to absolute than to rank-order stability: it is a theory of the normal changes that differentiate the personalities of people of different ages. The same people might tend to have relatively successful resolutions of successive stages (i.e., rank-order stability) even while different themes characterize their personalities at each stage (absolute instability). Indeed, Erikson's notion that resolution of each stage lays a foundation for resolution of the next implies just such rank-order stability: the same people who do well in one stage are likely to do well in the next.

The most important consideration, however, is that Erikson's stage theory and trait psychology operate at different levels of analysis. In McAdams' (1995) terms, the characteristic themes or preoccupations of each stage are level 2 'personal concerns' rather than level 1 traits. Eriksonian themes are more fine-grained, more difficult to identify with particular patterns of behaviour, more subtly qualitative, more contextualized by social experience and time of life. They are the sorts of personality characteristics that seem to be more changeable by nature, more responsive to new life situations and people's changing sense of self than the broad, basic tendencies embodied by the Big Five or Big Three. But this does not mean that the two languages of analysis and description – traits and Eriksonian themes – are unrelated. For instance, someone who lacks basic trust would be expected to score low on Agreeableness. Themes of industry surely have something to do with Conscientiousness or Constraint, as do themes of identity with Openness. Perhaps Erikson's stages give us a way to think about how our basic underlying dispositions are manifested in, and to some extent moulded by, changing patterns of developmentally-specific and socially-shaped lived experience. That's an ugly mouthful to say, but you should say it a couple of times to digest it anyway. Ugly or not, it may come closer to the truth than simply opting for one approach – the stability of traits versus the instability of personal preoccupations – and neglecting the other.

CONCLUSIONS: WHY DO PERSONALITY STABILITY AND CHANGE MATTER?

This chapter has examined a range of questions about personality change and continuity. These issues are so interesting because they are so central to our worldviews and to the basic assumptions we hold about human nature. You may have noticed that the theories we reviewed in the second part of this book take positions on the malleability of personality. Biological approaches, especially those based on behavioural genetics, tend to emphasize stability, seeing personality development largely as the unfolding of innate behavioural tendencies mediated by brain processes that are beyond conscious control.

Psychoanalytic theories tend to take an equally sceptical approach to personality change, but for different reasons. Adult personality is seen as being substantially determined by childhood experiences within the family. In addition, personality is conceptualized as a set of hard-won compromises between desires and defences, and any modification of this balance of opposed forces is resisted by fiercely conservative psychological defences.

In contrast with biological and psychoanalytic approaches, cognitive theories imply that personality is changeable. If personality is made up of ways of perceiving, thinking, and believing, then it should be modifiable by any of the processes by which cognitions change: trial-and-error learning, insight, imitation, education. The behaviourist approach from which cognitive psychology split off was even more consistent with malleability. If behaviour is governed by its consequences, as behaviourists believed, then all it should take for personality to change is for the pattern of rewards and punishments that the person receives to be altered. If these 'reinforcement contingencies' can be changed, by having people expose themselves to different environments or by engineering their environments to respond to them differently, then their dispositions should also change.

None of these theoretical approaches take absolute positions. Even the strongest advocate of the biological basis of personality might allow that personality can change in response to pharmaceutical treatment – as in the 'cosmetic' personality change some writers attribute to drugs like Prozac – or that our genetic inheritance dictates patterns of personality change over time. (After all, genes govern the transformations our bodies undergo as we mature, not just how we differ in enduring ways from one another.) Psychoanalysts argue that personality can change after gruelling years of psychoanalytic treatment. Likewise, cognitivists recognize that the cognitive system is conservative, often resisting change by ignoring information that challenges it or assimilating it to established ways of thinking. And behaviourism faltered partly because it had trouble accounting for the resistance of some behaviours to change in response to new patterns of reward and punishment. Nevertheless, the evidence we have considered regarding personality change and stability has definite implications for the personality theories we hold.

People have worldviews, just as theories do. If your worldview is primarily cynical, tragic, or pessimistic you will probably believe that people don't really change, and that they have an essential nature that is determined once and for all by their early life circumstances, their biology, or their existential predicament. If your worldview is more optimistic, romantic, or otherwise sunny, you will probably have faith in the power of people to change, overcoming obstacles and flaws along the path to self-improvement or fulfilment. The evidence of this chapter is highly relevant to these deep, often unacknowledged ways of looking at the world, and offer some support for both positions. Personality is both resistant to change and capable of it: it shows inertia in some respects, such as the relative stability of fundamental, highly heritable traits, and transformation in others, such as the changing identity themes that Erikson brought to light.

Some interesting research has investigated people's beliefs about personality change and stability. Carol Dweck and her colleagues (e.g., Dweck, 1999; Levy, Plaks, Hong, Chiu, & Dweck, 2001) have studied people's 'person theories', by which they mean core assumptions about human nature. They contrast people whose theories are 'static', implying that human attributes are fixed, as distinct from 'dynamic', implying malleability. They have found that people who hold static views – 'entity theories' – are more prone to exaggerate differences between groups to which they belong and other groups, and to endorse stereotypic beliefs about people in these groups. They are more likely to attribute group differences to innate factors, to avoid outgroup members, and to be more prejudiced. The implications of entity theories may also extend to how people think about themselves as well as others. Research suggests that entity theorists will be less likely to try to change undesirable aspects of their own behaviour. All of these findings suggest that apparently abstract, almost philosophical beliefs about human nature have very real implications for how we think and behave as social creatures. If we believe that people are not malleable, even if this belief is a tacit assumption that we barely recognize, we tend to see the social world as composed of fixed entities whose behaviour is driven by enduring internal dispositions. We correspondingly under-estimate the extent to which other people's behaviour – and perhaps our own as well – springs from social influences, the demands of the situation, or mental processes. This seems to be a recipe for an unfortunate lack of empathy and humanity towards those who are different from us.

Of course, even if it is true that holding a static view of personality may have some undesirable social consequences, this view still has some truth to it. With any luck, this chapter has given you a picture of the state of scientific knowledge about the malleability of personality, a picture that doesn't permit any extreme position on the issue. Perhaps the chapter may even lead you to consider your own beliefs about the fixedness of human nature, and their possible implications.

Chapter summary

- By definition, personality is at least somewhat stable over time, but how stable it is remains an important research and theoretical question.

(Continued)

(Continued)

- Longitudinal studies suggest high levels of 'rank-order stability' – stability in people's positions on trait dimensions relative to their peers – of personality traits, especially in adulthood. This stability may reflect a variety of genetic and environmental factors, and it increases with age.
- Studies of 'mean-level change' – change in the average level of traits from one age to another – demonstrate that personality is also malleable. Studies reveal predictable trajectories of mean-level change over the adult life-span, as well as changes from one historical period to another.
- Personality develops out of temperament, and there appear to be several meaningful continuities between dimensions of infant and child temperament and adult personality trait factors.
- Personality development cannot be reduced entirely to mean-level change in temperament or personality dimensions. Theorists such as Erikson propose that different stages of life involve different themes and concerns.
- The malleability or fixity of personality matters for psychological theory and practice. It may even matter in everyday thinking: people who believe personality is fixed tend to stereotype others.

Further Reading

- Caspi, A., Roberts, B.W., & Shiner, R.L. (2005). Personality development: Stability and change. *Annual Review of Psychology, 56*, 453–84.

Caspi and colleagues are perhaps the foremost researchers on personality change and stability, and this review article presents the state of the art in this field.

- Dweck, C.S. (1999). *Self-theories: Their role in motivation, personality, and development.* Philadelphia, PA: Psychology Press.

Dweck pioneered the study of people's beliefs about the stability vs. malleability of human attributes, such as intelligence and personality, and this book reviews the many implications of these different 'self-theories'.

(Continued)

(Continued)

- Erikson, E.H. (1963). *Childhood and society* (2nd ed.). New York: W.W. Norton.

Erikson's account of personality development is no longer influential or fashionable, but it remains interesting for readers who want an intimate portrait of different stages of life rather than a dry review of empirical studies.

- Heatherton, T.F., & Weinberger, J.L. (Eds.) (1994). *Can personality change?* Washington, DC: American Psychological Association.

This book contains a fascinatingly diverse assortment of chapters addressing personality change and stability.

- Roberts, B.W., Walton, K.E., & Viechtbauer, W. (2006). Patterns of mean-level change in personality traits across the life course: A meta-analysis of longitudinal studies. *Psychological Bulletin, 132,* 1–25.

This recent study complements the Srivastava et al. (2003) article discussed in the current chapter, combining many previous studies to show how mean levels of the major personality dimensions tend to change over the adult life-span.

- Shoda, Y., Mischel, W., & Peake, P.K. (1990). Predicting adolescent cognitive and self-regulatory competencies from preschool delay of gratification: Identifying diagnostic conditions. *Developmental Psychology, 26,* 978–86.

Shoda and colleagues describe some of their work on the remarkable ability of childhood delay of gratification to predict important life outcomes in adolescence and early adulthood.

- Srivastava, S., John, O.P., Gosling, S.D., & Potter, J. (2003). Development of personality in early and middle adulthood: Set like plaster or persistent change? *Journal of Personality and Social Psychology, 84,* 1041–53.

Srivastava et al.'s paper describes a huge cross-sectional internet-based study of personality which revealed predictable patterns of change of the five personality factors.

- Twenge, J.M., & Campbell, W.K. (2001). Age and birth cohort differences in self-esteem: A cross-temporal meta-analysis. *Personality and Social Psychology Review, 5,* 321–44.

This meta-analytic study demonstrates the striking rise in average self-esteem over the past few decades (at least among American undergraduates), and provides some evidence on what may be responsible for this increase.

8

The Assessment of Personality

Learning objectives

- To appreciate the complexities involved in the assessment of personality.
- To understand psychometric 'validity' and 'reliability', the basic concepts that define the quality of personality measurement.
- To recognize the strengths and weaknesses of alternative forms of personality assessment: interviews, inventories, and projective methods.
- To develop a basic understanding of alternative assessment methods.
- To recognize the difficulties involved in drawing valid inferences from personality test data.

This chapter examines the methods psychologists have developed for measuring individual differences in personality. Desirable psychometric features of assessment methods – the various forms of test validity and reliability – are outlined, and a number of popular assessment methods are reviewed. The strengths and weaknesses of interviews, personality inventories, and projective tests are discussed, followed by two interesting but less commonly employed alternative assessment methods. Finally, we examine some of the problems associated with the use of personality assessment data in making judgments about people.

At this point in the book you could be forgiven for thinking that psychologists are interested in personality only for the purposes of academic research and theorizing. However, this view is quite mistaken. In the course of their professional activities, many psychologists apply personality theory and research in a wide variety of practical contexts. Industrial and organizational psychologists frequently take personality into account in personnel selection, looking for dependable employees who will not steal, be frequently absent, or cause accidents and disciplinary problems. Counselling psychologists assess their clients' personalities when advising them about career choices or solutions to life problems. Clinical psychologists often try to improve their understanding and treatment of their patients by evaluating the personality traits and dynamics in which their symptoms are embedded.

If personality information is to be used in any of these applied settings, psychologists must have systematic procedures for obtaining it. As you may have guessed from the title of this chapter, the development of assessment procedures is a major preoccupation of personality psychologists. Over the years, a huge variety of methods has emerged for assessing personality characteristics, and many psychologists have devoted themselves to studying the complex issues surrounding personality measurement. In this chapter, we will explore the alternative methods of personality assessment that are available and consider their advantages and disadvantages. Before examining the details of these methods, however, it is useful to step back for a little while and consider the broader aims of personality measurement.

MEASURING PERSONALITY

At first blush, the thought of measuring something as elusive as personality may seem foolish or even absurd, like trying to take the temperature of happiness or to weigh beauty. After all, personality characteristics are not quantities that can be directly perceived, and often they seem to be more like concepts dreamed up in the minds of psychological theorists than attributes of actual people. We also know that two people can often have quite different opinions about the personality of a shared acquaintance, suggesting that judgments of personality are quite subjective. In short, personality characteristics appear on the surface to be unlikely candidates for measurement because they are unobservable, because they are theoretical 'constructs', and because they are in the eye of the beholder. For these reasons the general public is often sceptical about the idea of measuring personality and other psychological variables, imagining that it amounts to measuring the unmeasurable.

But is this scepticism about psychological measurement justified? Strictly speaking it isn't. All that is required for something to be measurable is for it to vary in detectable ways and for there to be some sensible procedure for assigning numbers to these variations. If some phenomenon varies by degrees then it can, in principle, be measured. People usually seem quite comfortable judging one person to have more of a certain personality characteristic than another for instance, to be more outgoing or hostile or rigid – so there is no rea-

quantified.

psychology that personality ment, or 'psychometrics', has discipline, and psychologists entific understanding. Instead sychologists argue, we should us empirical research. That is, lity measurements?

, and psychologists have paid eaks the issue of measurement mponents: *reliability* and *valid-* h reliable and valid. These two

asure, the extent to which its characteristic being measured. ree main varieties: consistency f the measure ('internal consis- different users of the measure nsistency over time in people's To the extent that these forms of rs from what psychologists call efore one that enables relatively nt components hang together in , it yields highly similar scores ides consistent scores from one easure is one whose components es when administered by differ- r over time. Such a measure has ot provide reliable information sychologists try to maximize test they correlate with one another, d in highly standardized ways to erent times.

Validity is another somewhat complicated concept, but it boils down to two questions: first, does a measure assess what it is intended to assess, and second, does it provide practically useful information? With regard to the first question, a valid measure is one that accurately reflects that psychological construct that it is supposed to measure. That is, a test of construct A should not in fact be measuring construct B or only measuring a portion of A. For example, a test of arrogance should not really measure self-esteem, and a test of general anxiousness should not only assess social anxiety. This kind of validity can be empirically demonstrated by showing that the measure correlates highly with other measures of the same construct (i.e., arrogance and anxiety ['convergent validity']) and does not correlate too highly with measures of distinct constructs (e.g., self-esteem and dominance on the one hand, depression and shyness on the other ['discriminant validity']). It can also be supported by showing that the content of the measure truly represents the construct of interest, rather than a related construct ('content validity').

With regard to the second question, a valid measure should yield information that enables psychologists to predict criteria that the construct should be associated with ('predictive validity' or 'criterion-related validity'). For example, a conscientiousness measure should be able to predict (i.e., correlate with) good work attendance, and a measure of trait anxiety should be able to distinguish patients suffering from anxiety-related disorders from those suffering from other disorders. Clearly measures that cannot predict real-life criteria such as these are practically useless. It is also worth noting that a measure that does not assess its intended construct – the first kind of invalidity – is unlikely to be able to predict criteria that the construct is associated with. For example, a test of 'conscientiousness' that actually measures the willingness to lie about one's virtuousness will probably not correlate with low absenteeism.

Reliability and validity are crucial psychometric properties of any assessment method. Without reliability and validity, assessments are incoherent, inaccurate, and practically ineffective. Fortunately, both can be established by empirical research on the correlations among measures and prediction criteria, and few measures are developed without attempting to maximize them. In addition to being individually crucial, the two properties are tightly linked such that validity cannot be high when reliability is low. That is, a measure that is inconsistent – one that is internally incoherent, yields different information to different examiners, and fluctuates over time – cannot predict validly. If assessment information is riddled with measurement error, that is, it has no practical value.

Let us briefly review our introductory discussions of personality measurement. They argued that personality characteristics are measurable in principle, and that we should take an empirical approach to the question of how well they are measured in practice. Although personality variables are unobservable, are often theoretical constructs, and are to some degree subjective, they can still be assessed rigorously and well. Unobservable variables and theoretical constructs are indispensable to scientific explanation, and some degree of subjectivity is inescapable. Careful evaluation of the reliability and validity of a personality measure can tell us how much assurance we can have in the information that it provides. If we want to have confidence in personality assessments, and to make practical judgments on the strength of them, then we need to establish their psychometric credentials.

INTERVIEW METHODS

One way to find out about another person is, of course, to talk to him or her. When this kind of conversation is formalized and used for the purpose of assessment it can be called an interview. Interviews have been a widely-used means of gathering personality information for some time, and have been especially popular in clinical settings, where psychologists and psychiatrists use them to diagnose mental disorders. Advocates of interviews argue that they are particularly effective assessment tools because they offer multiple sources of information about the person being assessed: their overt answers to questions, their appearance, and non-verbal signs such as intonation, facial expressions, and mannerisms. In addition, they maintain, interview methods enable skilled interviewers to explore areas of special interest in greater depth and with greater flexibility than other assessment methods allow, thereby providing a unique window on the person's universe.

Interviews vary widely in the extent to which they are standardized. In more 'free-form' interviews, interviewers are allowed to explore the domain to be assessed with as much flexibility in general approach and in the wording and order of questions as they wish. In more 'structured' interviews, interviewers are required to examine specified topics and to follow detailed instructions for question wording and order. 'Semi-structured' interviews permit an intermediate level of flexibility and organization. Psychoanalytically-oriented psychologists generally favour less-structured interviews, because they give interviewers the freedom to explore the person's conflicts, defences, and resistances in all their uniqueness. Researchers and non-psychodynamic psychologists tend to favour more structured interview methods because they yield more standardized and explicit information.

Varying degrees of interview standardization have been popular over the years. Recently, psychologists have come to favour more structured interviews, largely in response to research indicating that unstructured interviews are often unreliable. Different interviewers who assess the same person using these interviews frequently show poor levels of agreement. There are several reasons for this unreliability. First, if interviewers are given flexibility to explore the person, they will ask different questions and obtain different information on which to base their assessments. Second, by giving the interviewer more power to decide how to conduct the interview, unstructured interviews increase the likelihood that each interviewer's distinctive personal experiences and theoretical biases will distort their assessments. Third, unstructured interviews make it more likely that the person being assessed will be influenced by the interviewer's attributes – such as appearance, age, and personality – and therefore respond differently to different interviewers. More structured interviews restrict the role of the interviewer and focus on the standardized content of the questions, thereby reducing this kind of influence. In sum, unstructured interviews allow increased flexibility at a high cost: increased subjectivity and unreliability in assessment, and consequently reduced validity.

Interview methods face additional problems as assessment tools. First, they are often time-consuming, frequently requiring highly trained interviewers to spend long periods with each interviewee. Second, the reliability of interviews is often adversely affected by their inescapably social quality. Compared to more impersonal assessment methods such as paper-and-pencil or computerized tests, face-to-face interviews often make people more concerned about creating a positive impression and therefore more likely to distort their responses. In addition, the intimacy of the interview setting encourages a social psychological phenomenon known as the 'self-fulfilling prophecy'. This phenomenon works as follows: the interviewer subtly communicates his or her initial impressions to the interviewee, who responds in a corresponding way that confirms the interviewer's initial impressions. For instance, an interviewer who comes to the interview with an initially unfavourable impression of the interviewee – whether or not this impression is justified – may behave in a brisk, dismissive, or condescending way that makes the interviewee anxious, awkward, or angry, thereby 'confirming' the interviewer's negative judgment. Moreover, initial impressions seem to be overly influential in interviewers' assessments even if the self-fulfilling prophecy does not occur. Assessment methods that are more impersonal reduce the risk of these sources of unreliability. Finally, relatively few structured interviews have been developed for the assessment of personality characteristics, more attention having been paid to assessing the symptoms of mental disorders, so their effectiveness as assessment tools is still somewhat unproven.

In general, then, most personality psychologists do not hold interviews in very high esteem as assessment methods. They are usually considered to be too unreliable, too invalid, and too time-consuming. However, it is important to mention two exceptions to this negative verdict, in which interviews are still considered to be valuable sources of personality information. First, interview methods are still widely used by clinical psychologists when they diagnose 'personality disorders' (see Chapter 9). These disorders are difficult to assess because people who suffer from them are often poor judges of how they interact with and are perceived by others, and of how deviant and self-destructive their behaviour is. For this reason, it seems wise to employ a clinically skilled interviewer, who is given some flexibility to delve into the interviewee's ways of thinking and behaving while still following a standard series of questions to ensure reliability. Research tends to show that this sort of semi-structured interview yields a more reliable and valid assessment of personality disorders than other, less flexible methods of assessment.

A second domain in which interview methods seem to have special value is in the assessment of 'Type A' personality, which refers to a combination of traits including hostility, impatience, and competitive achievement striving (see Chapter 2). Type A personality appears to be particularly well assessed by an ingenious structured interview which illustrates the special possibilities of interviews as assessment devices. In this interview (Rosenman, 1978), the interviewee is asked a series of standard questions about Type A tendencies. However, the interviewer does not merely record the content of the interviewee's overt responses, but also notes properties of the person's speech that are indicative of Type A tendencies (e.g., its loudness, abruptness, speed, and explosiveness) and aspects of their general demeanour (e.g., boredom, irritability, and hostility). In addition, the interviewer deliberately tries to arouse hostility by sharply challenging or interrupting the interviewee's responses. Consequently, this interview combines self-report with behavioural observation, in a reasonably natural interpersonal situation where Type A behaviour might be manifested. Indeed, the interview appears to be a better way to assess Type A personality than alternative methods.

PERSONALITY INVENTORIES

Interviews generally allow some flexibility in how questions are worded, arranged, and answered. Personality inventories allow none. **Inventories** – also known as questionnaires or scales – present respondents with a standard list of printed statements, in a standard order, and with a fixed set of response options. Respondents use these options to express their agreement or disagreement with each item, usually with a pen or pencil. Their responses are assigned ratings which are summed over groups of items to yield numerical scores. At every step, that is, personality inventories are standardized.

Personality inventories were first developed by Sir Francis Galton in the late 19th century, and since then thousands have been constructed, especially since World War II. They have become the most numerous and widely employed form of personality measure, largely because they are relatively easy to develop and use. Although their basic format of item lists and explicit response options does not vary, they differ in two main ways. First, some inventories measure a single characteristic, whereas others use multiple scales to measure personality in a more comprehensive fashion. As a result, some single-trait inventories have as few as ten items, while other inventories may have more than 500 items distributed among more than 20 scales. Second, their response formats vary, with some inventories offering two verbal options (e.g., 'True/False') and others offering rating scales with as many as nine numbered options (e.g., from 1 'strongly disagree' to 7 'strongly agree').

The development of personality inventories is usually guided by some mixture of theoretical analysis and empirical research. Typically a large number of items are written to reflect a preliminary understanding of the construct or constructs to be measured. These provisional items are then pre-tested on a sample of respondents so that psychometrically stronger items can be selected and weaker ones eliminated. Items may be selected according to their ability to distinguish predefined groups, their consistency with other items, and their correspondence to latent variables identified by factor analysis (see Chapter 2). For instance, potential items for a hostility inventory might be eliminated if they fail to differentiate violent from non-violent criminals, if they fail to correlate with most other items, and if they are not associated with a factor which underlies most other items. Items that survive this statistical culling are usually combined to form the new inventory. This inventory is then administered to a new sample of respondents along with other measures, so that its validity can be established. In short, inventory construction is a heavily statistical process in which efforts are made to ensure the various forms of reliability and validity.

Personality inventories have a variety of practical advantages. Compared to interviews, they are easy and quick to administer and score. They are also highly efficient, in that they can be given to many people at once, and without an examiner present. Indeed, the administration and scoring of inventories are readily computerized, and programmes now exist that can generate interpretive reports for several of them. Compared to inventories, other assessment methods are cumbersome.

Inventories also have certain disadvantages. Because they rely on self-report, personality inventories are particularly vulnerable to what are known as **'response biases'**. Interviewers can probe and scrutinize the interviewee's responses for evidence of dishonesty and distortion, but inventories depend on the respondent to answer truthfully and sincerely. Several response biases have been identified, including 'yea-saying' (or 'acquiescence') and 'nay-saying' (tendencies to agree and disagree with test items regardless of their content); 'faking good' and 'faking bad' (tendencies to deceptively present the self in an overly favourable and unfavourable light); and 'social desirability' (the tendency to respond in socially approved ways, but without deceptive intent). Carelessness, the tendency to respond in an unconsidered or random fashion, can also be described as a bias. All of these biases weaken test validity because they reduce the extent to which test scores accurately reflect the respondent's standing on the disposition being measured.

Developers of personality inventories have usually been alert to response biases and the threat that they pose to validity, and often take active steps to counteract them. Yea-saying and nay-saying are easily neutralized by making sure that roughly equal numbers of items within a scale require agreement and disagreement to be scored in a certain direction. For example, 'I am very outgoing' and 'I dislike meeting new people' require different responses to indicate a consistent disposition, and a test will not ascribe such a disposition to people who consistently agree or disagree if both kinds of items are used. Other response biases can be detected using special 'validity scales'. Faking good and social desirability can be detected by 'lie scales' containing statements that only the most saintly among us could endorse or deny, such as 'I have never told a lie' and 'I never find dirty jokes amusing'. Subtler scales have also been developed to pick up more sophisticated forms of positive self-presentation, such as guardedness and defensiveness. Faking bad, which commonly occurs in some clinical and legal settings where it is called 'malingering', can be assessed by scales containing a diverse variety of self-denigrating statements and psychological symptoms. Careless responding can be detected by scales that contain items that very few people answer in a particular way, so that someone who does so repeatedly is suspected of the bias. Alternatively, highly similar items can be repeated in the inventory, and inconsistent responses taken as evidence of carelessness. In short, self-report inventories can be protected against response biases. However, as it is often difficult to determine how to adjust test scores when a bias is detected, this protection is far from absolute.

PROJECTIVE METHODS

The preceding section argued that objective personality inventories have some attractive features, but are also subject to some potentially serious limitations. Standardized item wording and unambiguous response options improve the reliability of these measures, but they cannot ensure that people responding to them do so validly. People may display a variety of biases and respond dishonestly, defensively, and carelessly. It is understandable that people may respond in evasive or self-protective ways, especially when items ask them about unflattering or socially undesirable behaviour. Sophisticated validity scales can partially compensate for these response tendencies, but cannot eradicate them.

A second potential problem with self-report inventories is that they might not be able to assess some important personality characteristics. Inventories typically depend on respondents having some amount of introspective access to their dispositions and psychological processes. But what if some thoughts, feelings, desires, and motives are not readily available to the respondent's introspection? Any personality measure that directly asks people about these things might meet with the person's incomprehension, their guesses about how they ought to respond, or their distorted beliefs about what they are like. So are there some parts of our personality of which we are unaware, and about which it is pointless to question us?

As you know by now (see Chapter 5), one major strand of personality theory answers this last question with a resounding 'Yes'. Psychoanalytically-oriented psychologists argue that many parts of the human personality are inaccessible to conscious awareness, and consequently they tend to be sceptical of self-report personality inventories. In place of inventories, they have designed personality assessment methods that do not depend on the respondent's introspective awareness, and actively attempt to bypass it.

The methods that these psychologists have designed are quite diverse, but they all require people to respond in an open-ended way to a set of ambiguous stimuli. They are usually referred to as '**projective tests**' because they demand that respondents 'project' their distinctive ways of giving meaning to experience – including their conflicts, anxieties, defences, cognitive styles, and preoccupations – onto the stimuli. The most widely used projective tests require people to respond to ambiguous visual stimuli, such as ink-blots or pictures, or ambiguous verbal instructions, such as to draw an unspecified person or to complete an unfinished sentence. Because respondents do not know what characteristics these projective tests are intended to assess, and may have no introspective access to these characteristics in any case, advocates argue that projective tests can penetrate the surface of the personality and avoid the distortions and biases of inventories.

The best-known projective test is the Rorschach Ink-Blot Test, which was published by Swiss psychiatrist Hermann Rorschach in 1921 but was loosely based on a popular 19th-century European parlour game. The test uses ten standard ink-blots which are symmetrical around the vertical axis (i.e., the left and right sides are mirror images) and printed on cards. Some blots are monochromatic, some are multicoloured. Respondents are asked to tell the examiner what each blot looks like to them, giving multiple responses if they see more than one 'percept'. They are also interviewed to explain what features of the blot led them to each percept.

Many schemes for Rorschach interpretation and scoring have been developed, focusing on an enormous variety of response elements. For instance, inferences may be based on the *content* of responses, so that a negative self-image, depression, and suicidal propensities might be inferred if a respondent's percepts contain many morbid images of death, injury, and decay. (One must be careful here; the author once tested someone who repeatedly saw bones in the ink-blots, but who turned out to be an undepressed X-ray technician.) Some content inferences are fairly direct and obvious, as in the case of morbid imagery, but others may refer to symbolic meanings, so that a wild animal might be inferred to represent a respondent's father. In addition to content, inferences may also be based on the *formal properties* of responses. These include the degree to which percepts clearly make use of the contours of the blot, rather than being arbitrarily imposed on it, and the extent to which percepts integrate separate components of the blot into coherent scenarios. Further response properties that Rorschach interpreters often consider include perceptions of movement, texture, and depth, reactions to the coloured portions of the blots, and peculiarities in the wording of responses.

Another well-known projective test is the Thematic Apperception Test (TAT), which was developed by the American psychologist Henry Murray and his colleagues (1938). Like the Rorschach, the TAT uses images printed on a set of cards. Unlike ink-blots, however, these images are structured and meaningful; they are rather vague and ominous black-and-white pictures depicting people in a variety of indoor and outdoor scenes. The respondent's task is to look at each card and tell a story about what is happening, what led up to it, and what the people in the picture are thinking and feeling. These stories are usually interpreted by the psychologist in terms of the respondent's needs, preoccupations, defence mechanisms, and ways of understanding personal relationships (i.e., 'object relations'; see Chapter 5).

Although projective tests such as the Rorschach and the TAT have an attractive rationale – who could deny the appeal of laying bare the hidden organization of personality by evading the person's defences? – they have been subjected to severe criticism over the years. Some have objected to the fact that the projective test interpretation demands a theoretical orientation that is antithetical to many psychologists, requiring the use of psychoanalytic concepts, terms, and doctrines (e.g., the crucial importance of early relationships with parental figures). Others criticize the rationale for projective tests for assuming that one artificial task, such as peering at ink-blots, can adequately reveal the person's general ways of apprehending the world, if such a general style even exists. Projective tests take it for granted that people's habitual ways of making sense of themselves, their interpersonal relations, and their environments will be imposed on any ambiguous stimulus. From a practical viewpoint, projective tests have been criticized for being time-consuming to administer and score, compared to the speediness of self-report inventories. In addition, they are not completely immune to defensive and distorted responding, as respondents can refuse to engage fully with the task by giving brief, guarded, or flippant responses. There is also evidence that people can 'fake bad' on projective tests, and that they are often subtly influenced by random features of the testing situation (e.g., they are more likely to draw a figure with a moustache if the examiner has one).

The most damning criticisms of projective tests, however, have focused on their lack of reliability and validity. When systematic research has been carried out, it has generally found disappointing levels of agreement between different projective test interpreters, and inadequate prediction by them of important criteria such as psychiatric diagnosis, suicide potential, and responsiveness to therapy. In the same way that the subjectivity and lack of standardization of unstructured interviews reduce their reliability, the flexibility of projective test interpretation makes it unlikely that two psychologists will draw similar inferences from the same projective response. And if psychologists cannot agree on what inferences should be drawn from a certain response, then, as we have seen, their inferences will tend to be invalid. This implies that projective tests will not become practically useful – reliable and valid – until their interpretation is standardized. A recent, comprehensive review of projective techniques (Lilienfeld, Wood, & Garb, 2000) found that most measures based on projective tests either had inadequate validity or no scientific evidence of validity. Even standardized projective techniques tend to be no more valid than objective measures of the same constructs, and generally do not improve the prediction of important psychological phenomena (i.e., 'incremental validity') over and above these quicker and cheaper alternatives.

In response to these criticisms of projective tests, and the proliferation of alternative systems for interpreting them, one scoring system for the Rorschach test has been developed that is superior to its predecessors. This system, created by Exner (1986), uses explicit, standardized rules for scoring responses, thereby improving the inter-rater reliability of Rorschach information. In addition, research suggests that scores based on Exner's rules are valid predictors of several important psychological variables, such as suicide risk. These developments suggest that projective methods are capable of yielding reasonably reliable and valid personality information when they are scored in standardized and well-researched ways. On the other hand, Exner's system appears to purchase its reliability and validity at the expense of the usual rationale for projective testing: the interpretation of the person's unique psychodynamics. The personality characteristics that its improved scoring system assesses – such as stress tolerance, emotional responsiveness, coping style, social isolation, and passivity – do not require deep psychodynamic inferences, and can be readily assessed by non-projective methods, such as inventories. In short, although the Rorschach test is a fascinating assessment tool, efforts to make it reliable and valid seem to remove what is unique to it and to projective methods in general. When the test is turned into a standardized measure that yields well-normed scores for a few personality characteristics, it no longer allows the sort of interpretation that originally motivated the development of projective tests. Part of the problem here may be the intrinsic difficulty of assessing the kinds of 'deep' or 'hidden' personality characteristics that these tests try to assess. It may simply be harder to assess whether people have separation conflicts or unconscious fears of their fathers than it is to assess their levels of extraversion or shyness. It is easier to see clearly the fish that swim near the surface than the fearsome creatures that inhabit the murky depths.

Projective tests remain popular among some personality researchers, who are often attracted to the rich narrative data that people produce in response to the TAT cards. Rigorous coding schemes have been used, for example, to assess people's use of defence mechanisms (Cramer, 1998) and their motives (McClelland, 1985). The TAT and Rorschach tests are also still widely taught to American clinical psychologists. Nevertheless, the enthusiasm for projective tests that was widespread in the 1950s and 1960s has subsided as their psychometric limitations have become clear, as psychoanalytic approaches to personality have become less popular, and as a great assortment of easy-to-use personality inventories has become available. Considerations of reliability and validity have made psychologists more sceptical about the power of projective tests to reveal the hidden depths of the personality, and more modest about what projective assessment can and should try to accomplish.

Illustrative study: Measuring personality using implicit methods

Projective tests attempt to evade the distortions that can affect self-report, and to lay bare the hidden dynamics of personality. Unfortunately, they tend to suffer from some serious psychometric weaknesses. Recent approaches to the study of 'implicit' cognition – cognition that is automatic or outside of conscious control – may offer a more rigorous way of assessing personality free of self-report biases. One interesting study of personality using implicit cognition methods was conducted by German psychologists Melanie Steffens and Stefanie Schulze König (2006). Steffens and Schulze König gave 89 undergraduates a popular self-report measure of the five-factor model (FFM), a set of tasks intended to assess behaviour reflecting the five factors, and five versions of the Implicit Association Test (IAT: Greenwald, McGhee, & Schwartz, 1998).

(Continued)

(Continued)

The IAT is a computer-based method for assessing the 'automatic associations' that exist between concepts in people's memory. It works in an ingenious way. In one 'block' on an IAT, labels for a pair of concepts appear on the top left of the computer screen (say, 'Sweets' and 'Happiness') and another pair that are alternatives to those concepts appears on the top right (say, 'Vegetables' and 'Sadness'). A series of words then flash up in the centre of the screen, and the participant is instructed to categorize each one as belonging to the left or the right concepts as quickly as possible, by pressing response keys on the left or right of the keyboard. The words include examples of all four concepts, such as 'cake' and 'ice-cream', 'joyful' and 'jolly', 'carrot' and 'potato', and 'gloomy' and 'depressed', and are presented in a random order. In the second block of the IAT, the same words flash up but the concept labels have been switched. Now 'Sweets' is paired with 'Sadness' and 'Vegetables' is paired with 'Happiness', and the participant must again categorize the words into the left or right concepts. The computer records the person's reaction times for words in the two IAT blocks.

If the paired concepts are closely associated, then it should be easy to do the categorization task. If we associate 'Sweets' with 'Happiness', then we should be able to quickly distinguish words that exemplify either of these concepts (e.g., 'cake' and 'joyful') from those that exemplify the other concepts (e.g., 'carrot' and 'gloomy'). However, if the paired concepts are not closely associated, then the task becomes slow and difficult. Deciding whether a word exemplifies 'Sweets' or 'Sadness' vs. 'Vegetables' or 'Happiness' is not easy if, like most people, you associate sweet things with happiness. Reaction times for the 'Sweets + Happiness' IAT block should therefore be shorter (i.e., faster) than for the 'Sweets + Sadness' block.

Steffens and Schulze König adapted the IAT to assess the five personality factors. Each factor was assessed by two IAT blocks. For example, in one block the concepts 'Self' and 'Conscientious' were paired (with 'Others' and 'Unconscientious' as the alternatives), and in the second block 'Self' and 'Unconscientious' were paired (with 'Others' and 'Conscientious' as alternatives). The stimulus words that participants had to categorize reflected self (e.g., 'me', 'mine'), others (e.g., 'you', 'your'), conscientious traits (e.g., 'disciplined', 'organized') and unconscientious traits (e.g., 'untidy', 'aimless'). If a participant showed quicker reaction times for the 'Self + Conscientious' block than for the

(Continued)

'Self + Unconscientious' block, it could therefore be inferred that she saw herself – automatically, rather than through some deliberate process of self-report – as relatively conscientious.

The findings of this study were striking. First, the IAT-based measures of the five factors correlated only weakly with the self-report questionnaire measures (mean $r = .07$). This finding suggests either that the two measures assess somewhat distinct phenomena or that one measure is flawed. If that were the case, suspicion would fall on the relatively unproven IAT measures, as the questionnaire has been extensively validated. Second, the IAT measures did appear to be valid: they predicted the behavioural tasks as well as or better than the questionnaire measures. For example, conscientiousness was assessed by a concentration task in which participants had to cross out as many copies of a particular letter in an array that contained many similar letters. More conscientious participants should be more careful and make fewer mistakes. The IAT measure of conscientiousness was more strongly correlated with performance on this task ($r = .36$) than the questionnaire measure ($r = .01$). In short, only the implicit measure of conscientiousness predicted conscientious behaviour.

As yet, implicit measures of personality have not been widely used, but they are likely to become more popular in the future. These measures are certainly not 'X-rays of the soul', but they may nevertheless help us assess personality in ways that evade some of the biases that influence self-report and that supply the rationale for projective tests. Studies such as this one suggest that implicit assessment of personality is promising, in part because they show that implicit measures may sometimes predict real-life behaviour when self-report measures do not.

ALTERNATIVE METHODS

Interviews, inventories, and projective tests do not exhaust the variety of assessment methods that have been developed by personality researchers, although they are by far the most numerous and widely used. Two alternative methods are particularly worthy of attention: the Q-sort method and the Repertory Grid.

The Q-sort method

The Q-sort method was originally developed as a means of assessing the self-concept: the person's understanding of himself or herself. It does so in an innovative way, requiring people to judge which personality attributes are more and which ones less important for defining who they are as unique individuals, instead of judging where they fall on these attributes relative to other people, the approach favoured by most personality tests. In short, Q-sorts allow people to describe themselves with reference to a purely personal, rather than normative, standard.

Q-sorts consist of a set of statements printed on cards, which people sort into several numbered piles according to how characteristic they are of themselves, ranging from 'least characteristic' to 'most characteristic'. The number of cards to be sorted into each pile is fixed in advance so that the distribution of cards is approximately normal, with few statements judged to be extremely characteristic or uncharacteristic and many judged to be intermediate between these extremes. For instance, in the popular California Q-sort (Block, 1978) there are 100 statements to be sorted into nine piles. Although at first it may seem arbitrary and restrictive, this 'forced-normal' distribution of cards has several advantages over simply presenting the same statements in an inventory with a rating scale. First, it makes people consider and judge each statement carefully and in the context of the others. Second, it does not allow them to yield to various response biases, such as indiscriminately agreeing or disagreeing with all statements (i.e., yea-saying and nay-saying). Third, it has certain statistical benefits for researchers. In return for these advantages, Q-sorts have the disadvantage of being somewhat time-consuming to complete.

Q-sorts are highly versatile methods for the intensive study of individuals. They can be used for a person's self-report and also for judgments of that person by an observer, therapist, or friend. People can also judge themselves in different ways, performing separate sorts for their 'real self' and 'ideal self', or for their personality before and after psychological treatment. Correlations between these alternative Q-sorts can reveal the extent of agreement between different observers, discrepancies between the person's self-understanding and the judgment of others, conflicts within the person, and changes in personality over time. Indeed, the Q-sort method has been used most prominently in studies of personality stability and change, allowing researchers to focus on the trajectories of individual lives rather than on normative patterns of personality change.

The Repertory Grid

The Repertory Grid test is similar in spirit to the Q-sort, in that it assesses each person's individuality in its own terms rather than in relation to group norms. However, the 'Rep Test' goes even further in its attempt to capture the person's uniqueness. Whereas the Q-sort uses a standard set of descriptive statements, allowing people to select which items in the set are most important for characterizing themselves, the Rep Test allows individuals to create the descriptive attributes in terms of which they will be assessed.

The radical idea that people should be understood in terms of their unique ways of understanding the world is one that readers will remember from the discussion in Chapter 6 of George Kelly's 'constructivist' approach to personality. Kelly developed the Rep Test as a way for psychologists, particularly clinical psychologists, to determine the 'constructs' that people habitually use in making sense of one another. Although the Rep Test can be administered in many ways, typically the person who is taking the test is presented with a list of role terms – such as mother, teacher, person who dislikes you, boyfriend/girlfriend – and is asked to name someone in their life who fits each role. The examiner then selects three of these names, and asks the person to state one important way in which two of them are alike but different from the third. The attribute that the person states in response to this request is called a **'personal construct'**, a way of differentiating people that is salient to him or her. The person repeats the process of eliciting constructs for many combinations of three names chosen by the examiner. The resulting set of constructs reveals the person's distinctive way of interpreting the interpersonal world in rich qualitative detail. An illustration of part of a Rep Test is presented in Figure 8.1. The first eight columns represent the role terms, the circles represent the specific roles that must be contrasted (i.e., two alike, one different), and the final two columns allow the person who is completing the test to fill in the two poles of each construct.

In settings where this kind of intimacy with the person's 'way of seeing' is crucial, as in some forms of psychotherapy, the Rep Test can have considerable value. In such settings, the information that it provides can usefully complement information derived from standardized inventories. For instance, an inventory might show that two people are high on neuroticism and depression, whereas the Rep Test might indicate that one person tends to construe others in terms of their dependability and warmth and the other in terms of their dominance and power. In one case, we might infer from the Rep Test that the person's distress is linked to their sensitivity to being abandoned and rejected (i.e., others being undependable and cold), and in the other case that the person's distress is linked to their sensitivity to feeling submissive, weak, and incompetent. These distinctive ways of construing others seem to suggest that therapy for the two people might focus on different themes.

MAKING USE OF PERSONALITY ASSESSMENTS

The previous sections of this chapter have presented a variety of methods for the collection of personality information. All of these methods are commonly

Your mother	Your father	Your spouse	Your closest friend of the same sex	A person you worked with who dislikes you	A person you'd like to know better	The most unsuccessful person you know	The happiest person you know	Column 1	Column 2
O			O			O		*Warm*	*Cold*
	O		O				O	*Honest*	*Dishonest*
		O	O		O			*Cool*	*Dorky*
		O			O	O		*Demanding*	*Easy-going*
O					O		O	*Old*	*Young*

Figure 8.1 Example segment of a Rep Grid

employed in applied settings, where they help psychologists to make decisions such as who to hire among several job applicants, what career a student should pursue, and whether to discharge a psychiatric patient who might be suicidal. All of these decisions are based on *predictions*: predictions that one applicant will perform better than others in the job, that the student will be most successful or fulfilled in a particular career, or that the patient will or will not attempt suicide if discharged. But how do psychologists use personality information to make predictions such as these?

This question may appear to be a simple one but it is actually quite complicated and controversial. Consider the position in which psychologists find themselves after conducting a personality assessment. Typically they have administered more than one measure to the respondent, perhaps involving some combination of interviews, inventories, and projective tests. Each measure may yield multiple pieces of information – such as different scales on an inventory – and these pieces may differ in their format, ranging from numerical scores on inventory scales to qualitative impressions drawn from an interview. Finally, this personality information often has to be combined with additional evidence, such as biographical details of the respondent (e.g., their work history, past suicidal behaviour) and assessments of other psychological attributes (e.g., cognitive abilities or attitudes). The daunting task facing the psychologist is to integrate all of these multiple and diverse sources of information into a single prediction, and to make this prediction as accurate (i.e., valid) as possible.

How psychologists should perform this integration is a matter of some debate, and two rival positions or philosophies can be distinguished. One position contends that psychologists should use assessment information as a basis for constructing a psychological portrait of the whole person. According to this position, a primary aim of a personality assessment is to arrive at a narrative understanding of the person, using theory, intuition, and personal experience to synthesize the assessment data. Predictions and judgments about the person can then be made from this synthesis. The other position contends that the psychologist's role should be more limited. Instead of constructing a portrait, the psychologist should use explicit rules and formulas, based on empirical research using many people, to make predictions and judgments from assessment data. They should specifically avoid the use of intuition, theory, and personal experience, as well as the urge to piece together a picture of the whole person, because doing so introduces elements of subjectivity that will weaken the validity of their predictions.

The contrast between these two positions should sound familiar by now. Remember that many of the criticisms of unstructured interviews and projective tests focused on the adverse psychometric consequences of their subjectivity and flexibility. Remember also how part of the rationale for these methods of assessment is their supposed capacity to yield a picture of the person's uniqueness and individuality. In contrast, objective assessment methods emphasize psychometric respectability and the comparison of individuals to group norms, and measure specific personality characteristics without aspiring to put them together into an integrated psychological portrait. Indeed, proponents of projective testing and unstructured interviews do tend to favour the view that assessment information should be used to construct psychological portraits, which has been dubbed the 'clinical judgment' position. Similarly, advocates of objective assessment tend to favour the 'rules and formulas' approach to the use of personality data, which is often referred to as the 'actuarial' or 'statistical judgment' position.

A great deal of research has been devoted to comparing the predictive validity of clinical and statistical methods in personality assessment. Much of this research was provoked by a ground-breaking book by Paul Meehl (1954), which reviewed a number of early studies and found overwhelming support for the superior validity of statistical methods. As Meehl's review showed, and more recent research has consistently confirmed, highly-trained psychologists who make predictions and judgments from a set of assessment data make more errors than simple statistical formulas and rules applied to the same data. Two additional points are worth making about this finding, which is now one of the best supported in all of psychology (Dawes, Faust, & Meehl, 1989). First, it holds true for all forms of assessment data, including scores from objective tests. Second, even if psychologists are given additional assessment information that is not available to the statistical formula, such as an interview, they still make less valid predictions than statistical procedures, and this additional information often makes their predictions *worse*.

The findings of this research are surprising to many people, and have been vigorously challenged by psychologists who favour the use of expert clinical judgment. How might we explain this apparent inferiority of clinical judgment? There appear to be several reasons, many of which have to do with human cognitive limitations. People are simply not very good at handling multiple sources of information at once, and making single, integrated judgments from them. We tend to follow a variety of simplifying strategies for information processing, rather than making the kinds of computations that formulas and rules involve. For example, judgments are often unduly influenced by the most striking or unusual piece of information, to the neglect of less salient but equally valid evidence. Similarly, people often make premature judgments based on a subset of the information, often the first data that they see. Furthermore, they commonly use their initial judgments to bias their evaluation of the remaining information, so that they pay attention to information that confirms the initial judgment and discount information that contradicts it. People are also quite poor at reasoning with probabilities, and consequently fail to correctly judge and take into account the likelihood of particular test results and prediction criteria. These probability judgments are vitally important given the uncertainty that is always involved in psychological predictions, and it is very well handled by statistical formulas.

In addition to being weakened by cognitive limitations such as these, clinical judgment is adversely affected by a few other factors. First, judgments are often distorted by psychologists' theoretical biases, which lead them to look for assessment information that is consistent with their pre-existing beliefs rather than consider the evidence disinterestedly. Second, psychologists may hold inaccurate beliefs about how certain assessment information is associated with prediction criteria. One example is the phenomenon of 'illusory correlation', in which psychologists believe in an intuitively plausible association between a test finding and a criterion – that men who see backsides in Rorschach blots are homosexual or that individuals whose projective drawings depict people with unusually large eyes are paranoid – that is, in fact, non-existent. Third, psychologists often base their judgments on their own clinical experiences, which may be limited and unrepresentative, so that the knowledge base from which they are making their predictions is flawed. Given all of these reasons why clinical judgment is prone to error, perhaps we should not be surprised that statistical judgment tends to do better.

The lessons of this chapter are perhaps a little deflating. The idea that psychologists can, with sufficient training, perform virtuoso acts of interpretation that unmask the hidden dynamics of the personality with startling insight and accuracy has been encouraged by movies and by court-appointed psychological 'experts'. The reality is more humble. Abundant evidence points to the modest conclusion that personality assessments can be reliable and yield valid predictions about a wide range of criteria. However, they perform best when they are conducted with standardized measures, with a focus on specific dispositions rather than holistic portraits, and with explicit prediction rules and statistical formulas. Attempts to make more ambitious and far-reaching inferences about the hidden complexities of the personality are generally ineffective: their validity crumbles under the subjectivity of the measures and the cognitive demands of clinical judgment. To modify an old saying, 'Give psychologists enough inferential rope and they will hang themselves'.

CONCLUSIONS

Personality characteristics can be assessed using a wide variety of methods, of which the most popular are interviews, objective inventories, and projective tests. Because all of these assessment methods serve practical purposes in which judgments and predictions must be made, it is important that they be psychometrically sound; that is, 'reliable' and 'valid'. Reliable measures are ones that assess a construct in a consistent and coherent fashion, yield similar scores when administered by different examiners, and yield scores that are stable over time. Valid measures are ones that assess the construct that they are intended to assess and are able to predict real-life criteria that the construct should be associated with.

Considerations of reliability and validity generally favour the use of objective over projective measures, and structured over unstructured interviews, although inventories are vulnerable to biased responding. Advocates of projective tests and unstructured interviews contend that these methods are best suited to assessing the person's underlying personality organization and psychodynamics, in all their uniqueness and individuality. However, it seems that the subjectivity and flexibility of these methods severely weaken the confidence that we can have in the 'deep inferences' that they yield.

A similar conclusion can be reached about the way in which psychologists make judgments and predictions based on personality information, regardless of the assessment methods used to generate it. Research shows that the inferences of experts are generally inferior to inferences made from statistical formulas based on empirical generalizations. The 'clinical judgment' of experts seems to be impaired by human cognitive limitations and biases, such as the difficulty of integrating multiple pieces of information and the tendency to take judgmental 'short-cuts'. For most purposes, personality assessment is best approached with standardized and empirically-validated methods, and with appropriate humility about how difficult it is to make valid inferences about another person's depths.

Chapter summary

- Personality assessment involves systematic methods for measuring individual differences. A variety of distinct methods have been developed for this purpose. All of these methods aim to yield valid and reliable assessments.
- Psychometric reliability refers to the extent to which a measure yields assessments that are consistent and does not contain measurement error. The components of the measure should be consistent with one another ('internal consistency'), different users of the measure should produce consistent assessments ('inter-rater reliability'), and the measure should yield consistent assessments when administered to the same person at different times ('retest reliability').
- Validity refers to the extent to which a measure assesses what it is intended to assess. It should therefore be correlated with other measures of the same construct, predict phenomena that should be associated with the construct.
- Interview methods of personality assessment can have problems with validity and reliability if they are unstructured and not standardized: various interpersonal processes can distort inferences drawn from them. They are also labour-intensive and costly.
- Personality questionnaires or inventories are very widely used, and constructing them generally involves extensive psychometric validation. Because they are based on self-report, however, they are subject to response biases.
- Projective methods aim to avoid the distorting influence of self-report by posing ambiguous tasks whose purpose is not transparent to the person being assessed. They generally aim to access hidden personality dynamics. However, these methods have been criticized for serious problems of validity and reliability.

(Continued)

(Continued)

- A number of additional assessment methods have been developed, tailored to overcome particular assessment problems or to assess personality characteristics that are not easily assessed using standard assessment (e.g., personal constructs).
- Having a set of validly and reliably assessed pieces of information about a person does not guarantee that valid and reliable inferences will be drawn about that person. Personality assessors are vulnerable to a number of biases that limit their ability to integrate personality information optimally.

Further reading

- Anastasi, A., & Urbina, S. (1996). *Psychological testing* (7th ed.). New York: Prentice-Hall.

This well-known textbook (or earlier editions of the same text) provides clear understandings of validity and reliability issues in psychological assessment.

- Dawes, R.M., Faust, D., & Meehl, P.E. (1989). Clinical versus actuarial judgment. *Science, 243*, 1668–74.

Dawes and colleagues have a strong reputation for cataloguing the errors that humans (including personality psychologists) make when drawing inferences from psychological test data. This paper presents some of the evidence of how fallible assessors can be.

- Lilienfeld, S.O., Wood, J.M., & Garb, H.N. (2000). The scientific status of projective techniques. *Psychological Science in the Public Interest, 1*, 27–66.

Lilienfeld and colleagues present a devastating critique of the use of projective measures such as the Rorschach Ink-Blot Test and the Thematic Apperception Test.

- Wiggins, J.S. (2003). *Paradigms of personality assessment.* New York: Guilford.

A strength of this somewhat advanced book is the balanced attention it gives to the eclectic variety of methods available for assessing personality characteristics.

9

Personality and Mental Disorder

Learning objectives

- To recognize the role that personality characteristics play in making people vulnerable to mental disorders.
- To understand the diathesis-stress model of vulnerability, and how it applies to particular mental disorders.
- To develop a basic understanding of the maladaptive forms of personality that are mental disorders in their own right ('personality disorders').
- To develop a basic understanding of the phenomenon of multiple personality.
- To comprehend the ways in which personality characteristics contribute to physical health and illness.

This chapter examines how the study of personality can illuminate mental disorders and physical illness. It begins by investigating the ways in which some personality characteristics make people vulnerable to develop particular mental disorders if they encounter stressful life events, taking depression and schizophrenia as examples. We then turn to maladaptive forms of personality that are themselves mental disorders, and examine the varied types of 'personality disorder'. Following this, the chapter examines the fascinating and puzzling phenomenon of dissociative identity disorder, a controversial condition in which a person appears to have several distinct and often mutually unaware personalities. Finally, the role of personality characteristics as sources of vulnerability for physical illness is reviewed, with an emphasis on heart disease and cancer, as well as the ways in which personality traits affect health-damaging and health-promoting behaviour.

Individual differences in personality are highly relevant to many applied areas of psychology. Psychologists who work in educational settings are interested in whether some teaching methods are more effective than others for people of differing personality. Psychologists who provide vocational guidance try to match people's personalities with appropriate careers, and those who are involved in personnel selection select people whose personalities fit them best to particular jobs. However, personality has been an especially important focus of attention for clinical psychologists, who specialize in treating, assessing, and researching mental disorders. Clinical psychologists are concerned with personality because many mental disorders can only be understood in the context of the traits and personality processes of the people who suffer from them. For example, some personality characteristics may place people at increased risk of particular disorders, and make them more likely to respond in disturbed ways to stressful life events. Personality characteristics may also influence the ways in which people express certain mental disorders, and have implications for how treatment should be conducted. In addition, some personality traits, when expressed in extreme ways, may themselves be thought of as mental disorders.

In this chapter we will examine some of these varied ways in which personality is relevant to the study and treatment of mental disorders. We will begin by investigating the role of personality characteristics as risk factors or sources of psychological vulnerability, using depression and schizophrenia as illustrations. In the process, we will also discuss how personality characteristics can shape the expression of particular mental disorders. We will then examine the so-called '**personality disorders**', disorders involving personality characteristics that are so exaggerated and inflexible that they may create serious interpersonal problems and emotional disturbances for people who suffer from them. Finally, we will move away from mental disorders and briefly examine the role that personality characteristics may play in physical illness, an exciting area of study in the growing fields of health psychology and behavioural medicine.

VULNERABILITY TO MENTAL DISORDERS

Mental disorders – disturbances of emotion, behaviour, and thinking such as phobias, psychoses, addictions, and depression – are major sources of suffering and disability in modern societies. However, these disorders are not evenly distributed in the population; some groups of people are more vulnerable to them than others. Finding out which groups of people are especially vulnerable to particular mental disorders – identifying their 'risk factors' – is therefore an important research question in clinical psychology. If we can identify groups of people who are vulnerable to a particular disorder, we can intervene with them to prevent the disorder from developing. At the same time, we can learn important clues about what causes the disorder; knowing who is at risk may tell us what it is about them that places them at risk.

Many risk factors have been discovered for a wide variety of mental disorders. These include demographic variables such as gender, social class, race, and age; genetic vulnerabilities revealed by family, adoption, and twin studies (see Chapter 4); cultural characteristics such as shared beliefs about the appropriateness of particular ways of expressing distress; life events such as traumas and other stressors; and aspects of social relationships such as marital difficulties and lack of social supports. In addition to these kinds of vulnerabilities, there is now a great deal of evidence that certain personality characteristics also make people susceptible to specific forms of mental disorder. In psychology such a vulnerability is commonly referred to as a **diathesis**, meaning a predisposition to develop a specific disorder that is intrinsic to the person, a part of their 'constitution'. The search for diatheses is an important goal for many researchers in personality and clinical psychology.

Personality diatheses make up an important class of risk factors for mental disorders, often enabling us to predict who will be affected by particular disorders at least as powerfully as other kinds of risk factor. However, it is important to understand what a diathesis is and what it is not.

A diathesis is not something that invariably leads the person who has it to develop a particular disorder: it only increases the *likelihood* that this will happen. Another way of saying this is that diatheses are 'probabilistic', not 'deterministic'. Only a minority of those who have a particular diathesis may go on to develop the disorder for which it makes them susceptible. Figure 9.1 presents three possible scenarios for the relationship between a hypothetical personality trait and the mental disorder for which it is a diathesis. A person's position on the trait is represented by the proportion of people in the population who fall below that person – known as a 'percentile' – so that someone with a percentile of 60 is higher on the trait than 60% of the population. In all three scenarios, even people who are extreme on the diathesis have a less than

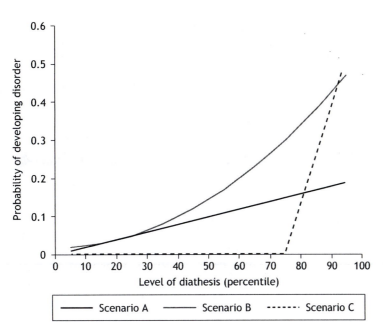

Figure 9.1   Possible relationships between diatheses and expression of mental disorders

50% chance of developing the disorder. In scenario A, everyone is at some risk of developing the disorder, and the risk rises steadily as a person's position on the diathesis increases. Scenario B differs only in that the risk accelerates as the person's level on the trait increases, meaning that the diathesis is especially potent among people who fall high on the personality trait. In scenario C, finally, people who fall low on the trait are at no risk of developing the disorder, which only affects people who have a relatively high level of the diathesis. All three of these scenarios may be true of some forms of mental disorder.

Now why is it that even people who have a high level of a diathesis for a particular mental disorder are still far from certain to develop the disorder? The answer is that most mental disorders are influenced by a complex variety of risk factors, of which personality is only one. Usually several risk factors must be combined before a person expresses a disorder, so that any one influence, such as a personality diathesis, will only lead to the disorder if other influences are also present. Someone who has a diathesis for a certain disorder but does not have other risk factors, such as poverty or harsh parenting, is therefore less likely to develop the disorder than someone who has these other risk factors. In addition, people who are predisposed to develop a disorder may also have what are known as 'protective factors', which *decrease* their likelihood of developing the disorder. For instance, someone whose personality makes her vulnerable to depression may also have a strong network of supportive friends and family that protects her against becoming depressed.

The existence of protective factors and the fact that most mental disorders are caused by multiple risk factors go a long way towards explaining why personality diatheses do not inevitably lead to disorder. However, a more complete explanation must also take into account the role of stressful life events in the causation of mental disorders. People who experience high levels of stress in their everyday lives – events or enduring circumstances that challenge their capacity to cope and adapt – have been shown to be at increased risk of most mental disorders. Note here that by this definition, stressful events need not be 'negative': events such as getting married, having a baby, and receiving a promotion also tax our capacity to adapt, and can make us more likely to develop a mental disorder. Consequently, one fundamental reason why personality diatheses are usually not sufficient to produce mental disorders is that life stress also plays an important role in determining who becomes disordered. Indeed, it is often the *combination* of diathesis and stress that best explains who becomes affected.

This simple idea is the basis for what are known as 'diathesis–stress models', which are ways of explaining the causation and development of mental disorders that are popular among psychologists. In essence, diathesis–stress models propose that for a particular disorder there is specific personality vulnerability that will only be triggered if a sufficient quantity of stress is present in the vulnerable person's life. If *either* the level of the diathesis *or* the level of life stress is low, the disorder is unlikely to develop. Only the combination of high levels of diathesis and stress is likely to result in disorder. Metaphorically, diatheses make people brittle, and life stress delivers the blows that make them crack.

This state of affairs is presented hypothetically in Figure 9.2, whose ten columns represent groups of people with increasing levels of the diathesis for a mental disorder: people in group 1 have no diathesis at all, and people in group 10 have a high level of it (45 units of risk). Imagine that life stress adds further risk: 10 units for mild levels of stress, another 10 for moderate levels of stress, and another 10 for high levels of stress. Imagine also that the disorder is expressed at a threshold level of 50 risk units. Figure 9.2 indicates that people in the four groups with the lowest level of the diathesis will never suffer from the disorder, no matter how much life stress they experience: they never reach 50 points. Groups 5 and 6 will express the disorder only if they experience high levels of stress, groups 7 and 8 if they experience moderate levels of stress, and the disorder will be triggered in members of groups 9 and 10 even if they only experience mild stress levels. The higher the level of one's diathesis, the less stress it takes to precipitate the disorder.

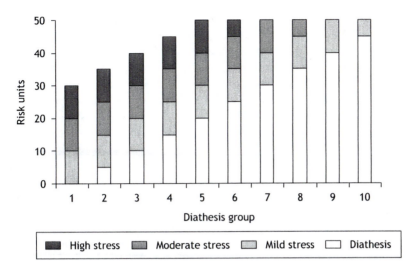

Figure 9.2   Relationship of diathesis levels, stress levels, and expression of a disorder

Diathesis–stress models of mental disorders have some interesting implications. First, they imply that the more of a diathesis a person has, the less life stress will be needed to produce a mental disorder in that person (i.e., the more brittle people are, the easier it will be to crack them). For example, if someone has an extremely high level of the predisposition to a certain disorder, a relatively minor disappointment, or upset, such as an argument with a romantic partner, may be sufficient to express it. Someone with a lower level of the diathesis, on the other hand, may develop the disorder only in response to severely traumatic experiences, such as the unexpected death of a loved one or rape.

A second interesting implication of diathesis–stress models is that people will respond in quite different ways to life stress. Not only will some people be more likely than others to develop a mental disorder of any kind, but different people will also tend to develop different disorders. Because each disorder has a diathesis that is somewhat specific to it, the disorder that each one of us is likely to develop if we are sufficiently stressed will depend on which of our diatheses is the strongest. Faced with the same level of adversity and trauma in our lives, one of us may become clinically depressed, another may engage in binge eating, another may develop delusions of persecution, and another may abuse alcohol, each depending on the particular kind of diathesis that is most prominent in our personalities. In short, our personalities play a major role in determining the distinctive ways in which we become psychologically distressed.

Diathesis–stress models are appealing in their simplicity and have some interesting implications. However, these models also have some limitations. Most importantly, they give personality a rather limited role in the causation of mental disorders. In the standard diathesis–stress model, the personality diathesis is assumed to increase the risk that a given disorder will develop, without influencing the specific form that the disorder takes. In addition, the diathesis is usually considered to be triggered by any kind of sufficiently severe life stress, rather than influencing the specific kinds of stresses that may be most harmful.

Both of these assumptions of the standard diathesis–stress model restrict the role of personality in mental disorder, and both can be disputed. It is quite possible that some personality characteristics not only make people vulnerable to specific disorders, but also shape the way that affected people experience and express these disorders. More than one diathesis may exist for a given disorder, with different diatheses yielding somewhat different expressions of the disorder. It is also possible, and likely, that specific personality characteristics make people especially susceptible to specific types of stress. After all, personality influences the distinctive ways in which people make sense of their environments and respond to them. In short, diathesis–stress models may need to be refined to allow a larger and more complex role for personality.

The issues that we have discussed surrounding diathesis–stress models may all seem a bit abstract and theoretical at this point. However, they are important if we want to understand the ways in which personality influences the development of different forms of mental disorder. To illustrate how personality characteristics make people vulnerable to mental disorders, determine the experiences that trigger their vulnerabilities, and influence the way they experience their disorders, let us now investigate two disorders that produce a terrible burden of human suffering: depression and schizophrenia.

Depression

Major depression, as it is known by mental health professionals, is a serious form of emotional disturbance that affects a relatively large and apparently growing proportion of the population (about 5% of people at any particular time, and about 12% of people at some time in their lives). People who are depressed commonly suffer from a wide variety of symptoms, such as a profoundly sad mood, a loss of interest and pleasure in their everyday activities, insomnia, an inability to concentrate and make decisions, loss of appetite and weight, fatigue, guilt, and intensely self-critical and hopeless thinking. Episodes of depression commonly last for months, often recur over a person's lifetime, and have many serious complications, including an increased risk of suicide, relationship and marital problems, occupational and academic difficulties, health complaints, and abuse of alcohol and other drugs.

Given the prevalence and terrible consequences of major depression, psychologists and psychiatrists have understandably been very interested in discovering factors that predispose people to develop the disorder. The search has yielded a wide variety of factors that make some people more likely to develop major depression than others. For example, being female is a risk factor, such that two to three times as many women as men develop the disorder. Having a close relative who has been depressed also makes a person more vulnerable to depression, as does living through the death of a parent in childhood. People experiencing other serious life events, such as divorce, unemployment, and physical illness, are particularly vulnerable to develop major depression, as are people who lack social supports, such as a close, confiding relationship with a spouse.

All of these vulnerabilities are clearly important in helping us predict who is at risk of developing major depression. However, none of them refer to personality characteristics. Instead, they refer to demographic attributes (female gender), family history, past and present life stresses, and social relationships. Nevertheless, psychologists have proposed and studied several personality dispositions that also place people at increased risk of developing major depression. Four of the most extensively researched dispositions are dependency, self-criticism, autonomy, and pessimistic explanatory style. We will consider each of these in turn.

Dependency

'Dependency' can represent a fundamentally healthy tendency to enjoy and seek out connections with others: unless we are hermits, we are all dependent on others for emotional and physical well-being and for our sense of who we are. However, in the context of depression-proneness dependency has a more pathological meaning, referring to an exaggerated need for the nurturance, guidance, and approval of others (Blatt & Zuroff, 1992). People who are dependent in this sense are deeply afraid of separation, abandonment, and disapproval, and are helpless and unable to make decisions when they are on their own. They constantly seek reassurance and advice, cling to others for support, behave submissively and passively in relationships, and tolerate being exploited because they dread losing their attachments.

Given that dependent people are heavily invested in their interpersonal relationships, it is not difficult to infer what kinds of stressful events are especially likely to tip them into depression. Not surprisingly, research has shown that highly dependent individuals are particularly vulnerable to become depressed in response to events involving interpersonal conflict, rejection, separation, and loss. These events might include romantic break-ups, arguments with family members or spouses, and the emigration or death of a loved one. Research has also suggested that when dependent people become depressed, they tend to exhibit a somewhat distinctive pattern of depressive symptoms. Although their depressions may involve all of the typical symptoms of the disorder, they are often dominated by themes of loss, emptiness and deprivation, by crying, and by active attempts to seek help.

Autonomy

Like dependency, 'autonomy' is a characteristic that can reflect a healthy independence and self-reliance that is highly esteemed in many cultures. However, some psychological writers have described a pathological form of autonomy that represents an excessive concern with personal achievement, and an aversion to being controlled by or dependent on others that may lead people to sever themselves from social supports. People who are overly invested in this kind of individualistic philosophy of life, they argue, may be vulnerable to depression if they fail in their striving for personal achievement. In other words, highly autonomous people are especially susceptible to become depressed in reaction to life stresses such as losing a job, being passed over for a promotion, failing to qualify for a competitive academic course, or having the manuscript of their novel rejected by a publisher.

When events such as these happen, pathologically autonomous people may question their belief in their personal competence and their ability to control their lives, resulting in a sense of defeat and powerlessness. Some research has found support for the role of autonomy as a vulnerability factor for depression, and for the special harmfulness of stresses involving achievement-related failure. Other research further suggests that when they become depressed, autonomous people often do exhibit a symptom pattern dominated by defeat, a belief that they cannot control events in their world, and a corresponding loss of motivation and initiative that leaves them apathetic and fatigued.

Self-criticism

Self-criticism is a third personality dimension that has been proposed as a diathesis for depression. Some people, theorists argue, are especially prone to punishing self-evaluations, holding themselves to unreasonably high or perfectionistic standards. Psychoanalytic writers would describe them as suffering from a harsh super-ego. Consequently these people are vulnerable to guilt, shame, and self-reproach in the course of their everyday lives, and if they experience significant negative events for which they feel responsible they may become clinically depressed. When depressed, as you might expect, highly self-critical people are likely to suffer from symptoms that represent extreme expressions of their personality: severe and sometimes quite irrational guilt, believing themselves to be worthless, evil and ugly, and ruminating about the flaws that they perceive in their character. Once again, we see a personality diathesis (self-criticism) that is linked to a particular class of life stressors (negative events for which the person feels responsible) that may trigger a particular set of symptoms (self-punishing).

Pessimistic explanatory style

Dependency, autonomy, and self-criticism are all personality dispositions that seem to make people vulnerable to depression. The final disposition that we shall examine differs from these in being conceptualized in explicitly cognitive terms. This disposition is based on a programme of research into the ways in which people explain life events, which we discussed in Chapter 6. Martin Seligman and his colleagues (Abramson et al., 1978) have shown that people's explanations for events differ along three 'causal dimensions', each of which has two opposed alternatives. First, events may be attributed to causes that are 'internal' (i.e., personal) or 'external' (i.e., influences outside of personal control). An internal explanation might invoke personal abilities or intentions as causes of an event, whereas an external explanation might refer to other people's behaviour, to social conventions, to chance, or to fate. Second, the causes of events may be judged to be 'stable' (i.e., enduring over time) or 'unstable' (i.e., changeable). Stable causes include personality traits, societal traditions, and genes, whereas unstable causes might include moods, the weather, or unusual chance circumstances. Third, some events are attributed to 'global' causes (i.e., causes whose implications are generalized and far-reaching), others to 'specific' ones (i.e., causes having relatively narrow implications which are limited to the event in question). Intelligence, social class and gender exemplify global causes, whereas luck, one's clothing, and skills restricted to particular tasks exemplify specific causes.

To illustrate this rather abstract review of the three explanatory dimensions, consider the following examples of explanations given by people who have just done poorly on an examination:

1. 'I did badly because I'm stupid.'
2. 'I did badly because the exam was unfair.'
3. 'I did badly because I had a toothache.'
4. 'I did badly because the educational system is biased against people like me.'

Explanation 1 invokes a cause that is internal, stable, and global. Stupidity, or low intelligence, is a characteristic that is intrinsic to the person, is unlikely to change, and is quite general in its implications for the person's life. Explanation 2, in contrast, points to a cause that is external, unstable, and specific: the unfairness of the exam was due to someone else, future exams are not all likely to be unfair, and because the unfairness was particular to just one exam it is unlikely to have broader implications for the person's future academic performance or life. Explanation 3 proposes a cause that is unstable and specific, like explanation 2, but differs in being internal rather than external: the person claims to have been distracted by a temporary state of mind which will probably not interfere with future activities. Explanation 4, finally, contrasts sharply with explanation 3, referring to a cause that is external, stable, and global: an ongoing system of discrimination perpetrated by others.

Research has shown that people exhibit consistent differences in their use of the three explanatory dimensions to make sense of events. These dispositions are referred to as their 'explanatory style'. People's ways of explaining negative events seem to be especially relevant to their vulnerability to depression, and it has been demonstrated that people who tend to attribute such events to stable and global causes are most vulnerable. In other words, people who explain negative events as outcomes of unchangeable and generalized causes – causes such as those invoked by explanations 1 and 4 – are said to have a 'pessimistic' explanatory style and are depression-prone. Why this is so is not difficult to imagine. Confronted with a personally-relevant negative event, they are likely to see it as difficult to avoid, likely to continue or recur, and wide-ranging in its harmful consequences. In contrast, people who attribute negative events to unstable and specific causes – like explanations 2 and 3 – are likely to see them as transient, one-of-a-kind disruptions whose consequences are limited, and hence easily overcome. Even if, from an 'objective' standpoint, a pessimistic explanation might be more accurate – perhaps the student in explanation 2 really is not very capable and blames the 'unfair' exam as an excuse for poor performance – optimistic explanations therefore appear to protect against depression.

Pessimistic explanatory style, then, is another personality diathesis for depression that can interact with a particular class of stressful events (i.e., negative ones) to produce depression. Some theorists (Abramson, Metalsky, & Alloy, 1989) have argued that people with this diathesis also tend to exhibit a characteristic pattern of symptoms when they become depressed. They propose that these people show prominent hopelessness and suicidal thinking, symptoms that are clearly consistent with a tendency to perceive negative events as unchangeable and devastating in their effects.

We have briefly reviewed four personality vulnerabilities for major depression, and found evidence that they are also associated with distinctive kinds of precipitating stresses and symptoms. It is important to recognize that these diatheses and stresses overlap: pessimistic people are likely to be self-critical, and a particular negative event, such as being insulted by one's employer, might at the same time represent an interpersonal conflict, a threat to personal competence, and a threat to self-esteem. Nevertheless, the important point to grasp here is that there are several somewhat distinct and psychologically meaningful pathways between personality and depression. All of these pathways suggest intriguing ways to understand and treat this crippling disorder.

Schizophrenia

Major depression provides a good illustration of the role that personality characteristics play in producing and shaping mental disorders. Schizophrenia provides another, which differs in interesting ways. Schizophrenia is a serious mental disorder that strikes about 1% of people at some time in their lives. The disorder is often long-lasting, with many affected people either suffering from its symptoms chronically or undergoing recurring episodes. In addition to being so enduring, the disorder is especially tragic because it severely impairs the capacity of people affected by it to engage in social relationships, to work, and to look after themselves, because these impairments often increase over time, and because the disorder usually first appears early in life, commonly in the early- to-mid-20s.

The symptoms of schizophrenia are often severe and disabling. People with schizophrenia often have deeply held delusions, which are erroneous and often bizarre beliefs like having thoughts inserted in their heads by other people, being persecuted by the secret police, being eaten from within by giant insects, or being a famous historical figure. They also commonly experience hallucinations, such as hearing voices commenting on their actions, seeing visions, or smelling odours of decay. Their thinking is often disorganized and confused, and their speech is frequently incoherent, rambling, and sprinkled with invented words. Because these symptoms – delusions, hallucinations, and disorganized thinking and speech – all represent an excess or distortion of normal psychological functions, they are sometimes referred to as 'positive symptoms'. In addition to these forms of peculiarity, schizophrenic people are often very withdrawn, have a profound loss of motivation and initiative, and show a lack of emotional responsiveness to events in their lives. These symptoms are sometimes described as 'negative symptoms' because they involve a decrease or loss of normal functions.

Schizophrenia is a disorder which appears to have a substantial genetic component, indicating that some people are at higher genetic risk of developing the disorder than others. Psychologists have been eager to learn whether this genetic diathesis is expressed as a set of personality characteristics. If there is such a personality diathesis for schizophrenia, which has an at least partly genetic basis, we might be able to identify people who are at risk of developing the disorder. Indeed, psychologists have been quite successful in characterizing a personality vulnerability for schizophrenia, which is generally known as '**schizotypy**' (Meehl, 1962).

Schizotypy is a personality disposition that has several distinct aspects, which usually first reveal themselves in childhood or adolescence. As adults, schizotypal people are usually very uncomfortable in close relationships, feeling anxious and often suspecting that others have hostile intentions towards them. They tend to be solitary, and when in social situations with unfamiliar people they often come across as awkward, stiff, and unable to carry out conversation or maintain eye contact. Compounding their social difficulties, schizotypal people are commonly odd, eccentric, or peculiar in their mannerisms, and their range of emotional responses is often restricted. In addition, schizotypal people tend to show a variety of unusual cognitive and perceptual characteristics. For example, they are very superstitious, sometimes experience disorted perceptions, and often believe that they have paranormal powers, such as being able to foretell the future or magically influence other people's behaviour. In childhood and adolescence many of these schizotypal personality characteristics are manifested in social isolation and anxiety, under-achievement in school, peculiarities of behaviour and appearance that lead to teasing by peers, and active and often bizarre fantasy lives.

Schizotypal people are at an increased risk of developing schizophrenia, although not all schizophrenic adults clearly exhibit pre-existing schizotypal traits and not all people who do exhibit these traits develop schizophrenia. The precise nature of the life stresses that trigger schizophrenia in the fraction of schizotypal people who develop the disorder is not entirely clear. However, a number of physical and social stresses do seem to be involved. These stresses illustrate the wide variety of environmental influences that are involved in mental disorder in vulnerable individuals. First, there is some evidence that events during and prior to birth are influential in some cases, possibly including exposure to a virus in the womb and oxygen deprivation due to difficulties during delivery of the baby. Second, there is evidence that chaotic or inadequate child-rearing during the school years may increase the risk of schizophrenia among vulnerable, schizotypal individuals. Third, general life stress in adulthood, such as living alone for the first time, suffering the break-up of a close relationship, or receiving angry criticism or excessive demands from family members, may also play a role in precipitating schizophrenia. However, none of these stresses cause schizophrenia in themselves, seeming only to do so among people who have the appropriate personality (and genetic) vulnerability.

The schizotypal diathesis is an interesting one in several respects. For one thing, it seems to be unlike many personality diatheses in being a matter of kind rather than a matter of degree (see Chapter 3). That is, people either belong to the category of schizotypes or they do not, and only the former seem to be at risk of developing schizophrenia. A second interesting aspect of schizotypy is that, like major depression, somewhat different forms of the diathesis may be precipitated by different kinds of stresses, and may result in somewhat distinctive patterns of symptoms. Some Danish research examining the children of people with schizophrenia – who are at increased risk of having the schizotypal diathesis – indicates that there are two rather distinct pathways linking the diathesis to the disorder of schizophrenia (Cannon, Mednick, & Parnas, 1990). On the one hand, some vulnerable children and adolescents tend to be socially withdrawn, emotionally unresponsive, and introverted, and often have a history of birth complications. If these individuals develop schizophrenia as adults they tend to exhibit 'negative' symptoms of the disorder (e.g., loss of motivation, profound apathy, flattened emotional expression). On the other hand, some children and adolescents with the schizotypal diathesis are impulsive, disruptive, and have peculiar mannerisms, rather than being quiet and emotionally bland. For these individuals, a chaotic family environment, including such factors such as frequent moves of home, abuse, and neglect, seems to be particularly important in triggering schizophrenia. If they do develop schizophrenia, they tend to exhibit 'positive' symptoms, such as paranoid delusions, hallucinations, and disorganized speech.

Major depression and schizophrenia provide two good examples of how diathesis–stress models explain the connections between personality and mental disorder. In both cases psychologists have discovered personality characteristics that place people at increased risk of developing the respective disorders, but are not sufficient to produce the disorders in themselves. In both cases, more than one kind of personality diathesis seems to exist, and these different diatheses seem to require somewhat different kinds of stressful events to precipitate the disorders. Moreover, the personality characteristics that make people vulnerable to the two disorders also seem to influence the ways in which they express the disorders, producing distinctive patterns of symptoms. To summarize, personality characteristics influence vulnerability, precipitating factors, and symptom patterns for mental disorders.

Our discussions of personality factors in mental disorder have focused on depression and schizophrenia, but it is worth mentioning in passing that there appear to be personality vulnerabilities for many other mental disorders. To give one example, social phobics – people who suffer from disabling anxiety in social situations such as parties and public speaking – commonly have had what is known as 'inhibited temperament' as infants and young children (Kagan, 1994). Such children are unusually shy, are easily over-stimulated, and react fearfully and with high levels of physiological arousal to unfamiliar situations. (They are also, Kagan claims, more likely than one would expect by

Table 9.1   *Personality vulnerabilities for selected mental disorders*

Disorder	Diathesis	Definition
Anorexia nervosa	Perfectionism	A tendency to set extremely high performance standards for oneself and to be distressed when these are not met
Bipolar disorder	Hypomanic temperament	A tendency to be overly optimistic, excitable, exuberant, energetic, hyperactive, and needing less sleep than other people
Obsessive-compulsive disorder	Thought–action fusion	A tendency to see thoughts and actions as equivalent, so that having a thought about a negative thing happening makes it more likely to happen, and is morally equivalent to doing that thing
Panic disorder	Anxiety sensitivity	A tendency to fear the physical symptoms of anxiety, such as racing heartbeat and shortness of breath

chance to be blue-eyed!) Having an inhibited temperament does not dictate that a child will, as an adult, become socially phobic, because many other influences such as life stress and home and school environment are also involved, but it does raise the odds.

To give another example, psychopaths – people who seem to lack the capacity for remorse and empathy with others, and who often engage in impulsive, violent, deceitful, and otherwise antisocial activities – seem to have the personality diathesis of unusually low fearfulness (Lykken, 1995). Once again, this diathesis does not in itself destine children to become psychopathic adults. However, by making children more impulsive and risk-seeking and less concerned and inhibited by the fear of punishment, the diathesis leaves them especially vulnerable to a variety of environmental conditions that push and pull them towards a psychopathic way of living. These conditions might include abusive, coercive, or neglectful parenting (fearless, impulsive children are apt to be frustrating and difficult to socialize), falling in with groups of older peers who introduce the child to petty criminality, being made homeless, repeatedly witnessing violent acts, and so on. In short, identifiable personality dispositions make people vulnerable for psychopathy, and these dispositions act in combination with identifiable life circumstances to produce disorder. Several additional empirically validated diatheses for mental disorders are summarized in Table 9.1, to convey a sense of the range of personality vulnerabilities that have been identified. Personality researchers are actively engaged in the important task of identifying more of these risk factors so as better to detect and intervene with people at risk.

PERSONALITY DISORDERS

Our extended discussions of depression and schizophrenia have focused on the role that personality dispositions play in making people vulnerable to mental disorders. However, in addition to influencing who develops particular disorders and how they express them, some personality dispositions can themselves be understood as disorders. These dispositions are known as 'personality disorders'. These disorders have recently become a major topic of investigation in clinical psychology, although they have been recognized forms of psychological disturbance since the 18th century, when European psychiatrists understood them in terms of moral and constitutional degeneracy.

In essence, the personality disorders are enduring dispositions that are inflexible and maladaptive, producing significant interpersonal difficulties and distress for people who have them. They therefore differ from most other mental disorders in several important respects. First, their primary symptoms involve problems in the person's relations with others rather than abnormalities of personal behaviour, emotions, or thinking, although such abnormalities often co-exist. Second, they are lasting rather than temporary or recurrent: unlike most mental disorders which *affect* or befall the person at distinct times, personality disorders are woven into the fabric of the person, partly defining who they *are*. Third, because personality disorders are intrinsic to the person's sense of self in a way that most disorders are not, they are seldom seen by the person as problems to be solved by psychological treatment. More often, the person sees other people as the source of their interpersonal difficulties, and only comes into treatment when their personality disorder gives rise to another disorder, such as depression.

Most of the personality disorders seem to reflect exaggerated or extreme forms of normal personality variation. Brief descriptions of the ten disorders recognized by the current diagnostic system (the DSM-IV-TR: American Psychiatric Association, 2000), are presented in Table 9.2. A wide variety of theories have been developed to make sense of personality traits and processes that underlie the descriptive features laid out in the table. Researchers have found that many of them can be captured well by Big Five personality traits (see Chapter 2), and that traits having to do with interpersonal behaviour are particularly important. Most disorders, that is, have a distinctive interpersonal style whose inflexibility causes difficulties in their personal relationships. In addition to these trait approaches, biological, cognitive, and psychoanalytic theories of the personality disorders have also been put forward. To illustrate the differences among these different conceptualizations, we will briefly consider the example of paranoid personality disorder.

As we see in Table 9.2, paranoid personalities are suspicious, distrustful, liable to see others as malicious and devious, and inclined to search for the

Table 9.2 *Descriptive features of the personality disorders*

Personality disorder	Core personality features
Paranoid	Pervasive distrust and suspicion of others, tendency to see others as exploiting, harming or deceiving the person and to read threatening hidden meanings into benign remarks or events
Schizoid	Pervasive detachment from social relationships (i.e., preference for solitary activities and lack of desire for close relationships) and restricted or cold emotional expression
Schizotypal	Pervasive peculiarities in beliefs, perceptions, speech, and behaviour, coupled with excessive social anxiety and isolation
Antisocial	Pervasive disregard for and violation of the rights of others, shown by deceitfulness, impulsiveness, aggressiveness, irresponsibility and remorselessness
Borderline	Pervasive instability of relationships, self-image and emotions, indicated by recurrent suicidal gestures, abandonment fears, impulsiveness, and mood-swings
Histrionic	Pervasive pattern of exaggerated emotionality and attention-seeking, shown by inappropriate exhibitionism, seductiveness, shallow displays of emotion, and self-dramatization
Narcissistic	Pervasive grandiosity, need for admiration, and lack of empathy for others, indicated by arrogance, self-importance, and feeling entitled to special treatment
Avoidant	Pervasive social inhibition, feelings of inadequacy, and over-sensitivity to negative evaluation, shown by fear of criticism and rejection
Dependent	Pervasive need to be taken care of, involving submissive and clinging behaviour and fears of separation
Obsessive-compulsive	Pervasive preoccupation with orderliness, perfectionism, and being in control, manifested by inflexibility, over-conscientiousness, excessive devotion to work, stubbornness, and miserliness

'truth' hidden behind ordinary phenomena. They are also grudging, unforgiving, unwilling to confide in others, quick to take offence, argumentative, secretive, and emotionally guarded. How might we account for these characteristics? In terms of the five-factor model, paranoid personalities fall high on Neuroticism, indicating proneness to negative emotions and emotional reactivity, and low on Agreeableness, suggesting a cold and aloof manner. They have an interpersonal style that is vindictive, bitter, domineering, and prone to aggression.

Cognitive theorists propose that paranoid personalities have distinctive schemas about themselves and others: they see themselves as vulnerable, morally righteous, and innocent, and others as malicious, abusive, and interfering. Because they hold such negative beliefs about the willingness and power of others to inflict harm on them, they believe that trust is risky and that they must always be vigilant for attacks. Consequently, they pursue an inter-personal strategy of wariness, suspicion, and pre-emptive counter-attack.

Psychoanalysts, finally, argue that the paranoid personality has an unconscious sense of personal weakness and inferiority, and an unconscious fear of being overwhelmed in close relationships, both of which may spring from early disruptions in their relations with their parents. Because of this self-image and this fear, they are very sensitive to being humiliated, dominated, and made passive by others, and are overly protective of their personal autonomy. In addition, they tend to employ the defence mechanisms of projection, disowning their self-doubts and aggressive wishes and attributing them to others, who they view as critical, contemptuous, and malevolent towards them. It is clear to see that these alternative accounts of paranoid personality offer a variety of insights into the personality structures and processes that underpin the disorder. Each of them identifies somewhat different core disturbances, and has distinct implications for how treatment of the disorder should be conducted.

Personality disorders present an intriguing field of study to personality researchers and theorists. However, the field also has more than its share of controversies. Some writers question the distinctness of the disorders, noting that most people who are diagnosed with a personality disorder receive more than one diagnosis (e.g., avoidant and dependent personality disorders often co-occur, as do antisocial, narcissistic, and paranoid personality disorders). Many writers therefore criticize the current system of diagnosing disorders, arguing that fewer disorders should be recognized, or that the existing diagnostic categories should be replaced with a few dimensions. Others argue that to diagnose someone with a personality disorder is to treat as a psychiatric disorder something that is really an expression of normal personality variation, an alternative philosophy of life, or a form of moral deviance.

Despite these controversies, however, few psychologists question the need to take personality disorders into account when assessing and treating other mental disorders. Personality disorders make people vulnerable to a variety of mental disorders; the reader will notice that dependent and schizotypal personality disorders correspond to some extent to diatheses for depression and schizophrenia that were discussed earlier. Personality disorders also complicate the treatment of other disorders, typically making the relationship with the therapist more difficult, reducing the patient's compliance with instructions and medication regimens, and generally making treatment slower and less beneficial. For these reasons, it is vitally important for us to further our understanding of personality disorders if we want to improve the effectiveness of psychological treatment.

Illustrative study: does the five-factor model help to illuminate personality disorders?

In collaboration with several Chinese colleagues, American psychologists Robert McCrae and Paul Costa (McCrae et al., 2001) sought to clarify how well abnormal personality can be understood in terms of the five-factor model (FFM). Many writers have argued that there is no sharp, categorical distinction between normal and abnormal personality, and that models of normal personality should therefore help to make sense of personality disorders (PDs). Disorders might simply reflect extreme positions on continuous FFM dimensions.

A considerable amount of research has shown correlations between PDs and FFM dimensions. McCrae et al. attempted to do so in a cultural setting where this sort of research had not previously been done: the People's Republic of China. Some writers have questioned whether personality disorders that were catalogued in the West can also be found elsewhere in the world, making McCrae et al.'s effort an important scientific exercise.

McCrae et al. obtained a sample of 1,909 Chinese psychiatric patients and administered to them a carefully translated questionnaire measure of the FFM and questionnaire- and interview-based measures of PDs. Expected or 'prototypical' FFM profiles for each PD were generated based on Western research — for example, the profile for paranoid PD includes high Neuroticism and Conscientiousness, and low Agreeableness — and the extent to which each participant fitted each profile was calculated. These FFM-based measures of PDs were then correlated with scores for the same PDs on the PD questionnaire and interview. If these different measures correlate well, then it would appear that FFM does a good job of making sense of the PDs in China: the same FFM profiles that capture PDs in Western nations would capture them in that country.

Consistent with the validity of the FFM's PD profiles in China, these profiles correlated reasonably well with the scores derived from the PD questionnaire and interview. The FFM, a prominent model of normal personality, appears to be a useful tool for understanding abnormal personality in China as well as in the countries where the model was developed.

MULTIPLE PERSONALITY

The personality disorders generally seem to reflect exaggerated expressions of normal personality dispositions. For this reason, many of us can recognize aspects of our own or our acquaintances' personalities when we read descriptions of these disorders. However, there is another disturbance of personality that seems so peculiar and striking that it is difficult to identify with it at all. This disturbance is often referred to as 'multiple personality disorder', although more recently the term 'dissociative identity disorder' has been put forward. For the sake of simplicity, we will refer to the disorder here as '**multiple personality**'.

In essence, multiple personality is the existence of two or more distinct personalities or identities, each of which takes control of the person's behaviour from time to time. Each personality has its own distinctive way of thinking and behaving, and is generally unaware of what the other personalities do when they are in charge. As a result, one personality is often unable to recall or account for long stretches of time when another personality was dominant, and may re-emerge to find itself in an unfamiliar place or activity. The person may wake up in an unfamiliar bed with someone they do not remember, or believe that someone impersonating them is withdrawing money from their bank account only to find that another personality was the culprit.

People diagnosed with multiple personality generally have a primary or 'host' personality, and one or more 'alter' personalities. These alters typically have their own names, ages, mannerisms, and emotional states, and often they are of a different gender to the host personality. Different personalities often emerge predictably in different situations, and switches between them often occur during stressful interactions with others. Whereas the host personality is usually sad, dependent, and passive, the alters are often childish, hostile, seductive, or otherwise uninhibited, and are often scornful of the other personalities. The personalities seem to share general knowledge and physical skills, but may differ in many other respects. There are reports of cases whose personalities had different allergies, eye-glass prescriptions, handedness (left versus right), menstrual cycles, and patterns of blood flow in the brain.

The existence of people with multiple personalities has proven to be a controversial issue for a variety of reasons. First, it seems simply inconceivable to many people that anyone could harbour distinct identities within a single body. The idea that each of us has a single personality, whose coherence and continuity over time we prize in ourselves and rely on in making sense of other people, is deeply rooted in Western cultures. We expect others to be consistent in their behaviour and beliefs, and distrust dramatic changes in either. People who hold contradictory beliefs or behave very differently from one time to another are distrusted, and their apparent lack of a solid 'centre' is often attributed to personal weakness or immorality, or to the undue influence of others. We might accept that people act differently in different social roles or situations, but we tend to see these differences as facets of a unitary self, shallow, socially-imposed performances rather than deep divisions between alternative personalities.

A second source of scepticism about multiple personalities has to do with the recent history of the diagnosis itself, which is unusual. Until 1980 fewer than 200 cases were reported worldwide, but present estimates suggest that there may currently be tens of thousands of cases. In addition to the apparently epidemic nature of multiple personality, it is strikingly restricted to North America, with very few cases having been recorded outside the USA. Some have even claimed that the disorder is one of an exotic family of 'culture-bound' disorders, like *koro* (the intense and sometimes epidemic fear among some South and East Asian men that their penis will disappear into their body). Even within the USA, the disorder tends to congregate in a few urban areas, where a small number of psychologists and psychiatrists claim to have seen very large numbers of patients.

In addition to the intuitive strangeness and geographic limits of multiple personalities, many people are sceptical of the disorder because of the bizarre, faddish, and cult-like phenomena that sometimes adhere to it. In recent years, as more and more attention has been paid to the disorder and organized groups and conferences for sufferers have emerged, the number of alters that diagnosed cases of multiple personality present has increased, from the two or three that were typical in early reports to an average of about 12, with some cases claiming more than 100. Lately, reports of animal alters have begun to appear regularly, as have claims by patients to have been abused in gruesome rituals perpetrated by organized satanic cults or aliens. Phenomena such as these strain the credibility of many people, and suggest to them that they are witnessing some mixture of fantasy, hysteria, and theatre.

Psychological theories of the origin and nature of multiple personality have been developed over the past two decades, building on important theoretical contributions made by the 19th-century French psychiatrist Pierre Janet. Recent theories differ in their details, but most of them begin with two apparently crucial facts about multiple personality. First, almost all people diagnosed with the disorder report having been severely sexually or physically abused as children. Second, these people tend to score very high on measures of a psychological characteristic known as 'suggestibility', which refers to the capacity to become absorbed in activities and to respond to social influences. Highly suggestible people are easily hypnotized; that is to say, they are easily sent into a trance-like state of consciousness in which they are unusually responsive to other people's suggestions.

Most recent theories of multiple personality put these two observations together in an intriguing way. They argue that in response to extreme and inescapable traumatic experiences, such as being repeatedly raped by a stepfather, some young children split their consciousness into one part that contains the traumatic memories and associated thoughts, and another part that has no recollection of the trauma. This splitting of consciousness is known as 'dissociation', and may represent a primitive attempt by the child to protect itself against the pain and catastrophic loss of trust and security that the traumatic abuse involves. In effect, the child tries to preserve some sense of intact selfhood by a kind of 'internal avoidance' of the trauma, in which it is isolated into a separate pocket of awareness and memory. This kind of reaction has been compared to the survival tactics of animals that freeze or play dead when confronted by predators. Children who have highly suggestible personalities may be predisposed to dissociate in this way, because they are unusually capable of entering trance-like states and deflecting their attention away from unpleasant experiences. In theory, then, some children engage in an 'auto-hypnotic' reaction to protect themselves against overwhelming stress. Although this reaction may be self-protective in the short term, in the long term it creates a disintegrated personality. Moreover, children who dissociate under severe stress may learn to use dissociation as a habitual defence mechanism, which may lead them to continue to split off new identities as they progress through life.

According to this theory of multiple personality, traumatic experiences in childhood fragment an initially unitary personality in people whose suggestibility makes them predisposed to dissociate. However, this theory remains controversial to some psychologists. One in particular, Nicholas Spanos (1994), argues that multiple personality is not caused by past traumas at all. Instead, it is created by therapists who believe that multiple personality is under-diagnosed, and by a culture that recognizes it as a legitimate way of expressing psychological distress, just as in other cultures and times possession by spirits has been recognized. Spanos proposes that therapists commonly using leading questions and hypnotic procedures to induce their patients to understand their often chaotic experiences in terms of distinct personalities. Because these patients are prone to sudden mood swings, the idea that they have several identities is readily planted in their minds by therapists who treat their desires, emotions, and recollections *as if* they were distinct and nameable identities. The suggestibility of the patients makes them susceptible to their therapists' convictions that they have multiple personalities, even if these convictions are communicated in subtle ways, and to elaborate each newly hatched identity into a fully-fledged character. Spanos has even conducted experiments in which, using simple hypnotic instructions, several multiple personality-like phenomena can be produced in ordinary people. In short, Spanos sees multiple personality as a way for suggestible people who are struggling with identity confusions and diffuse psychological problems to make sense of their experiences. It also allows them to enact multiple social roles and personality states – such as confident sexuality, anger, authority, and innocence (i.e., the alters) – that they were unable to express prior to 'becoming a multiple'.

The two theories of multiple personality could hardly be more incompatible. One views the personalities as truly distinct products of traumatic experiences, while the other sees them as labels for poorly integrated psychological states, labels that are transformed into distinct identities by a collusion of patient and therapist. One sees multiple personality as a real disorder that is finally being recognized by enlightened mental health professionals after years of ignorance, the other as a hysterical epidemic that can be likened to previous epidemics of witchcraft and demonic possession. Wherever the truth may lie, it is clear that people diagnosed with multiple personality are not simply play-acting: they believe sincerely and passionately that their personalities are not merely roles to be enacted or personas to be juggled. The solution to the puzzle of multiple personality will be found somewhere in the grey area between two metaphors: the actor playing a series of parts and the sheet of glass shattered into pieces by a hammer.

The controversy over multiple personality is sure to continue, and it is currently the focus of vigorous debate. At this point, however, it is enough to contemplate the controversy as another fascinating intersection between the psychology of personality and mental disorder.

PERSONALITY AND PHYSICAL ILLNESS

Up to this point we have focused exclusively on the links between personality and mental health. However, it would be unfortunate to complete our investigation of this topic without discussing the connections between personality and illnesses that primarily affect the body. Although these links are proving to be highly complex, two of them are particularly well-established and noteworthy.

Type A personality and coronary heart disease

Coronary heart disease (CHD) is a major – often *the* major – cause of death in industrialized nations. The disease is caused by a narrowing of the arteries that supply blood to the heart ('coronary atherosclerosis'), due to the gradual build-up of accumulations of fatty substances, called 'plaques', on the artery walls. The formation of plaques reduces the flow of blood to the muscles of the heart, eventually producing chest pain ('angina pectoralis') and heart attacks ('myocardial infarction') when a portion of the heart, deprived of oxygen, dies.

Many risk factors have been found for CHD, of which the foremost are high blood pressure, smoking, blood cholesterol levels, fat intake, and being male. However, one personality disposition, termed 'Type A' personality by the cardiologists who first proposed it (Friedman & Rosenman, 1974), also appears to place people at risk of the disease. They described Type A people as competitive, hostile, impatient, and devoted to personal achievement, and found them to be about twice as likely to develop symptoms of CHD than people who do not exhibit these traits ('Type B' personalities). Later research has shown that the Type A construct has several rather distinct components, only some of which are linked to CHD risk, with the evidence pointing to hostility as the active ingredient (Smith & Spiro, 2002). Psychologists have related this dispositional hostility to an excessive need for unfettered personal control, a tendency to set high standards for one's performance, and a cynical belief that life is a competitive struggle where other people can be expected to act unfairly.

Knowing that hostility is a diathesis for CHD has led researchers to ask what mechanisms might link this trait to the physiological processes that result in coronary atherosclerosis. The mechanisms appear to be complicated. However, the fundamental pathway seems to be that hostile people tend to show high levels of physiological reactivity to psychological stresses. In response to stress, they show an unusually intense activation of the physiological system that readies the body for active effort and underlies fear and anger. This activation may promote atherosclerosis by several means – by generating large blood pressure and heart rate fluctuations and chemical secretions that damage the walls of the coronary arteries, and by releasing fatty molecules that contribute to arterial plaques – and may also play a role in triggering heart attacks among people whose atherosclerosis has progressed significantly. In short, psychologists have taken great steps to understand the personality diathesis as well as its mechanisms of harmful influence on the body.

Pessimism and cancer

Psychological researchers have made similar progress in understanding the role of personality in cancer, a collection of disorders which involve the proliferation of abnormal cells that form tumours in different parts of the body. Because the body normally fights cancers by killing abnormal cells with its immune system – a system that combats disease by identifying and destroying 'foreign' particles such as bacteria, viruses, and disordered cells – psychological processes that impair immune function have been the focus of most work. This research has yielded a description of the cancer-prone (or 'Type C') personality, and an account of the processes that link it, via reduced immune function, to the development and rapid progression of cancers.

The picture of the cancer-prone personality that has emerged over the past two decades includes a group of related dispositions, of which depression, hopelessness, helplessness, and low emotionality (i.e., a stoical, 'rational', repressed, and passive approach to life). Note that these characteristics could develop in response to cancer rather than predisposing people to it, so researchers have had to show that people who have the characteristics prior to the onset of cancer are at increased risk of developing it later. The evidence points to these characteristics being associated with reduced immune function in several rather complex ways. However, one well-supported pathway links hopelessness, helplessness, and depression – all associated with the pessimistic explanatory style discussed earlier in this chapter – and a physiological system that coordinates responses to uncontrollable stress and the perceived inability to cope. These responses include subjective sadness, withdrawal, and conservation of bodily resources (e.g., passivity), and are commonly triggered in response to experiences of loss and clinical depression. Activation of this physiological system leads to the release of hormones that have been shown to reduce the immune system's capacity to destroy cancerous cells, which is carried out by its roving 'natural killer' cells. As with CHD, then, we have a pathway which connects a personality diathesis, a series of physiological processes, and the increased likelihood of a serious set of illnesses.

Additional links between personality and health

In addition to the well-researched role of Type A personality and pessimism as diatheses for heart disease and cancer, personality dispositions have a variety of additional influences on health and illness. First, some dispositions may not directly influence the physiological processes that increase the risk of illness – such as the narrowing of coronary arteries and the impairment of immune function – but indirectly influence health by affecting behavioural risk factors. For example, any personality disposition that is associated with smoking, excessive drinking, or risky sexual practices will be indirectly associated with the health problems that are linked to these behaviours. If, as seems to be the case, more extraverted and neurotic people tend to be smokers, they will be more prone to the health risks associated with smoking. Similarly, sensation-seekers tend to be more likely to contract venereal diseases via their increased likelihood of taking sexual risks (Kalichman, Heckman, & Kelly, 1996).

Personality dispositions may be indirectly linked to physical illness in a second way. Besides being associated with behavioural risk factors for illness, some personality dispositions may be associated with what can be called preventive, protective, or health-promoting behaviour. Whereas some kinds of behaviour place the person at risk of illness, others – such as seeking regular medical check-ups, avoiding excessive sun exposure, maintaining a good diet and exercise, and taking sexual precautions (e.g., condom use) – reduce the risk of illness. Any personality disposition that reduces a person's likelihood of engaging in protective behaviour will therefore be associated with an increased risk of illness. Conscientiousness traits appear to have especially strong links to the practice of health-promoting behaviours (Bogg & Roberts, 2004). Similarly, people who tend not to be concerned about their future well-being, who are fearful of learning unpleasant information about themselves, or who are unrealistically optimistic about their personal risk of illness will probably be deficient in their protective behaviour. Consequently, these dispositions – lack of conscientiousness, impulsivity, neuroticism, and unrealistic optimism – may be linked to ill-health. On the other hand, optimism appears to be health-promoting because it enables effective coping with stress and extraversion is healthy because it is associated with efficient seeking of social support.

A third way in which personality dispositions may influence health in addition to their role as diatheses is by influencing recovery and the risk of recurrence of illnesses. For instance, any disposition that makes people less likely to comply with medical treatments – impulsivity or low conscientiousness, perhaps (Kenford, Smith, Wetter, Jorenby, Fiore, & Baker, 2002) – should be associated with lower or slower rates of recovery. Similarly, people's habitual coping styles probably influence how well they respond to the stress of illness, and hence their likelihood of suffering another episode of the illness. Personality dispositions that make people vulnerable to the first episode of an illness may be quite different from the dispositions that make people vulnerable to a second. For instance, one study found that Type A personality *improves* the prognosis of patients who have suffered a heart attack: people who are aggressive and impatient in pursuing their recovery seem to recover better than those who are not.

In summary, then, there is a variety of ways in which personality dispositions may be linked with physical illness: as diatheses, as predictors of behavioural risk factors, as predictors of deficient protective or preventive behaviour, and as predictors of recovery and recurrence. All of these sorts of links are under active investigation in the burgeoning fields of health psychology and behavioural medicine. The importance of this work is obvious. First, it offers promising avenues for the development of psychologically-informed interventions for preventing some of the most deadly and debilitating conditions that afflict humanity. Perhaps we can successfully change Type A personality and the pessimistic explanatory styles that place people at risk of premature death and poor response to medical treatment. Second, it challenges the naïve division between mind and body, showing how the whole person, as an integrated *system*, is implicated in health and illness.

Although there are many reasons to be excited by research on the intersection of personality and illness, it is important not to become over-enthusiastic.

These links are often enormously complicated, and definitive research is very hard to conduct. In addition, it is very important to remember that the associations between personality dispositions and illness are not particularly strong, and that they contribute to vulnerability alongside many non-psychological risk factors. Unfortunately, when people learn that psychological processes play a role in illness they sometimes engage in what could be called the 'psychosomatic fallacy', imagining that illness is *caused* by a character flaw for which the ill person is responsible. This kind of stigmatizing and victim-blaming should be avoided, and is certainly not warranted by the evidence.

CONCLUSIONS

Personality characteristics are important sources of vulnerability for a variety of mental disorders, as well as for some physical illnesses. Several traits have been identified as diatheses for such crippling mental disorders as major depression and schizophrenia, as well as physical illness such as coronary heart disease and cancer. None of these diatheses are capable of producing their disorder without the contribution of other influences, such as life stresses and non-psychological risk factors. Often, the combination of personality diathesis and environmental stress is especially potent in producing mental disorder. However, personality plays a powerful role in the development of mental disorders, acting not only as a risk factor but also as an influence on the kinds of stress that are harmful to different people and on the ways in which people express and experience their disorder. Finally, some forms of personality variation can themselves be considered mental disorders. These personality disorders, as well as multiple personality, have emerged as intriguing and clinically important topics of investigation, and are open to a wide and fascinating variety of explanations.

Chapter summary

- Personality psychology intersects with clinical psychology and health psychology in several intriguing ways. Personality characteristics render people vulnerable to particular kinds of mental disorder, in extreme cases they constitute disorders in themselves, and they play a role in physical illness and health.
- Personality vulnerabilities ('diatheses') increase the risk for major mental disorders. Disorder usually occurs only when a diathesis is triggered by life stress, with less stress necessary the greater the level of vulnerability.

(Continued)

(Continued)

- Major depression and schizophrenia are two serious mental disorders that have well-established personality vulnerabilities.
- Personality disorders are extreme, inflexible maladaptive personality variants that are associated with significant distress and interpersonal difficulties for people who are affected. Ten distinct forms are recognized by the current psychiatric classification, and these can be explained.
- Multiple personality ('dissociative identity disorder') is a controversial and rare condition in which the person appears to have several distinct personalities, which are often mutually unaware.
- Personality characteristics appear to be linked to physical illnesses. Type A personality (hostility, impatience, competitiveness) confers an increased risk of heart disease; pessimism may also be associated with cancer risk.
- In addition, a number of traits are associated with risky and self-damaging behaviours that increase the risk of illness indirectly, or with patterns of compliance with treatment that increase the risk of poor clinical outcomes (e.g., slow recovery or recurrence of the illness).

Further reading

- Alloy, L.B., & Riskind, J.H. (eds.) (2005). *Cognitive vulnerability to emotional disorders*. Mahwah, NJ: Erlbaum.

This diverse collection of chapters takes a cognitive approach to the factors that place people at risk for the development of disorders involving depression, anxiety, disturbed eating, and much more.

- Claridge, G., & Davis, C. (2003). *Personality and psychological disorders*. London: Hodder Arnold.

Claridge and Davis offer a thought-provoking and clear explication of the relationship between personality variation and major mental disorders.

- Kihlstrom, J.F. (2005). Dissociative disorders. *Annual Review of Clinical Psychology, 1*, 227–53.

(Continued)

(Continued)

For readers interested in multiple personality ('dissociative identity disorder'), Kihlstrom provides a review of current research and theory.

- Lenzenweger, M.F., & Clarkin, J.F. (2004). *Major theories of personality disorder* (2nd ed.). New York: Guilford.

This book contains several excellent chapters that present diverse theoretical perspectives (from the psychodynamic to the biological) on personality disorders.

- Smith, T.W., & MacKenzie, J. (2006). Personality and risk of physical illness. *Annual Review of Clinical Psychology, 2,* 435–67.

This is a cutting-edge review of the empirical evidence concerning the role of personality in physical health and illness.

- Zuckerman, M. (1999). *Vulnerability to psychopathology: A biosocial model.* Washington, DC: American Psychological Association.

Zuckerman's book exemplifies the diathesis–stress model of mental disorders, examining the ways in which personality increases risk of the triggering of mental disorders.

10

Psychobiography and Life Narratives

Learning objectives

- To understand the personological approach to the study of individual personalities.
- To recognize the methodological difficulties involved in making biographical sense of lives, and the weaknesses of many psychobiographies.
- To appreciate how these difficulties and weaknesses can be overcome.
- To understand the concept of 'life narrative' and how it illuminates an important dimension of the self.
- To understand some of the ways in which life narratives can be described and studied.

How personality theory and research can be used to make sense of individual lives is the focus of this chapter. We begin by examining the contentious practice of 'psychobiography', a form of biographical investigation and writing that is informed by personality psychology. Some of the theoretical and methodological problems that plague psychobiographies are discussed, followed by some of the steps that can be taken to improve their validity. We then turn to the systematic study of the stories that people tell about their own lives, and how these 'self-narratives' represent an important aspect of the self.

Adolf Hitler is the person many of us would name if we were asked to identify a historical figure who embodies evil. He was largely responsible, most historians would agree, for a war in which perhaps 50 million people lost their lives, and prosecuted a remorseless policy of extermination towards millions of Jews, homosexuals, handicapped people, 'mental defectives', Gypsies and Slavs.

Numerous attempts have been made to make sense of Hitler as a person (e.g., Redlich, 1999; see Rosenbaum, 1998, for a review). Not all of these are psychological in nature. Some writers see him as merely a symptom of the turbulent historical and political forces surging through Germany in his time. By this account, Nazism and the Holocaust were, in a sense, just waiting to happen whether or not a Hitler arose to lead and harness them, and therefore did not depend in any deep way on his personal dispositions. Others view Hitler through a theological lens, focusing on religious concepts of evil, sin, and so on. A large number of writers, however, have attempted to understand Hitler's psychology in the hope that it will illuminate the origins and dynamics of his behaviour.

Sexuality has been a dominant focus of attention for Hitler's more psychological biographers. One of the most exotic explanations makes reference to Hitler's supposed 'genital deficiency'. The tamer version of this explanation proposes that he had a congenital deformity of the penis. The more colourful alternative is that during a schoolboy prank, in which he supposedly attempted to urinate in a billy-goat's mouth, the goat objected and bit off one testicle. This story is supported by a medical examiner who examined Hitler's charred body after he had killed himself in his bunker as Berlin fell to the Allies. His scrotum – described as 'singed but preserved' – was found to lack a left testicle. Writers have argued that one or other of these genital abnormalities caused Hitler intense shame, rendered him sexually dysfunctional, and poisoned his relationships with women. It has been written that his genital condition led him to react against any femininity within himself by developing a harsh form of hyper-masculinity. This manifested itself in cruelty, mistrust of women, and the sensuousness and emotionality that they represented to him, and hatred of homosexuals and other supposedly 'feminized' groups such as Jews. Some writers have reported that Hitler had an unusual sexual perversion involving urine ('undinism'), and that the horror of participating in this may have been at least partially responsible for the suicide or attempted suicide of many of the women with whom he was intimate.

Other writers have attempted to comprehend Hitler's personality from non-sexual angles. It has been claimed that he had a physically abusive father. His anti-Semitism has been seen as rooted in his perception that a Jewish doctor mishandled the treatment of his dying mother, or as a form of displaced self-hatred because his paternal grandfather may have been Jewish. Various writers have labelled Hitler's personality psychopathic and borderline, described it as death-loving, or attributed it to a brain disorder called 'post-encephalic sociopathy'. Others have rejected efforts to attribute mental disorders to him and described him simply as an unusually cold-hearted and Machiavellian politician. A variety of symptoms and behavioural problems have been reported, ranging from hallucinations, hysterical (i.e., psychologically-caused) blindness, hypochondria, and amphetamine abuse. The combined evidence of these bewilderingly diverse psychological analyses points to a clearly disturbed man, but whether they bring us closer to an understanding of a terrible genocide is perhaps debatable.

PSYCHOBIOGRAPHY

Attempts such as these to make sense of Adolf Hitler's personality are examples of '**psychobiography**'. Biographies, of course, are accounts of individual lives, and what sets psychobiographies apart from run-of-the-mill biographies is their use of psychological knowledge, in the form of theory and research. A psychobiography therefore tries to situate the events of someone's life in a psychological analysis of their personality and its development.

Numerous psychobiographical studies have been published over the years. Freud conducted the first, an analysis of Leonardo da Vinci in 1910, and later collaborated on a psychobiographical study of US president Woodrow Wilson. Erik Erikson, whose eight stages of human development we encountered in Chapter 7, published widely-read psychobiographical studies of Martin Luther, founder of Protestantism, and of Mahatma Gandhi, the non-violent architect of Indian independence. Other psychobiographies have tackled famous politicians (e.g., Ronald Reagan, Margaret Thatcher, Saddam Hussein, Richard Nixon), writers and intellectuals (e.g., Virginia Woolf, Charles Darwin), and cultural icons (e.g., Elvis Presley), among many others (Schultz, 2005).

Psychobiography is one expression of a branch of personality psychology that Henry Murray, its originator, dubbed '**personology**'. Personologists try to make sense of individual lives through detailed analysis of single cases, rather than by extracting general rules or observations about groups of people, and they tend to use qualitative rather than quantitative research methods. Their focus is not just on individual personalities, in their unique complexity, but also on *lives*: they aim to understand the life-history of the person as it unfolds through time, not just to take a snapshot of the person at a particular moment.

This description of psychobiography and the personological approach should resonate with some of the themes and issues that you have come across earlier in this book. First, psychobiography clearly relates to personality development (Chapter 7), in its focus on whole lives, extended through time. Second, psychobiography is, in a sense, a form of personality assessment (Chapter 8), an effort to make informed judgments about the person on the basis of systematically collected evidence. Third, psychobiographers tend to make use of psychoanalytic theory in their work (Chapter 5). Although this is not strictly necessary, and other personality theories can be (and have been) used in psychobiographical studies, psychoanalytic theories would seem to have several advantages: they address psychological development, they are well-suited to the intensive analysis of individuals, as in clinical case studies, and they claim to penetrate beneath the surface of the personality to its underlying dynamics.

It may not surprise you to learn that psychobiography has been a controversial activity, often seen as somewhat disreputable by historians and mainstream biographers (Elms, 1994). In part this disrepute reflects the controversies surrounding two of the common threads of psychobiography mentioned above, namely psychoanalytic theory and psychological assessment. Some of the criticisms that have been thrown at psychobiography reflect the reservations that many people hold about the problematic nature of psychoanalytic theory and inference, and the limitations of certain forms of assessment. We will discuss some of these problems below, as well as a few others.

WEAKNESSES OF PSYCHOBIOGRAPHY

Psychoanalytic theory

As we saw in Chapter 5, psychoanalysis is a controversial but influential approach to the understanding of personality. It has greater ambitions than many personality theories: to explain personality development, provide a basis for the treatment of mental disorders, interpret cultural phenomena, and, most of all, to go beneath the sometimes tranquil surface of the personality to the unpleasant truths (repressed wishes, sexual desires, unconscious fantasies, and so on) that lie beneath. It has also received a greater amount of criticism than most other theories, focusing particularly on the untestability of its theories, the weak and generally unscientific nature of its evidence base, the implausibility of some of its claims regarding human motivation and development, and the problems that plague psychoanalytic inference. The fact that with notable exceptions (e.g., Bowlby's 1991 attachment theory-based analysis of Charles Darwin) most psychobiographers make some use of psychoanalytic theory in their work leaves them open to many of the same criticisms.

Let's take an example from a psychobiography of Richard Nixon, the US president from 1969 to 1974 who left office in disgrace after it became known that he had supported the burglary of his opponents' offices to steal documents in the Watergate affair. Volkan, Itzkowitz, and Dod (1997) paint a portrait of a man who was highly moralistic but also willing to engage in criminal activities, who played the tough guy but was troubled by anxiety, and who was frequently paranoid and mistrustful of others. They also make a series of psychoanalytic inferences that might strike many readers as far-fetched and, more importantly, as going well beyond the available evidence. For example, they suggest that Nixon was especially troubled by leaks of information from the White House because they represented to him a loss of bowel control, and his personality was unconsciously dominated by such anal themes. Similarly, they argue that skills in public speaking were due in part to a sublimation of his childhood tendency to be a cry-baby, and that an inflammation of the blood vessels that he suffered reflected the operation of unconscious self-punishment. Speculations such as these are not uncommon in psychobiographies that employ psychoanalytic ideas, and to the extent that the theory can be questioned, so can the psychobiographical insights that are produced.

Inference problems

Volkan et al.'s (1997) interpretations of Nixon's personality are problematic not only because they make some questionable theoretical assumptions – for example, that unconscious guilt can cause tissue damage, that the leakage of information by one's staff is likely to be unconsciously understood as a leakage of faecal matter by one's anus – but also because the grounds for making the interpretations seem inadequate. It appears unlikely that the sort of evidence on which these inferences about Nixon's psychological dynamics were made could support them. Interpretations like these seem to go well beyond the available evidence, and rely on a form of theory-based guesswork. Such guesswork is difficult and unreliable enough when there is a living, breathing person in the psychoanalyst's consulting room, where new evidence such as dreams can at least be gathered and mental processes studied in real time. How much more difficult is it when the person is unavailable for contact and the evidence is incomplete and second-hand?

You may recall the problems with psychoanalytic inference that were discussed in Chapter 5. You will also remember the discussion of the problems with projective testing and with clinical prediction in Chapter 7 on psychological assessment. These problems can all arise in psychobiography. As with projective tests, inferences are often made about the subject's unconscious dynamics, and these inferences are often based on psychoanalytic theory, as in the case of Nixon. Similarly, the psychobiographer is required to assemble many different pieces of evidence about the person into an overall assessment, the very situation that has been shown to produce unreliable predictive judgments in clinical psychologists trying to integrate the results of multiple psychological tests. What's more, psychobiography is really not predictive at all in the sense of making judgments about the future: it usually tries to make sense of lives that have been completed, or are at least well advanced. Psychobiography is 'postdictive' not predictive, an exercise in making guesses about what has already happened. In hindsight many things look clearer than when looking into the future, and so postdictions are often more confident than they should be. For all of these reasons – the psychoanalytic licence to make judgments about the unconscious, the need to make a consistent assessment of the person out of many pieces of evidence, and the over-confidence of hindsight – psychobiographers run the risk of making serious inferential errors.

One such error – an attempt to extract deep underlying meaning from inadequate evidence – was a serious problem in the first psychobiography (Elms, 1994). Freud discussed Leonardo da Vinci's life in relation to his possible homosexuality, his illegitimacy (he was born out of wedlock to a peasant woman), his parents' separation, his remarkable creativity, and much more besides. At one point, Freud interpreted an event that Leonardo reported as an early childhood memory but that Freud took to be a fantasy. Leonardo wrote that a vulture had come down to him, opened his mouth, and repeatedly thrust its tail into it. Perhaps one does not need to be a psychoanalyst to infer a sexual meaning here, but Freud was and he did. He interpreted the fantasy as evidence of Leonardo's intense erotic relationship with his mother and of his subsequent homosexuality, based on his theory of the Oedipus complex. The interpretation was based in part on the fact that vultures are symbols of motherhood, and are sexually ambiguous (the Egyptian goddess Mut was depicted as a vulture with breasts and a penis). Unfortunately, however, Leonardo had not remembered being assaulted by a vulture at all, but by a kite, a bird with no similar mythological significance. 'Vulture' was an error in the translation of Leonardo's recollection from which Freud was working. This example of an error due to the combination of inference about unconscious meanings and faulty evidence serves as a cautionary lesson for psychobiographers.

Nature of psychobiographical evidence

One reason why psychobiographical inference can be unreliable is that the evidence on which it is based is often of low quality or limited quantity. Making reliable judgments about people is difficult enough, as we have seen in Chapter 8, when we are assessing them with psychological tests. It is doubly difficult when, as in most psychobiographies, the author never even meets the subject and must rely on the historical record. In essence, psychobiographers are attempting to put their subjects on the couch, but these subjects are often dead or otherwise unavailable (and there is no couch). Some of the information on which inferences about personality are made, such as letters and diaries or reports on historical figures by writers of their day, may be systematically distorted. The subject's self-reports may tend to neglect or gloss over psychologically important material, or information that presents them in a poor light, and reports on them by other writers may be biased by the writers' own interests and purposes. Data from validated psychological tests are almost never available, and even if the subject is alive and consents to interviews with the psychobiographer, these interviews are prone to the same difficulties that beset that method of assessment (see Chapter 8).

Determinism

Critics of psychobiographies sometimes complain that they over-simplify the lives of their subjects by emphasizing a single dominant cause that is taken as a source of all the person's distinctive characteristics and behaviour. That cause might be a childhood trauma, a troubled relationship with a parent, or some other encompassing explanation. Erikson referred to one form of this over-simplifying determinism as 'originology': the idea that a life's shape is determined by some traumatic event in its first few years. Needless to say, the psychoanalytic approach offers some encouragement to this idea, given the importance it places on the early psychosexual development of the child and the fundamental role that family relationships are taken to play in personality formation. However, as we have seen in Chapter 7, personality is not set like plaster at age 30, let alone 3, and change is at least as much a fact of life in the study of personalities as is continuity from childhood. Moreover, single events rarely have the power to exert life-long influence over a person's personality. Some psychobiographies have even taken the point of origin back to the time of birth: one writer (Whitmer, 1996) located the source of Elvis Presley's distinctive personality in the fact that he had a stillborn twin brother, Jesse, and that his intrauterine bond with this twin exerted a lasting influence on his life.

Another form that determinism can take in psychobiographical studies is a neglect of non-psychological factors in the person's behaviour. Numerous writers, for example, have speculated about the oddities of Britain's King George III (1738–1820), who had recurring episodes of incessant talking, delusions, deep confusion, agitation, and excitement in which he sometimes foamed at the mouth. Many have argued that King George suffered from some form of madness, and have speculated about the psychological dynamics that might explain it. Medical scholarship, however, indicates that his behaviour was probably due to porphyria, a metabolic disease that causes psychiatric symptoms (Runyan, 1988). Similarly, the empirical fact that personality traits are to a considerable degree heritable (Chapter 2) implies that the sorts of environmental factors on which psychobiographers focus – the life events, family relationships, and the like – do not tell the whole story of a person's adult personality. Another way in which non-psychological factors can be neglected is a lack of consideration of the cultural or historical context. Especially when the psychobiographer is investigating a figure from a very different background, or one who lived centuries ago, it may be difficult to judge what is normal or abnormal in the person's behaviour or upbringing. Social norms have often been wildly different in other times and place, and what might at first blush seem to be clearly pathological behaviour may turn out to have been entirely typical in its context, when the appropriate historical or anthropological background is discovered.

The challenge for the psychobiographer, then, is to recognize that early events and relationships can be important determinants of a life's course, but must always be placed in the context of the many other factors, emerging throughout the life-span, that alter, dilute, or compensate for these early experiences. Similarly, psychobiographers must not spare basic research on the historical and cultural context in which their subject's life was led.

'Pathography'

Another common pitfall of psychologically informed biographies is an emphasis on abnormality or mental disorder. Psychobiographies sometimes seem to concentrate primarily on the dark side of their subjects, and to speculate that their behaviour had disturbed roots. Of course, this concentration makes for fascinating reading and strong book sales, and finding what is hidden – which tends to be more negative than what is open to public view – is one of the reasons why we want to read about famous people. However, psychobiographies can sometimes seem to show an excessive emphasis on abnormality, complete with clinical jargon. Some readers object that this sort of work can be little more than a hatchet job masquerading as science: an attempt to discredit a person while pretending to adopt the impartial stance of a psychological professional. This strikes some people as especially dubious when the subject of the psychobiographer is no longer alive to rebut a negative portrayal, and when the inferences that are made about deviant desires are made without the sort of careful clinical evaluation that would be required if the person were receiving a real psychological assessment.

Sometimes this focus on abnormality appears as a kind of reductionism: the person is assigned a psychiatric diagnosis, and this becomes the primary explanation for most of their behaviour. Does it really help to understand

Hitler's complexity to classify him as a psychopath, or to classify Elvis as having a 'split personality', as some psychobiographers have done? It may well be true that subjects of psychobiography had mental disorders, and that these disorders had important implications for how their lives proceeded, but people cannot, of course, be reduced to their disorders (any more than they can be reduced to their gender, ethnic background, social class, and so on). As we saw in Chapter 9, although some mental disorders have a pervasive influence on behaviour and are woven into the fabric of the personality (i.e., personality disorders), others are superimposed on it rather than being part of it, are not lasting, and may have little relationship to enduring personality dispositions. Responsible psychobiographers must therefore recognize the existence of mental disorders in their subjects – as in Virginia Woolf's bipolar disorder or Charles Darwin's anxiety – without taking these disorders as all-consuming explanations.

A final concern with pathography is that it often leaves unanswered the important question of life success. The subjects of psychobiographies have often led accomplished and creative lives, and an exclusive focus on their psychological problems and dark motives makes it difficult to understand where this accomplishment and creativity came from. Although the famous and influential are not immune to psychological disturbance, of course, it is difficult to view life successes merely as symptoms or to explain how, in spite of disturbance, greatness came about. Pathographies are therefore unsatisfying portraits of real people, in much the same way that standard biographies that dwell too much on the desirable qualities of their subjects – sometimes dubbed 'hagiographies', a term referring to accounts of lives of the saints – are unsatisfying. One-dimensionally positive or negative biographies dehumanize their subjects: without a little ambivalence a life story lacks depth, complexity, and credibility.

IMPROVING PSYCHOBIOGRAPHIES

At this point you might think that psychobiography is hopelessly riddled with problems, and that perhaps we would be better off without it. However, it is important to remember that there are also many problems with orthodox biographies, which can also be full of incorrect inferences, wrong-headed theories, deterministic explanations, and so on. It also seems fair to say that an account of someone's life that failed to grapple seriously with the person's psychology would be seriously lacking. 'Just the facts' may be an appropriate motto for a police report, but it is inadequate when we want to make sense of real lives: something is missing in a life story that focuses exclusively on dates, places, and social context with no appreciation of the person's psychological individuality. Psychology, and personality psychology in particular, has amassed a body of knowledge and a set of methods of inquiry that should be able to enrich biographical studies. Rather than abandoning psychobiography, then, perhaps we should try to improve it and find ways to safeguard it against the problems we have identified.

One attempt to do so was made by Runyan (1981), who offered a set of guides for choosing between alternative psychobiographical explanations. As an example, Runyan examined 13 distinct explanations that have been offered for why Vincent van Gogh cut off his ear. These included that the act was a symbolic self-castration based on a conflict over homosexual impulses; that it was an emulation of Jack the Ripper's mutilation of his victims, which had received much media attention at the time; that it imitated the practice of bull-fighters who gave the severed ear of the bull to the lady of their choice, just as Vincent gave his to a favourite prostitute; and that it was an attempt to stop the auditory hallucinations that troubled him. Runyan notes that human behaviour often has multiple causes, so that no single explanation need be correct, but that nevertheless there are principled ways to decide between the alternatives.

First, explanations should be logically sound and have no internal contradictions. Second, they should account for multiple aspects of the relevant events, the more comprehensively the better. Weaker explanations may appear to make sense of one aspect of the situation but be unable to account for many others. Third, better explanations should be able to pass attempts to falsify them. It should be possible to derive predictions from them and see whether these are supported. Fourth, explanations should be consistent with what we know about people in general. If an explanation departs markedly from ordinary human psychology, it is likely to be mistaken. Finally, a good explanation should be more credible than other explanations, when these are directly compared. These guidelines for improving psychobiographical explanation may seem somewhat obvious at some level, but they are radical in their implications for how psychobiographers should work. Rather than simply coming up with free-wheeling interpretations of a person's life, they should approach psychobiography as an attempt to build a systematic scientific theory of the individual. Like a theory, a psychobiography should be internally consistent, capable of accounting for a wide variety of facts, able to survive efforts to falsify it, and consistent with other well-supported theories, and it should be critically examined in relation to competing theories.

Psychobiography has a long way to go before it can be considered a science, and it will always involve a certain amount of non-scientific (but not necessarily unscientific) interpretation of meaning. However, writers such as Runyan (1981) show how it cannot be exempt from scientific criteria if it is to be credible. Other writers have proposed additional methodological advice to psychobiographers in an effort to improve it. Alexander (1990), for example, offers a series of criteria for deciding what information psychobiographers should pay attention to, in the vast quantities that may be available. Among these, for example, he proposes that people should heed: (a) what the person says most frequently ('frequency'; e.g., repetitious themes); (b) what they say or write first ('primacy'; e.g., early memories); (c) what they emphasize ('emphasis'); (d) what they say that seems peculiar and jarring ('isolation'); (e) what they present as unique and unprecedented in their lives ('uniqueness'); and (f) what they say that they are not ('negation'; e.g., 'I am not like my mother'). Considerationss such as these, which are based on solid psychological research evidence, help to establish the 'salience' or importance of information about a person. Like Runyan's criteria for choosing between explanations, these criteria should help to improve the quality and credibility of psychobiographies.

LIFE NARRATIVES

As we have seen, psychobiographies are psychologically informed accounts of individual lives. They are, in effect, stories – although not entirely fictional – about particular individuals, generally those who are famous. However, not all life stories are told by professional psychobiographers about celebrated people. Some are told by ordinary people, about ordinary people: themselves. Psychologists who study **'life narratives'** argue that every one of us is engaged in an ongoing process of telling his or her own life story, and that such autobiographical life stories are crucial aspects of the self.

This narrative approach to the study of personality is different from most of the approaches that we have encountered to this point in several respects. First, unlike most personality research, studies of life narratives emphasize the uniqueness of the individual rather than attempting to fit each person into a standard descriptive framework, such as a set of trait dimensions. Accordingly, studies of life narratives tend to focus on single individuals rather than large samples of people. Second, studies of life narratives are 'person-centred' rather than 'variable-centred'. The focus of attention is on understanding the individual person rather than examining the relationships that personality characteristics have with one another or with other variables (e.g., how extraversion is related to attachment style or to age). Third, whereas most personality psychology is relatively static, aiming to give a snapshot of people at a particular time, the narrative study of lives is intrinsically temporal. Lives unfold through time and must be understood as extended through past, present, and future. Finally, whereas most personality psychology employs quantitative research methods and seeks to clarify the causes of behaviour, the narrative approach to personality is not normally quantitative and aims to enlighten us about the meanings of behaviour (Josselson, 1995). Rather than trying to formulate explanatory laws about the causes and effects of personality characteristics, that is, narrative psychologists try to interpret the complexities of individual lives in terms of human intentions, motivations, and beliefs.

If you cast your mind back to the end of Chapter 3, you will remember that after reviewing a variety of alternative units for describing personality it was proposed that they represent a distinct level of personality: Level II (personal concerns, such as motives, values, and constructs) vs. Level I (traits). McAdams (1995), who proposed this distinction, further argued that there is a third level of personality that is distinct from both traits and personal concerns, which he refers to as the level of 'integrative life stories'. Levels I and II offer a picture of the person as a static list of characteristics, but beginning in adolescence, at least, people seek a sense of personal identity that gives them unity, purpose, and coherence over time. People need to have an answer to the question 'Who am I?' that has a historical or temporal component: that presents them as a unique person with a connected past, present, and imagined future. Such Level III life stories, self-narratives or 'personal myths' are the basis of personal identity, which you will remember from Chapter 7 as a core developmental task of adolescence in Erikson's theory.

To refer to identity as a life story or **self-narrative** is to propose that we are all engaged in a process of self-construction or 'self-narration'. There is no single life story that is discovered and fixed early in adulthood. Rather, people continually and actively revise their life story to encompass, connect and integrate new events, new hopes, and fears, and new understandings of their pasts. There is no single 'true self' or identity, on this view, just a revisable history of the self. The events of one's life do not dictate a particular life story, and the same events can, in principle, be narrated in quite different ways, much as we can tell a story seriously or for laughs. Indeed, some writers argue that psychotherapy works by enabling people to develop new and more satisfying ways of understanding (or narrating) their pasts (Spence, 1980).

MAKING SENSE OF SELF-NARRATIVES

Psychologists have developed a variety of ways of assessing and analysing people's life stories. Given the complexities of these narratives, their irreducible uniqueness to each person, it is a challenge to describe them in a systematic way. Even so, there is a rich tradition of work in literary studies for making sense of stories, and many of the concepts that can be employed in the analysis of novels, myths, movies, and plays can be put to use in the autobiographical narratives that everyday people produce. Four core concepts that are of particular interest are narrative tone, narrative themes, characters, and narrative forms. McAdams has been at the forefront of the study of self-narratives, and our discussions lean heavily on his work.

Narrative tone

Perhaps the simplest characteristic of life narratives is their overall evaluative quality or tone. Some life stories are consistently positive, presenting past events in a favourable light and looking towards the future with optimism. Note that a life story does not need to be without sadness and adversity to have such a positive tone. The narrator may acknowledge problems, losses, or setbacks but present them as opportunities for growth rather than as crippling blows that destroyed their faith in the world, others, or themselves. Stories with a negative tone, in contrast, are full of sadness, pessimism, resignation, and distrust. However, they need not be litanies of sorrow and hardship. The narrator may report past happiness that has since been lost forever or that turned out to be illusory. What makes narrative tone positive or negative is therefore not simply the desirability or undesirability of the events that compose the story, but the psychological attitude towards them, whether it is one of hope and trust or of pessimism and disillusion.

McAdams (1996) has argued that the roots of narrative tone can be traced to the earliest stages of personality development. According to attachment theory, people who were securely attached to caregiving figures in infancy and early childhood develop just the sort of confidence, openness, optimism, and trust in others that shine through in stories with a positive tone. Insecurely attached infants – those whose attachment style is avoidant or anxious-ambivalent (see Chapter 2) – are more likely to think of other people, and also the world beyond, as unreliable and unsafe. Similarly, Erikson's theory of psychosocial development views the first stage, Trust vs. Mistrust, as the foundation for a basic sense of security and optimism: trust not just in other people, but in the world's capacity to provide us with what we want and need. Although it is controversial to propose that early childhood experiences of caregiving and attachment are directly carried forward into adult patterns of behaviour in this way, there is an obvious resonance between the meaning of these early experiences and later narrative tone.

Narrative themes

A second aspect of life narratives refers not to their overall emotional colour, but to the sorts of themes that appear in their content. Themes refer to 'recurrent patterns of human intention' (McAdams, 1996, p. 67), specifically the kinds of desires and motives that animate the characters in the narrative. What kinds of desires, needs, and preoccupations are repeatedly expressed by people in the story? In a self-narrative, of course, these desires and motives are largely those of the self.

There could in principle be as many themes as there are motives, or perhaps more, given that different themes might exist when a certain motive is fulfilled or thwarted. However, McAdams (1996) suggests that themes can usefully be classified according to broad motivations such as those identified by McClelland and colleagues (e.g., McClelland, 1985). You will remember from Chapter 3's brief discussion of motivation that McClelland proposed that human behaviour springs from needs for power, achievement, and intimacy. You may also remember from Chapter 7 that these needs are typically assessed using projective methods, specifically the Thematic Apperception Test (TAT). The TAT is a method that explicitly requires people to generate stories about ambiguous pictures and, as its name suggests, it aims to extract the themes that appear in these stories. If strivings for influence (power), success relative to others (achievement), and love (intimacy) are core motivational themes in TAT stories, they may similarly be core themes in self-narratives.

McAdams proposes that McClelland's three basic needs can be simplified further into two distinct types of theme. 'Communal' themes are simply those in which the primary motive is intimacy. Self-narratives with communal themes emphasize the person's striving for connection, love, submergence in a larger group or in a close relationship. Successfully or unsuccessfully, the character seeks union with others. 'Agency' themes, in contrast, are those in which the character is driven by desires for independence, autonomy, and personal efficacy. The character strives to assert and enhance the self as an independent agent. Power and achievement needs are both *agentic* in this sense, placing emphasis on distinguishing the self from others through personal effort rather than linking the self to others.

Self-narratives may therefore be dominated by agentic or communal themes, although many will contain both to some extent. One person's life story may be a tale of drive for career accomplishment, triumphs over setbacks, and ultimate glory in personal achievement or a position of influence. Another's may tell of relationships forged and lost, of romantic joys and disappointments, and of successes and failures shared with important social groups. Yet another person's self-narrative may record one-dimensional striving for personal accomplishment in the early years of life that gives way – perhaps after a crisis or flash of insight – to a belated appreciation of the importance of relationships and family.

The relative importance of these themes in self-narratives is likely to alter as people age, and may also vary by gender. Agentic themes may often diminish in importance, perhaps especially for men at mid-life. Men who have striven for personal accomplishment, conforming to the high value many cultures place on male agency and independence, may often question the meaningfulness of what they have achieved at this time. Another common variant runs in the opposite direction. An early life remembered as overly submerged in relationships or groups – caring for others or being trapped in the tight embrace of a family or group – is left behind as the person seeks independence and self-realization. This sequence may be more common among women. The important thing to remember, however, is that self-narratives are always works in progress, and the themes that they contain may be reworked over the course of life.

Characters

All stories are populated by human characters, or at least by entities that have been endowed with human-like attributes (e.g., anthropomorphized animals or aliens, intelligent robots, or gods). Self-narratives are no different. The self is the main figure in its own life story, accompanied by a supporting cast of significant others. However, even though the self may be the primary figure, it may not be represented by a single character. McAdams (1996) proposes that in life stories the self is often carried by multiple characters. The need for multiple characters comes from the sheer complexity of our selves, both real and imagined. First, people tend to hold several social roles at the same time (wife, mother, daughter, employee, club president), each with its own set of expectations for appropriate behaviour. Second, people are often internally conflicted or confused about their personal identity, holding an inconsistent view of who they are or ought to be. Third, over the life-course the definition of self may change, so that it is meaningful to talk about past and future selves. Finally, given that self-narratives are not only histories but also look towards the future, we must also consider possible selves, which can be desired (successful novelist) or dreaded (homeless person).

According to McAdams, we simplify this multiplicity of self by constructing what he calls 'imagoes'. An imago is an image of the self that is simplified and personified, in the sense of being a 'stock character' that exemplifies one core component of self. These imagoes resemble figures of myth or legend, as they stand in for a particular idea or quality. Rarely does a person's self-narrative contain only a single imago, but neither do life stories contain distinct imagoes for every possible social role or facet of the personality. Instead, people refine their multiple aspects or roles into a few imagoes, each of which encompasses several such aspects and roles. A woman's roles as wife, mother, and employee might be personified in a 'caregiver' imago, whose relevance extends beyond each specific role, whereas a 'maker' imago embodies her roles as a productive and organized employee and club president. By this means, people have available a small set of story characters that can capture their internal conflicts and confusions without being unmanageably complex.

Just as self-narratives may have communal and agentic themes, the characters who embody these motives can be classified as communal or agentic imagoes. McAdams (1996) proposes a variety of possible imago figures, many drawn from Greek mythology. Communal imagoes include the lover, who strives for passionate intimacy in close relationships; the caregiver, who nurtures others with devotion and self-sacrifice; and the friend, who seeks a loyal and cooperative relationship with equals. Agentic imagoes include the warrior, who embodies vigour, courage, and self-assertion; the traveller, who is always in motion and seeks novelty, freedom from constraint, and adventure; and the sage, who seeks wisdom and deep knowledge above all. Commonly self-narratives will include conflict between an agentic and a communal imago, reflecting the conflict between autonomy and relatedness that figures in many life stories. Different imagoes may become prominent at different times in the narrative, as if jostling for the starring role, and the narrative is given dramatic tension by this conflict.

Narrative form

Narrative tone sets the overall emotional quality of the story, themes provide the recurring motivational content, and characters supply the cast, who embody this content. None of these narrative elements capture the ways in which stories unfold through time. Narrative form, the final element, refers to the temporal trajectory of stories, and to the assortment of distinct trajectories that appear repeatedly.

One interesting model of narrative form was developed by Ken and Mary Gergen (1983), who argued that many self-narratives seem to follow a few basic patterns. These narrative trajectories can vary on a dimension of positive versus negative evaluation, so that different points on a trajectory represent desirable or undesirable states of affairs. Thus, a narrative form represents a particular way in which a life story unfolds in good or bad ways. The Gergens propose seven basic forms, many of which can be observed in literary works such as novels. These forms are presented in Figure 10.1.

The simplest form, depicted in the first graph, is the 'stability' narrative. In it, the person sees his or her life as unchanging over time, maintaining a steady way of living and fixed attributes from the past into the imagined future. The evaluative tone of such narratives can be consistently positive or negative: people may see their lives as comfortably settled and have a fixed self-definition, or they may see themselves as stuck in an unending rut. Change rather than stability is the basic feature of the 'progressive' and 'regressive' narratives depicted in the second graph, which reflect life trajectories that gradually rise or decline. Progressive narratives reflect a sense of continual self-improvement that is popular in self-help books, according to which people can move from a

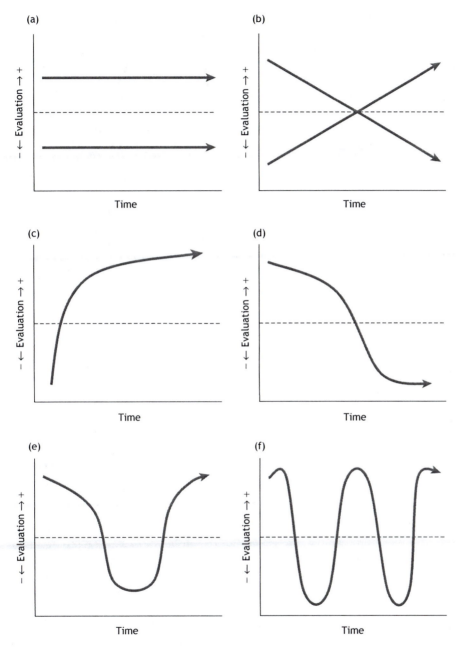

Figure 10.1   Narratives forms from Gergen and Gergen (1983): a) stability (positive & negative); b) progressive & regressive; c) *'happily-ever-after'*; d) tragic; e) comedy-melodrama; f) romantic saga

lacklustre present towards a golden future by following a few simple steps. This sort of self-narrative appears to be very widespread. People are motivated to see themselves as steadily improving, and in the service of this goal they may remember their past self as if it were less positive than it was in fact (Ross, 1989). Regressive narratives, in contrast, portray the self as on a steady downward path from earlier glories.

Other narrative forms are more complex. Instead of reflecting a straightforward linear pathway, they have points at which the story changes direction or turns, and they may involve combinations of the simpler forms. The 'happily-ever-after' narrative, presented in the third graph, involves a combination of the progressive and stability forms: things get better and better until they reach a stable plateau of contentment (e.g., an older person looking back on life leading up to retirement, or a younger one looking forward to marriage and Prince Charming). The 'tragic' narrative, presented in the fourth graph, represents a similar variation on the regressive form, with the decline being relatively sudden and abrupt, a turning point often brought about by a loss or fall from grace. Typically the narrative themes are agentic: a heroic individual acts contrary to social convention and as a result is isolated from others by a cruel world. Like regressive narratives, tragedy has a negative tone, but this is made more poignant by the suddenness of the decline.

The final two narrative forms are more complex still. Gergen and Gergen (1983) describe as 'comedy-melodrama' a self-narrative in which events become increasingly troubled, as in tragedy, but the problems are then rapidly overcome and happiness is restored. The dominant narrative themes in this form tend to be communal: the trouble is often resolved through love or togetherness. The 'romantic saga', finally, is a narrative form in which cycles of progressive and regressive elements are repeated. Someone with this sort of narrative identity sees himself or herself in heroic, questing terms, engaged in a continuing process of overcoming ill-fortune or evil. As in tragedy, the narrative themes tend to be agentic; however, the tone is more positive, as the heroic individual battles successfully against all obstacles.

The Gergens did not propose that their seven narrative forms were exhaustive, or that every possible life story could be assigned to just one form. More complex narratives can be described. For example, McAdams (2006) discusses an intricate 'redemption narrative' that he found to be common among highly generative mid-life Americans. According to this narrative, people see themselves early in life as having a special gift or advantage and experience empathy for the suffering of others. They come to develop a firm belief system that rules their life, experience a series of episodes where bad events are swiftly followed by good ones that redeem them, feel a conflict between desires to advance the self and to connect with others, and look forward to contributing more to society. This redemption narrative form has an upward gradient, as in the progressive form, a strong sense of personal consistency, as in the stability narrative, and also romantic elements, as in the alternation of bad then good events and the struggle between different motives. The narrative forms are building blocks from which self-narratives may be constructed.

FINAL NOTES ON SELF-NARRATIVES

Self-narratives link up life events into a coherent plot, but theorists emphasize that there is no necessary connection between the actual events of someone's life and the narrative form that they superimpose on them. Life is often quite ambiguous, in the sense that there are often many alternative ways in which it can be made coherent. For example, it is quite possible to think about a normal student 'career' at university in any of the following ways: as a dreary time when nothing much changed, as a continuing upward path to enlightenment or maturity, as a steady dimming of one's youthful spark, as a climb to the goal of being an employed graduate, as a tale of disillusionment and missed opportunity, or as a cycle of tests of personal strength and of intellectual or social challenges to be overcome. The important basic observation that writers on self-narratives make is that the way we comprehend our lives, as stories, may have profound implications for how we behave and how we view our identities. For this reason, self-narratives are fundamentally important aspects of our personalities.

Self-narratives are not the only kinds of narratives, of course. A culture contains a large repository of narratives, whether in the form of books, television shows, and movies, or as myths, oral histories, and fables. We are constantly exposed to our culture's available scripts. Many of these narratives exemplify the forms presented here. One important theoretical question in the study of self-narratives is what relation self-narratives bear to the narratives that circulate within a culture. Gergen and Gergen are quite clear on this point: 'life and art are interdependent' (p. 261). How we make sense of our life stories is influenced by the narratives and narrative forms that we are exposed to, so that we will tend to construct self-narratives that borrow from and conform to cultural patterns. McAdams, for example, argues that the redemption narrative is a typically American product, embodying themes of self-reliance, spiritual destiny, and having a special place in the world that appear consistently in the nation's intellectual history, early autobiographies, and current cinema. In short, self-narratives not only supply us with coherent individual selves: they connect us to the shared values and ways of thinking of our culture.

Illustrative study: love stories across cultures

The psychology of life narratives generally focuses on the intensive study of individuals, but it is possible to investigate stories using more standard research methods. In an interesting cross-cultural study, Australian-based psychologist Todd Jackson and Chinese psychologists Hong Chen, Cheng Guo, and Xiao Gao (2006) adopted a narrative perspective to examine the ways in which love stories are constructed by American and Chinese couples. Previous research has pointed to a number of cultural differences in these stories. Chinese people appear to emphasize more the selfless, pragmatic, painful, and fatalistic aspects of love. Americans emphasize more the erotic, romantic, and happy aspects.

Jackson et al. made use of a questionnaire measure of love stories developed by Sternberg (1996), whose items assess 25 different types of love stories. For example, 'Travel' stories involve the belief that love is a shared journey, 'War' stories portray love as a series of battles, and 'Mystery' stories envision loving relationships as mysterious arrangements in which people should remain somewhat unfathomable to their partners. The researchers had members of married or dating couples (142 American and 140 Chinese) complete sections of the questionnaire relating to 12 of the love-story types. Using factor analysis (see Chapter 2), they examined whether love stories were conceptualized differently in the USA and China, and whether they had different associations with relationship satisfaction.

Jackson et al. found some common themes in the two samples. Both Chinese and American participants thought of love stories in terms of threat and objectification (i.e., seeing partners as difficult to understand or frightening), devotion and care, pragmatism (i.e., following certain steps to ensure relationship success), and sexuality. However, differences also emerged. Threat appeared to be more bound up with conflict among Chinese participants and with seeing the partner as incomprehensible or alien among Americans. Fantasy ('happily ever after', 'perfect match' and related fairy tales) was more prominent in the American sample. In addition, there were cultural differences in the story dimensions that predicted relationship satisfaction. In the Chinese sample, endorsement of themes of devotion, care, and pragmatism were associated with greater relationship satisfaction, and endorsement of threat themes was associated with lesser satisfaction. In the American sample, greater satisfaction was associated with themes of devotion and fantasy, and lesser satisfaction with themes

(Continued)

(Continued)

of objectification and threat. In addition, for the Americans but not the Chinese, people who endorsed similar love-story themes to their partner tended to be more satisfied with their relationships.

Jackson et al.'s study is a far cry from psychobiography, but it reveals how taking stories seriously as topics of psychological study can offer valuable insights into social and cultural processes. The study's findings also help us to understand the power of stories to influence people's well-being: how we narrate our relationships may have a bearing on how pleasant they are.

CONCLUSIONS

Psychobiography and the psychology of life narratives are attempts to make sense of whole lives in their fullness and complexity. Their aim is to produce and understand coherent psychological portraits of individuals in a way that is informed by personality theory and research. Psychobiography, for example, is intrinsically difficult because of the complexity of individuals and the obstacles that stand in the way of making reliable inferences about them. Information about people is often inaccurate or incomplete, there are often many alternative explanations of their behaviour, and their motives, thoughts, and wishes are often obscure, even to themselves. In addition, the subjects of psychobiographies are engaged in a process of making narrative sense of their lives, and the sense they make may conflict sharply with how they appear to others. For all of these reasons it is not surprising that psychobiography can be done badly.

Even if that is true, the fact remains that understanding whole persons and whole lives is an ultimate goal of personality psychology. It is no less important a goal for being hard to reach. The chapters of this book have all presented ways of addressing some aspects of the person, and with any luck they show how personality psychology can assemble scientifically justified understandings of people that can be put together to understand whole persons and lives. The book started with a poem, went on a variety of forays into scientific psychology, and ended with some literary-sounding discussions of narrative form. In a sense we have travelled full circle. Understanding persons requires this sort of broad view, and a combination of scientific rigour and humanistic imagination. This necessary breadth and complexity, and this mixture of hard and soft ways of understanding, is part of what makes the psychology of personality so fascinating. I hope I've convinced you of that.

Chapter summary

- 'Personology' is the branch of personality psychology concerned with the intensive study of individual lives. One primary example of it is psychobiography, the use of psychological research and theory in biographical writing.
- Psychobiography has been a controversial exercise for several reasons. It often relies on questionable psychoanalytic theories of personality development, makes inferences on the basis of problematic or weak historical evidence, creates over-simplified explanations that refer the subject's personality to a single determining event and reduces the subject to a diagnosis.
- Despite these serious problems, psychobiographies can be improved by following a set of systematic guidelines for responsible interpretation. These refer to the selection of evidence and the responsible and scientifically-informed testing of alternative explanations.
- Psychobiographies are narratives of other people's lives, but people also construct stories of their own lives ('self-narratives'). These stories are important components of personal identity, one critical aspect of the self.
- These can be investigated rigorously by examining their emotional tone, themes, characters, and form (i.e., the trajectory through time of the self, whether upward, downward, or mixed).

Further reading

- Elms, A.C. (1994). *Uncovering lives: The uneasy alliance of biography and psychology.* New York: Oxford University Press.

This is an important text that discusses some of the difficulties involved in psychobiographical research, and some of the weaknesses to which it is prone.

- Gergen, K.J., & Gergen, M.M. (1983). Narratives of the self. In T.R. Sarbin & K.E. Scheibe (Eds.), *Studies in social identity* (pp. 254–73). New York: Praeger.

(Continued)

(Continued)

The Gergens' work is theoretically difficult, but this chapter makes a strong case for the value of considering the self as (among other things) an evolving story that can be told and re-told in many different ways.

- McAdams, D.P. (1996). *The stories we live by: Personal myths and the making of the self*. New York: Guilford.

McAdams is the most prominent scholar in the field of life narratives. This book lays out his approach in a very clear and compelling way, and shows how life narratives can be studied systematically but without over-simplification.

- Runyan, W.M. (1981). Why did Van Gogh cut off his ear? The problem of alternative explanations in psychobiography. *Journal of Personality and Social Psychology, 40*, 1070–77.

This short classic article is a fascinating account of the difficulties in making definitive explanations of behaviour on the basis of historical data, in the context of a particularly puzzling event.

- Schultz, W.T. (2005). *Handbook of psychobiography*. Oxford: Oxford University Press.

Schultz's handbook is an excellent resource for students of psychobiography, bringing together some new contributions as well as reprinting a number of classic papers.

SECTION 4
INTELLIGENCE

11

Intelligence and Cognitive Abilities

Learning objectives

- To recognize the names of some major tests along with the typical scoring systems and the stability and reliability of these scores.
- To develop an understanding of the different theoretical models for intelligence that have been proposed, including the hierarchical and multiple intelligence models.
- To understand the evidence for these different perspectives.
- To know the measured heritability of intelligence, and know what this concept describes.
- To recognize how intelligence changes across the life-span.
- To understand how developments in imaging are giving us insight into the role of brain volume and connectivity in intelligence.

This chapter introduces the science of human intelligence. Intelligence influences how well we perform many tasks, and how well we learn. While school and beginning a complex new job are times when intelligence differences are clear and important, intelligence has many other effects, from managing the tasks of life through to health outcomes and longevity. The chapter begins with a 'hands-on' look at the types of test used to measure intelligence. We then examine how these tests developed, reviewing concepts such as 'IQ'. Moving to models of intelligence, we show how theories have distinguished between a general ability common to all tasks, and specific abilities in restricted domains such as spatial processing, or language. Next we shift focus to the very basic cognitive correlates of intelligence such as reaction time and working memory, and the biological bases of intelligence are introduced, focusing on the genetic and environmental causes of intelligence, and their reflection in brain development and structure. In the final section, we examine important practical properties of tests, such as their stability and potential bias. With this material understood, the educational and social correlates of ability are discussed, along with their implications for educational and social policy.

> What we measure with [intelligence] tests is not what the tests measure – not information, not spatial perception, not reasoning ability. These are only means to an end. What intelligence tests measure, what we hope they measure, is something more important: the capacity of an individual to understand the world about [him or her] and [his or her] resourcefulness to cope with its challenges. (Wechsler, 1975, p. 139)

- Try and write down a definition for the word '*esoteric*'.
- If 5 machines can make 5 widgets in 5 minutes, how long will 100 machines take to make 100 widgets?
- In the figure below, which shape would complete the puzzle?

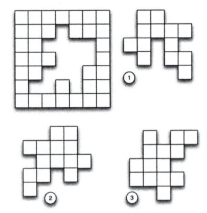

How accurate were your answers ?[1] These tasks assess verbal, mathematical, and spatial ability. Are there other types of ability? Are each of these abilities related to the others or independent? Why? Do these items reliably measure

---

[1] Answers: '*esoteric*' is an adjective describing knowledge which is understood by or available to only a restricted or special group. 100 machines will take just 5 minutes to make one hundred widgets (a common incorrect answer is 100, seeing a syllogism with 5 machines taking 5 minutes to make 5 widgets). The puzzle piece is 3.

intelligence? Are they valid? Could they be biased? Why do people differ on these tasks? If someone gets these types of item correct, what practical guide does that give us to their ability in the workplace or other areas of importance such as social life or neuropsychological function after brain damage? Do genes play a role in why people differ in how well they perform on these tests? Can changes to the environment change scores on such items? The answers to these questions are the subject of intelligence research, and of this chapter.

Many of the things we will discuss were examined first by British polymath Sir Francis Galton. Along with contributions to African exploration, analysis of finger prints, composite photography, meteorology, and developing the correlation test (see Chapter 2), to name but a few of his diverse achievements, he also established the study of ability differences as a science (Wright Gillham, 2001). Galton observed that differences in ability fell along a continuum and that the distribution of these differences followed a bell-curve shape (for which he coined the phrase 'normal distribution' in 1875). He saw that this ability dimension could be discerned in people's practical achievements. Furthermore, he understood the need for theory to explain these unsuspected relations between ability and achievements in life. Finally, Galton examined how ability ran in families, and conceived of the twin-study as a method of testing for the effects of genes and culture on intelligence. The one thing that Galton did not do, and which has proven to be basic to advances in modern intelligence research, is develop a test of intelligence. While observers have distinguished between 'ability' and other faculties such as personality at least since Aristotle, the period of greatest advance in the scientific study of intelligence begins more or less with the advent of tests for ability at the beginning of the 20th century.

BINET AND THE ORIGINS OF INTELLIGENCE TESTING

The French psychologist Alfred Binet (1857–1911) pioneered the psychometric approach to intelligence, having been commissioned by the French government to develop a method of measuring ability to learn, so as to detect children who would face difficulties in the school system. Together with Theodore Simon, Binet published the first intelligence test in 1905 — a test that has guided most subsequent tests of intelligence. Unlike Galton, Binet did not search for a single or 'theoretically basic' measure of intelligence. Instead, he tested items from diverse areas and simply kept those items which worked, evolving the test over time based on feedback from the predictive success of the items.

Binet's test development was guided by two principles (Matarazzo, 1992):

1. Binet believed that intelligence increases through childhood: therefore if a given item is a valid measure of ability, older children should find it easier than do younger children.

2. Binet also believed that the rise in intelligence across childhood was not due to developments in sensory acuity or precision, nor was it a direct result of special education or training.

These two beliefs led to Binet's lasting contributions to intelligence test construction. First, and despite seeking to assess ability at school, he avoided any items that required experience or that resembled schoolwork. Second, he focused on tests of abstract reasoning on which, despite not being directly taught at school, performance improved with age:

> It is the intelligence alone that we seek to measure, by disregarding in so far as possible the degree of instruction which the child possesses ... We give him nothing to read, nothing to write, and submit him to no test in which he might succeed by means of rote learning. (Binet & Simon, 1905)

Here we can see that Binet explicitly distinguishes between ability and achievement: he aims to predict subsequent achievement not from current learning or achievements, but from a measure of abstract reasoning ability. Binet's attempt to reduce dependence on special training or experience can be seen if we examine the types of item used in the 30-item 1905 Binet–Simon test of intelligence:

- Unwrap and eat a sweet.
- Define abstract words and name simple colours.
- Remember shopping lists.
- Order weights (3, 6, 9, 12, and 15 grams) and lines (3 cm, 4 cm).
- Make rough copies of a line-drawn square, diamond, and cylinder.
- Construct sentences containing given words (e.g., 'Paris', 'fortune', and 'river').

Binet expected that all the children he tested would have been exposed to these materials many dozens of times, and that children's ability to reason and manipulate with these types of stimulus would not be dependent on differences in experience.

Within each of these item categories, various levels of difficulty (defined by the average age at which the problem could be answered correctly) were constructed. For instance, Binet found that copying a cylinder was more difficult (needed more intelligence) than copying a diamond, which in turn was more demanding than copying a square. Binet found that a typical 5-year-old could copy a square but not a diamond, and that a typical 8-year-old could copy a diamond but not a cylinder, which could in turn be copied from memory by an average 11-year-old.

Because Binet's test development has been of such lasting value, it is worth examining an item of this test in more detail. Let us take the example of figure copying. First of all, Binet controlled the test situation. He showed the child a simple figure, and then removed it from view, asking them to draw the stimulus from memory. He also specified the criteria for marking, noting that accuracy of detail and neatness of the child's copy are unimportant. By presenting the stimulus (rather than simply saying 'draw a diamond') he removed some of the role of experience and vocabulary from the situation. By removing the stimulus from view during the actual copy, he removed the possibility of a direct perceptual copy, forcing the child to rely on an internal representation. These insights to the testing situation enhance test reliability and validity (see Chapter 8).

In addition to these insights in increasing the reliability of the test by controlling presentation and marking, the outcomes of the test itself help us develop a construct of intelligence. As noted above, Binet found that a square could be copied from memory by the average 5-year-old child, a diamond by age 8, and a cylinder by age 10. Why was this? What are some possible reasons why a problem is solvable at one age, but not earlier?

The problem was not perceptual or manual but rather analytic: the 8-year-old who fails at copying the diamond will have been quite able to copy the square, despite both shapes being composed of the same lines and vertices. Binet explored whether the problem was practice (which could increase with time). However, he found that the ability to copy was hard to train, and, moreover, that training on one figure did not transfer to other equally hard figures. This suggested that, as Binet had thought, intelligence does not result from particular experiences or training, but develops largely independent of experience.

MENTAL AGE

The next insight that Binet exhibited related to how to score an ability test. Because large-scale testing meant that Binet knew at what age the average child could complete each item, his test could be scored in terms of a 'mental age'. Binet developed this use of a single mental-age score for two reasons. First, he found that items within a category could be arranged in terms of the mental age required to complete them. Second, he also found that children who could complete an item in one category to a given level of difficulty typically completed items from other categories to the same level of difficulty.

While Binet believed there were many distinct abilities (hence his wide choice of tests), and was initially agnostic as to the structure of intelligence, he came to speak of ability as a unitary construct. This is an important point and is worth reiterating. For example, if a 5-year-old could normally draw a square but not a cylinder, and could normally make a sentence containing the word 'cake' but not 'fortune', then an average 5-year-old could both define 'cake' and draw a square: these apparently very different abilities somehow went together, defining a coherent 'mental age'. It was this mental age that Binet felt identified whether children would be able to cope at a given level of schooling (which was, after all, his primary task).

Binet found that children's mental age could diverge considerably from their chronological age, and that this accounted for their needing extra help at school. Some children performed as well as average children several years older, and some children achieved scores typical of children several years younger than themselves. If two children of different ages were found to have the same level of mental age, the younger one could be thought of as more intellectually able, given his or her age. To express these two concepts, Binet developed a distinction between mental age and chronological age.

- Chronological age – How old is this child?
- Mental age – how old would the average child be who performed at this child's level of performance?

The Binet–Simon test was therefore scored not in terms of the number of items correct, but in terms of the average chronological age of a child who would achieve this score, taking this as the effective mental age of the tested subject, with the child's chronological age reported for comparison.

THE CONCEPT OF 'IQ'

We noted above that Binet scored his test in terms of a mental age for a child, to be read along with the child's chronological age. William Stern (1912) saw that these two numbers were related and could be used to express a single value – the intelligence quotient or 'IQ':

$$IQ = \text{Mental age/Chronological age} * 100.$$

While this definition was functional for work with children under 17, the definition is no longer used, as scores on intelligence tests do not continue to rise with chronological age after 16–18 years of age, leading to an obvious problem: if you are an average 17-year-old (the age at which raw scores peak), and therefore have an IQ of 100 (17/17 * 100), what will your IQ be when you are 55, assuming your ability remains the same? You would have a mental age of 17 and a chronological age of 55, giving an IQ of just 31 (17/55 * 100)!

The solution to this dilemma was realized by Wechsler (1975) who recognized that the key insight to Binet's scoring system was not the use of a mental

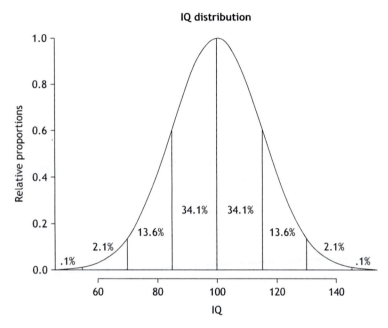

Figure 11.1   The Normal or "Gaussian" Distribution of Ability

Ability is distributed in a normal or bell-curve, with most people clustered in the middle, and fewer people achieving very high or very low scores. Most modern IQ tests are scored with a mean of 100 and a standard deviation of 15 (SD: a measure of the spread or width of the curve). The figure is marked with vertical lines at each standard deviation, and you can see that a little over 2/3s of people (68.2%) fall within 1 SD of the mean.

age, but the *deviation* of a child's mental age from that of the average children of his or her own age. This led to the adoption in nearly all tests of a so-called 'deviation IQ' – no longer the result of dividing mental age by chronological age, but instead based on a person's percentile score within their age cohort. In this system, the average person at any given age is given an IQ of 100, with scores above and below this scaled to give a standard deviation (SD) of 15. This is displayed in Figure 11.1, which shows the 'normal distribution' or bell-curve of IQ scores, with most people clustered in the middle around 100, and fewer people scoring either above or below this mean value. Some values to remember are that 95% of scores lie within ±2SD of the mean, i.e., between 70 and 130. Correspondingly, a score over 145 is obtained by only one person in 1,000.

THE WAIS-III: AN EXAMPLE OF A MODERN IQ TEST

In order to best understand the material of the rest of the chapter, it will be helpful to see the kinds of items in a modern ability test, what they are (and are not), and to begin to think about why they have been chosen, and how they will relate to human circumstances and outcomes.

Perhaps the most widely used and validated test of human intelligence is the Wechsler Adult Intelligence Scale, or WAIS, now in its third revision (Wechsler, 1997). This test contains 13 sub-tests, spanning many, if not all, of the types of item that have seen wide currency in validated tests of ability. For reasons of copyright and of test security, the items are not shown. (It is important that the exact items of the test do not become common knowledge, lest this disrupt their valid use in selection and assessment, especially in forensic and medical contexts, such as neuropsychological assessment.) The WAIS is administered individually by a trained tester practised in the particular time limits and delivery requirements of this test. The test takes an hour or more. (Not all intelligence tests are as time-consuming, complex, and labour-intensive as this: the popular Raven's tests [Raven, Raven, & Court, 1998] takes 30 minutes or less, focuses on a single task and can be administered to a group.)

Verbal comprehension

1. *Vocabulary*: word meanings:

    - 'What does "seasonal" mean?'
    - 'Fluctuating with the time of year' would earn more points than 'like the weather'.

2. *Similarities*: finding what is common to two words:

    - 'Why are a boat and a car alike?'
    - 'Both are means of transport' would earn more points than 'Both made of metal'.

3. *Information*: general-knowledge questions:

    - 'Why do we have elections?'
    - 'To allow people to decide how they wish their country to be run' would earn more points than 'it happens every five years'.

4. *Comprehension*: understanding practical problems, proverbs, and social norms:

    - 'What does 'Make hay while the sun shines' mean?'
    - 'The time to achieve objectives is often limited, and needs to be taken advantage of' would earn more points than the more literal 'farmers have to be quick with hay, or it will rot'.

Perceptual Organization

5. *Picture completion*: detecting missing elements in drawings of common objects.

6. *Block design*: a spatial test, in which subjects reproduce two-dimensional patterns using cubes with a range of differently coloured faces.

   • Make the pattern on the right using blocks shown on the left:

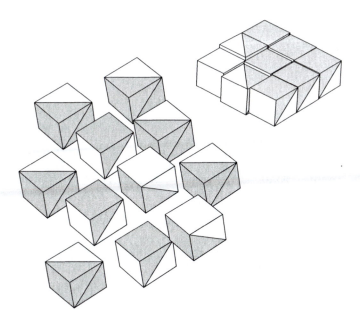

7. *Matrix reasoning*: find the missing element in an array of patterned panels:

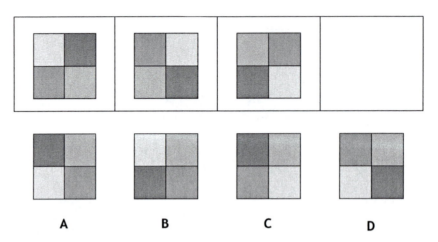

8. *Picture arrangement*: arrange a series of cartoon drawings into a story order.

Working memory

9. *Arithmetic*: mental arithmetic problems posed in practical situations:
   - If 1 boy takes 6 hours to make 12 widgets, how long will 3 boys take to make 6 widgets?

10. *Digit span*: the longest verbally presented number sequence that can be recalled correctly in forward, or reverse, order:
    - Read out loud at a rate of 1 per second, increasing in length until the subject reliably fails.
    - Backward span: asked to recall increasing digit strings in reverse order, again until reliably unable to do so without error.

11. *Letter-number sequencing*: given a sequence of letters and numbers in random order, mentally reorder and recall the letters and numbers separately.
    - '7 Z J 4 K 9 B 8 F 2'→'24789, BFJKZ'.

Processing speed

12. *Digit symbol-coding*: re-code as many items as possible in a short time-period, using a table to map symbols such as '£, ∂, π' into corresponding digits.

13. *Symbol search*: mark as many lists as containing or not containing a particular-target symbol as possible in a given time period.

THE STRUCTURE OF ABILITY

Although all scientists must deal with the same data, their explanations (theories) of these data may diverge, at least in the short term. In intelligence testing, two main approaches to explaining intelligence have been followed: one emphasizing the generality of ability, and the other focusing on differences between abilities. The first, both chronologically and in terms of its simplicity, is general-ability theory, developed by Charles Spearman in the first quarter of the 20th century.

Charles Spearman and general intelligence

As noted above in relating the experience of Binet, one of the most powerful facts that confronts any student of cognitive ability is the positive relationship shown across diverse-ability measures, suggesting the existence of an organized factor underlying this correlation.

The earliest empirical studies of general cognitive ability were conducted by Charles Spearman (1863–1945) who termed this general intelligence factor 'g' (Spearman, 1904). Spearman argued that g was not a single faculty or module and therefore could never be measured directly or observed in a single behaviour. Instead, Spearman argued that intelligence was a property common to all cognitive processes, and he thought of intelligence as a 'mental energy', energizing diverse faculties and functions.

Binet, working on the atheoretical principle of keeping items that distinguished younger from older children, found that his test was improved by keeping items from a broad range of domains. In similar fashion, Spearman, working from a more theory-driven perspective, argued that a good test of intelligence must concentrate not on developing a single type of question that measures g, but on incorporating the widest possible diversity of test items, the common element of which would emerge as general ability. This need for a wide range of items he called 'indifference of the indicator', suggesting that as g should affect all kinds of ability, the particular measures chosen didn't matter, and the more different measures the better.

Spearman collected and studied the patterns of correlations among large numbers of distinct ability tests, observing that the clearest pattern was that all the tests, from whatever domain, correlated positively with each other: this he called 'positive manifold'. Spearman developed the statistical method of factor analysis (see Chapter 2) in part to show that these consistently positive correlations reflected an underlying general factor, implying that different ability tests are all influenced by a common underlying cause. The existence of such a g factor is well illustrated by the 13 WAIS-III sub-tests presented earlier. When

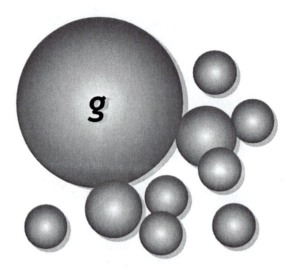

Figure 11.2   Graphical depiction of Spearman's 2-Factor theory

Notes: A large general factor (g) accounting for around half the variance in all ability, and specific factors, some of which are related to groups of tests, such as verbal ability, and some of which are very specific.

the WAIS-III was given to a representative group of several thousand adults, the average correlation of each sub-test with all of the others was a very substantial .49. The general-ability factor has been confirmed in hundreds of data sets collected over the last century, where it accounts for 50% of the variance in any comprehensive and diverse battery of tests (Carroll, 1993).

Even other animals show a kind of *g* factor. While humans have evolved novel adaptations such as generative language (Corballis, 2003), other species also appear to show general ability, suggesting that intelligence is not a simple product of language. Individual animals differ in their ability, and these differences cluster along a general factor explaining around 40% of the differences between them (Galsworthy et al., 2005). This raises the possibility of studying the biology of ability in animals, an area that has been neglected.

g is not the last word (or letter) on the structure of ability, however. In 1904, Spearman proposed that any test of ability could be decomposed into it *and* one or more specific components (see Figure 11.2). In 1937, he elaborated this theory, noting that not only did all tests correlate with each other (*g*), and single tests tended to contain variation unique to themselves (specifics), but tests also formed broad clusters such as 'verbal' 'spatial', or 'attention'. These came to be known as 'group factors'. This is suggested in Figure 11.2 by some slightly larger components of ability amongst the smaller, very specific elements.

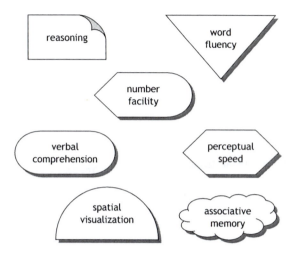

Figure 11.3   Thurstone's seven primary mental abilities

However, it was the work of Thurstone, who we will examine next, that most clearly emphasized these group factors.

The hierarchical model of ability: different levels of order

While Spearman focused on the common element of all ability measures, other researchers focused on the differences between abilities, and the fact that individuals could be found who were strong on one type of ability and weak on another. Principal among those emphasizing this point of view was Lewis Thurstone (1887–1955), who developed a theory of 'primary mental abilities', identifying seven major different types of ability (see Figure 11.3).

Simply identifying different kinds of ability, of course, does not put Thurstone's model at odds with Binet or Spearman: both researchers acknowledged that different kinds of ability exist. The major distinction was that Thurstone argued that these abilities were independent. He proposed that the apparent evidence of a general-ability factor was an artefact of testing; for instance, due to the fact that many tasks called on more than one primary mental ability. For example, a verbally presented mathematical puzzle might be aided by spatial imagery. In a related suggestion, Thurstone and his followers argued that *g* was merely an 'averaging' of a person's ability on multiple independent domains. This view that there is no underlying correlation to be found across all abilities remains today in the form of multiple intelligence theory (Gardner, 1983), which is discussed below.

Of course, if half of the variability in ability is due to a single general factor, two questions arise: What is the basis for this factor? And What is the structure of the other 50% of ability? The basis of g is addressed through the rest of this chapter, but before turning to that, it is important to understand how the overall structure of human intelligence is understood by contemporary researchers. Carroll (1993) concluded that while half of the differences in any large test battery were due to general ability, the remaining differences had a three-tier structure similar to that intimated above by Spearman: underneath g lies what Carroll called stratum-II factors, or what Spearman called group factors. Beneath this, on what Carroll called stratum-III, lie the abilities specific to a single test or a very narrow domain of ability. These are quite similar in scope to what cognitive psychologists now identify as cognitive modules. This structure is well-exemplified by turning again to the structure of the WAIS. Using what is called 'confirmatory factor analysis' the 13 sub-tests of the WAIS-III have been shown to group into four cognitive 'domains' (see Figure 11.4). Scores on the four domains inter-correlate .8 on average, supporting a single, general factor influencing each of the four abilities.

Crystallized and fluid intelligence

An alternative model of the structure of intelligence is somewhat related to that of Spearman, distinguishing between fluid ability and crystallized ability (Cattell, 1963). As we have seen above, intelligence tests can contain items that assume very little specific knowledge as well as items for which the person must have already learned the correct answer and stored it in memory. The theory of **fluid intelligence** and **crystallized intelligence** (Gf–Gc) was developed by Cattell in the 1940s and extended by Horn (1998). Cattell distinguished between fluid ability — the solving of problems where prior experience and knowledge are of little use — and crystallized knowledge — education and experience, which would develop over time. Cattell and Horn argued that fluid ability should be more heritable and crystallized ability should show greater effects of family and cultural environment. The predictions have not been borne out, however (Horn, 1998), and it seems likely that both fluid and crystallized ability reflect a single effect of general ability up until adulthood. During adulthood, genetic and environmental ageing factors begin to act on intelligence, with fluid ability showing greater sensitivity to these effects and declining much faster than crystallized ability (Craik & Salthouse, 2000).

Gardner: multiple intelligences

Howard Gardner (1983) proposed a theory of multiple intelligences, based on studies of 'savants' who have islands of preserved high ability despite scoring

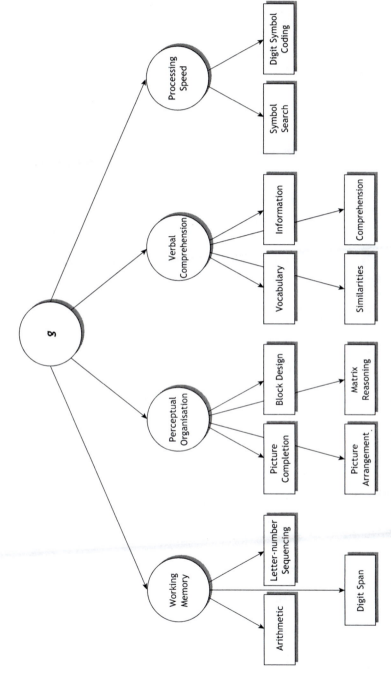

Figure 11.4 Three-level structure of the WAIS-III

very poorly on most ability measures, neuropsychological patients who have lost relatively circumscribed ability (e.g., the ability to recognize faces), and experts showing virtuoso performance within a limited domain such as music. Gardner used these groups to contrast against the normal developmental progression observed and measured by Binet. Gardner proposed that intelligence should include musical, bodily-kinaesthetic, linguistic, logical-mathematical, spatial, and inter- and intra-personal ability. This in itself is not controversial: Spearman was very specific in suggesting that the best possible measure of *g* should include all possible abilities, and most theories of general intelligence include linguistic, logical, and spatial tasks, as well as acknowledging that behaviour results from the activity of a great range of specialized brain 'modules'. What distinguishes Gardner's theory is not its recognition of multiple abilities, but his hypothesis that these abilities do not form a general factor. In this sense Gardner is repeating the argument of Thurstone that primary mental abilities are independent (Thurstone also identified seven primary abilities, although not the same seven). As Gardner has not developed any scales to assess his proposed abilities, this theory remains to be tested, although the stubborn fact remains that research consistently demonstrates positive correlations among different ability tests and a powerful *g* factor. It does appear, for example, that intra- and inter-personal skills correlate with general ability (Mayer et al., 1999), and that even pop dancing (presumably kinaesthetic intelligence) is correlated with much more general cues of personal competence (Brown et al., 2005).

COGNITION AND BIOLOGY

A major goal of research into the nature of human intelligence has been to determine its biological (or neural) bases. The major experimental correlates of ability are processing speed and working memory, brain volume, and brain connectivity, and these are discussed next.

Reaction time and inspection time

In a typical reaction time experiment, participants sit before a box with an array of 1–8 buttons, each with an adjacent light. When one of these lights illuminates, participants must lift their finger (often known as decision time) and move to press the correct button (often known as movement time). Hiding or inactivating some of the stimuli can produce a range of choices from 1 to 8 (see Figure 11.5).

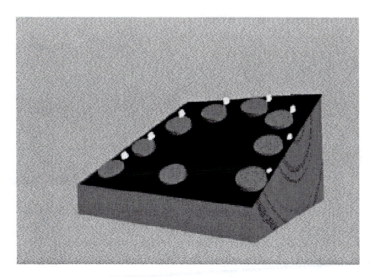

Figure 11.5   The Jensen Reaction Time Box

Each of 8 buttons has a light immediately above it. The subject rests their finger on the central 'home' key until one of the lights is illuminated, at which time they lift their finger from the home key (reaction time) and move to depress the appropriate response key (movement time).

Early on, the German psychologist Hick showed that reaction time increases linearly with the amount of information a subject must process in order to complete the reaction. Thus, perhaps surprisingly, lifting off the home key takes longer when one of four lights may illuminate, than when only one of two lights can be chosen to illuminate on a trial. This effect of information processing demand on reaction time (RT) is known as 'Hick's law'. Many dozens of studies since the 1970s have shown a correlation between rate of reaction and IQ. The largest study completed to date, studying over 900 adults, gave results representative of these many studies, indicating a correlation of .49 between IQ and four-choice RT, and a correlation of .26 between IQ and the variability of RT (Deary, Der, & Ford, 2001).

In addition to faster reactions to stimuli, researchers have examined the speed of the perceptual process itself in intelligence: the so-called 'inspection time'. Inspection time (IT) refers to the smallest duration for which a stimulus can be presented – before being removed ('masked') – and the participant can still accurately report what the stimulus was. One of the reasons why researchers are interested in IT is that unlike many tasks for

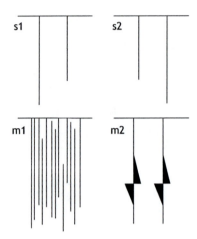

Figure 11.6   Inspection Time Stimulus

In the Inspection Time task, subjects are shown 1 of either s1 (long line left) or s2 (long line right) and are asked to report which side the long line was on. After some practice trials, a mask is introduced: commonly a group of distracting lines (m1) or else a lightning-flash (m2) that obscures the line lengths. The exposure time of the line stimulus before it is masked is varied by computer, and, by varying this duration and scoring correct and incorrect responses across a range of durations, an inspection time score can be calculated which indicates how many milliseconds exposure time before the mask a subject needs to achieve a certain percent correct, often 76%.

assessing intelligence – e.g., defining rare words, maths tasks – it is almost completely independent of culture or social learning. The typical stimulus used in an IT study is just a long and short line side by side, and the task is simply to report which of the two lines is longer (see Figure 11.6). Given a one-second exposure to the stimulus before it is covered by a mask, all participants can complete this task accurately on every trial. However, despite all participants knowing how to perform the task accurately, as the exposure duration is systematically reduced, some subjects remain accurate while others begin to make many errors. This error rate correlates highly with tested IQ. The effect was first reported by Australian researcher Ted Nettelbeck (1982). Since that time many dozens of studies have confirmed the effect, with a recent meta-analysis of 92 studies totalling over 4,000 subjects, suggesting that IT performance correlates .51 with general ability (Grudnik & Kranzler, 2001).

Brain volume and connectivity

The relationship between brain volume and intelligence has been a topic of a scientific debate since at least the 1830s. Claims of such a relationship have been severely criticized by historian of science Steven Gould as being 'pseudo-scientific', based on unconscious bias or even bogus data (Gould, 1996). On its face, the idea that something as crude as brain size should be associated with intelligence does seem questionable. However, the scientific evidence now seems to rebut Gould's criticism, and brain volume appears to be one of the strongest biological correlates of intelligence. The first rigorous report of a relation between brain volume and ability came from Nancy Andreasen (Andreasen et al., 1993), a cognitive scientist interested in creativity and exceptional performance, and numerous studies followed. A recent meta-analysis of 37 studies of the relationship between intelligence and brain volumes derived from modern brain imaging techniques, has shown that the correlation is approximately .33 (McDaniel, 2005). It is somewhat higher for females than for males, and also higher for adults than for children. For all age and sex groups, however, brain volume is positively correlated with intelligence.

The genetics of brain structure has begun to be studied, and some studies linking heritability of brain structure to IQ are now available. A recent review of the genetics of brain structure and intelligence (Toga & Thompson, 2005) concluded that the predominant determinant of both intelligence and brain structure is genetic. Two twin-study reports in the journal *Nature Neuroscience*, indicate that brain size and ability are both heritable, that they correlate around .4, and that this correlation is due to shared genetic effects. This finding implies the existence of genes that control the growth of brain tissue and that also influence ability. Thompson et al. (2001) showed that although the volume of cortical grey matter is genetically influenced over all of the brain, this effect is particularly marked in the brain's frontal and language areas. The volumes of these areas correlated particularly strongly with IQ, and were much more similar in identical twins than in dizygotic twins. This similarity therefore probably has a genetic basis. Brain imaging research also shows that activation in the brain's frontal lobes – such as during tasks that demand controlled attention – correlates .51 with IQ (Gray, Chabris, & Braver, 2003).

Thompson's results were soon confirmed in a much larger study by Dutch researcher Danielle Posthuma and colleagues (Posthuma, De Geus, Baare, Hulshoff, Kahn, & Boomsma, 2002). Her team found the heritability of brain volume to be very high (about .85), and that all of the effect of increased brain volume on increased IQ scores was due to genetic effects, rather than to environmental influences that might raise both brain size and cognitive ability. These twin study results were extended again by University of California researcher Richard Haier and his colleagues (Haier, Jung, Yeo, Head, & Alkire, 2004), who measured both the volume of particular brain regions and the activation of those regions during IQ test performance. Haier et al. replicated the brain volume–IQ correlation, and also found that the same regions that were larger in more intelligent participants were also most strongly activated during test-taking in all participants.

The brain consists not only of dense collections of nerve cells and their helpers (which appear grey in brain scans) but also of long fibres (axons) connecting these processing regions. These axons appear white because they have an insulating sheath of myelin which speeds conduction of the impulses from one grey matter nucleus to another. The organization and integrity of these fibre connections is related to ability, with correlations between .44 (Schmithorst, Wilke, Dardzinski, & Holland, 2005) and .51 (Jung et al., 2005). In sum, the modern literature on brain correlates of intelligence indicates that the number of neurons (i.e., brain volume) and amount of connectivity together enhance the types of processing required for high ability.

ENVIRONMENTAL EFFECTS ON INTELLIGENCE

Much research has been devoted to attempting to understand the effects of environmental factors on intelligence. Some of this research has aimed to develop interventions to minimize or remediate the effects of early childhood deprivation on cognitive ability. While simplistic solutions such as listening to Mozart for a short period of time have garnered great attention (Rauscher, Shaw, & Ky, 1993), only to be rejected by closer scrutiny (Stough, Kerkin, Bates, & Mangan, 1994; Chabris, 1999), other effects bear closer scrutiny.

Schooling

Several natural experiments suggest that schooling raises IQ. One example is 'entrance staggering', which occurs when children of near identical age enter school one year apart because of birthday-related admission criteria. This creates two groups of children who would be expected to have roughly equivalent IQ (i.e., they are roughly the same age), and so any differences between them should reflect school effects. The data indicate that children who have been in school longer have higher mean IQ scores. A different kind of natural experiment occurs when schooling is interrupted for a period of time for some children but not others. Green, Hoffman, Morse, Hayes, and Morgan (1966) reported that when the schools in one Virginia county closed for several years in the 1960s to avoid racial integration, the intelligence test scores of children who did not attend school dropped by about .4 standard deviations (six points) per missed year of school. A third natural experiment occurs when children from the same family attend different schools. Jensen (1977) reported that children learn so little at some schools that older siblings have systematically lower scores than their younger brothers and sisters attending better schools. It can be concluded that attending school raises intelligence, and that some schools do a better job of this than others.

It is clear that any skilled performance requires practice, not only from the evidence of virtuoso musicians, be they Yehudi Menuhin or Jimi Hendrix constantly carrying and practising their instrument, but also from experimental studies (Charness, Feltovich, Hoffman, & Ericsson, 2006). This literature on skilled performance demonstrates few, if any, cases exist of exceptional performance without a large investment of time, and shows that some forms of practice are much better than others. Simple repetition is much worse than practice aimed at specific technique goals and reinforced with immediate feedback. Education appears to provide such structured practice.

Head Start and Abecedarian studies

The first major intervention study attempting to remediate a poor or impoverished environment was 'Project Head Start', a programme giving deprived children systematic exposure to educational materials and experiences for one to two years. The results were disappointing in that while the programme did raise test scores during the course of the programme, these gains faded with time (Lee, Brooks-Gunn, Schnur, & Liaw, 1990). Building on this experience, longer interventions were planned, beginning in early infancy and continuing through pre-school, of which the best example is the Carolina Abecedarian Project. This project studied 111 pre-schoolers, providing a full-day, five-day week out-of-home pre-school intervention, from age 6 months and continuing for five years (see Figure 11.7). The study also had appropriate controls to allow careful evaluation of the intervention. The results indicated that infants at age 2 in the programme were scoring higher on cognitive tests than control infants who had not received the intervention. Importantly, at age 12 – seven years after the programme had been completed – the experimental group maintained a five-point IQ advantage over controls, and this IQ advantage was fully reflected in school and academic achievement (Ramey & Ramey, 2004).

The Flynn Effect

In the 1980s, New Zealand-based researcher James Flynn reported on an apparently very large and consistent rise in IQ scores around the world since

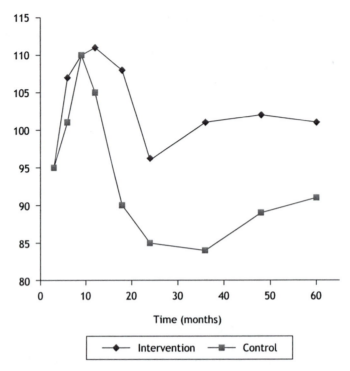

Figure 11.7   Abecedarian 5-year Intervention Data

Standardized scores on nine pre-school measurement occasions for treatment group (approximately 50 children with nutrition and health care intervention, plus full-day day-care five days a week for five-years) and control (nutritional and health care only) in the Abecedarian high-risk pre-school study (Ramey & Ramey, 2004).

intelligence testing began: around three IQ points per decade, and a full standard deviation since 1940. This came to be known as the 'Flynn Effect' (Dickens & Flynn, 2001). The gains were largest in 'culture fair' types of test (i.e., tests that do not rely extensively on learned material that may be less familiar to some cultural groups than to others) and smallest on knowledge-based tests such as the Scholastic Aptitude Test (SAT), where scores have actually declined (Dickens & Flynn, 2001).

Several explanations have been proffered. Flynn himself argued that intelligence has not in fact increased, but rather that 'We have wrongly defined intelligence'. He argues that the results are so dramatic they cannot be real. For example, results from the Netherlands indicate that in 1952 only .38% of the population had IQs over 140 ('genius'), while by 1982, scored by the same norms, 12% exceeded this figure! Flynn argued that he could not see a commensurate increase in genius products and that what had changed was 'abstract problem solving ability', perhaps due to teaching that emphasizes this skill. He and Dickens have suggested that perhaps there is now a better alignment of (especially school) environments to the genetic requirements of individuals (Dickens & Flynn, 2001).

Others, citing the parallel increase in height over the same period (the average Dutch young adult male is now over six feet [1.83 metres] in height), suggested that changes in nutrition or a reduction in childhood developmental stress and infection may account for the effect. Recent studies suggest that the rise in IQ, whatever its cause, ceased in the 1990s (Teasdale & Owen, 2005) and may now have reversed, so younger readers should worry more about declines than relying on continuing effortless rises in ability.

GENETIC EFFECTS ON INTELLIGENCE

Heritability

As we saw in Chapter 4, behavioural genetics is the study of genetic contributions to differences between members of a population. It examines the extent and nature (e.g., specific genes) of these contributions. You will recall that 'heritability' can vary from 0 to 1, and represents the proportion of variation between people that is due to genetic effects. The proportion of variability that is left unexplained by these effects is due to shared environment (i.e., effects shared within families) and non-shared environmental effects that are unique to the individual. It is important to remember that heritability can be very high even when tremendous amounts of environmental experience are known to be required for a behaviour to develop. For instance, every word in an individual's vocabulary is learned. However, in countries like the UK and Australia or New Zealand where all children attend school, and where systematic exposure to written words is available in everyone's environment, the number of words learned hinges on genetic differences. Thus, reading is highly heritable in these countries (Bates, Luciano, Castles, Wright, Coltheart, & Martin, in press).

Many large studies estimating the heritability of IQ have been conducted, and these yield estimates between .5 and .8 (Deary, Spinath, & Bates, 2006). *g* has been shown to be highly heritable in many studies, and the results of these are summarized in Table 11.1. Most of the different types of relationships presented have been examined in six or more studies, usually with at least several hundred participants.

Table 11.1   *Summary of world literature on familial effects on IQ (adapted from T. J. Bouchard, Jr. & McGue, 1981)*

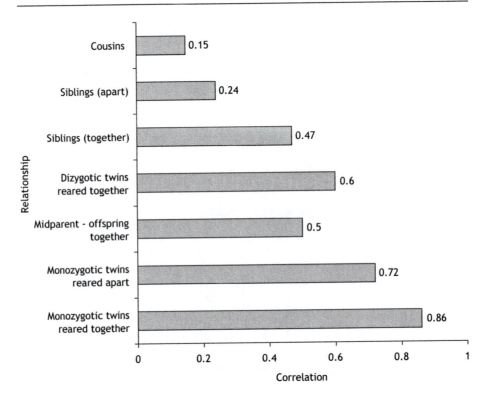

Effects of age on heritability

Genetic and environmental effects on ability are not constant, but evolve quite dramatically over time (see Figure 11.8). As the figure shows, early on in life, particularly before school starts, the contribution of family environment to children's IQ scores is quite high (about .6). However, children develop and, particularly from adolescence onwards, heritability climbs steeply, reaching around .8 in 60-year-olds. This suggests that as we develop and gain more control over our environments, the role of particular family, cultural, or social status variables on ability becomes minimized. As people mature, they may begin to exercise active choice over their environment, seeking out environments and activities that are based on their internal, genetically-based personal preferences and abilities.

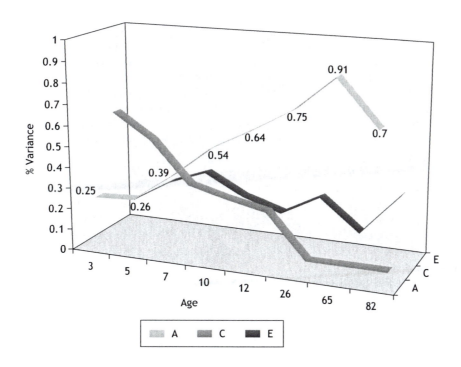

Figure 11.8   Genetic and Environmental Components of Intelligence from age 3 to age 82

Notes: A (pale) is the observed heritability, C (medium) is the effect of shared or family environment factors such as SES and home, and E (dark) is the remaining effects, which are unique to each individual and include measurement error. The Figure shows that at very young ages family environment has a large effect on cognitive ability, but that by young adulthood, this has been replaced with large effects of genes, which continue to rise in relative importance into old age, possibly declining again as people reach their 80s.

The data are combined results from (Bartels, Rietveld, Van Baal, & Boomsma, 2002; McClearn et al., 1997; Posthuma, de Geus, & Boomsma, 2001; Reynolds et al., 2005; Spinath & Plomin, 2003)

Limitations of heritability research

In many samples used in heritability research, people from the lowest socio-economic status (SES) levels are under-represented, and most samples also under-sample non-white populations. The heritability of intelligence may differ for people from different social backgrounds. One suggestion that this is the case comes from studies of children from impoverished backgrounds who are adopted into high SES families. Although the studies reported above show limited effects of family environment on IQ by middle childhood, these adopted children show increases in IQ when compared to children who remain in the impoverished environment, their IQ often increasing to the same level as that of biological children in the adoptive family (van Ijzendoorn & Juffer, 2005). Studies such as these suggest that very poor environments have substantial negative effects on IQ, and that removing a child from such environments may have positive effects, even at age 3 or later.

The hypothesis that heritability is lower among people from very poor family environments was tested in a sample of 331 pairs of twins, aged 7 years old, who were selected from the National Collaborative Perinatal Project in the USA. The heritability of IQ was .71 in the highest SES group within the sample, but only .10 in the lowest SES groups. The effect of family environment within this subset of low SES children was a very substantial .58 (Turkheimer, Haley, Waldron, D'Onofrio, & Gottesman, 2003). This finding is consistent with the average heritability (around .4 at age 7) reported from the UK TEDS sample (shown in Figure 11.8). As the average heritability of IQ rises quite dramatically after age 7, and family effects correspondingly decrease, it is unclear whether differences in the SES groups would remain as the children grow older.

The results of behavioural genetic studies of intelligence can be summarized in terms of two major effects: one surprising and one perhaps less surprising. The less surprising finding is that some family environments, concentrated among those of lower SES, can have large negative impacts on IQ, and these large negative effects appear to be remediable by exposure to stable and enriched environments. Perhaps more surprising is the finding that the effect of family environment on intelligence diminishes outside of the most impoverished social backgrounds, suggesting, perhaps comfortingly, that most families can provide adequate environments for cognitive development.

Molecular genetics

With the advent of the human genome project, researchers are beginning to discover the individual genes that underlie human intelligence (Deary, Spinath, & Bates, 2006). In the case of IQs below 70, defined as the threshold of mental retardation (MR), mental ability is often affected by major chromosomal disruption such as Trisomy 21 (presence of an extra copy of chromosome 21, leading to Down's Syndrome). MR affects over 2% of the population, with around 50% more males than females being affected (Chelly, Khelfaoui, Francis, Cherif, & Bienvenu, 2006). Of the almost 30,000 genes carried by each human being, over 300 have been associated with mental retardation, and there are many other genetic effects on retardation for which the gene responsible remains unknown. Many causes of MR related to larger chromosomal abnormalities can now be detected in early screening, raising the possibility of aborting foetuses known to carry MR, and the attendant ethical and moral questions. The growing ability to detect the much larger group of small changes within genes that are likely to affect brain development adversely will only intensify this debate.

Unlike MR, which is often due to major genetic abnormalities, Plomin and Kovas (2005) have argued that mild mental retardation (defined as IQ between one and two SDs below the population mean) is part of the normal spectrum of intelligence variation. The heritable variance within that normal spectrum is distributed across many hundreds or even thousands of genes, each having very small effects. The first genome-wide search for genes for intelligence was conducted in 2005 by Danielle Posthuma and colleagues (Posthuma et al., 2005), and indicated that a gene or genes on chromosome 6 are related to intelligence. A recent report (Burdick et al., 2006) has implicated Dysbindin, a gene at this site.

CORRELATES OF ABILITY

Cognitive ability has been shown to predict a variety of real-world outcomes. One of the clearest correlates of intelligence is school performance. Replicating Binet's original insight, it seems that aptitude for school, as measured by tests such the American SAT, simply is g (Frey & Detterman, 2004), and that g predicts school grades better than any other measure apart from the student's previous year's grades. The correlation between IQ scores and school grades is about .50, meaning that IQ explains about 25% of the differences between people in exam results. The other 75% is due to random factors affecting school grading, as well as individual differences in personality such as Conscientiousness and Openness that affect study habits, and external factors such as encouragement of learning by peers, family, and teachers. Childhood IQ also predicts the total years of education that people undertake (Neisser et al., 1996). How much people can learn can be dramatically affected by the teaching they receive, but the gap in educational outcomes between higher and lower IQ people remains when teaching is held constant. If you think about it, this makes sense: IQ was designed to detect ability to respond to teaching.

After school, performance at work has been repeatedly shown to be best predicted by general ability (Ree & Earles, 1992). At work and across a range of occupations, IQ accounts for about 30% of differences between people in job performance (Schmidt & Hunter, 1998). Because IQ test scores may be the best predictor of economic success in Western society (Schmidt & Hunter, 1998), these differences have important societal outcomes (Gottfredson, 1997). IQ scores account for around one-quarter of the differences between people in social status and around one-sixth of the differences in income. These effects are mostly due to people's individual intelligence, rather than to their parents'

SES, as cognitive ability still strongly predicts status and income even when the effect of parental background is statistically removed (Neisser et al., 1996).

Intelligence is also related to several other important life outcomes, both positive and negative (Gottfredson, 1997). Some are relatively easy to understand, such as the propensity to invest in financial markets. Other relationships are weaker and harder to relate directly to ability, such as links between lower IQ and juvenile offending (Moffitt, Gabrielli, Mednick, & Schulsinger, 1981), and risk for as well as severity of mental illness (Macklin et al., 1998). Intelligence is also related to mortality and longevity, with higher IQ people tending to live longer (Whalley & Deary, 2001). Understanding effects such as these is the focus of a new area of study known as 'cognitive epidemiology'.

Illustrative study: why lower IQ predicts earlier death

Scottish psychologists Ian Deary and Geoff Der (2005) set out to study explanations of the surprising finding that people with lower IQs tend to die younger, a find that has been replicated several times. For example, an earlier study found that if two people had IQs that differed by one standard deviation, the person with the lower IQ was only 79% as likely as the person with the higher IQ to live to age 76. Remarkably, in that study IQ was measured at age 11, indicating that childhood ability predicts adult longevity.

Deary and Der examined whether the greater mortality risk of people with lower IQs might reflect their less efficient information processing. They studied a representative sample of 898 Scottish adults in 1988, when they were aged about 54 to 58. These participants completed measures of verbal and numerical ability and a set of reaction time tasks, and indicated their education, occupation, and some lifestyle data. The researchers were notified by the National Health Service of any deaths among the participants until the end of 2002. By this time 20.6% had died. Statistical analysis showed that cognitive factors (lower IQ, slower and more variable reaction times) predicted who died even after controlling for other predictors associated with mortality risk (i.e., being male, smoking, lower social class). Moreover, reaction times were more strongly associated with death than was IQ, and appeared to explain the association between lower IQ and death. The authors speculate that reaction times may reflect an important aspect of the person's physical integrity, although the precise mechanism linking reaction times to mortality remains unclear.

STABILITY OF IQ

There is strong evidence that intelligence has high rank-order stability, even over long durations. IQ at age 18 is predicted very well by measures taken at age 12 (r = .89) or even age 6 (r = .77) (Jones & Bayley, 1941). If we average several test sessions at each age band to remove testing error, these correlations become even higher: for instance, the correlation of an average of measures taken at ages 11, 12, and 13 years with the average of two tests taken at 17 and 18 years is an astonishing .96, suggesting that IQ changes very little from age 11 onwards. Ability scores also remain stable across the life-span. Deary, Whalley, Lemmon, Crawford, and Starr (2000) had access to intelligence test scores for all children aged 11 in Scotland in 1932. They were able to bring 100 of this sample back to do the identical test 66 years to the day after the original test. The scores correlated .73, despite more than half a century having elapsed and the sample now being aged 77 years old.

BIAS

To be used legally, and to meet the ethical standards of relevant professional organizations, measures of intelligence must pass a strict set of statistical tests aimed at detecting bias. Bias detection is essentially a form of validity testing, examining whether any differences in scores between groups of people are due to the test having reduced validity for one group. In short, bias lowers test validity. Three major types of **test bias** can be distinguished: internal, situational, and external.

Internal bias arises and can be detected when test items behave differently for different groups. Items should have the same ordering of difficulty from easiest to hardest for all groups, and a group difference in this difficulty ordering would suggest that the items concerned are biased – i.e., difficult in ways unrelated to intelligence – for or against one group. For instance, a person who did not speak English would find the question 'What sound does a dog make?' much harder than they would assembling a jigsaw to form a dog. English speakers would find the verbal question easier. This inverted pattern of item difficulties indicates that the verbal question is internally biased against non-English speakers.

Situational bias is caused not so much by some property internal to the test, but by differences in how the test is administered to different groups. Testers might have a bias to assume that answers given by members of a group will be wrong, and therefore spend less time prompting them for a correct answer than they would for members of another group. Other types of situational bias might arise if one group of people is less familiar with the testing environment or more nervous in it.

External bias can be detected when a test makes systematically different predictions for one group than for another. For instance, IQ tests predict school grades and incomes. If a given IQ test under-predicted grades or income for one group – i.e., predicted mean levels that are lower than the true levels – then we would suspect the test was biased.

An example of the way in which bias is a practical matter as well as a matter of test construction can be found in the early use of intelligence tests in the American Army during World War I. Robert Yerkes, a highly respected American psychologist, was asked to develop tests that would allow the American Army to select men for different roles within the military. Yerkes responded by developing the Army Alpha and Army Beta tests, which came into use towards the end of the war. Both tests could be reliable and valid if administered to the correct population. The Army Alpha depended heavily on written information, and assumed exposure to a particular American culture. For instance, it required people to know what the 'Crisco' company manufactured (patent medicine, disinfectant, toothpaste, or food products). For army recruits who were recent immigrants or non-English speakers this test was clearly biased, and this bias was easily detected in the results of the test. First, *internal bias* was obvious: items that were easy for most English-speaking Americans were much harder for immigrants. These recruits should have been referred to the Army Beta: a non-verbal test administered individually by testers acting out the instructions. However, the test-givers, instead of referring non-English speakers for testing with the Army Beta, inappropriately tested these recruits on the Army Alpha. This use of a linguistically inappropriate test probably also created *situational bias*. Both of these biases were revealed in the failure of Army Alpha to make valid predictions about the performance of non-English-speaking recruits.

GROUP DIFFERENCES IN INTELLIGENCE

One of the most controversial and lasting aspects of intelligence testing has been the detection of group differences. One of the earliest impacts of systematic intelligence research was to disconfirm the then widely-held view that males were more intelligent on average than females, a view that was used to justify unequal access to education and democratic participation into the 20th century. Intelligence researchers demonstrated the fallacy of sex differences in intelligence, and also became active within the government of the day to push for social change based on their findings. The most reasonable conclusion to draw in 2006 is that male and female intelligence is equal on average, likely differing by less than one IQ point. However, several strands of evidence indicate that males have slightly greater variability in IQ than females (see Figure 11.9).

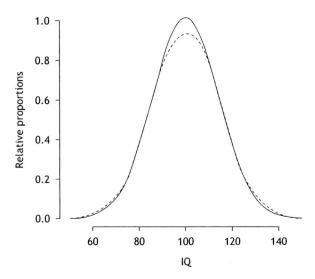

Figure 11.9   Sex differences in IQ: Both sexes have the same mean, with male scores (dotted line) being slightly more variable

Research on cognitive differences between racial groups has been more contentious. Readers are referred to Rushton and Jensen (2005) and the accompanying commentaries for a recent review of the literature. These contributions outline both what is known and unknown in this area of study, and help to appreciate the ethical and scientific issues involved in how the research findings should be interpreted, or whether they should be interpreted at all.

What most researchers do agree on is that there is a large difference in the average test scores of self-reported black and white groups, and that this difference persists to this day even in relatively affluent societies such as the UK and USA. The magnitude of this difference (around 1.1 standard deviations or 16 IQ points: Neisser et al., 1996) is accepted mostly because the samples in which it has been demonstrated are among the largest and most representative ever collected in psychology (e.g., nation-wide testing for college entrance [the Scholastic Aptitude Test and Graduate Record Examinations] and in corporate and military employment screening: see Roth, Bevier, Bobko, Switzer, & Tyler, 2001).

While the difference is a matter of record, the cause of the difference has been one of the longest and most heated debates in psychology. Two elements of the race–IQ question have proven most controversial: the first is the existence of race itself as a meaningful biological construct; the second is the origin of the observed racial differences in test scores.

The existence of race has been controversial, because if racial groupings themselves have no biological basis, then neither could the observed test score differences. The validity of the concept of race has been hotly contested, with many arguing either that there is no biological basis for race, or that any biological correlates of race are of such little importance that research should ignore them (Rose, 2005). Early biological analyses used blood-type to differentiate groups and concluded that most variation between people occurred within racial groups, rather than between them (Lewontin, 2001). However, the advent of human genome technologies means that millions of genetic markers are now available, allowing a more detailed examination of possible racial differences. Analysis of these markers appears to validate common racial groupings, indicating that self-reported race is 96% aligned with genetic marker data (Tang et al., 2005). Therefore, although racial groupings are not categories with crisp boundaries, and more variability occurs within them than between them, they have some utility for understanding differences between people including, for instance, risk and appropriate treatment for many medical disorders (Tang et al., 2005).

Even if racial groupings are not biologically meaningless, however, this does not mean that race-based differences in mean IQ have a biological basis. It is entirely possible that environmental factors that differ between racial groupings – potentially including nutrition, social norms, poverty, discrimination – contribute to these differences. Although IQ tests generally do not suffer from significant internal or external bias where race is concerned, it is possible that situational biases might exist. For example, Steele and Aronson (1995) demonstrated that when African American students were led to believe that a difficult verbal task was diagnostic of their intelligence they performed more poorly on it than when the task was not presented in this way. They argue that being made aware of a negative stereotype about one's group creates feelings of threat and vulnerability that impair performance. When black participants are administered intelligence tests, aware that lower intelligence is part of the stereotype of their group, their performance may therefore be adversely affected. As a result, their intelligence may be under-estimated and the racial stereotype invalidly 'confirmed'. This 'stereotype threat' phenomenon may at least partly account for racial disparities in measured intelligence.

CONCLUSIONS

We can end with a definition of intelligence, provided by 52 researchers on intelligence as:

> a very general mental capability that, among other things, involves the ability to reason, plan, solve problems, think abstractly, comprehend complex ideas, learn quickly and learn from experience. It is not merely book learning, a narrow

academic skill, or test-taking smarts. Rather, it reflects a broader and deeper capability for comprehending our surroundings – 'catching on,' 'making sense' of things, or 'figuring out' what to do. (Gottfredson, 1997)

Through studying this chapter, you will have seen that 'making sense' develops over childhood and early adolescence, that there are different elements to this trait which correlate with each other, around half the differences falling under a general-ability factor, with support for several groupings beneath this and different ageing profiles for fluid and crystallized ability. Development over childhood is reflected in measurable cortical changes, and is influenced positively by exposure to cognitively demanding environments with opportunities for structured practice, such as school. The tests are stable over long periods of time, and predict a broad range of outcomes, from school to work, mental well-being, and, ultimately, longevity. Intelligence test scores vary between different groups, with sex differences in variance (men more variable than women) and quite large differences between cultural groups. While researchers and educators agree on the magnitude of these differences (mean differences between groups can be over a standard deviation, about as big as the average difference between siblings within a family) they differ on their causes. Within deprived groups, heritability appears to be lower. Alongside the effects of environment, genetic differences exert considerable control over differences between people in their ability, and this effect grows with time, at least until the mid-60s, where some 70% of variance between people is explained by genetic effects. Some portion of the effect of these gene effects is summarized in the biological variables of head size (brain volume) and the integrity and connectivity of white matter, and genes are being studied which affect cognitive development and function. Ability tests themselves have developed over the century since their invention, with the most valid measures containing a broad array of abstract skills, and with testing guides that must be followed to avoid bias, and ensure reliability and validity. When followed, the 'IQ' test is among our most stable, powerful tools developed by psychologists, with applications in medical research, neuropsychological assessment, human resources, and education.

Chapter summary

- Binet assessed intelligence by assembling items that differentiated between typical children at various ages, scoring his test in terms of mental age, which formed the basis of the later 'intelligence quotient' or IQ.

(Continued)

(Continued)

- The 'deviation IQ' was first adopted by Wechsler, and differs by comparing an individual's performance against age norms, so that IQ tests have a mean of 100 and a standard deviation of 15.
- Like personality, the structure of ability is hierarchical, but unlike personality, all abilities appear to lie within a single domain.
- Authors emphasizing primary mental abilities (Thurstone) or a general ability (Spearman) are reconciled in this hierarchical model, in which *g* binds together more basic groups of ability, which in turn contain more specific lower-level abilities.
- Cognitive ability and the volume and connectivity of the central nervous system are related, according to imaging studies.
- Ability develops throughout childhood, and stimulation from early childhood onward, especially in the form of school-type activities, appears to be the major influence on the development of ability.
- Programmes for raising intelligence have had little lasting effect, but for children in deprived environments, full-time daycare-based care and stimulation throughout the pre-school years may have a lasting positive effect.
- Large rises in intelligence test scores in the latter half of the last century may demonstrate the effects of improved physical environment (reduced infection, improved nutrition), improvements in education, or increased practice at school of puzzle-like thinking.
- Estimates of the heritability of intelligence average around .5, with lower values in the very young, and higher values in older subjects. Specific genes underlying this heritable pattern are being investigated.
- Behavioural genetic research indicates that family environment matters rather little after school begins.
- IQ scores are amongst the most stable measures we have of a person over time.
- Intelligence tests yield reliable race-based differences, but the causes of these differences remain obscure.

Further reading

- Brown, W.M., Cronk, L., Grochow, K., Jacobson, A., Liu, C.K., Popovic, Z., et al. (2005). Dance reveals symmetry especially in young men. *Nature, 438*, 1148–50.

(Continued)

(Continued)

A brief paper relating pop dancing (one of Gardner's multiple intelligences) to evolutionary fitness.

- Deary, I.J., Spinath, F.M., & Bates, T.C. (2006). Genetics of intelligence. *European Journal of Human Genetics, 14,* 690–700.

A recent review of research on the genetics of ability.

- Mayer, J.D., Caruso, D., & Salovey, P. (1999). Emotional Intelligence meets traditional standards for an intelligence. *Intelligence, 27,* 267–98.

Re-introducing affect into intelligence testing.

- Neisser, U., Boodoo, G., Bouchard, T.J., Jr, Boykin, A.W., Brody, N., Ceci, S.J., et al. (1996). Intelligence: Knowns and unknowns. *American Psychologist, 51,* 77–101.

A comprehensive, but brief and straightforward review of intelligence, produced in the wake of the bell-curve controversy.

- Ramey, C.T., & Ramey, S.L. (2004). Early learning and school readiness: Can early intervention make a difference? *Merrill-Palmer Quarterly, 50,* 471–91.

A summary of the Abecedarian project outcomes.

- Ree, M.J., & Earles, J.A. (1992). Intelligence is the best predictor of job performance. *Current Directions in Psychological Science, 1,* 86–9.

How intelligence relates to work.

Glossary

Affect A general term to refer to emotions and moods.

Agreeableness One of the Big Five personality factors, involving dispositions to be cooperative, interpersonally warm, and empathic.

Anal stage The second stage of psychosexual development in psychoanalytic theory's genetic model, in which the focus of interest is the anus and the primary developmental issue is control.

Attachment style The tendency to approach close or romantic relationships in a particular way, as indicated by trust, dependence, and desired closeness to relationship partners. Three styles are generally recognized: secure, avoidant, and anxious-ambivalent.

Attributional style The tendency to explain events using a particular combination of causal dimensions, the standard dimensions being internal vs. external, stable vs. unstable, and global vs. specific. A pessimistic attributional style is one in which negative events are habitually explained in terms of internal, stable, and global causes. This concept is sometimes also referred to as 'explanatory style'.

Authoritarianism A personality trait involving rigidity, punitiveness, conventionality, distrust of introspection, and submission to authority.

Behavioural approach system (BAS) In Gray's theory, a neuropsychological system that underpins impulsivity, is sensitive to the possibility of rewards, and motivates people to seek them.

Behavioural inhibition system (BIS) For Gray the neuropsychological system that is the basis for anxiety, is sensitive to the possibility of punishment, and motivates people to avoid it.

Behaviourism A school of theory and research that addressed the relationships between environmental stimuli and observable behaviour, and held that mental states were not appropriate subjects of psychological investigation.

Big Five A popular model of the five primary dimensions of personality – Agreeableness, Conscientiousness, Extraversion, Neuroticism, and Openness to experience – derived from factor-analytic research on trait terms ('lexical' studies).

Character The component of personality associated with integrity, self-control, and other morally-relevant dispositions. It is often analysed in terms of character strengths and virtues.

Conscientiousness One of the Big Five personality factors, involving dispositions to be organized, reliable, self-controlled, and deliberate.

Coping The methods or 'strategies' that people use to manage stressful life events, generally by attempting to control the events themselves or their emotional reactions to them.

Correlation The degree of association between two variables, measured on a scale from −1 to +1.

Crystallized intelligence According to Cattell, the component of intelligence that depends on acquired knowledge based on education and life experience, assessed by tests of vocabulary and general knowledge, for example.

Defence mechanism Within psychoanalytic theory, the methods (e.g., repression, denial, projection) employed by the Ego to defend itself against the anxiety caused by troublesome thoughts, wishes, and impulses.

Diathesis A personality characteristic that confers increased vulnerability to a mental disorder, which is triggered if the person experiences a sufficient amount of life stress.

Ego In the structural model of psychoanalytic theory, the mental agency that mediates between desire (Id), conscience (Super-Ego), and external reality. It employs a repertoire of defence mechanisms to accomplish this task.

Emotional intelligence A set of abilities involving the perception, recognition, understanding, and regulation of emotions.

Entity theory The belief or 'lay theory' that a psychological attribute, such as personality or intelligence, is fixed or unchangeable. The opposite belief, an 'incremental theory', posits that the attribute is malleable.

Extraversion A Big Five personality dimension that also appears in Eysenck's system, involving sociability, high activity levels, and interpersonal dominance. The absence of these dispositions is Introversion.

Factor analysis A statistical procedure for determining the dimensions that underlie a set of observed variables.

Five-factor model A popular model of the five primary dimensions of personality: Agreeableness, Conscientiousness, Extraversion, Neuroticism, and Openness to experience. Essentially equivalent to the 'Big Five' but derived from factor analyses of questionnaire items rather than lexical studies.

Fluid intelligence According to Cattell, the component of intelligence that depends on general mental fluency and flexibility rather than acquired knowledge.

g The general component of intelligence that underlies all cognitive abilities.

Heritability The proportion of the differences in a characteristic between people in a population that is explained by genetic differences between people, varying from 0 to 1.

Humanistic psychology A theoretical approach to the study of personality that emphasized motives for personal growth and self-realization, and held a very optimistic view of human nature.

Id In the structural model of psychoanalytic theory, the mental agency that is the repository of drives and their associated wishes and impulses.

Idiographic An approach to the study of personality that emphasizes intensive analysis of the individual's uniqueness.

Intelligence A broad, general cognitive ability, reflected in reasoning, problem-solving, abstract thinking, mental speed, and capacity to learn.

Interactionism A theoretical position according to which behaviour is a joint function of situational and dispositional factors.

Interest A preference for or tendency to engage with a particular kind of activity, such as a particular kind of vocation or leisure activity.

Inventory A form of assessment device requiring structured responses – usually self-ratings – to a standard series of test items.

Latency In psychoanalytic theory, a period of psychosexual development in middle childhood during which sexual drives are largely dormant.

Life narrative A biographical story of a person's life history.

Locus of control The general expectation that events in one's life are under one's personal control (internal locus) or due to factors outside one's control, such as luck, fate, or other people (external locus).

Mean-level change The extent to which the average level of a characteristic, such as a personality trait, differs for people of different ages.

Motive   A force that directs and energizes behaviour in particular directions. Motives may be largely outside of awareness (e.g., drives, needs) or consciously accessible and future-oriented (e.g., goals, strivings).

Multiple personality   Now known as Dissociative Identity Disorder, this is a rare mental disorder in which the person appears to have more than one distinct personality, with these personalities often mutually unaware.

Neuroticism   A Big Five personality dimension that also appears in Eysenck's system, involving emotional instability, proneness to experience negative emotions, vulnerability, and low self-esteem.

Neurotransmitter   A brain chemical involved in the transmission of impulses between neurons. Variation in the typical concentrations of these in the brain may be associated with differences on personality trait dimensions.

Nomothetic   An approach to the study of personality that emphasizes the development of generalizations and laws of behaviour.

Object relations   The mental representations – including unconscious ones – of self, others, and interpersonal relations that are the focus of a school of psychoanalytic theory that goes by the same name.

Openness to experience   A Big Five trait dimension involving dispositions towards imaginativeness, aesthetic sensibility, intellectual interests, and unconventionality.

Oral stage   In the genetic model of psychoanalytic theory, the earliest stage of psychosexual development, in which the mouth is the erotic focus and dependency is the primary developmental issue.

Personal construct   In Kelly's theory, a pair of polar alternatives (e.g., 'warm vs. cold', 'old vs. young') that people use to make sense of, or 'construe', their experiences. Objects or events are construed as similar to or different from these alternatives.

Personality disorder   An extreme, inflexible, and maladaptive personality variant associated with distress, interpersonal problems, and impaired social and occupational functioning.

Personology   A school of personality psychology that focuses on the intensive study of individual lives through time, often examined using case-study and psychobiographical methods.

Phallic stage   The third psychosexual stage in psychoanalytic theory's genetic model, in which erotic interest shifts to the genitals and the difference between the sexes is a major theme. The stage terminates in the Oedipus complex.

Preconscious   In the topographic model of psychoanalytic theory, the intermediate level of the mind in which mental content that is potentially conscious resides.

Projective test   A form of personality assessment that employs ambiguous stimuli and open-ended responses in order to examine people's typical ways of imposing ('projecting') meaning on their experience, often in an attempt to delve beneath the conscious surface of the personality.

Psychobiography   The use of systematic psychological research and theory to advance the biographical understanding of individual lives, most commonly historical figures.

Psychoticism   A major trait dimension in Eysenck's system, involving aggressiveness, coldness, egocentricity, and creativity.

Rank-order stability   The extent to which levels of a characteristic, such as a personality trait, are associated from one time to another, as assessed by a 'retest correlation'.

Reliability   The extent to which a measure yields consistent assessments: the components of the measure should be consistent with one another ('internal consistency'), different users of the measure should agree in their assessments of people who they assess ('inter-rater reliability'), and the measure should yield consistent assessments when the same person is assessed on different occasions ('retest reliability'). The greater the reliability of a measure, the less its measurement error.

Response bias   The systematic tendency for people completing assessments to respond in ways that distort their responses, for example yea- or nay-saying (excessive yes or no responses independent of item content), faking bad (responding more disturbed than the person truly is), and social desirability (responding in an effort to conform to social norms).

Schizotypy   An abnormal personality variant involving social anxiety and susceptibility to unusual ideas and experiences, which appears to confer vulnerability for schizophrenia.

Self-complexity   The degree to which the self-concept is composed of multiple distinct aspects such as social roles.

Self-efficacy   The expectation that one's behaviour can effectively achieve its goals.

Self-esteem   The global evaluation, from highly negative to highly positive, that people attach to their self-concept.

Self-monitoring A personality trait referring to the degree of consistency between a person's inner self and their public self-presentation: low self-monitors have high levels of consistency and do not shape their public behaviour to their audience; high self-monitors adjust their behaviour to situational demands, and are therefore less consistent.

Self-narrative One component of the self-concept, involving a story-like conception of how one's life has unfolded over time which may follow a variety of narrative trajectories.

Shared environment In behavioural genetics, those environmental influences of behaviour that are shared within families, such as social class and parental education. The remaining, non-shared environmental influences are unique to each individual.

Situationism A theoretical position holding that behaviour is primarily a function of the situation or context in which it occurs, rather than of the person's enduring and consistent dispositions. This position directly conflicts with the trait perspective.

Social learning theory A personality theory that modified behavioural learning theories by including cognitive constructs such as expectancies.

Super-Ego In the structural model of psychoanalytic theory, the mental agency that represents internalized social norms in primitive form, primarily in the form of prohibitions.

Temperament The component of personality that is believed to be biologically based, present at birth or at least early in development, and is often related to emotional expression.

Test bias The tendency for a test to yield assessments that are less valid for one or more social groups than for another, such as having content that is unfamiliar to a group, being administered in different ways for different groups, or under- or over-predicting outcomes for particular groups.

Trait An internal disposition to think, feel, or behave in particular ways, understood to be consistent across situations and through time, especially when referring to non-intellectual dispositions (i.e., 'personality traits').

Type A form of personality variation in which a subset of people belong to a distinct category that share a particular characteristic, rather than varying by degrees along a personality dimension, as in standard personality trait models.

Unconscious In psychoanalytic theory, a level of the mind whose contents (thoughts, wishes, and impulses) are prevented from entering awareness and that has its own, irrational cognitive processes.

Validity   The extent to which a measure accurately assesses the construct that it is intended to assess, and predicts phenomena that should be associated with that construct. It can be broken down into several forms. 'Content' validity refers to the extent to which the measure's elements accurately refer to the construct, 'convergent' and 'discriminant' validity refer to it being associated with other measures of the same construct and not associated with measures of other constructs, and 'predictive' validity refers to the measure's capacity to predict outcomes linked to the construct.

Value   An abstract, consciously accessible goal (e.g., 'freedom', 'respect for tradition') that applies across many situations and motivates people to behave in accordance with it.

References

Abramson, L.Y., Seligman, M.E.P., & Teasdale, J.D. (1978). Learned helplessness in humans: Critique and reformulation. *Journal of Abnormal Psychology, 87*, 49–74.

Abramson, L.Y., Metalsky, G.I., & Alloy, L. (1989). Hopelessness depression: A theory-based subtype of depression. *Psychological Review, 96*, 358–72.

Ackermann, R., & DeRubeis, R.J. (1991). Is depressive realism real? *Clinical Psychology Review, 11*, 565–84.

Adams, H.E., Wright, L.W., & Lohr, B.A. (1996). Is homophobia associated with homosexual arousal? *Journal of Abnormal Psychology, 105*, 440–5.

Adorno, T.W., Frenkel-Brunswik, E., Levinson, D.J., & Sanford, R.N. (1950). *The authoritarian personality*. New York: Harper.

Alexander, I.E. (1990). *Personology: Method and content in personality assessment and psychobiography*. Durham, NC: Duke University Press.

Allport, G.W. (1931). What is a trait of personality? *Journal of Abnormal and Social Psychology, 25*, 368–72.

Allport, G.W., & Odbert, H.S. (1936). Trait-names: A psycho-lexical study. *Psychological Monographs, 47* (No. 211).

American Psychiatric Association (2000). *Diagnostic and statistical manual of mental disorder: DSM-IV-TR*. Washington, DC: Author.

Andreasen, N.C., Flaum, M., Swayze, V., O'Leary, D.S., Alliger, R., Cohen, G., et al. (1993). Intelligence and brain structure in normal individuals. *American Journal of Psychiatry, 150*, 130–4.

Arbelle, S., Benjamin, J., Golin, M., Kremer, I., Belmaker, R.H., & Ebstein, R.P. (2003). Relation of shyness in grade school children to the genotype for the long form of the serotonin transporter promoter region polymorphism. *American Journal of Psychiatry, 160*, 671–6.

Bandura, A. (1986). *Social foundations of thought and action: A social cognitive theory*. Englewood Cliffs, NJ: Prentice-Hall.

Barrick, M.R., & Mount, M.K. (1991). The Big Five personality dimensions and job performance: A meta-analysis. *Personnel Psychology, 44*, 1–26.

Bartels, M., Rietveld, M.J., Van Baal, G.C., & Boomsma, D.I. (2002). Genetic and environmental influences on the development of intelligence. *Behavioural Genetics, 32*, 237–49.

Bates, T.C., Luciano, M., Castles, A., Wright, M., Coltheart, M., & Martin, N.G. (2007). Genetics of reading and spelling: Shared genes across modalities, but different genes for lexical and nonlexical processing. *Reading and Writing*.

Baumeister, R.F., Campbell, J.D., Krueger, J.I., & Vohs, K.D. (2003). Does high self-esteem cause better performance, interpersonal success, happiness, or healthier lifestyles? *Psychological Science in the Public Interest, 4*, 1–44.

Benet-Martínez, V., & Waller, N.G. (2002). From adorable to worthless: Implicit and self-report structure of highly evaluative personality descriptors. *European Journal of Personality, 16*, 1–41.

Binet, A., & Simon, T. (1905). Méthodes nouvelles pour le diagnostic du niveaux intellectuel des anormaux. *L'année psychologique, 11*, 191–241 (E. Kite, Trans.). Reprinted in *The development of intelligence in children* (pp. 41–88). Baltimore, MD: Williams & Williams.

Blatt, S.J., & Zuroff, D.C. (1992). Interpersonal relatedness and self-definition: Two prototypes for depression. *Clinical Psychology Review, 12*, 527–62.

Block, J. (1978). *The Q-sort method in personality assessment and psychiatric research.* Palo Alto, CA: Consulting Psychologists Press.

Bogg, T., & Roberts, B.W. (2004). Conscientiousness and health behaviours: A meta-analysis. *Psychological Bulletin, 130*, 887–919.

Bouchard, T.J., & McGue, M. (1981). Familial studies of intelligence: A review. *Science, 212*, 1055–9.

Bower, J.E., Kemeny, M., Taylor, S.E., & Fahey, J.L. (1998). Cognitive processing, discovery of meaning, CD4 decline, and AIDS-related mortality among bereaved HIV-seropositive men. *Journal of Consulting and Clinical Psychology, 66*, 979–86.

Bowlby, J. (1969). *Attachment and loss: Vol. 1. Attachment.* New York: Basic Books.

Bowlby, J. (1991). *Charles Darwin: A new life.* New York: W.W. Norton.

Brown, W.M., Cronk, L., Grochow, K., Jacobson, A., Liu, C.K., Popovic, Z., et al. (2005). Dance reveals symmetry especially in young men. *Nature, 438*, 1148–50.

Burdick, K.E., Lencz, T., Funke, B., Finn, C.T., Szeszko, P.R., Kane, J.M., et al. (2006). Genetic variation in DTNBP1 influences general cognitive ability. *Human Molecular Genetics, 15*, 1563–8.

Bushman, B.J., & Baumeister, R.F. (1998). Threatening egotism, narcissism, self-esteem, and direct and displaced aggression: Does self-love or self-hate lead to violence? *Journal of Personality and Social Psychology, 75*, 219–29.

Campbell, J.D. (1990). Self-esteem and clarity of the self-concept. *Journal of Personality and Social Psychology, 59*, 538–49.

Cannon, T.D., Mednick, S.A., & Parnas, J. (1990). Antecedents of predominantly negative and predominantly positive symptom schizophrenia in a high-risk population. *Archives of General Psychiatry, 47*, 622–32.

Cantor, N. (1990). From thought to behavior: 'Having' and 'doing' in the study of personality and cognition. *American Psychologist, 45*, 735–50.

Carroll, J.B. (1993). *Human cognitive abilities: A survey of factor-analytic studies.* New York: Cambridge University Press.

Caspi, A., & Herbener, E.S. (1990). Continuity and change: Assortative mating and the consistency of personality in adulthood. *Journal of Personality and Social Psychology, 58*, 250–8.

Caspi, A., Sugden, K., Moffitt, T.E., Taylor, A., Craig, I.W., et al. (2003). Influence of life stress on depression: Moderation by a polymorphism in the 5–HTT gene. *Science, 301*, 386–9.

Caspi, A., Taylor, A., Moffitt, T.E., & Plomin, R. (2000). Neighbourhood deprivation affects children's mental health: Environmental risks identified in a genetic design. *Psychological Science, 11*, 338–42.

Cattell, R.B. (1943). The description of personality: Basic traits resolved into clusters. *Journal of Abnormal and Social Psychology, 38*, 476–506.

Cattell, R.B. (1963). The theory of fluid and crystallized intelligence: A critical experiment. *Journal of Educational Psychology, 54*, 1–22.

Chabris, C.F. (1999). Prelude or requiem for the 'Mozart effect'? *Nature, 400*, 826–7.

Charness, N., Feltovich, P.J., Hoffman, R.R., & Ericsson, K.A. (Eds.). (2006). *The Cambridge handbook of expertise and expert performance.* New York: Cambridge University Press.

Chelly, J., Khelfaoui, M., Francis, F., Cherif, B., & Bienvenu, T. (2006). Genetics and pathophysiology of mental retardation. *European Journal of Human Genetics, 14*, 701–13.

Church, A.T., & Lonner, W.J. (1998). Personality and its measurement in cross-cultural perspective. Special issue of the *Journal of Cross-Cultural Psychology, 29*.

Cohen, J. (1992). A power primer. *Psychological Bulletin, 112*, 155–9.

Corballis, M.C. (2003). *From hand to mouth: The origins of language.* Princeton, NJ: Princeton University Press.

Costa, P.T., & McCrae, R.R. (1992). *Revised NEO Personality Inventory (NEO PI-R) and NEO Five-Factor Inventory. Professional manual.* Odessa, FL: Psychology Assessment Resources.

Costa, P.T., & McCrae, R.R. (1994a). Set like plaster? Evidence for the stability of adult personality. In T.F. Heatherton & J.L. Weinberger (Eds.), *Can personality change?* (pp. 21–40). Washington, DC: American Psychological Association.

Costa, P.T., & McCrae, R.R. (1994b). Stability and change in personality from adolescence through adulthood. In C.F. Halverson, G.A. Kohnstamm, & R.P. Martin, (Eds.), *The developing structure of temperament and personality in infancy and childhood* (pp. 139–50). Hillsdale, NJ: Erlbaum.

Côté, S., & Miners, C.T.H. (2006). Emotional intelligence, cognitive intelligence, and job performance. *Administrative Science Quarterly, 51*, 1–28.

Craik, F.I.M., & Salthouse, T.A. (Eds.). (2000). *The handbook of aging and cognition* (2nd ed.). Mahwah, NJ: Erlbaum.

Cramer, P. (1998). Freshman to senior year: A follow-up study of identity, narcissism, and defence mechanisms. *Journal of Research in Personality, 32*, 156–72.

Dawes, R.M., Faust, D., & Meehl, P.E. (1989). Clinical versus actuarial judgment. *Science, 243*, 1668–74.

Deary, I.J., & Der, G. (2005). Reaction time explains IQ's association with death. *Psychological Science, 16*, 64–9.

Deary, I.J., Der, G., & Ford, G. (2001). Reaction times and intelligence differences: A population-based cohort study. *Intelligence, 29*, 389–99.

Deary, I.J., Spinath, F.M., & Bates, T.C. (2006). Genetics of intelligence. *European Journal of Human Genetics, 14*, 690–700.

Deary, I.J., Whalley, L.J., Lemmon, H., Crawford, J.R., & Starr, J.M. (2000). The stability of individual differences in mental ability from childhood to old age: Follow-up of the 1932 Scottish Mental Survey. *Intelligence, 28*, 49–55.

DeNeve, K.M., & Cooper, H. (1998). The happy personality: A meta-analysis of 137 personality traits and subjective well-being. *Psychological Bulletin, 124*, 197–229.

Depue, R.A., & Collins, P.F. (1999). Neurobiology of the structure of personality: Dopamine, facilitation of incentive motivation, and extraversion. *Behavioural and Brain Sciences, 22,* 491–530.

De Raad, B. (2005). The trait coverage of emotional intelligence. *Personality and Individual Differences, 38,* 673–87.

Dickens, W.T., & Flynn, J.R. (2001). Heritability estimates versus large environmental effects: The IQ paradox resolved. *Psychological Review, 108,* 346–69.

Digman, J.M. (1989). Five robust personality dimensions: Development, stability, and utility. *Journal of Personality, 57,* 195–214.

Donaghue, E.M., Robins, R.W., Roberts, B.W., & John, O.P. (1993). The divided self: Concurrent and longitudinal effects of psychological adjustment and social roles on self-concept differentiation. *Journal of Personality and Social Psychology, 64,* 834–46.

Driessen, M., Herrman, J., Stahl, K., Zwann, M., Meier, S., Hill, A., Osterheider, M. & Petersen, D. (2000). Magnetic resonance imaging volumes of the hippocampus and the amygdala in women with borderline personality disorder and early traumatization. *Archives of General Psychiatry, 57,* 1115–22.

Dweck, C.S. (1999). *Self-theories: Their role in motivation, personality, and development.* Philadelphia, PA: Psychology Press.

Elms, A.C. (1994). *Uncovering lives: The uneasy alliance of biography and psychology.* New York: Oxford University Press.

Emmons, R.A. (1999). Motives and life goals. In R. Hogan, J. Johnson, & S. Briggs (Eds.), *Handbook of personality psychology* (pp. 485–512). New York: Academic Press.

Erikson, E.H. (1963). *Childhood and society* (2nd ed.). New York: W.W. Norton.

Exner, J.E. (1986). *The Rorschach: A comprehensive system, Vol. 1: Basic foundations* (2nd ed.). New York: Wiley.

Eysenck, H.J. (1947). *Dimensions of personality.* London: Routledge & Kegan Paul.

Eysenck, H.J. (1967). *The biological basis of personality.* Springfield, IL: Charles C. Thomas.

Eysenck, H.J. (1990). Biological dimensions of personality. In L.A. Pervin (Ed.), *Handbook of personality: Theory and research* (pp. 244–76). New York: Guilford.

Fazio, R., Jackson, J.R., Dunton, B., & Williams, C.J. (1995). Variability in automatic activation as an unobtrusive measure of racial attitudes: A bona fide pipeline? *Journal of Personality and Social Psychology, 69,* 1013–27.

Feldman Barrett, L., & Russell, J.A. (1999). The structure of current affect: Controversies and emerging consensus. *Current Directions in Psychological Science, 8,* 10–14.

Fiske, A.P., Kitayama, S., Markus, H., & Nisbett, R. (1998). The cultural matrix of social psychology. In D.T. Gilbert, S.T. Fiske, & G. Lindzey (Eds.), *The handbook of social psychology* (pp. 915–81). Boston, MA: McGraw-Hill.

Fiske, D.W. (1949). Consistency of the factorial structures of personality ratings from different sources. *Journal of Abnormal and Social Psychology, 44,* 329–44.

Fleeson, W. (2001). Towards a structure- and process-integrated view of personality: Traits as density distributions of states. *Journal of Personality and Social Psychology, 80,* 1011–27.

Folkman, S., & Lazarus, R.S. (1980). An analysis of coping in a middle-aged community sample. *Journal of Health and Social Behavior, 21,* 219–39.

Folkman, S., & Moskowitz, J.T. (2004). Coping: Pitfalls and promise. *Annual Review of Psychology, 55,* 745–74.

Fraley, R.C., & Shaver, P.R. (1998). Airport separations: A naturalistic study of adult attachment dynamics in separating couples. *Journal of Personality and Social Psychology, 75*, 1198–212.

Franz, C.E. (1994). Does thought content change as individuals age? A longitudinal study of midlife adults. In T.F. Heatherton & J.L. Weinberger (Eds.), *Can personality change?* (pp. 227–49). Washington, DC: American Psychological Association.

Freud, S. (1923). *The ego and the id.* In J. Strachey (Ed. and Trans.), *The collected works of Sigmund Freud, Vol. 14.* London: Hogarth Press.

Frey, M.C., & Detterman, D.K. (2004). Scholastic assessment or *g*? *Psychological Science, 15*, 373–8.

Friedman, H.S., Tucker, J.S., Tomlinson-Keasey, C., Schwartz, J.E., Wingard, D.L., & Criqui, M.H. (1993). Does childhood personality predict longevity? *Journal of Personality and Social Psychology, 67*, 278–86.

Friedman, M., & Rosenman, R.H. (1974). *Type A behavior and your heart.* New York: Knopf.

Funder, D.C. (1997). *The personality puzzle.* New York: W.W. Norton.

Galsworthy, M.J., Paya-Cano, J.L., Liu, L., Monleon, S., Gregoryan, G., Fernandes, C., et al. (2005). Assessing reliability, heritability and general cognitive ability in a battery of cognitive tasks for laboratory mice. *Behavioural Genetics, 35*, 675–92.

Gardner, H. (1983). *Frames of mind: The theory of multiple intelligences.* New York: Basic Books.

Gergen, K.J., & Gergen, M.M. (1983). Narratives of the self. In T.R. Sarbin & K.E. Scheibe (Eds.), *Studies in social identity* (pp. 254–73). New York: Praeger.

Glenn, N.D. (1980). Values, attitudes, and beliefs. In O.G. Brim & J. Kagan (Eds.), *Constancy and change in human development* (pp. 596–640). Cambridge, MA: Harvard University Press.

Goleman, D. (1995). *Emotional intelligence.* New York: Bantam.

Gosling, S.D., & John, O.P. (1999). Personality dimensions in nonhuman animals: A cross-species review. *Current Directions in Psychological Science, 8*, 69–73.

Gosling, S.D., Ko, S.J., Mannarelli, T., & Morris, M.E. (2002). A room with a cue: Personality judgments based on offices and bedrooms. *Journal of Personality and Social Psychology, 82*, 379–98.

Gottfredson, L.S. (1997). Mainstream science on intelligence: An editorial with 52 signatories, history, and bibliography. *Intelligence, 224*, 13–23.

Gould, S.J. (1996). *The mismeasure of man* (2nd ed.). New York: W.W. Norton.

Gray, J.A. (1981). A critique of Eysenck's theory of personality. In H.J. Eysenck (Ed.), *A model for personality* (pp. 246–76). New York: Springer-Verlag.

Gray, J.R., Chabris, C.F., & Braver, T.S. (2003). Neural mechanisms of general fluid intelligence. *Nature Neuroscience, 6*, 316–22.

Green, R.L., Hoffman, L.J., Morse, R.J., Hayes, M.E., & Morgan, R.F. (1966). *The educational status of children during the first school year following four years of little or no schooling*: Charlotteville, Virginia Department of Health, Education and Welfare.

Greenwald, A.G., & Farnham, S.D. (2000). Using the Implicit Association Test to measure self-esteem and self-concept. *Journal of Personality and Social Psychology, 79*, 1022–38.

Greenwald, A.G., McGhee, D.E., & Schwartz, J.L.K. (1998). Measuring individual differences in implicit cognition: The Implicit Association Test. *Journal of Personality and Social Psychology, 74,* 1464–80.

Grudnik, J.L., & Kranzler, J.H. (2001). Meta-analysis of the relationship between intelligence and inspection time. *Intelligence, 29,* 523–35.

Grünbaum, A. (1984). *The foundations of psychoanalysis: A philosophical critique.* Berkeley, CA: University of California Press.

Haier, R.J., Jung, R.E., Yeo, R.A., Head, K., & Alkire, M.T. (2004). Structural brain variation and general intelligence. *Neuroimage, 23,* 425–33.

Hall, C.S., & Lindzey, G. (1978). *Theories of personality* (3rd ed.). New York: Wiley.

Hamer, D. (1997). The search for personality genes: Adventures of a molecular biologist. *Current Directions in Psychological Science, 6,* 111–14.

Hampshire, S. (1953). Dispositions. *Analysis, 14,* 5–11.

Harter, S. (1993). Causes and consequences of low self-esteem in children and adolescents. In R. Baumeister (Ed.), *Self-esteem: The puzzle of low self-regard* (pp. 87–116). New York: Plenum Press.

Haslam, N. (1997). Evidence that male sexual orientation is a matter of degree. *Journal of Personality and Social Psychology, 73,* 862–70.

Haslam, N., Bain, P., & Neal, D. (2004). The implicit structure of positive characteristics. *Personality and Social Psychology Bulletin, 30,* 529–41.

Haslam, N., Bastian, B., & Bissett, M. (2004). Essentialist beliefs about personality and their implications. *Personality and Social Psychology Bulletin, 30,* 1661–73.

Haslam, N., & Kim, H.C. (2002). Categories and continua: A review of taxometric research. *Genetic, Social and General Psychology Monographs, 128,* 271–320.

Hazan, C., & Shaver, P. (1987). Romantic love conceptualized as an attachment process. *Journal of Personality and Social Psychology, 52,* 511–24.

Heaven, P.C.L., & Bucci, S. (2001). Right-wing authoritarianism, social dominance orientation and personality: An analysis using the IPIP measure. *European Journal of Personality, 15,* 49–56.

Heine, S.H., Lehman, D.R., Markus, H.R., & Kitayama, S. (1999). Is there a universal human need for positive self-regard? *Psychological Review, 106,* 766–94.

Helson, R., Mitchell, V., & Moane, G. (1984). Personality and patterns of adherence and non-adherence to the social clock. *Journal of Personality and Social Psychology, 46,* 1079–96.

Hogan, J. (1989). Personality correlates of physical fitness. *Journal of Personality and Social Psychology, 56,* 284–8.

Holland, J.L. (1997). *Making vocational choices: A theory of vocational personalities and work environments* (3rd ed.). Odessa, FL: Psychological Assessment Resources.

Horn, J. L. (1998). A basis for research on age differences in cognitive capabilities. In J.J. McArdle & R.W. Woodcock (Eds.), *Human cognitive abilities in theory and practice* (pp. 57–91). Mahwah, NJ: Erlbaum.

Howard, A., & Bray, D. (1988). *Managerial lives in transition: Advancing age and changing times.* New York: Guilford.

Jackson, T., Chen, H., Guo, C., & Gao, X. (2006). Stories we love by: Conceptions of love among couples from the People's Republic of China and the United States. *Journal of Cross-Cultural Psychology, 37,* 446–64.

Jemmott, J.B. (1987). Social motives and susceptibility to disease: Stalking individual differences in health risks. *Journal of Personality, 55,* 267–98.

Jensen, A.R. (1977). Cumulative deficit in IQ of Blacks in the rural South. *Developmental Psychology, 13,* 184–91.

John, O.P. (1990). The 'Big Five' factor taxonomy: Dimensions of personality in the natural language and in questionnaires. In L. Pervin (Ed.), *Handbook of personality: Theory and research* (pp. 66–100). New York: Guilford.

John, O.P., Caspi, A., Robins, R.W., Moffitt, T.E., & Stouthamer-Loeber, M. (1994). The 'little five': Exploring the nomological network of the five-factor model of personality in adolescent boys. *Child Development, 65,* 160–78.

John, O.P., & Srivastava, S. (1999). The Big Five trait taxonomy: History, measurement, and theoretical perspectives. In L.A. Pervin (Ed.), *Handbook of personality: Theory and research, Vol. 2* (pp. 102–38). New York: Guilford.

Jones, H.E., & Bayley, N. (1941). The Berkeley Growth Study. *Child Development, 12,* 167–73.

Jordan, C.H., Spencer, S.J., Zanna, M.P., Hoshino-Browne, E., & Correll, J. (2003). Secure and defensive high self-esteem. *Journal of Personality and Social Psychology, 85,* 969–78.

Josselson, R. (1995). Imagining the real: Empathy, narrative, and the dialogic self. In R. Josselson & A. Lieblich (Eds.), *Interpreting experience: The narrative study of lives, Vol. 3* (pp. 27–44). Thousand Oaks, CA: Sage.

Jung, R.E., Haier, R.J., Yeo, R.A., Rowland, L.M., Petropoulos, H., Levine, A.S., et al. (2005). Sex differences in N-acetyl-aspartate correlates of general intelligence: A 1H-MRS study of normal human brain. *NeuroImage, 26,* 965–72.

Kagan, J. (1994). *Galen's prophecy: Temperament in human nature.* New York: Basic Books.

Kalichman, S.C., Heckman, T., & Kelly, J.A. (1996). Sensation seeking as an explanation for the association between substance abuse and HIV-related risky sexual behavior. *Archives of Sexual Behavior, 25,* 141–54.

Kelly, G. (1955). *The psychology of personal constructs.* New York: W.W. Norton.

Kenford, S.L., Smith, S.S., Wetter, D.W., Jorenby, D.E., Fiore, M.C., & Baker, T.B. (2002). Predicting relapse back to smoking: Contrasting affective and physical models of dependence. *Journal of Consulting and Clinical Psychology, 70,* 216–27.

Kernis, M.H., Cornell, D.P., Sun, C.R., Berry, R.J., & Harlow, T. (1993). There's more to self-esteem than whether it's high or low: The importance of stability of self-esteem. *Journal of Personality and Social Psychology, 65,* 1190–204.

Lavine, H., & Snyder, M. (1996). Cognitive processing and the functional matching effect in persuasion: The mediating role of subjective perceptions of message quality. *Journal of Experimental Social Psychology, 32,* 580–604.

Lee, V.E., Brooks-Gunn, J., Schnur, E., & Liaw, F.R. (1990). Are Head Start effects sustained? A longitudinal follow-up comparison of disadvantaged children attending Head Start, no preschool, and other preschool programs. *Child Development, 61,* 495–507.

Lesch, K.-P., Bengel, D., Heils, A., Sabol, S.Z., Greenberg, B.D., Petri, S., Benjamin, J., Muller, C.R., Hamer, D.H., & Murphy, D.L. (1996). Association of anxiety-related traits with a polymorphism in the serotonin transporter gene regulatory region. *Science, 274,* 1527–31.

Levy, S.R., Plaks, J.E., Hong, Y., Chiu, C., & Dweck, C.S. (2001). Static versus dynamic theories and the perception of groups: Different routes to different destinations. *Personality and Social Psychology Review, 5,* 156–68.

Lewontin, R. (2001). *The triple helix: Gene, organism and environment.* New York: Harvard University Press.

Leyens, J.-P., Yzerbyt, V., & Schadron, G. (1994). *Stereotypes and social cognition.* London: Sage.

Lilienfeld, S.O., Wood, J.M., & Garb, H.N. (2000). The scientific status of projective techniques. *Psychological Science in the Public Interest, 1,* 27–66.

Lillard, A.S. (1998). Ethnopsychologies: Cultural variations in theories of mind. *Psychological Bulletin, 123,* 3–32.

Linville, P.W. (1987). Self-complexity as a cognitive buffer against stress-related illness and depression. *Journal of Personality and Social Psychology, 52,* 663–76.

Little, B.R. (1989). Personal projects analysis: Trivial pursuits, magnificent obsessions, and the search for coherence. In D.M. Buss & N. Cantor (Eds.), *Personality psychology: Recent trends and emerging directions* (pp. 15–31). New York: Springer-Verlag.

Little, B.R., Lecci, L., & Watkinson, B. (1991). Personality and personal projects: Linking big five and PAC units of analysis. *Journal of Personality, 60,* 501–25.

Loehlin, J.C. (1992). *Genes and environment in personality development.* Newbury Park, CA: Sage.

Lopes, P N., Salovey, P., Cote, S., & Beers, M. (2005). Emotion regulation abilities and the quality of social interaction. *Emotion, 5,* 113–18.

Lykken, D. (1995). *The antisocial personalities.* Hillsdale, NJ: Erlbaum.

Macklin, M.L., Metzger, L.J., Litz, B.T., McNally, R.J., Lasko, N.B., Orr, S.P., et al. (1998). Lower precombat intelligence is a risk factor for posttraumatic stress disorder. *Journal of Consulting and Clinical Psychology, 66,* 323–6.

Macmillan, M. (1997). *Freud evaluated: The completed arc.* Cambridge, MA: MIT Press.

Markus, H., & Nurius, P. (1986). Possible selves. *American Psychologist, 41,* 954–69.

Marshall, G.N., Wortman, C.B., Vickers, R.R., Kusulas, J.W., & Hervig, L.K. (1994). The five-factor model of personality as a framework for personality–health research. *Journal of Personality and Social Psychology, 67,* 278–86.

Martin, R.P., Wisenbaker, J., & Huttunen, M. (1994). Review of factor analytic studies of temperament measures based on the Thomas–Chess structural model: Implications for the Big Five. In C.F. Halverson, G.A. Kohnstamm & R.P. Martin (Eds.), *The developing structure of temperament and personality in infancy and childhood* (pp. 157–72). Hillsdale, NJ: Erlbaum.

Maslow, A.H. (1962). *Towards a psychology of being.* New York: Van Nostrand.

Matarazzo, J.D. (1992). Psychological testing and assessment in the 21st century. *American Psychologist, 47,* 1007–18.

Matsumoto, D. (2006). Are cultural differences in emotion regulation mediated by personality traits? *Journal of Cross-Cultural Psychology, 37,* 421–7.

Matthews, G., Roberts, R.D., & Zeidner, M. (2004). Seven myths about emotional intelligence. *Psychological Inquiry, 15,* 179–96.

Mayer, J.D., Caruso, D.R., & Salovey, P. (1999). Emotional intelligence meets traditional standards for an intelligence. *Intelligence, 27,* 267–98.

Mayer, J.D., Salovey, P., & Caruso, D.R. (2004). Emotional intelligence: Theory, findings, and implications. *Psychological Inquiry, 15,* 197–215.

McAdams, D.P. (1995). What do we know when we know a person? *Journal of Personality, 63,* 365–96.

McAdams, D. P. (1996). *The stories we live by: Personal myths and the making of the self.* New York: Guilford.

McAdams, D.P. (2006). *The redemptive self: Stories Americans live by.* New York: Oxford University Press.

McAdams, D.P., de St. Aubin, E., & Logan, R. (1993). Generativity in young, midlife, and older adults. *Psychology and Aging, 8,* 221–30.

McClearn, G.E., Johansson, B., Berg, S., Pedersen, N.L., Ahern, F., Petrill, S.A., et al. (1997). Substantial genetic influence on cognitive abilities in twins 80 or more years old. *Science, 276,* 1560–3.

McClelland, D.C. (1985). *Human motivation.* Glenview, IL: Scott Foresman.

McCrae, R.R., Yang, J., Costa, P.T., Dai, X., Yao, S., Cai, T., & Gao, B. (2001). Personality profiles and the prediction of categorical personality disorders. *Journal of Personality, 69,* 155–74.

McDaniel, M.A. (2005). Big-brained people are smarter: A meta-analysis of the relationship between in vivo brain volume and intelligence. *Intelligence, 33,* 337–46.

Mealey, L. (1995). The sociobiology of sociopathy: An integrated evolutionary model. *Behavioural and Brain Sciences, 18,* 523–99.

Meehl, P.E. (1954). *Clinical vs. statistical prediction: A theoretical analysis and a review of the evidence.* Minneapolis, MN: University of Minnesota Press.

Meehl, P.E. (1962). Schizotaxia, schizotypy, schizophrenia. *American Psychologist, 17,* 827–38.

Meehl, P.E. (1992). Factors and taxa, traits and types, differences of degree and differences in kind. *Journal of Personality, 60,* 117–74.

Metalsky, G.I., Halberstadt, L.J., & Abramson, L.Y. (1987). Vulnerability to depressive mood reactions: Toward a more powerful test of the diathesis–stress and causal mediation components of the reformulated theory of depression. *Journal of Personality and Social Psychology, 52,* 386–93.

Meyer, G.J., & Shack, J.R. (1989). Structural convergence of mood and personality: Evidence for old and new directions. *Journal of Personality and Social Psychology, 57,* 691–706.

Mischel, W. (1968). *Personality and assessment.* New York: Wiley.

Moffitt, T.E., Gabrielli, W.F., Mednick, S.A., & Schulsinger, F. (1981). Socioeconomic status, IQ, and delinquency. *Journal of Abnormal Psychology, 90,* 152–6.

Murray, H.A. (1938). *Explorations in personality.* New York: Oxford University Press.

Neisser, U., Boodoo, G., Bouchard, T.J., Jr, Boykin, A.W., Brody, N., Ceci, S.J., et al. (1996). Intelligence: Knowns and unknowns. *American Psychologist, 51,* 77–101.

Nettelbeck, T. (1982). Inspection time: An index for intelligence? *Quarterly Journal of Experimental Psychology: Human Experimental Psychology, 2,* 299–312.

Norem, J.K., & Cantor, N. (1986). Anticipatory and post hoc cushioning strategies: Optimism and defensive pessimism in 'risky' situations. *Cognitive Therapy and Research, 10,* 347–62.

Palys, T.S., & Little, B.R. (1983). Perceived life satisfaction and the organization of personal project systems. *Journal of Personality and Social Psychology, 44*, 1221–30.

Paradise, A.W., & Kernis, M.H. (2002). Self-esteem and psychological well-being: Implications of fragile self-esteem. *Journal of Social and Clinical Psychology, 21*, 345–61.

Paunonen, S.V., & Ashton, M.C. (2001). Big Five predictors of academic achievement. *Journal of Research in Personality, 35*, 78–90.

Peterson, C., & Barrett, L. (1987). Explanatory style and academic performance among university freshmen. *Journal of Personality and Social Psychology, 53*, 603–7.

Peterson, C., & Seligman, M.E.P. (2002). *Character strengths and virtues: A handbook and classification.* New York: Oxford University Press & American Psychological Association.

Peterson, C., Seligman, M.E.P., & Vaillant, G.E. (1988). Pessimistic explanatory style is a risk factor for physical illness: A thirty-five year longitudinal study. *Journal of Personality and Social Psychology, 55*, 23–7.

Plomin, R., DeFries, J.C., McClearn, G.E., & Rutter, M. (1997). *Behavioural genetics* (3rd ed.). New York: Freeman.

Plomin, R., & Kovas, Y. (2005). Generalist genes and learning disabilities. *Psychological Bulletin, 131*, 592–617.

Posthuma, D., De Geus, E.J., Baare, W.F., Hulshoff Pol, H.E., Kahn, R.S., & Boomsma, D. I. (2002). The association between brain volume and intelligence is of genetic origin. *Nature Neuroscience, 5*, 83–4.

Posthuma, D., de Geus, E.J., & Boomsma, D.I. (2001). Perceptual speed and IQ are associated through common genetic factors. *Behavioural Genetics, 31*, 593–602.

Posthuma, D., Luciano, M., Geus, E.J., Wright, M.J., Slagboom, P.E., Montgomery, G.W., et al. (2005). A genomewide scan for intelligence identifies quantitative trait Loci on 2q and 6p. *American Journal of Human Genetics, 77*, 318–26.

Rafaeli-Mor, E., & Steinberg, J. (2002). Self-complexity and well-being: A review and research synthesis. *Personality and Social Psychology Review, 6*, 31–58.

Ramey, C.T., & Ramey, S.L. (2004). Early learning and school readiness: Can early intervention make a difference? *Merrill-Palmer Quarterly, 50*, 471–91.

Rauscher, F.H., Shaw, G.L., & Ky, K.N. (1993). Music and spatial task performance. *Nature, 365*, 611.

Raven, J., Raven, J.C., & Court, J.H. (1998). *Manual for Raven's advanced progressive matrices* (1998 Ed.). Oxford: Oxford Psychologists Press.

Redlich, F. (1999). *Hitler: Diagnosis of a destructive prophet.* New York: Oxford University Press.

Ree, M.J., & Earles, J.A. (1992). Intelligence is the best predictor of job performance. *Current Directions in Psychological Science, 1*, 86–9.

Reivich, K. (1995). The measurement of explanatory style. In G.M. Buchanan & M.E.P. Seligman (Eds.), *Explanatory style* (pp. 21–48). Hillsdale, NJ: Erlbaum.

Reynolds, C.A., Finkel, D., McArdle, J.J., Gatz, M., Berg, S., & Pedersen, N.L. (2005). Quantitative genetic analysis of latent growth curve models of cognitive abilities in adulthood. *Developmental Psychology, 41*, 3–16.

Roberts, B.W., & DelVecchio, W.F. (2000). The rank-order consistency of personality traits from childhood to old age: A quantitative review of longitudinal studies. *Psychological Bulletin, 126*, 3–25.

Roberts, B.W., Walton, K.E., & Viechtbauer, W. (2006). Patterns of mean-level change in personality traits across the life course: A meta-analysis of longitudinal studies. *Psychological Bulletin, 132,* 1–25.

Roccas, S., Sagiv, L., Schwartz, S.H., & Knafo, A. (2002). The Big Five personality factors and personal values. *Personality and Social Psychology Bulletin, 28,* 789–801.

Rogers, C. (1961). *On becoming a person.* Boston, MA: Houghton Mifflin.

Rose, S. (1998). *Lifelines: Biology, freedom, determinism.* London: Penguin.

Rose, S. (2005). *Lifelines: Life beyond the gene.* London: Vintage.

Rosenbaum, R. (1998). *Explaining Hitler: The search for the origins of his evil.* New York: Random House.

Rosenman, R.H. (1978). The interview method of assessment of the coronary-prone behavior pattern. In T.M. Dembroski, S.M. Weiss, J.L. Shields, S.G. Haynes, & M. Feinleib (Eds.) *Coronary-prone behavior* (pp. 55–69). New York: Springer-Verlag.

Rosenthal, R. (1990). How are we doing in soft psychology? *American Psychologist, 45,* 775–7.

Rosenthal, R., & Rubin, D.B. (1982). A simple, general purpose display of magnitude of experimental effect. *Journal of Educational Psychology, 74,* 166–9.

Ross, M. (1989). Relation of implicit theories to the construction of personal histories. *Psychological Review, 96,* 341–57.

Roth, P.L., Bevier, C.A., Bobko, P., Switzer, F.S.I., & Tyler, P. (2001). Ethnic group differences in cognitive ability in employment and educational settings: A meta-analysis. *Personnel Psychology, 54,* 297–330.

Rotter, J.B. (1966). Generalized expectancies for internal versus external control of reinforcement. *Psychological Monographs, 80,* 1–28.

Rowatt, W.C., Cunningham, M.R., & Druen, P.B. (1998). Deception to get a date. *Personality and Social Psychology Bulletin, 24,* 1228–42.

Rozin, P., & Royzman, E.B. (2001). Negativity bias, negativity dominance, and contagion. *Personality and Social Psychology Review, 5,* 296–320.

Runyan, W.M. (1981). Why did Van Gogh cut off his ear? The problem of alternative explanations in psychobiography. *Journal of Personality and Social Psychology, 40,* 1070–7.

Runyan, W.M. (1988). Progress in psychobiography. In D.P. McAdams & R.L. Ochberg (Eds.), *Psychobiography and life narratives* (pp. 295–326). Durham, NC: Duke University Press.

Rushton, J.P., & Jensen, A.R. (2005). Thirty years of research on race differences in cognitive ability. *Psychology, Public Policy, and Law, 11,* 235–94.

Sandstrom, M.J., & Cramer, P. (2003). Girls' use of defence mechanisms following peer rejection. *Journal of Personality, 71,* 605–27.

Schmidt, F.L., & Hunter, J.E. (1998). The validity and utility of selection methods in personnel psychology. *Psychological Bulletin, 124,* 262–74.

Schmithorst, V.J., Wilke, M., Dardzinski, B.J., & Holland, S.K. (2005). Cognitive functions correlate with white matter architecture in a normal pediatric population: A diffusion tensor MRI study. *Human Brain Mapping, 26,* 139–47.

Schultz, W.T. (2005). *Handbook of psychobiography.* Oxford: Oxford University Press.

Schwartz, S.H. (1992). Universals in the content and structure of values: Theoretical advances and empirical tests in 20 countries. In M. Zanna (Ed.), *Advances in experimental social psychology, Vol. 25* (pp. 1–65). New York: Academic Press.

Schwartz, S.H. (1994). Are there universal aspects in the structure and contents of human values? *Journal of Social Issues, 50,* 19–45.

Seligman, M.E.P., Nolen-Hoeksema, S., Thornton, N., & Thornton, K.M. (1990). Explanatory style as a mechanism of disappointing athletic performance. *Psychological Science, 1,* 143–6.

Seligman, M.E.P., & Schulman, P. (1986). Explanatory style as a predictor of productivity and quitting among life insurance salesmen. *Journal of Personality and Social Psychology, 50,* 832–8.

Shoda, Y., Mischel, W., & Peake, P.K. (1990). Predicting adolescent cognitive and self-regulatory competencies from preschool delay of gratification: Identifying diagnostic conditions. *Developmental Psychology, 26,* 978–86.

Silverman, L., & Weinberger, J. (1985). Mommy and I are one: Implications for psychotherapy. *American Psychologist, 40,* 1296–308.

Simpson, J.A., Rholes, W.D., & Phillips, D. (1996). Conflict in close relationships: An attachment perspective. *Journal of Personality and Social Psychology, 71,* 899–914.

Skinner, E.A., Edge, K., Altman, J., & Sherwood, H. (2003). Searching for the structure of coping: A review and critique of category systems for classifying ways of coping. *Psychological Bulletin, 129,* 216–69.

Smith, H.S., & Cohen, L.H. (1993). Self-complexity and reaction to a relationship breakup. *Journal of Social and Clinical Psychology, 12,* 367–84.

Smith, T.W., & Spiro, A. (2002). Personality, health, and aging: Prolegomenon for the next generation. *Journal of Research in Personality, 36,* 363–94.

Snyder, M. (1974). The self-monitoring of expressive behavior. *Journal of Personality and Social Psychology, 30,* 526–37.

Spanos, N.P. (1994). Multiple identity enactments and multiple personality disorder: A sociocognitive perspective. *Psychological Bulletin, 116,* 143–65.

Spearman, C. (1904). 'General intelligence,' objectively determined and measured. *American Journal of Psychology, 15,* 201–93.

Spence, D.P. (1980). *Narrative truth and historical truth: Meaning and interpretation in psychoanalysis.* New York: W.W. Norton.

Spinath, F.M., & Plomin, R. (2003). *Amplification of genetic influence on g from early childhood to the early school years.* Paper presented at the IVth Meeting of the International Society for the Study of Intelligence, Irvine, USA, 4–6 December.

Srivastava, S., John, O.P., Gosling, S.D., & Potter, J. (2003). Development of personality in early and middle adulthood: Set like plaster or persistent change? *Journal of Personality and Social Psychology, 84,* 1041–53.

Steele, C.M., & Aronson, J. (1995). Stereotype threat and the intellectual performance of African Americans. *Journal of Personality and Social Psychology, 69,* 797–811.

Steffens, M.C., & Schulze König, S. (2006). Predicting spontaneous Big Five behavior with Implicit Association Tests. *European Journal of Psychological Assessment, 22,* 13–20.

Stern, W. (1912). *The psychological methods of intelligence testing* (G. Whipple, Trans.). Baltimore, MD: Warwick & York.

Sternberg, R.J. (1996). Love stories. *Personal Relationships, 3,* 59–79.

Stewart, A.J., Franz, C.E., & Layton, L. (1988). The changing self: Using personal documents to study lives. *Journal of Personality, 56,* 41–74.

Stough, C., Kerkin, B., Bates, T.C., & Mangan, G. (1994). Music and spatial IQ. *Personality and Individual Differences, 17*, 695.

Tang, H., Quertermous, T., Rodriguez, B., Kardia, S.L., Zhu, X., Brown, A., et al. (2005). Genetic structure, self-identified race/ethnicity, and confounding in case-control association studies. *American Journal of Human Genetics, 76*, 268–75.

Taylor, S.E. (1983). Adjustment to threatening events: A theory of cognitive adaptation. *American Psychologist, 38*, 1161–73.

Taylor, S.E., & Brown, J.D. (1988). Illusion and well-being: A social psychological perspective on mental health. *Psychological Bulletin, 103*, 193–210.

Teasdale, T.W., & Owen, D.R. (2005). A long-term rise and recent decline in intelligence test performance: The Flynn Effect in reverse. *Personality and Individual Differences, 39*, 837–43.

Tellegen, A. (1985). Structures of mood and personality and their relevance to assessing anxiety, with an emphasis on self-report. In A.H. Tuma & J.D. Maser (Eds.), *Anxiety and anxiety disorders* (pp. 681–706). Hillsdale, NJ: Erlbaum.

Terracciano, A., et al. (2005). National character does not reflect mean trait levels in 49 cultures. *Science, 310*, 96–100.

Thompson, P.M., Cannon, T.D., Narr, K.L., van Erp, T., Poutanen, V.P., Huttunen, M., et al. (2001). Genetic influences on brain structure. *Nature Neuroscience, 4*, 1253–8.

Toga, A.W., & Thompson, P.M. (2005). Genetics of brain structure and intelligence. *Annual Review of Neuroscience, 28*, 1–23.

Tooby, J., & Cosmides, L. (1990). On the universality of human nature and the uniqueness of the individual: The role of genetics and adaptation. *Journal of Personality, 58*, 17–67.

Turkheimer, E., Haley, A., Waldron, M., D'Onofrio, B., & Gottesman, I. (2003). Socioeconomic status modifies heritability of IQ in young children. *Psychological Science, 14*, 623–8.

Twenge, J.M. (1997). Changes in masculine and feminine traits over time: A meta-analysis. *Sex Roles, 36*, 305–25.

Twenge, J.M. (2000). The age of anxiety? Birth cohort change in anxiety and neuroticism, 1952–1993. *Journal of Personality and Social Psychology, 79*, 1007–21.

Twenge, J.M. (2001a). Changes in women's assertiveness in response to status and roles: A cross-temporal meta-analysis, 1931–1993. *Journal of Personality and Social Psychology, 81*, 133–45.

Twenge, J.M. (2001b). Birth cohort changes in extraversion: A cross-temporal meta-analysis, 1966–1993. *Personality and Individual Differences, 30*, 735–48.

Twenge, J.M., & Campbell, W.K. (2001). Age and birth cohort differences in self-esteem: A cross-temporal meta-analysis. *Personality and Social Psychology Review, 5*, 321–44.

Twenge, J.M., Zhang, L., & Im, C. (2004). It's beyond my control: A cross-temporal meta-analysis of increasing externality in locus of control, 1960–2002. *Personality and Social Psychology Review, 8*, 308–19.

van Ijzendoorn, M.H., & Juffer, F. (2005). Adoption is a successful natural intervention enhancing adopted children's IQ and school performance. *Current Directions in Psychological Science, 14*, 326–30.

Vazire, S., & Gosling, S.D. (2004). E-perceptions: Personality impressions based on personal websites. *Journal of Personality and Social Psychology, 87*, 123–32.

Volkan, V.D., Itzkowitz, N., & Dod, A.W. (1997). *Nixon: A psychobiography*. New York: Columbia University Press.

Watson, D., & Clark, L.A. (1984). Negative affectivity: The disposition to experience aversive emotional states. *Psychological Bulletin, 96*, 465–90.

Watson, D., & Clark, L.A. (1992). On traits and temperament: General and specific factors of emotional experience and their relation to the five-factor model. *Journal of Personality, 60*, 441–76.

Watson, D., & Clark, L.A. (1993). Behavioral disinhibition versus constraint: A dispositional perspective. In D.M. Wegner & J.W. Pennebaker (Eds.), *Handbook of mental control* (pp. 506–27). Upper Saddle River, NJ: Prentice-Hall.

Watson, D., & Tellegen, A. (1985). Toward a consensual structure of mood. *Psychological Bulletin, 98*, 219–35.

Wechsler, D. (1975). Intelligence defined and undefined: A relativistic appraisal. *American Psychologist, 30*, 135–9.

Wechsler, D. (1997). *Wechsler Adult Intelligence Scale III*. San Antonio, TX: Psychological Corporation.

Westen, D. (1998). The scientific legacy of Sigmund Freud: Toward a psychodynamically informed psychological science. *Psychological Bulletin, 124*, 333–71.

Whalley, L.J., & Deary, I.J. (2001). Longitudinal cohort study of childhood IQ and survival up to age 76. *British Medical Journal, 322*, 819–22.

Whitley, B.E. (1999). Right-wing authoritarianism, social dominance orientation, and prejudice. *Journal of Personality and Social Psychology, 77*, 126–34.

Whitmer, P.O. (1996). *The inner Elvis: A psychological biography of Elvis Aaron Presley*. New York: Hyperion.

Wiggins, J.S. (1997). In defence of traits. In R. Hogan, J. Johnson, & S. Briggs (Eds.), *Handbook of personality psychology* (pp. 95–115). New York: Academic Press.

Williams, R. (1976). *Keywords: A vocabulary of culture and society*. London: Fontana.

Wilson, D.S. (1994). Adaptive genetic variation and human evolutionary psychology. *Ethology and Sociobiology, 15*, 219–35.

Woolfolk, R.L., Novalany, J., Gara, M.A., Allen, L.A., & Polino, M. (1995). Self-complexity, self-evaluation, and depression: An examination of form and content within the self-schema. *Journal of Personality and Social Psychology, 68*, 1108–20.

Wright Gillham, N. (2001). *A Life of Sir Francis Galton: From African exploration to the birth of eugenics*. London: Oxford University Press.

Zuckerman, M. (1991). *Psychobiology of personality*. New York: Cambridge University Press.

Zullow, H.M. (1990). Pessimistic rumination in popular songs and newsmagazines predicts economic recession via decreased consumer optimism and spending. *Journal of Economic Psychology, 12*, 501–26.

Zullow, H., & Seligman, M.E.P. (1990). Pessimistic rumination predicts defeat of presidential candidates, 1900–1984. *Psychological Inquiry, 1*, 52–61.

Index